Educational Assessment in the 21st Century

Claire Wyatt-Smith · J. Joy Cumming
Editor

Educational Assessment in the 21st Century

Connecting Theory and Practice

 Springer

Editors
Prof. Claire Wyatt-Smith
Faculty of Education
Mt Gravatt Campus
Griffith University
176 Messines Ridge Road
Mt Gravatt QLD 4122
Australia
c.wyatt-smith@griffith.edu.au

Prof. J. Joy Cumming
Faculty of Education
Mt Gravatt Campus
Griffith University
176 Messines Ridge Road
Mt Gravatt QLD 4122
Australia
j.cumming@griffith.edu.au

ISBN: 978-1-4020-9963-2   e-ISBN: 978-1-4020-9964-9

DOI 10.1007/978-1-4020-9964-9
Springer Dordrecht Heidelberg London New York

Library of Congress Control Number: 2009920277

Printed on acid-free paper

Springer is a part of Springer Science+Business Media (www.springer.com)

Foreword

Signs of Change: Assessment Past, Present and Future

Another Time, Another Place . . . Examinations Then and Now

In the Temple of Literature in Hanoi, Vietnam, a series of stone stelae records the names of the handful of illustrious examination candidates who, in each century, passed the national examination to become a Doctor of Literature. Beginning in the 11th century, the exams were conducted personally by successive kings who pursued Confucian ideals that found expression in the enormous value placed on the pursuit of wisdom and learning.

In the 21st century we are both puzzled and impressed by this tradition. Puzzled by such an explicit commitment to a meritocracy in an essentially feudal society; impressed by this enthusiasm for learning and the pursuit of wisdom at the highest level of society.

Yet, there are also important similarities between the 11th and 21st centuries. Then, as now, assessment was associated with excellence, high standards, prestige and competition—success for the chosen few; disappointment for the majority. Then, as now, the pursuit of excellence was embedded in a social context that favoured the elite and determined success in terms of the predilections of the powerful. Then, as now, the purpose of the assessment, the way it was conducted and its impact on society all reflected the social and economic priorities of the day.

However, where examinations in the form that we would recognise today existed in pre-modern societies, they were typically of a consistent pattern. They were extremely hierarchical in organisation, in that only a tiny minority could be successful. They were typically oral or written in mode. Their content normally concerned the mastery of designated classical texts, and they were conducted primarily for the purpose of selection.

In the 21st century, examinations and other forms of assessment serve a much wider range of purposes and take a greater variety of forms. They are also commonly used for the certification of competence, to monitor educational standards and to provide learners with feedback, as well as continuing as in previous eras to serve an important social function in providing for selection. In each case, however, the same four dimensions of variability may be identified. These are purpose, mode, content and organisation. This fourfold characterisation may usefully be used to compare key aspects of examination systems that have existed in different times and places in order to explore their link to the social context in which they are embedded. The use of the four themes of purpose, mode, content and organisation for analysis of assessment practices provides a framework within which to understand the particular challenges for assessment in the 21st century and how these might differ from the formal assessment systems that began to be widely used in the West during the 19th century. Central to any such analysis is a recognition of the different assumptions shaping educational practices in pre-modern, traditional societies, since these differences in turn shape the way in which the purpose, mode, content and organisation of assessment are determined.

Assessment as a Modernist Project

Although, as suggested above, the use of examinations to determine relative merit and competence has a long history in human society, it was really only with the post-Enlightenment emergence of 'modern' society in the West that such use became widespread and, eventually, defining within educational provision. The emphasis on individual rights and responsibility, rationality and scientific progress that characterised Western societies, at least during this period, provided fertile soil for the growth of examinations since examinations provided a powerful tool for the application of these principles in the organisation of educational provision and social opportunity. Initially, at least, these 'modern' examinations were similar in many respects to those that had long been used in other parts of the world and in other contexts. The dominant purpose continued to be the provision of fair competition by means of which the 'best' candidates could be chosen. As before, too, practicalities would dictate that the principal mode for conducting such competitions would be either oral or written interrogation. In terms of content, the ability to demonstrate mastery of classic texts only very gradually came to be complemented by the new disciplines being created by the development of scientific research and associated discoveries.

However, there was also a very significant difference from the examinations characteristic of pre-modern societies. This difference concerned the widespread development of bureaucratic systems for their delivery. National examination boards, university examination syndicates and other similar organisations began to emerge in order to make possible the systematic and rigorous administration of examinations to many hundreds of candidates, rather than to an elite few. Gradually, these systems necessarily also came to control the content of the examination, the way it was conducted and the designation of the associated qualification. Disseminated around the world during the colonial era, examinations and the organisations that ran them thus began to be able to exercise an unprecedented degree of international influence on both the shape of educational provision and the regulation of social opportunity and status in countries across the world. The strength and scope of this influence grew steadily during the 19th and 20th centuries, with the advent of the 21st century witnessing examinations and assessment being used ubiquitously to provide for selection, for certification, for accountability and for international comparisons of educational standards. The advent of the 21st century also heralded the early stages of a movement to promote the use of assessment as a tool to support learning itself.

Assessment as a Post-modern Project

Although the new century is less than a decade old, it is already apparent that the belief in the power of science to solve the world's problems that so characterised the post-Enlightenment era is being rapidly eroded. 'Post-modernism', instead, is recognising the increasingly fractured nature of society and the limitations of science to provide solutions to the great issues of our time, such as the sustainability of the planet, poverty and social cohesion. For many, the certainties of modernism have been replaced by post-modern doubts about the possibility of progress. Recognition of the fallibilities of science has brought with it an increased recognition of the importance of diversity and subjectivity. Changes in the nature of work, globalisation, the information revolution and the increasingly social nature of contemporary challenges also suggest different priorities for education systems. These will in turn require different priorities for assessment practices.

  With the erosion of faith in the search for certainty through science has come the associated recognition that the assessment of educational performance cannot be an exact science either; that the involvement of human beings in every aspect of its design, execution and use makes it irrevocably a social project and thus subject to all the vagaries that any kind of human activity implies. This has led to the beginnings of a more humanistic approach to assessment. By contrast with the pursuit of maximum accuracy in educational measurement, which largely defined the 20th-century approach to examinations, testing and assessment, the agenda for assessment in the 21st century shows signs of a growing preoccupation with 'fitness for purpose' and impact on learning. During the 20th century, research and development in examinations and assessment tended to focus overwhelmingly on issues of 'mode'—how to test better—more accurately, more equitably, more efficiently and even more humanely. By the same token, comparatively little consideration has been given to how to make the other three dimensions of purpose, context and organisation more fit for purpose, despite the fact that the latter are fundamental in shaping the priorities that decisions about mode must address.

  Perhaps it is for this reason that, despite a growing recognition of the limitations of a scientific approach to assessment, the 21st century is nevertheless finding it hard to escape from the assessment thinking and practices that were characteristic of the 20th century. As a consequence the purpose, mode, content and organisation of examination and assessment practices around the world today remain strikingly similar to those that prevailed a century or more ago, despite the scale of the changes that have taken place in society during that time. There can be very few technologies indeed that have developed conceptually so little over the course of the past 100 years. It would appear that the examination systems that evolved with the modernist era have proved to be just as enduring as their precursors in pre-modern times.

However, if the design and application of these social phenomena have proved remarkably resistant to change, their influence has continued to spread. The combination of bureaucratic administration, widespread social penetration and global dispersal which the 20th-century development of examinations and assessments of all kinds produced, had produced a megalith so deeply rooted in public consciousness and so powerful in its influence that alternatives are almost literally inconceivable. Thus, as a result, the dawn of the 21st century heralds a situation in which, while there is increasingly broad recognition among assessment professionals, teachers, researchers and even policy makers that there is a need for substantial change of approach to assessment, any significant re-balancing in the way we use assessments, in the way we conduct them, in the content that is included and in the way in which assessments are organised, remains elusive.

However, there are hopeful signs that the historical preoccupation with the use of assessment in the form of examinations and tests to manage competition for scarce opportunities is likely to be re-balanced in favour of an emphasis on certification. Assessment procedures are needed that are capable of determining achievement across a very wide range of content and skills, in many different contexts and at a great variety of levels. Assessment procedures need to be able to engage students with diverse cultural and personal backgrounds, to provide a fair means of judging students with disabilities and other kinds of special needs. For this and for many other reasons, there is increasing interest in the potential of assessment procedures that can be delivered electronically and so save both time and money while providing personalised feedback.

New areas of competence such as planning and managing one's own learning and meta-cognition are growing rapidly in importance, by contrast with more traditional forms of knowledge and understanding. In the much-bruited 'knowledge economy', the fostering of creativity and the development of transferable skills, such as analysis, team work and problem solving, are already a central concern. To the extent that this is so, assessment in the 21st century seems likely to be characterised by a much more radical departure from tradition than in the previous two centuries, as written tests give way to the accreditation of real-life practice, and occasional 'big-bang' examination events are replaced by 'just-in-time' online assessments and on-demand, personalised 'micro assessments'. This is not just a question of developments within a paradigm; it concerns the evolution of a fundamentally new one.

Central to the emergence of such a new assessment paradigm and the element upon which all the other changes are likely to depend, is likely to be the dimension of organisation and the development of new forms of delivering assessments. It seems likely that the monolithic, traditional examination systems underpinned by substantial administrative bureaucracies are likely to evolve into much more distributed systems. In typically post-modern style, the 'grand narratives' of assessment and certification characterised by a few main gatekeepers and a limited range of qualifications are likely to become fragmented into smaller, more flexible units and credits that individuals can mix and match. The traditional 'rites of passage' of school-leaving and university entrance examinations, degree finals and professional qualifications are likely to be gradually replaced by the ability to accumulate credit at different times and levels. Individuals will be able to study for credit in different settings such as school, college, university or work, at different times—pre-work, during work and post-work, during retirement and through different means such as e-tests and work-based assessment as well as through more traditional performance assessments. The credits obtained will accumulate into a personal portfolio—a record of achievement that provides a unique and self-managed narrative on each individual's life-long learning.

If this seems a rather fanciful scenario in the face of the apparently unquenchable international obsession with traditional examinations and tests, it is important to recognise that there are already significant straws in the wind that testify to the emergence of a more 21st-century version of educational assessment. Tertiary students can already accumulate credits as well as whole qualifications. Qualifications are becoming cumulative and expressed in terms of national qualification frameworks with levels that stretch from school through to the highest reaches of university study. Experience at work can be accredited as contributing towards academic qualifications through the accreditation of prior learning. The increasingly wide range and scope of available accreditation are breaking down the traditional qualification 'highways'. The availability of new types of qualification and new accrediting bodies is both testimony to, and supportive of, this trend. In the United Kingdom, for example, commercial companies like McDonald's can now award their own qualifications within a nationally recognised framework of levels of achievement and credit.

Perhaps most fundamental of all is the transformative potential of e-assessment. On the one hand, it can help both to guide and to motivate learning by providing rapid, individualised and constructive feedback. On the other hand, through simulated authentic tasks, it can provide convenient and flexible access to all kinds of academic and professional accreditation.

The chapters in this book illustrate many of these trends. Some explore the rapidly developing potential of e-assessment. Others address the way in which the breaking down of uni-dimensional forms of assessment will help to foster great equality of opportunity. Still others consider the 'data-environment' and how the skilful use of available information can be used by teachers better to guide interventions in relation to a particular individual's learning.

The Way Forward. . . ?

History is a good teacher. It allows us to marvel at what seem to us to be the rather quaint idiosyncrasies of another era. History strips reality of the subjective, of the emotions, while laying bare the grand narratives that informed the choice of particular policies and practices. The present is a poor pedagogue by comparison. The clutter of social debris accumulated since the inception of mass education, in particular, makes it difficult to achieve a genuinely contemporary perspective on the utility of current assessment practices. But the title of this book challenges us to do this, to understand the changing exigencies that shape education for today's world and, hence, the approaches to assessment that these call forth.

What will the world in 2100 or even 2200 make of the education policies and practices of 2010? The grand narratives of today suggest, at best, a difficult future for the world, characterised by the impact of global warming, food and water shortages and the pressures of an ever-expanding population. These in turn are likely to lead to an increase in violence and terrorism, inter-ethnic strife and a continually widening disparity between rich and poor, North and South. It is a pessimistic future, a future in which the close association between levels of education and national prosperity has become overlaid by other priorities. The priorities for education systems are thus likely to change.

As this book makes clear, the challenge for assessment in the 21st century will be to reflect these newly emerging educational priorities. Assessment procedures will be needed that support the preparation of the next generation with the skills and values that they will need to manage the emerging global challenges. For if, as is widely recognised, assessment that drives individual effort and aspiration; that communicates system priorities and that provides the currency of social opportunity, for education to begin to address changing global priorities, the assessment systems that shape it will need to change also.

This book presents evidence of the overwhelming need for a fresh appraisal of current practices in this respect, whether these concern the assessment of individual student achievement, teacher and school accountability or education system management. It suggests that there is a need to reconsider current assumptions and practices with regard to all four of the assessment dimensions identified earlier— purpose, mode, content and organisation. If contemporary educational assessment practices are one of the most powerful institutions of today's society, then the burden of this book is that they cannot be allowed to operate without the closest of critical scrutiny concerning their fitness for purpose. At whatever level assessment decisions are made, whether this is in the classroom or at that of national policy, it is essential to ensure that the approaches being used are the most fruitful that can possibly be achieved within the constraints of what is practically and technologically possible at any given time. Sadly, the lack of any real change in assessment thinking and practice in recent decades suggests that, so far, this has not been the case; that tradition and political expediency rather than fitness for purpose have been the main influences on assessment practice.

The purpose of assessment during the 20th century has been overwhelmingly the generation of summative data. The content addressed has concerned primarily cognitive tasks. The mode has been the largely traditional vehicle of paper-and-pencil tests and the organisation through large testing and assessment providers. Could it really be the case that stubborn persistence of this out-moded thinking and the technologies of a bygone age are now finally to change? This book offers hope. It suggests that after more than a century of modernist-inspired educational assessment practices in which the pursuit of scientifically defensible measurement has substantially eclipsed issues of utility, fairness, flexibility and relevance, we may well be standing at the threshold of significant change. Could it be, finally, that the grand narratives of intelligence and ability, which were regarded as the key to the determination of life chances, are beginning to yield to a more practical discourse of multiple experiences, skills, knowledge and dispositions?

This book describes some of the starting points for this journey and helps to point the way. It suggests that in time, the assessment procedures of the 21st century will be as fitting to the needs of the contemporary world as those of pre-modern Asia were to theirs. Perhaps then there will be no need for anyone to go to the temple to pray for success.

Gloucestershire, UK   Patricia Broadfoot

Acknowledgements

Any book is the sum of parts of the efforts of many individuals, and this is especially true for an edited book. Our first appreciations are to our chapter authors. We approached you all, valuing your insights into assessment issues and your high professional standing in your fields. Thank you so much for agreeing to contribute to this book within your busy professional lives. Together, your chapters become one more contribution to the goal of improving the educational opportunities for all students.

We also need to thank especially Peta Colbert, who has assisted with chapter editing and the book's creation from the beginning. You are a valued long-term colleague, and it is a pleasure to have the opportunity to work with you. We appreciate your skills and willingness to engage with the creative process and with the assessment dialogues contained within to ensure streamlined and fluent prose across the book.

Our editorial consultant, Renée Otmar, has been invaluable for her editorial eye on each chapter as well as for ensuring the authors met timelines, as much as was within her control! Renée, our authors have commented on how pleasant their interactions with you have been in the development of this book and how smooth the process has been.

The development of this book is a part of our academic work. However, it also reflects the deep beliefs we hold of the importance of assessment in the education of all. We completed this work while we met our other academic commitments and management responsibilities. Thus, inevitably, the support of our families has been a major contribution to its completion. We thank you for your unquestioning support.

Finally, we would like to say that, as co-editors, we have enjoyed once more the opportunity to collaborate within a productive partnership, and look forward to more to come.

Claire Wyatt-Smith
J. Joy Cumming

Contents

List of Figures

List of Tables

Contributors

Michael Arthur-Kelly Michael Arthur-Kelly is associate professor in special education at The University of Newcastle, New South Wales, Australia. He has particular interest in research to practice in instructional design and effectiveness, classroom and behaviour management and support for students with multiple and severe disabilities. His teaching background includes extensive experience in regular and special schools, and he currently serves as a board member or editorial consultant to several educational journals published in Australia and internationally.

Randy Elliot Bennett Randy Bennett is a Distinguished Scientist in the Research and Development Division at Educational Testing Service (ETS) in Princeton, New Jersey. Since the 1980s, he has conducted research on the applications of technology to testing, including presenting and scoring open-ended test items on the computer, multimedia and simulation in testing, and generating test items automatically. For his work, Dr. Bennett was given the ETS Senior Scientist Award in 1996 and the ETS Career Achievement Award in 2005.

Patricia Broadfoot Patricia Broadfoot is a professor and vice chancellor of the University of Gloucestershire, in the United Kingdom. She has researched extensively in her specialist academic fields of educational assessment and comparative education and has published many books and over a hundred articles in these fields, for which she was awarded a DSc from the University of Bristol in 1999. Professor Broadfoot has edited two leading international journals and has been a provider of educational consultancy for policy makers both in the United Kingdom and internationally.

Susan M. Brookhart Susan M. Brookhart is an education consultant based in Helena, Montana, in the United States. She was formerly professor and department chair in the School of Education at Duquesne University, where she currently is a senior research associate in the Center for Advancing the Study of Teaching and Learning. Dr. Brookhart is 2007–09 editor of *Educational Measurement: Issues and Practice*, a journal of the National Council on Measurement in Education. She has written or co-authored seven books and more than 40 articles on assessment.

J. Joy Cumming Joy Cumming is professor of education at Griffith University in Queensland, Australia. Formerly a secondary school teacher of mathematics and

English, and as an educator and researcher for over 35 years, Professor Cumming has researched and published extensively in her area of expertise—assessment—particularly within the areas of literacy and numeracy. She has been a consultant to national and state governments in Australia on many issues in policy and practice in assessment. The impact of legislation and policy on assessment practices and accountability led to her recent completion of a Juris Doctor (law) degree in order to understand legal perspectives in these areas. Professor Cumming's main focuses are on the individual child in education and access to appropriate education for all, with many recent publications focusing on children's rights, assessment and the law.

Glenn Finger Glenn Finger is Deputy Dean (Learning and Teaching) (2007–08), Faculty of Education Executive, at Griffith University in Queensland, Australia and was formerly the deputy director of the Centre for Learning Research (2005–06). Dr. Finger has extensively researched, published and provided consultancies in the use of Information and Communication Technologies (ICTs) to enhance learning. He has more than 50 peer-reviewed publications and major reviews, including being the lead author of the book *Transforming learning with ICT: Making IT happen* (Pearson Education, 2007).

Caroline Victoria Gipps Caroline Gipps trained as a primary school teacher and psychometrician before entering a career in research. She worked at the National Children's Bureau, the National Foundation for Educational Research and the University of British Columbia, before joining the Institute of Education, University of London as a researcher, professor of education and then dean of research. Professor Gipps became deputy vice chancellor at Kingston University in 1999 and vice chancellor of the University of Wolverhampton in 2005. She has published widely on assessment, primary education and equity issues and has an international reputation in educational assessment.

Drew H. Gitomer Drew Gitomer is an Education Testing Service (ETS) Distinguished Researcher. His research interests include policy and evaluation issues related to teacher education, licensure, induction and professional development. Dr. Gitomer's research has also focused on the design of assessments, particularly those that support improvement of instruction. He was senior vice president for research and development at ETS from 1999 to 2004. Dr Gitomer is co-editor of *Educational Evaluation and Policy Analysis*. He earned a PhD in cognitive psychology from the University of Pittsburgh.

Patrick Griffin Patrick Griffin holds the chair of education (assessment) at The University of Melbourne, Australia, and is director of the Assessment Research Centre. He is the deputy dean and associate dean for knowledge transfer in the Melbourne Graduate School of Education. He has published numerous books and journal articles on assessment and evaluation topics. Professor Griffin is a project team leader for UNESCO in southern Africa and a World Bank consultant in Vietnam and China. He has developed a system of teacher assessment recently signed into law by the Vietnam government, to be applied to more than 380 000 teachers and to be replicated in China. His work currently focuses on item-response modelling applications in interpretive frameworks for criterion-referenced performance and developmental competence assessment.

Stephanie Gunn Stephanie Gunn is a research fellow at Griffith University in Queensland, Australia. She has been involved in educational research for nearly 20 years, including as National Coordinator, Literacy and Numeracy Projects for the Australian government, where she assisted in the development of national policies on literacy and numeracy. Ms. Gunn has been co-author on several large government-funded projects. Her current research includes work on a large Australian Research Council-funded project that is exploring standards-driven reform in assessment, with a focus on teacher judgment and moderation.

Romina Jamieson-Proctor Romina Jamieson-Proctor is the Associate Director of Education at the University of Southern Queensland, Australia. She has had first-hand involvement with the use of computer-based technologies in classrooms since 1980. She has also been extensively involved in teacher education programs and professional development activities focusing on the use of information and communications technologies (ICTs) in education, and demonstrating to teachers how they can effectively integrate and create ICT applications that transform curriculum, teaching and learning to meet the needs of the 21st-century learners. Associate Professor Jamieson-Proctor has also had extensive experience managing national and industry-sponsored research projects investigating the impact of ICT on teaching and learning.

Deb Keen Deb Keen is an associate professor in the School of Education and Professional Studies at Griffith University, Queensland, Australia and a member of the Griffith Institute for Educational Research. She has extensive experience as a psychologist, educator, administrator and researcher with individuals who have developmental disabilities. Associate Professor Keen's research interests are primarily in the areas of educational, communication and behavioural interventions for individuals with autism across the lifespan. Current research projects include early intervention with families, and engagement and learning in children with autism.

Ann Kelly Ann Kelly is a lecturer in the School of Education and Professional Studies at Griffith University in Queensland, Australia. She has over 20 years' experience in adult literacy and vocational education, as a teacher, curriculum writer, professional development officer and researcher. Dr. Kelly's current research interests include understanding how the term 'literacy' is conceptualised and applied in a range of practices, investigating mature-aged workers' identities and capacities and their implications for training initiatives, and using ethnomethodology and conversation analysis to explicate how work and vocational training are enacted.

Gunther Kress Gunther Kress is professor of semiotics and education at the Institute of Education, University of London. His interests are in understanding principles of meaning-making and communication in contemporary social environments. This includes having a continuing interest in the development of a social semiotic theory of multimodal communication. For Professor Kress, this involves a focus on the processes and forms of communication in 'environments of learning', whether in institutions or outside formal institutional sites, and more specifically it entails a focus on the relations between sign-making, meaning and knowledge, and between sign-making, learning and the formation of identity. Current research projects are 'Museums, exhibitions and the visitor' (funded by the Swedish Research Council) and 'Gains and losses: Changes in teaching materials 1935–2005' (funded by the Economic and Social Science Research Council, United Kingdom).

Gabrielle Matters Gabrielle Matters is a principal research fellow at the Australian Council for Educational Research (ACER), Head of ACER Brisbane and Executive Secretary of the International Association for Educational Assessment. She is adjunct professor, Faculty of Education, Queensland University of Technology, with a doctorate in the field of psychometrics. Professor Matters has been keenly interested in educational assessment throughout her career as a classroom teacher (physical sciences), school administrator, researcher, advisor, test designer and author. She has held executive management positions within the Australian education sector and has worked with education systems internationally.

Graham Samuel Maxwell Graham Samuel Maxwell is an educational consultant and researcher specialising in assessment policy and practice. He began his professional career in 1962 as a teacher of mathematics and science. After 30 years of teaching and research on assessment in the School of Education, The University of Queensland, Australia, Dr. Maxwell spent 3 years as deputy director of the Queensland Studies Authority. Recent consultancies have concerned assessment, moderation and standards in schools and universities in the United Kingdom, the United States and Australia.

Gordon Stobart Gordon Stobart is professor in education at the Institute of Education, University of London. He is editor of the international journal *Assessment in Education: Principles, Policy and Practice*. He is also a member of the Assessment Reform Group, which campaigns for better use of formative assessment in teaching and learning. Professor Stobart's most recent publication is *Testing times—The uses and abuses of assessment* (Routledge, 2008).

Sverre Tveit Sverre Tveit is a postgraduate student at the University of Oslo, Norway, and Griffith University, Queensland, Australia. He is a former board member of the school-student union of Norway (2001–03), which has been a significant voice calling for reforms in the regulations and practice forms for student assessment. On the union's initiative, in 2007, Mr. Tveit edited a book in which students, teachers, researchers and other experts identified weaknesses in the present system and suggested new regulations and practice forms for student assessment in Norway.

Claire Wyatt-Smith Claire Wyatt-Smith is professor of education and dean of the Faculty of Education at Griffith University in Queensland, Australia. She has been chief investigator on a number of Australian Research Council (ARC) projects and other funded research studies focusing on teacher judgment, standards and evaluative frameworks as these apply in policy and practice. Current research includes an investigation of the dependability of teacher assessment for statewide reporting in Queensland. A current ARC project includes a longitudinal study of standards-driven assessment reform in middle schooling, the focus being on teacher judgment and moderation, both face-to-face and ICT-mediated.

Chapter 1
Framing Assessment Today for the Future: Issues and Challenges

J. Joy Cumming and Claire Wyatt-Smith

Assessment—and its interface with curriculum, teaching and learning—has always been a significant component of classroom practice. Research has indicated that typical teachers spend between one-third and one-half of their class time engaged in one or another type of assessment or learning evaluation activity (Stiggins & Conklin, 1992). However, research has also expressed concern that the knowledge that teachers hold about assessment matters has been limited, with scant attention paid to this area in teacher-preparation programs (Christie et al., 1991; Louden et al., 2005; Matters, 2006).

Over the past decade, the significance of the roles of assessment and accountability in education has only increased. On the one hand, educators are developing ways to improve practical knowledge and application of assessment and development of assessment cultures among teachers through projects and policies such as Assessment for Learning (Black, Harrison, Lee, Marshall, & Wiliam, 2003; Black & Wiliam, 2004; Harlen, 2005; Kellis & Silvernail, 2002; National Research Council, 2001). On the other hand, governments and policy makers around the world have strengthened the role of externally mandated and reported assessment for accountability purposes.

This book examines educational assessment research, policy and practice in the rapidly changing world of the 21st century. Assessment not only continues to be a key activity of teachers, but also has become a key focus of educational research throughout the world, with the field often represented as contested. While traditional issues of validity and reliability continue to have high salience, there are a myriad of issues that are also pressing for educational assessment on the international scene. These include assessment, the law and accountability; the value of testing for international benchmarking and public reporting; assessment practices that take account of cultural and social diversity; assessment practices that go beyond traditional paper-and-pencil tests to include other modes; assessment and technological innovation; the matter of what counts as authentic assessment, especially in relation

J.J. Cumming (✉)
Faculty of Education, Mt Gravatt campus, Griffith University, 176 Messines Ridge Road,
Mt Gravatt QLD 4122, Australia
e-mail: j.cumming@griffith.edu.au

C. Wyatt-Smith, J.J. Cumming (eds.), *Educational Assessment in the 21st Century*,
DOI 10.1007/978-1-4020-9964-9_1, © Springer Science+Business Media B.V. 2009

to professional and vocational education; and assessment issues relating to inclusion and disability.

Two major factors have informed this book. First, the book has arisen as a result of the previously mentioned clear and growing pressure from various stakeholders for education accountability. This has been reflected in increased measurement initiatives, including the prominence given to large-scale testing and reporting initiatives, and national introspection on outcomes from international comparative tests. Such measurement activities are not a stand-alone force, however, in the education and assessment fields. Also evident are strong moves in some countries to endorse alternative modes of assessment beyond traditional paper-and-pencil tests—the assessment mode limits usually required in large-scale testing—and to develop teachers' assessment capabilities in their daily classroom practice as well as to serve accountability purposes. These radically different directions in research inevitably make competing demands on education researchers, as well as those involved in policy and practice. It is timely, therefore, for this book to bring together cutting-edge research and theoretical discussion from all perspectives and to open out and explore the ways forward for assessment in a new century characterised by an unprecedented change and growth in knowledge.

Thus, the second factor that informed the development of this book is our chosen approach. In previous research and publications, we have applied a multidisciplinary and multitheoretical approach in our work (Cumming & Wyatt-Smith, 2001). A multitheoretical approach to education research has also been advocated by others (for example, Beach, Green, Kamil, & Shanahan, 1991, and more recently, Green, Camilli, & Elmore, 2006). This book aims to be encompassing of different disciplines that inform the methodologies and approaches underlying different theoretical understandings about, and practices in, assessment.

The field of assessment research needs to move beyond tensions posited as diametrically opposed in ways that are unhelpful for improving practice or assisting the classroom practitioner. Notions of assessment for measurement and assessment for learning work, in part, to maintain a long-standing perceived disparity between objectivity and subjectivity. We consider it important to move forward. The field of assessment can now be characterised in terms of the myriad of 21st-century issues that confront it and that call for public and scholarly scrutiny and discussion. The authors in this book situate assessment in differing contexts, providing a research, policy and practice nexus for assessment in the 21st century, with impacts of changes, such as technology, inclusive practices, cultural diversity and learning for the workplace, as well as accountability-driven reform.

What the Authors Were Asked to Do

In order to shape this book and meet our commitment to readers to provide a multitheoretical and multidisciplinary approach to assessment, we asked our authors to provide chapters with a difference. Each chapter, and its respective author/s, frames its own space and presents a distinctive 'voice' in the book. While in our initial framing we envisaged the dimensions of assessment issues of interest for the 21st century and identified potential authors with expertise in each dimension, the authors were free to amend our suggested topic or to offer alternative topics of interest to them. We knew that the standing of each of our authors in their field would ensure interesting and provocative commentary for our readers. However, each chapter becomes a self-contained exposition on assessment. We did not just ask authors to contribute in their areas of special interest, but we also asked authors to provide brief overviews to inform the reader about the theoretical and methodological frameworks underpinning their writing. This is contained within each chapter itself in some writings, or as an appendix in others. Further, our authors were asked to provide their own definitions for key terms and concepts in their chapters, again either within the chapters or in an attached glossary. Thus, throughout this book you may find definitions of terms across a range of chapters that may or may not be congruent. We consider these contextual definitions of assessment concepts valuable in demonstrating the social and cultural meanings we bring to bear on our research work. In this book, particular theories are not prioritised and meanings are not singular in direction. Thus, we hope the book is informative for readers, not only for the breadth of discussion on assessment issues for the 21st century, but also for the demonstration of different ways of knowing, learning and 'doing' assessment.

In the next part of this chapter, we provide an overview of the contents of the book as a guide to you as the reader. We highlight the main focuses of the authors and synthesise very briefly the many complex and exciting ideas embedded in each chapter. We endeavour to provide some sense of orientation of the authors in each chapter, but leave to you a fulsome engagement with, and examination of, the theoretical and methodological framings of each. We also leave to your own discovery the excitement and depth of the insights of the authors and their conclusions for future directions.

The Contributions of the Authors

First, we express our thanks to Patricia Broadfootfor providing the Foreword to this book. Broadfoot provides a historical and sociocultural overview of assessment that serves as a constant—dare we say—'benchmark' for the practices we see around us in education today. We understand that in strongly competitive societies in the past, examinations were used to stratify social class and opportunity. What is harder to understand in a world in which equitable opportunity and education for all are the espoused goals of our nations, we appear to perpetuate systems that promote competition, failure and success, especially when such success appears, in part at least, to reflect the social capital of the student. Broadfoot examines the various roles for assessment in our 21st-century world, defining four dimensions that we should consider to compare the present with the past: 'purpose, mode, content and organisation' (see page v–vi). She reminds us that in our post-modern construction of assessment at the beginning of the 21st century, we are having doubts about the perfection of science as a measure of student learning. The direction for the new century is for more 'humanist' and individualised focuses on assessment and student-learning enhancement. New directions will need to consider the diversity of learners and learning, of what is to be learned and how it can be demonstrated. Broadfoot posits a new scenario of portfolios, transportability and tailored assessment. We believe that the considerations of our authors provide the means to move us forward in the pursuit of a new paradigm for assessment for the remainder of the 21st century.

The chapters in this book have been characterised under three main groupings, although this is not to imply similarity or singularity of thoughts within the chapters. However, as the authors' perspectives emerged, we identified three major concerns. The first four chapters—by Gunther Kress; Randy Bennett and Drew Gitomer; Glenn Finger and Romina Jamieson-Proctor; and Claire Wyatt-Smith and Stephanie Gunn—explore the new dimensions for assessment in the 21st century that are having or will have an impact on assessment. These include the impacts of globalisation, new technologies and new understandings of the role and significance of frameworks and communication in enactments of educational assessment. We characterise these chapters as dealing with issues of creativity, innovation, new skills and capabilities and changing communication practices.

Gunther Kress starts his discussion with the proposition that 'dealing with learning and assessment invokes theories of communication and meaning' (see page 19). He challenges readers to consider how to recognise learning and the data or evidence that would count, showing that learning has occurred. Through his probing of these two issues, Kress focuses on the notions of learning in specific contexts and how the making of meaning, sign and concept relate to context.

Working from the perspective of a semiotic theory of learning, Kress presents the case for new principles of recognition of learning that challenge the traditional dominance of the linguistic modes of speech and writing. His chapter calls into question how these modes have been given pre-eminence and provokes a conscious attempt at recognising meaning-making and learning in all modes. The powerful message from Kress is that 'what is not recognised will not and cannot be assessed', leading to what he refers to as 'severe misrecognition of learners' capacities and actions' (see page 38).

Any discussion of assessment for the future must necessarily encompass the issue of technology. The relationship between technology and assessment can have many forms: technology as a tool to undertake traditional forms of assessment; the interplay of the impact of technology on assessment; assessment of technology in education; and new views as to how assessment is shaped when technology is assumed as a 21st-century focus. Randy Bennett and Drew Gitomer provide an exhilarating perspective of the way in which assessment should be construed in a technologically driven world—the world that is already around us in the 21st century. Bennett and Gitomer link technological advances to advances in understanding individuals and the nature of learning. They challenge current accountability agendas to be more informed and informing. Their challenge involves the incorporation of cognitive science developments, developments in psychometric measurement approaches and technological developments that allow presentation of 'richer assessment tasks' with some automation of 'scoring' (see page 43). Bennett and Gitomer commence by contextualising their thoughts in the United States' educational context, concerns about quality and equality of educational experiences for all students and the limited educational value of consequent accountability agendas for student improvement. However, as we note for other chapters, the United States' experiences and policy preoccupations, rightly or wrongly, are not theirs alone. Bennett and Gitomer challenge themselves to create a better accountability system that is modern, informed by good assessment practices and educationally of value, allowing monitoring of student progress to inform and enhance student learning. Their proposed solution encompasses the themes that emerged independently from so many of our authors—concerns that assessment should be able to identify individual strengths and weaknesses with customised reports for different audiences, should be based in some theory of learning and development, should provide authentic and meaningful engagement for students, should recognise the social and cultural nature of learning and knowledge and should be supported by professional development and assessment-cued teachers. It is in the final enactment of their solution that technology becomes a central support.

Glenn Finger and Romina Jamieson-Proctor also examine assessment through the lens of technology—not just the application of technology as a form of assessment, but also the issues relating to assessment of learning in the area of information and communications technologies (ICTs), the interaction of assessment forms and the nature of ICT knowledge. Agreeing with Bennett and Gitomer, and Finger and Jamieson-Proctor, we take as given that technology and technological developments will be major influences on the directions that education and assessment will take in the 21st century. If they are not, then the outcome will be an education of students constructed by adults that is an anachronism in the modern world. The technological changes to come cannot be envisaged, just as the technological resources available to children at this time are beyond the dreams of the mid-20th century. However, understanding the nature of knowledge in ICT contexts and the import for teaching, learning and assessment are relatively new educational endeavours. Finger and Jamieson-Proctor explore this issue for teachers from the perspective of TPCK—technological pedagogical content knowledge—building on the pedagogical theories of Shulman (1987). They provide examples of ICT use for assessment, such as development of ePortfolios for students. As this chapter demonstrates, the opportunities are limited only by our own capacity to engage with the technologies afforded. Finger and Jamieson-Proctor argue that it is important for assessment schema to go beyond a focus on the knowledge that students have of technologies to 'how students are able to use ICT for learning in a range of curriculum contexts' and how such use facilitates the 'development of creative, complex and critical thinking' (page 67). Finger and Jamieson-Proctor provide a comprehensive examination of the current state of the art in learning with, and assessment of, ICT and the many tools already available to teachers and emerging innovations. Most importantly, they identify that the challenge for the future will be teachers maintaining ICT proficiency at the same rate as students and the need for educators to have 'a strong understanding of how students are learning in the 21st century' (page 78).

Claire Wyatt-Smith and Stephanie Gunn explore the need for theoretical underpinnings to assessment in the 21st century, given the range of purposes and activities being implemented. They argue that an approach to assessment as 'meaning-making' (Delandshere & Petrosky, 1998) provides a way to examine and shape assessment purposes and practices. Wyatt-Smith and Gunn support their theoretical propositions with empirical evidence collected during research conducted in Queensland, Australia. The assessment system of Queensland for accreditation in the senior years of schooling, using teacher judgment, has been internationally known for 30 years. Wyatt-Smith and Gunn explore enactments of such approaches in the earlier years of schooling and explore the ways in which such judgments are made: the dynamics between social contexts and teacher expectations in shaping judgments and the contexts of increasing external accountability demands and influence on classroom practices. While the discussion is set in Queensland and Australia, these contexts have clear international generalisability. Drawing on arguments about the import of these for issues of student equity and the need to address the diversity of students, Wyatt-Smith and Gunn emphasise the need for evidence as an underpinning essential element in assessment. However, such evidence itself is part of the sociocultural context of educational enactments. Wyatt-Smith and Gunn elaborate four 'lenses' to explore assessment as meaning-making, applying them as a framework to explore the empirical evidence from their research. As the exploration unfolds, implications not only for assessment theory and practice but also for teacher professionalism and assessment cultures emerge. This chapter shows that as we have moved into the 21st century with enhanced expectations of the role of assessment to improve learning, we need to move further with our expectations of our own understandings of the theory of assessment itself.

Another broad theme identified by the authors in this book was the consideration of a range of assessment issues we characterise as 'Building social capital: Difference, diversity and social inclusion'. An underlying theme in these chapters, by Caroline Gipps and Gordon Stobart, Susan Brookhart, Deb Keen and Michael Arthur-Kelly, and Joy Cumming, is the effect of assessment on students' demonstration of achievement and the interaction of assessment and student. Again, these concerns have been examined from a range of perspectives: equity issues for individual students in the pursuit of best educational opportunities for all; equity issues through the examination of available national and international standardised test data; equity issues and new ways of enhancing assessment practices with students with disabilities; and assessment and equity issues as they emerge from law.

Caroline Gipps and Gordon Stobart address the issue of fairness in assessment, moving from technical definitions of 'fairness' to conceptions of fairness that consider the contexts of assessment and social and cultural issues—assessment as a 'socially embedded activity'. Most broadly, they argue that fairness needs to consider access and opportunity, not just equality of scores or achievement outcomes. Equal outcomes may be fair to one group of students but not to another, and unequal outcomes may be 'fair and just' for all (see page 106). Gipps and Stobart elaborate the theme of the origins of assessment discussed by Broadfoot in the 'Foreword', the emergence of assessment in society for selection purposes, within a framework at the time considered fair and promoting merit. The influence of these origins on assessment development and the emergence of the psychometric paradigm through the 20th century are considered in parallel with the social assumptions that underpin these developments and the social capital that enables performance. While the development of the 'assessment' paradigm was seen as an educational response to the measurement paradigm development of the 20th century, in itself this development is not socially or culturally neutral. Gipps and Stobart posit that fairness from a sociocultural perspective can only be achieved through new constructions of validity. Through three examples from different social, cultural and assessment contexts, the authors demonstrate that fairness and equity cannot be assumed, but must be carefully monitored in any assessment environment. Most importantly, they see the pursuit of fairness in assessment, and opportunity for the individual, as a major and ongoing challenge for educational assessment. We need to continue to make apparent biases and assumptions and to maintain vigilance and the 'political will' if we value a goal of fairness for all.

Susan Brookhart provides a comprehensive analysis of international and national assessment data and research study outcomes across many dimensions to examine assessment equity and gender effects. Necessarily, her analyses are based on the standardised measures used in, and outcomes from, such studies, with the types of standardised assessments ranging from multiple-choice formats to extended performance assessments. She investigates findings for a range of curricula, including English, mathematics and science, and for different student age groups. However, Brookhart's discussion is not just to identify whether different achievement outcomes can be related to the gender of a student, but also to examine the nature of any differences, whether differences are due to an interaction between the gender of a student and an assessment process (the answer appears to be 'no') and how any such differences are interpreted by educators. Her concern is with what students can do and the pedagogical implications for differences demonstrated by achievement studies. Brookhart's initial analyses show that while consistent effects are found for reading, favouring girls over boys, the effects for mathematics are less clear and consistent and are likely to be curriculum and pedagogy related. Somewhat similar outcomes are found for other areas, particularly when results are analysed in conjunction with other demographic data. There appears to be a clear interaction between the construct being assessed, the groups of students and gender outcomes. Brookhart notes that where differences are found, individual variation can be more significant: 'individual boys and girls, and individual schools, may be very different from the average' (page 125). Her concluding discussion regarding future directions to ensure equity in assessment considers the importance of individual items. However, her final thoughts and recommendations offer a different challenge to assessment research, calling for more understanding of 'economic and cultural patterns in achievement, which may be more amenable to change' (page 133).

Deborah Keen and Michael Arthur-Kelly consider the implications of assessment for students who have always had specific attention in education research: students with disability. However, their discussion shifts the discourse from a deficit model of limited expectations for these students to an empowering model in order to chart progress through acts of assessment tied closely and intrinsically to instruction and goal setting. Such assessment is occurring in a context in which change is 'incremental', but where identification of effective and ineffective instruction and the level of intensity of instruction needed for each individual student are critical. Keen and Arthur-Kelly continue the theme of our work that all individuals are able to learn and are entitled to learning opportunities. Their focus on student engagement with learning, and ways to assess such engagement, brings a new dimension to considerations of assessment theory from mainstream perspectives. Keen and Arthur-Kelly support their argument by drawing on empirical data from research with students with autistic spectrum disorder. They describe curriculum-based assessment for students with disability, drawing on research originating in the United States. They state that '[i]t is now generally agreed that assessment and intervention are best focused on maximising the individual learning outcomes achieved by the student, from a strengths perspective' (page 142). Keen and Arthur-Kelly pose 'big' questions in their assessment profiles, including the 'best support' for students and life-long learning, with goals including 'curiosity, increased independence . . . and self-actualisation' (page 144) and the intensive curriculum planning necessary to work with students with disability. Their chapter provides positive and challenging directions for the education and assessment of students with disability. We ponder whether their principles apply only to students with disability or whether they represent ideal frameworks for the education of all students.

In the final chapter in this section of the book, examining issues of fairness, cultural diversity and social capital, Joy Cumming explores assessment issues from the perspective of education law. Education law, including legal challenges relating to assessment, is already a major area of study in the United States, but is only emerging in case law in England and is relatively limited in Australia and many other nations. However, individual students, teachers and parents have a growing expectation of their rights and empowerment as individuals, whether or not such rights are indeed present in a nation's laws. When administrative recourse to right-perceived wrongs fails, people are turning to the courts for justice. In this chapter, Cumming examines the status of legal challenges in assessments, the frameworks in which such challenges can occur and the burdens that must be met by those who feel they are wronged—the plaintiffs—in order to succeed in court. The area of education law is not recognised in its own right in the law courts, and challenges must be won or lost within the fields that have emerged from other contexts such as administration law, discrimination law or negligence law. Cumming's analysis shows that the construction of equity in law for an individual is not necessarily of the same meaning that educators would ascribe. Indeed, the courts may be perceived as harsh in their resolution of educational matters that clearly have had considerable negative impact on the lives and opportunities of individuals. Nevertheless, cases raising a range of assessment matters have been successful, and precedents for much broader future actions around educational assessment matters have been established through key cases in England, such as Phelps (2001). Cumming considers the assessment areas where educators need to take care, to reduce the likelihood of litigation and the subsequent distribution of resources to the legal community, rather than to educational provision.

Our final characterisation of the chapters in this book reflects the impact of specific contexts on assessment outcomes, whether drawing on geographical, political, paradigmatic or policy frameworks.

Patrick Griffin has explored the ways in which schools and teachers can use the array of standardised test data available in Australia, and in schools in other nations, for formative purposes to reform teaching and enhance student learning. Drawing on psychometric models of assessment, including item-response modelling, Griffin follows the work developed at the Australian Council for Educational Research[1] in the use of developmental scales to identify the quality and developmental progress of a student's achievement against the item demands and constructs of such tests. Griffin notes that a developmental approach in interpreting data allows teachers to scaffold learning for individual students and to create 'personalised and clinical approaches to intervention' (page 185). When standardised tests are developed using a criterion-referenced approach, the developmental scales and student performance against criteria can be identified. In his chapter, Griffin provides guidelines on ways that teachers can map content and examine student performance and progress. He explores the resources that teachers need in order to undertake intervention and plan future instruction with individual students, suggesting enhanced communication among teachers as an active form of professional development. Griffin's chapter includes description of a successful school enactment of the principles that he proposes. He concludes by considering the import of his arguments, not only for teacher professional development but also for teacher education. Griffin's chapter commences with a focus on individualised use of student assessment data for formative purposes to improve learning, but progresses to a systemic examination of the use of data for change and pedagogical enhancement. Given the maintained focus of governments on educational accountability, it is likely that systemic assessment data will continue to grow in Australia and elsewhere. It, therefore, is sensible to explore how this can be used most effectively for the purposes for which it was intended.

Gabrielle Matters also examines the way that teachers, and schools, can use a range of assessment data to improve instruction and student learning. Her focus, in the main, is similar to that of Griffin: the standardised-test information available to schools from external accountability regimes. However, Matters argues that considerable detailed information is available to schools and teachers within such school data and suggests ways in which the interaction between students and assessments should be scrutinised to examine and improve student performance. She further argues that future developments of assessments should ensure that information at such a level is of a quality that it can serve these functions. One key to quality for Matters is the care taken in the identification of the construct, the 'conceptual

---

[1] In 1992, the National Council for Measurement in Education gave ACER its Annual Award for 'outstanding dissemination of educational measurement concepts to the public' for this work.

framework' (page 210) that is being assessed and against which student progress is being measured. She explores the value of each individual item within an assessment context, and indeed the interaction of the item and the individual student within the specific context. Drawing on a learning model incorporating 'presage–process–product', Matters posits that the individual student has as much a 'causally central role in the learning process' as teachers and schools, and hence in the assessment process (page 211). Both Matters and Brookhart have noted that individuals have varied backgrounds and experiences and are the product of 'nature' and 'nurture'. As Wyatt-Smith and Gunn also noted, this source of difference, however, should not be used to justify or explain different outcomes or to remove responsibility from educators for learning outcomes for each student. Examination of the nature of an assessment item and an individual student's responsiveness to the item rather than just correctness of response can provide insight into the student's development. Difficulty of an item is not just a statistical description but also represents a different interaction for each student, according to context. Examination of items and responses can highlight misconceptions and lead to improved instruction. As Matters notes, such examination may even reveal some flaws in the assessment items and tests themselves. Her overall conclusions reiterate her call for more focus on development of quality assessments, in any form, and much more focus on using available assessment information for learning improvement.

Sverre Tveit brings the perspective of a student to educational assessment issues, albeit the perspective of a student now engaged in graduate studies. Tveit's account of the Norwegian assessment experience of the past two decades provides an insight into the impact of differing agendas on education experiences, goals and assessment practices. Tveit was a member of the School-Student Union of Norway at a time when the government decided to implement major national changes to assessment. The Norwegian government's action was in response to perceived national 'failure' on international tests such as PISA, considering the high expenditure of the nation on education. Tveit provides an overview of pedagogical development in Norway, drawing on a range of policy documents as well as personal experience. He describes the assessment regimes of Norway at local and national levels and the various attempted changes by the government—in conjunction with the opposition demonstrated by students, educators, assessment experts and politicians in opposition. His chapter provides a very clear exposition of the impact of external factors on national practice and the political roles that education and assessment play across the world today. Tveit's overview demonstrates a system exhibiting local authority and national accountability of teachers in a way uncommon to most other nations, with the concept of official, random examinations for students as a monitor of overall schooling effectiveness and student preparedness. Most importantly, Tveit examines the system of assessment in Norway with the critical eye of a student, seeking evidence for research-based underpinning of practice and teacher professional development, and consistency in goals and purposes. He makes a number of propositions for future reform of assessment in Norway. While Tveit's exploration of assessment is set in a singular assessment culture, his descriptions of theory, practice and issues will resonate throughout the international community.

The assessment context for the chapter by Ann Kelly is vocational education. She adopts a situated approach and calls for an extension to current assessment of skills development. Worldwide, vocational assessment has been moving to a competency-based approach. The competences reflect identified component skills, both lower order and higher order, in the development of guild knowledge (see page 246). Thus, the expectation underpinning this approach was that apprenticeships could become part of formal educational contexts, in the same way that general education became institutionalised at the commencement of the 20th century, to cope with the needed growth in education for the Industrial Revolution. Aspects of the apprenticeship could be identified and confirmed. A further advantage envisaged for formal vocational education and a competence approach was the capacity to allow apprentices to proceed at their own learning and developmental paces. However, the formalisation of apprenticeships and vocational education into competences has left many considering that the essence of guild knowledge is missing—competences can become superficial rather than rich descriptions of a skill base (page 246). In her chapter, Kelly has unpacked this issue and explored a way in which the richness of skills development can be explored, using the methodology of conversational analysis to examine authentic enactment of an area of communication competences. Such an analysis allows the identification and assessment of the tacit knowledges that underpin performance. While this analysis provides a telling instance of elaborated assessment in a vocational context, it also demonstrates central themes that emerge from the authors of this book: assessment is most effective when the individual is targeted; individual performance needs elaboration in order to be effective, making high demand on assessment processes; and the situated context of assessment interacts with the performance.

Standards as conceptual identities emerge in the discussions of a number of our authors. Within each chapter, the conceptual identity each author attributes to 'standards' should emerge for the reader. In his chapter, Graham Maxwell provides a theoretical and policy-based consideration of the situated constructions of 'standards' commonly being used around the world and the many contexts that influence such construction of concepts. Maxwell provides an analytical framework, elaborating four dimensions that can be considered to explore the contextual use of a concept of standards: type, focus, underlying characteristic or construct and purpose. Maxwell shows that cultural contexts provide very different interpretations for standards, from conceptions of standards as a form of curriculum framework to conceptions of standards as indicators of levels of performance. Within the latter, many different meanings are still visible in practice. He notes the constant tension between descriptions of performance against standards or others (notionally criterion-referenced and normative standards) despite the basis of both in guild knowledge. The one has always informed the other—we only understand perfection by understanding what is not perfection, and we need a model as a comparator. Overall, Maxwell exhorts educators to identify and clarify the meanings we ascribe to our constructions of a 'standard' to enable common conversations about intentions and to clarify the social and cultural contexts that frame these conversations. Throughout his explorations of these frameworks and meanings, Maxwell keeps a central imperative on their impact for the individual learner, working from the central 'purpose of education [which] is to enable the advancement of the personal knowledge and capabilities of each student to the fullest extent possible and to prepare them for further learning and development throughout their life' (page 264). It is Maxwell who notes that the children entering school today can expect to live during most of the 21st century and many will enter the 22nd century.

In working through the chapters in the book and exploring the ideas presented by our authors, readers will notice commonalities and differences, which we now consider.

Assessment Commonalities in Diversity

There can be no doubt that education in this century is a dynamic and exciting discipline. Students and teachers are engaging in learning dialogues of unprecedented complexity in recognition of changing times, changing needs, changing social groupings and, not least, changing technology. Educational policy is seen as a significant political area, with resultant high focus on educational content and delivery. Each of these dimensions of current educational contexts has import for educational assessment, ensuring that the traditional concept of 'testing' is to modern educational practice as the quill is to textual recording.

In this book, we have drawn together the voices of international experts in educational assessment, talking about the issues with which they are concerned and providing opportunity to identify possible directions for future action. Even though the book is intended to be comprehensive, it can only touch on the issues and practices engaging educational assessment. What we hope we have portrayed successfully are the ongoing and increasing complexity and significance of the role of good educational assessment in modern education practice and the challenges that present in attaining such a goal.

The 21st century has commenced with high expectations, not just for student outcomes but also for the professionalism of teachers and authorities—of clarity of purpose, approach and language, of recognition of different theoretical framings of assessment and, not least, of an overall care for the educational opportunities for all students.

The authors in this book have written from a range of different theoretical and methodological framings of assessment, reflecting what are often referred to as different paradigms.

Beyond points of difference, however, there are several calls that readers will hear resonating across the chapters. We refer deliberately to these as 'calls', in that they invite action in the fields of research, policy and practice. While readers will no doubt hear such calls differently, in this chapter we offer our framing—our hearing—of these. Throughout the chapters, a recurring call is for assessment to be relevant to the needs of the individual learner, in order to improve their educational opportunities and life outcomes and to provide the individual learner the opportunity to voice their needs. This goes beyond the long-standing stance for learner-centred approaches to a recognition of learner agency and the active contributions of the learner to inform how learning, and therefore assessment, should occur. The gravity of this call is to the fore when there is also the clear connection between educational, and more specifically, assessment opportunities and life opportunities. All too often in the past, assessment has worked to limit, even prescribe, such opportunities, inevitably impacting on what and how individuals achieve in social, workplace and civic spheres.

An expansion on this is the need to go beyond policies of inclusion (which can focus on stereotypical and group identification drawing on a deficit perspective) to develop policies that recognise diversity and the complexity of the individual learner. Increasingly, teachers report that one of their main challenges in classroom practice is how to provide responsive teaching and assessment to diverse learners. Many of our authors recognised such challenges and demonstrated that assessment needs to chart student learning from the perspective of an underpinning theory of learning progress and development—whether such a theory is based on cognitive science, psychometric analyses, curriculum theories or combinations of these. From the standpoint of an underpinning theory of learning progress and development, the purposes of standards can be moved away from being a 'standardising' influence. More specifically, they need to be rethought and clearly defined in terms of their role in supporting learners and teachers in progressing learning and in understanding differences across learning development.

There is also the strong call in the chapters for 'salient' or revealing evidence to support such charting and assessment of learning development, whether from formal or informal bases. Constant, therefore, is the need for sources of information and documentation. Related to this is the recurring challenge for assessment to take seriously the issues of equity by unpacking how the judgments of progress are being made. At play here are critical matters of the types of information that count as evidence and the ways in which the evidence is treated. Further, the chapters open spaces for different niche approaches to assessment and highlight the need for assessment researchers to theorise assessment practices in greater depth, elaborating and clarifying contexts and assumptions. This is particularly to the fore, for example, in how our chapters have conscientiously included commentary on the impact of technology on assessment, explored from various dimensions. What differentiates the 20th century from the beginning of the 21st century is the exponential and unbelievable development of new methods of communication, representing knowledge, and making knowledge available. Within this framework of the developments of the past 30 years—from clunky computer terminals with limited capacity to hand-held devices more powerful than computers of a decade ago and from a paper-based society to the development of the World Wide Web and the Internet in the past two decades—change in practices in education and assessment is inevitable.

Last but not least, there is a call for opportunities to enhance the professional development of teachers. This development is taken to include the repertoires of assessment practices that teachers rely on, especially in relation to student diversity and inclusion as well as teachers' own knowledge of what counts as quality assessment and ways to promote student learning. This, of course, becomes critical, given the intensified policy interest in accountability of school decision making and transparency in how judgements, including grading decisions, are arrived at.

Looking Backwards, Looking Forwards: Developing an Interactionist Perspective

A decade ago, Delandshere & Petrosky (1998) reported how, in the then recent past, there had been 'a shift in the rhetoric (if not yet the practice) of assessment' (p. 15). They went on to identify how, by 1998, 'much more emphasis [had] been placed on the support of learning and teaching than on the sorting and ranking of individuals' (p. 15). This observation informed their characterisation of how, at that time, 'the field of assessment [was] challenged by many conflicting purposes that create interesting problems', referring in particular to the challenges associated with how 'performance assessment systems are implemented for their potential impact on instruction and, more generally, as a way to promote systemic change in schools' (p. 15).

The chapters in this book provide clear evidence of how the field of assessment, and further, the practice of assessment, has strengthened the focus on how assessment can support learning and teaching. Across the chapters, the concentration on assessment to improve the quality of learning is to the fore. Also clear is a shift in rhetoric away from 'the problems' of assessment through to opportunities for rethinking assessment. The chapters provide frames for seeing how such rethinking is occurring in relation to the changing contexts of education, developments in learning theory and different ways of thinking about the nature of knowledge itself.

Further, the book as a whole presents new insights into the nature of assessment that go beyond the notion of assessment as evidence-based practice. There is recognition of how assessment is contextualised practice, linking in complex ways to social, cultural and policy/political contexts. This opens the space for a new appreciation of the forces at play in shaping how assessment occurs and should occur. In regard to the latter, there are, of course, the forces that are tied to ongoing and rapid changes in ICTs, bringing with them new interaction possibilities, as well as new ways to use, represent and create knowledge.

It might be interesting for readers to revisit the idea, introduced earlier, that while we, as editors, made choices about the writers who would be invited to contribute chapters, taking account of what we knew of previous writings, we were not seeking to give greater prominence to any particular theoretical tradition or approach in the field of assessment. Therefore, on reflection, we know that different paradigms in assessment research focus on measurement versus assessment paradigms, with the former seen as having psychological and psychometric bases and the latter being more socially constructivist based. The authors in this collection show, however, that such characterisations may be too simplistic for assessment directions for the 21st century. Instead, there is emerging a new appreciation of how theoretical and disciplinary stances, and contexts and modes for enacting assessment, are fundamentally interactionist. Beyond this, there are some signs of movement towards a multitheoretical assessment approach. Readers will observe, for example, that writers working within the psychometric paradigms explored and considered sociocultural contexts, while, overall, the different assessment paradigms recognised the need for theoretical progressions of learning. Such signs hold promise for paradigmatic change, whereby assessment practices incorporate technological change and offer both new performance and new learning contexts that take account of new student cohorts.

We hope that you as readers find this book a valuable addition to your library on assessment. We encourage you to delve into the chapters and to make your own reflections on the influence of the different theoretical and methodological frameworks of the authors on their work. We invite you to consider whether the frameworks are necessarily incompatible or whether they can all be perceived to contribute to our understanding of learners and learning and to contribute to the research, policy and practice imperatives that have identified the significant role that assessment plays in education at this point in the 21st century.

References

Beach, R., Green, J. L., Kamil, M. L., & Shanahan, T. (Eds.). (1991). *Multidisciplinary perspectives on literacy research.* Urbana, IL: National Council of Teachers of English.

Black, P., & Wiliam, D. (2004). The formative purpose: Assessment must first promote learning. In M. Wilson (Ed.), *Towards coherence between classroom assessment and accountability.* Chicago, IL: National Society for the Study of Education.

Black, P., Harrison, C., Lee, C., Marshall, B., & Wiliam, D. (2003). *Assessment for learning: Putting it into practice.* Buckingham: Open University Press.

Christie, F., Devlin, B., Freebody, P., Luke, A., Martin, J. R., Threadgold, T. et al. (1991). *Teaching English literacy: A project of national significance on the preservice preparation of teachers for teaching English literacy—Volume 1.* Canberra: Department of Employment, Education and Training.

Cumming, J. J., & Wyatt-Smith, C. M. (Eds.). (2001). *Literacy-curriculum connections: Implications for theory and practice.* Melbourne: ACER Press.

Delandshere, G., & Petrosky, A. R. (1998). Assessment of complex performances: Limitations of key measurement assumptions. *Educational Researcher, 27*(2), 14–24.

Green, J., Camilli, G., & Elmore, P. (Eds.). (2006). *Handbook of complementary methods in education research.* Mahwah, NJ: LEA (for AERA).

Harlen, W. (2005). Teachers' summative practices and assessment for learning—tensions and synergies. *The Curriculum Journal, 16*(2), 207–223.

Kellis, M., & Silvernail, D. (2002). *Considering the place of teacher judgment in Maine's local assessment systems.* Maine: Center for Educational Policy, Applied Research, and Evaluation, University of Southern Maine.

Louden, W., Rohl, M., Gore, J., McIntosh, A., Greaves, D., Wright, R. et al. (2005). *Prepared to teach: An investigation into the preparation of teachers to teach literacy and numeracy.* Canberra: Department of Education, Training and Youth Affairs.

Matters, G. (2006). *Assessment approaches in Queensland senior science syllabuses. A report to the Queensland Studies Authority.* Brisbane: ACER.

National Research Council. (2001). *Knowing what students know: The science and design of educational assessment.* Washington: National Academy Press.

Phelps v Hillingdon London Borough Council [2001] 2 AC 619.

Shulman, L. S. (1987). Knowledge and teaching: Foundations of the new reform. *Harvard Educational Review, 57,* 1–22.

Stiggins, R. J., & Conklin, N. F. (1992). *In teachers' hands: Investigating the practices of classroom assessment.* Albany, NY: State University of New York Press.

Part I
Creativity and Innovation in Assessment: New Skills and Capabilities, and Changing Communication Practices

Chapter 2
Assessment in the Perspective of a Social Semiotic Theory of Multimodal Teaching and Learning

Gunther Kress

The world of meaning is multimodal. It always has been and now, for a variety of reasons, that awareness is once again moving onto centre stage. In education, a range of questions arises from this recent recognition. Among these, the two linked questions are becoming insistently urgent: 'How do we assess learning expressed in multimodal texts, objects and processes?' and 'What theories are needed to deal with *assessment* in this environment?' The framework proposed here is that of a *social semiotic theory of multimodality*. It provides a 'take' on *meaning*—and hence by implication on *learning*—and it provides a view on the characteristics and uses of *modes* in representation. It asserts that *modes* have different *affordances*; potentials, capacities as well as limitations for making meaning: a result jointly of the *materiality* of modes—sound, for instance, being different *materially* to movement or to colour—and often long histories of the shaping of these materials in specific societies. *Multimodality* asserts that societies use many means of making meaning beyond those of *speech* and *writing* and insists that they all be taken into consideration in domains in which *meaning, learning, knowing* and the *'(e)valuations'/assessments* of these are the issue.

Multimodality, as such, is not a theory. It describes the field in which meaning is made; hence, the need for the social semiotic theory. However, the two together enable an account of communication, of meaning, of learning and, with that, of assessment, in which these issues can be treated as distinct and yet remain connected, in theory and in practice.

Dealing with learning and assessment invokes theories of communication and meaning. Teaching is communication, as is learning; they are reciprocal aspects of one relation. Learning is the obverse of making meaning; they are two sides of one sheet of paper, as Ferdinand de Saussure (1983) might have said. Learning is the result of a semiotic/conceptual/meaning-making engagement with an aspect of the world, as the result of which the learner's semiotic/conceptual resources for

G. Kress (✉)
Faculty of Culture and Pedagogy, Centre for Multimodal Research, Institute of Education, University of London, London, UK
e-mail: g.kress@ioe.ac.uk

C. Wyatt-Smith, J.J. Cumming (eds.), *Educational Assessment in the 21st Century*,
DOI 10.1007/978-1-4020-9964-9_2, © Springer Science+Business Media B.V. 2009

making meaning and therefore for acting in the world are changed—they are augmented. Learning happens in specific environments; environments of learning make available specific semiotic/conceptual resources in particular configurations. The characteristics of these environments and the shape of the configurations have large effects on possibilities of learning.

Assessment deals with a relationship between that which was to be learned—a curriculum—and that which has been learned. Two major issues for assessment are how to 'recognise' learning, say, when it appears in a mode not expected or legitimated and what might constitute data of that which has been learned. A common means is to 'ask' someone, in some way or the other: what they (thought that they) might have learned or how they felt that they had learned. I use the notion of signs of learning (Jewitt & Kress, 2001). These indicate changes in resources and capacities as a result of the processes of learning in the modes used by the learner in the assessment task.

There is then the issue of assessment itself, and differences such as those between (e)valuation and assessment. These have been the substance of a vast academic endeavour, captured in shorthand by the two terms of formative and summative assessment. Given that valuation happens in all environments in respect to all our actions, always, a theory of assessment ideally applies to all such environments and all forms of evaluation. At that point, questions focus on those metrics that can or might be used in different instances of (e)valuation.

Communication

A minimal sketch of a theory of communication may serve as a basis for much of the discussion that follows. I develop this sketch around three entirely different examples: one is that of the operating theatre (see Fig. 2.1), the second comes from a 'visitor study' in a museum (see Fig. 2.3a and b) and the third is the BBC website for children (see Fig. 2.2). All three examples also function as *sites of learning*; each in significantly different ways, and so the question in each case is: 'How would we assess what has been learned?'

Assume that we take the situation in Fig. 2.1 as the normal condition of communication—rather than notions of communication based on versions of diadic interaction, versions of which, in many modified forms, have haunted, and still haunt, mainstream conceptions of communication, even if by negation.

Figure 2.1 shows an operating theatre. An operation is in its very early stage. In the forefront of the image stands the scrub nurse; behind her, to the right, is the lead surgeon, and on the left is the trainee-surgeon—a qualified medical doctor training to be a surgeon; behind them, separated by a screen, is the anaesthetist; at the very back, barely visible on the right, is an operating theatre technician. In other words, there are representatives of four related, entirely integrated, yet distinct, professions. First and foremost, the situation is one of (communication in) a situation of professional practice. It is also an environment of learning, and so the questions posed here are 'What has been learned?' and 'How can we assess that learning?'

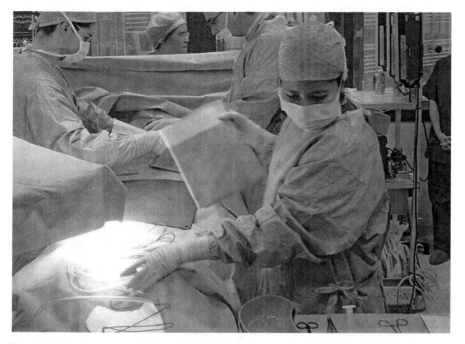

Fig. 2.1 Operating theatre (Source: Roger Kneebone)

Fig. 2.2 The CBBC homepage

Communication here is multimodal: by speech at times, by gaze and by actions—passing an instrument, reaching out for an instrument and by touching. At all times, communication is 'prompted': a gaze produces a spoken comment, which produces an action; a look at the screen by both surgeons produces a guiding touch by the one of the other's hand and an outstretched hand is met by an instrument being passed. Communication has happened when attention by one or more of the participants has focused on a prompt of some kind and that prompt has been interpreted by that participant.

This (rudimentary sketch of a) theory of communication is based on two assumptions: communication happens as a response to a prompt; and communication has happened when there has been an interpretation. Both, together, are fundamental. First, it means that interpretation is central, and so therefore is the interpreter. Without interpretation there is no communication. Secondly, it recognises that the characteristics and the 'shape' of the prompt constitute the 'ground' on which the interpretation happens. The prompt engages the attention of one or more of the participants; the participant's attention is shaped by their interest (where, by interest, I mean the momentary 'condensation' of a social history, a sense of who I am in this social situation, as well as a clear sense of the social environment in which the prompt occurred).

To restate this in the frame of learning and assessment: learning happens in a complex social environment; with distinct social groupings present; they need to communicate across the boundaries of their differences; individuals' interest frames their attention to what thereby becomes the prompt for their learning. It is the interpretation of that curricular prompt that can be called learning.

Communicational environments are complex. They consist of a plethora of phenomena that can, potentially, act as prompts; whether they are or not depends on the interest of a participant; her or his interest directs their attention to the prompt; this 'interested attention' frames an aspect of the communicational environment as a prompt; the characteristics and the 'shape' of the prompt provide the ground on which the interpretation proceeds; the participant engages with features of the prompt and forms their interpretation.

The action that follows the prompt is based on the interpretation. It is a sign of, and based on, that interpretation. If we switch our view from communication to one of (communication-as-) learning, then this is a sign of learning. In this perspective, meaningful assessment can only ever be based on that interpretation.

Reading as Design

The rudimentary theory sketched here takes the new communicational world as given, rather than tinkering with older models based on different (social) givens in order to patch them up for contemporary uses. It re-centres attention in communication upon the *interpreter* of a *message-prompt*, rather than on the initial maker of the message. Through the lens of *learning*, the effect is a corresponding shift in focus from the teacher and teaching to the *learner* and learning.

There is a homologous situation in relation to reading. The 'old' page of writing embodied notions of authority and authorship, in which the author had assembled (knowledge-as-) text on behalf of readers, displayed on the lines of the printed page. Readers engaged with that knowledge/text in the order laid down by the author—an order of syntax, of lines, of pages and chapters. The reader's task was to decode and acquire the knowledge as it had been produced and set out by an author. Contemporary sites of display—whether of information books (published by, for example, Dorling & Kindersley), of the screens of computer games or of websites, such as the children's BBC homepage (CBBC) in Fig. 2.2, assume and act on the basis of a quite different engagement.

Unlike the traditional page, designed with a (pre-)given order of engagement/reading encoded in a 'reading path' (Kress & van Leeuwen, 2006), this website requires the reader's *ordering-as-design*. It is the reader's interest that determines how they engage with the page and the order in which its elements are encountered: the reader's interest shapes the design of this page.

With this site, too, the question of modes of representation is in the foreground. On a first traverse of the site, it is not at all clear that content conveyed lexically through the mode of writing will be the first point of engagement; nor is the order of reading determined by the spatial order of placement of the elements on the site. 'Reading' conforms to the theory of communication outlined. However, if 'reading' follows the route of prompt, interest, attention, framing and engagement, it becomes ever more difficult to imagine and to maintain that for such readers learning does not follow the same route as reading. Readers who read according to a design of their interest—even though on the ground of someone else's prompt—are likely to take much the same attitude in relation to their semiotic engagement with (all) other domains in their world.

It might be objected that reading for pleasure is one thing and that reading/engagement for learning in any institutional site of learning is another; there is, after all, the issue of power. But before I pass on: 'How would we assess what learning there had been as a result of the engagement with this site?' and 'What would constitute materials to be assessed?'

My third example comes from a research project on visitor studies, 'The museum, the exhibition and the visitor'. The research (funded by the Swedish Research Council) was conducted in Sweden and England. The visitor studies were conducted at the Museum of National Antiquities in Stockholm, on an exhibition on Swedish pre-history, and at the Museum of London, based on two exhibitions, 'London before London' and 'Roman London'. Museums cannot, usually, exercise power directly in relation to either communication or learning of their visitors. In both the Stockholm and the London components of the study, visitors were invited to participate as couples (grandparent and child, friends, married couples, etc.) in order to understand how and what sense they made of a specific exhibition in a museum.

Those who accepted were filmed on video as they made their way through the exhibition. They were given a camera to take images of objects or ensembles that took their interest, and at the conclusion of their visit they were asked to 'draw a

map' that represented their sense of the exhibition. They were also asked to participate in a brief interview. The aim was to obtain signs of learning. So each of these
four 'takes' was seen as possible data for 'signs of learning'. Below, as an example,
are two maps drawn by a member of two couples.

When an exhibition is designed, its designer(s) have specific aims: to show
objects, images or reconstructions, or to tell stories of the pre-history of a community or place—and they also have specific social purposes in mind. These are
rarely overtly stated in the exhibition, though in interviews with curators or cura-
torial teams it is clear that much discussion precedes, framed by policies of the
museum. Semiotically speaking, an exhibition is a message; it is meant as a prompt
to the visitors who come to engage with it. Pedagogically speaking, an exhibition
(re)presents a curriculum for the visitor seen as a learner. In that context, the maps
are indications of how aspects of the overall design message have engaged the
visitor's interest; they are signs of learning.

Whether from the perspective of *communication* or of *learning*, the maps are
of equal interest. They are not, of course, a full account of the meanings made by
either of the visitors (a woman and a man). Nevertheless, they give a clear sense of
a difference in interest, of a consequent difference in attention and framing and of
distinctly different *interpretations* of the same *prompt*.

Most immediately, they show a different sense of what a 'map' is or does based
on different conceptions of what is to be mapped. In one case, the notion of the map
is very much a spatial one—the exhibition was arranged as a sequence of 'rooms'
as distinctly separate spaces. The question posed, seemingly, was: 'What was the
space that I traversed and what interesting objects did I encounter?' In the other
case, the notion of the map is 'conceptual': the question posed, seemingly, was
'What are (the) significant elements of this exhibition, and in what order shall I
present them?' For the first mapmaker, 'space' and sequence of spaces, a sense of
'movement through', with specific objects of interest included, define 'map' and
the exhibition overall; for the second visitor, a map is defined as a spatially ordered
representation, as a classification of salient elements.

From the same prompt, with a seemingly clear 'reading path'—the fixed suc-
cession of 'rooms'—each of the two visitors has fashioned their own design and a
distinct interpretation. Whose interest has been dominant here: the curator's or the
visitor's? Has the curator succeeded more in one case and less so in the other? Has
one visitor couple 'failed' in their experience of the exhibition?

These are questions for the curator—and they are the motivation for engaging
in 'visitor studies'. Looking with the lens of learning and assessment, these are *the*
questions. 'Failure' or 'success' is a concept curators use in relation to either exhibition or visitor; for the pedagogue/assessor, they very much are *the* notions, though
most often used in relation to the learner/student. This goes directly to conceptions
of learning and to the social conditions in which learning happens. 'Has what I have
provided as the curricular issue been learned?' is the teacher's/assessor's question.
Would the teacher/assessor recognise these 'maps' as signs of learning, willing to
accept them as indications of learning, either because of their modal expression as
image and not as writing or speech—generically as report or story—or in terms of

their divergence from the curriculum: 'these are nothing like a map'? Recognition or refusal/inability to recognise signs of learning has effects directly on possibilities and forms of assessment.

These aspects are dealt with by a social semiotic theory of communication/sign-making/meaning-making/learning in the way I have indicated. The first criterion is the visitor's or learner's interest. 'What principles did each of the visitors/learners apply in their engagement with the curriculum of the exhibition?' 'What consequences follow for the pedagogue?' Then come considerations of the path that the (curator as) teacher might have wanted the (visitor/) learner to take.

The curator might wish to understand the reasons for the differences in interpretation. One is provided by the notion of interest. As it happened, one of the visitors was an archaeologist and her interest is expressed in her map, but that is the case equally in all the maps. The teacher ought perhaps to be just as interested in these differences and in their origins; though that is not the usual path taken in forms of assessment in schools.

The matter of modes arises with the question of rhetoric and design; that is, it goes to the initial conception of the exhibition and from there to the overall 'shaping' of the exhibition, in the selection of its objects, in the salience given to particular themes and to the modes chosen in representing specific meanings: for instance, in its layout, in its lighting, in the use of written text and of image. Are three-dimensional objects more salient, more 'attractive', more noticeable than written captions? Is movement more salient than longer written accounts/explanations? Are painted scenes more engaging than three-dimensional tableaux? What effect does lighting have in creating affect and mood? Is the distance at which visitors are able to engage with objects, or whether they are able to touch an object, a significant matter? The question of affect has to be addressed in the case of the exhibition: the wrong affect will 'turn off' potential visitors. But affect is equally significant in all sites of learning, institutional or not.

In the map of Fig. 2.3, a three-dimensional space is represented in the mode of two-dimensional image; spaces that were rounded, irregularly shaped and of different sizes are shown as square, as regular in shape and uniform in size. Selection by the mapmaker has changed rooms with many objects into rooms with few or none. The maps, in other words, are representations shaped by principles of selection; by transduction, the change from one mode to another mode with deep changes in meaning; and by transformation, changes in ordering and configurations of elements within one mode also with changes in meaning.

Curators might see themselves first and foremost as communicators, and their response to these representations might be shaped by a wish for better, more 'effective' communication. Yet, museums are increasingly seen as educational environments, particularly by governments that fund them. Whether as communicators or educators, they are likely to be interested in those characteristics of their audience that seem to have an effect on both.

Seen from the perspective of teaching, effectiveness is judged in terms of assessment of some form or other. What has been learned is now the centre of attention. The question appears in several ways, each dependent on a different kind of

a

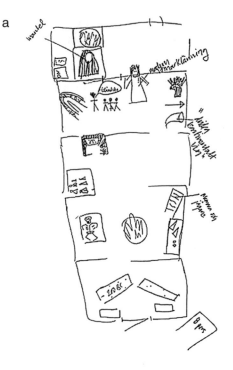

b

Fig. 2.3 (**a**) Map of a museum exhibition; (**b**) map of a museum exhibition

recognition such as: 'Whose interests count in terms of curriculum and learning: those of the authority or those of the learner?' 'How can we assess learning expressed in modes other than those that are dominant in formal educational settings?' 'What theoretical and practical means do we have to assess learning in different modes; how do we assess multimodally?' 'What knowledge about mode and meaning, and therefore about multimodal assessment, do we actually have?'

While the first question is one about recognition of 'authority': 'How can we recognise learning when it does not conform to our expectations of what was to be learned?' the second question is about the 'means': 'How was the curriculum expressed modally and how is what has been learned now represented modally?' 'What is actually recognised as means of representation of learning, as means of knowing?' It is a question of 'visibility': 'what is visible to the 'eye of assessment'? 'What is it possible, actually, for the assessor to see?' The questions of recognition and of visibility are addressed by a social semiotic theory as it deals with meaning in all social relations and semiotic forms, and they are dealt with by a multimodal approach, with its insistence that meaning is made in all modes. One might say that most of the issues in assessment of a traditional kind boil down to the single question: Whose interests rule?

Semiosis, Meaning and Learning

Learning is not a term that belongs in semiotics. So, can there be a *social semiotic* theory of learning? And what might we mean by *learning*? Notions of *learning* are products of the theories in which they are developed. Theories are historical, social and, hence, ideological products of the manifold social and political forces of the time of their making and use; theories of *learning* are no exception. *Learning* in institutional settings is a political matter, and as such subject to power in the service of ideology. Beyond that, there is the question of disciplinary difference: psychological, linguistic, social and anthropological, never mind the pedagogical theories of learning, which will each produce distinctly different understandings of *learning*.

In addition, can one ever talk about learning-as-such, or can we only ever talk of learning in specific contexts? Contemporary theorising favours the latter view. These questions point in two directions: one asks: 'Is learning always shaped in essential respects by the structures, resources, participants and environments of the occasions of learning?' The other asks: 'Is there learning as such, irrespective of the circumstances in which it takes place?'

Both questions are central to multimodal social semiotics, because they focus on the role of the social and the material resources in and through which meaning is made and by which learning therefore takes place. One cannot have a theory of learning without a theory of meaning, however implicit that may be; a theory of learning always entails a theory of meaning. Meaning is the stuff of semiotics; hence, semiotics is inevitably and centrally implicated in any theory of learning.

Semiotically, sign-making is meaning-making, and learning is the result of these processes.

The term 'learning' has tended to be used when these processes happen in specific institutions with particular purposes and forms of power, which provide institutionally organised sets of entities as a curriculum and with which learners are required to engage. Usually, there are associated metrics for assessment in the environment of a pedagogy, whose aim is the making of social subjects according to purposes of the social group standing behind the educational institution.

While the core concept of learning is the concept, the core concept of semiotics is the sign, an entity in which meaning and form are fused (Kress, 1996, in-press/2009). In conventional (Saussurian-derived) semiotics, the relation of form and meaning is taken to be an arbitrary one, sustained by convention; in social semiotics, that relation is seen as 'motivated': form is apt for expressing meaning in the sign. This is crucial, as the concept of arbitrariness goes directly against the core notion of sign-making (rather than sign-use) in social semiotics, and against the sign- and (concept-)maker's agentive and 'interested' role in the making of meaning, sign and concept.

This approach has a direct effect on assessment. If the sign in its form—say, either one of the two maps—is the result of its makers' interest and is an apt reflection of that interest, then the form gives an indication of what has been learned. The maker of the sign has made the form of the sign to be an apt expression of the meaning to be represented. For the recipient of the sign, therefore, the shape, the form of the sign, is a means of forming a hypothesis about the maker's interest and about the principles that they brought to their engagement with the prompt that led to the making of the sign—whether the experience of the visit to the museum exhibition or the experience of a series of lessons in the classroom. When the 'recipient of the sign' is an assessor, the question is: 'What metric will be applied?' Will it be a metric oriented to authority—a metric that indicates the distance from what ought to have been learned, whether in terms of modes used or in terms of conformity to the authority of the teacher/assessor; or will it be a metric oriented to the learner's interest and that evaluates the principles the learner brought to the engagement with the curriculum?

The makers of the maps have made signs. In neither case was there any such prior sign to be used. In the making of these map signs, one or more of what are regarded by the mapmakers as criterial features of the exhibition are selected. The signs were made for reasons that were entirely motivated by the interest of the maker in the circumstances at the time of their making.

Sign-making, meaning-making and learning are, in this case as in all others, distinguishable only on the basis of different disciplinary perspectives on what is essentially the same phenomenon. In the case of the two maps, the prompt was the same; what differed were the map-makers' interests.

If we take the museum examples as instances of learning, then the question of how to assess what was to be learned can only be done by recourse to multimodal means. Modally, what was to be learned is distinct from the representations of which document was learned. As I mentioned, three-dimensional objects have been transducted into two-dimensional images; 'spaces' have become images; the transformational process of selection has led to the deletion in the maps of most of what was there in the 'curriculum' of the exhibition.

Interest

Before further exploring the issue of multimodal assessment, I want to re-emphasise two notions: that of *interest* and that of the *principles* used in the engagement with an aspect of the world shaped by interest. I use examples from two primary schools in (north) London. The children are 7 years old. The topic of the (biology) lesson was 'Frog's spawn'. Here are two *signs of learning,* each from a child in one of the two classes.

The examples illustrate *sign-making* as *learning*. The *interest* of the sign-maker selects what is criterial for them about an entity at the moment of its representation. What the sign-maker takes as *criterial* determines what they will represent about that entity; only what is *criterial* is represented. Representation is always partial.

The maker of the text of Fig. 2.4a decided to 'spread' the meaning he wished to represent across two modes: image and writing. While the maker of Fig. 2.4b uses writing to represent 'the most interesting thing, namely 'that the tadpoal are the blak spots', the maker of Fig. 2.4a uses image to show the black spots in his carefully drawn image of frog spawn. Is the teacher likely to see this as a very nice picture or as a careful visual account of a scientific fact?

Both sign-makers took the black spots to be criterial, though they chose to represent them in different modes. In Fig. 2.4a, the drawing precedes the writing, and in this way it frames the writing in significant ways. In Fig. 2.4b, the 'same' fact is embedded in the written judgment: 'the most interesting thing . . .' Again, the question posed for the teacher is whether to accord embedding of fact to written evaluation higher status than the embedding/framing by the drawing, or the other way around—that is, accord to the child's presentation of empirical reality as prior a higher status or to treat them as alternative accounts, both of which are worth exploring with the class.

I am not, here, so much interested in a detailed analysis of the two texts—for instance, that the maker of Fig. 2.4(a) foregrounds the explanation of the (for him new) concept 'when frogs are born there called frogs born', while the maker of Fig. 2.4(b) foregrounds her knowledge 'I already knew that frogs have Baby's'. I am interested in the principle of recognition as a heuristic device for the teacher. For me, that includes the recognition of both makers' interest in precision, which appears, among other things, in their transcription of the language they hear.

'. . . so they cont do nofing . . .' where the transcription of the north London vowel in 'cont' as /o/ and of the 'standard language' consonant /th/ in 'nofing' as /f/ are signs of acute hearing and accuracy in transcription; as are the /ay/ in 'thay', and the

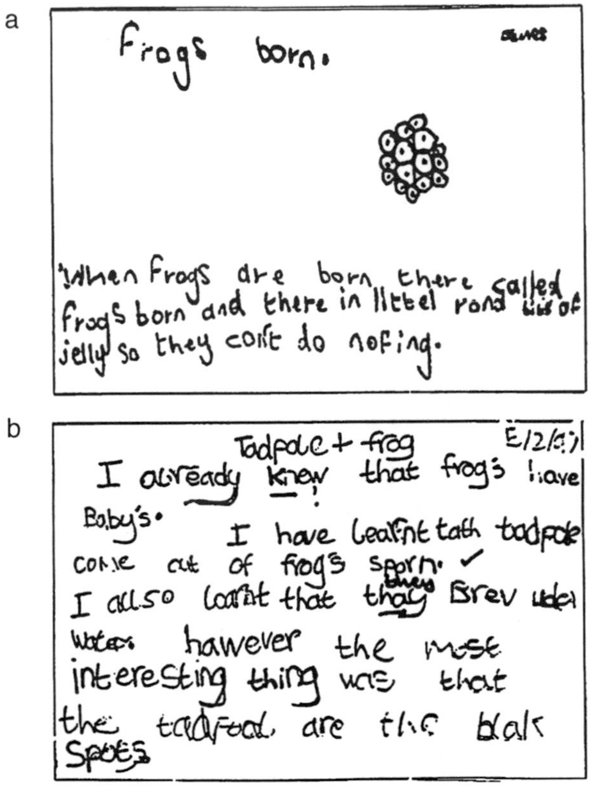

Fig. 2.4 (a) Frogs born; (b) frog's sporn

(voiced) /v/ as a transcription of the 'standard language' voiced /th/ in 'Brev'; as is
the loss through nasalisation of the /n/ in 'uder water'.

And not least, of course, precision appears in their 'transcription' of the unknown
term 'frog spawn'—semantically transcribed as 'frogs born' and syntactically
transcribed as 'frogs sporn'—that is, 'frog's sporn', a nonsense term lexically, yet
syntactically well motivated.

All signs are metaphors that embody the interest of the maker of the sign, whether
the sign of a letter as transcript of a sound; of a concept, such as the black spots in
frog spawn, as image or as word; or of an unknown word/concept, as in 'frogs born'
or 'frogs sporn'. Given the principle that signs function as concepts, we can say that
concepts are the result of the work of the sign-maker and represent their interest in
relation to the world that is in focus. As a consequence, the semiotic, as much as the
conceptual resources of the individual, is the result of their work in their engagement
with their (social and cultural) world.

This can be translated into a view of learning in two ways. One is to say: what
the sign-maker does, settles—if only for this moment—the world of signs and the
state of his inner world. In this case, it has settled his understanding of what frogs
born/frogs sporn is. With that, it has for a moment changed his capacities for making

a Draw a line to join the things which are the same.

b

Fig. 2.5 (a) Benjamin: classification 1; (b) Benjamin: classification 2

(new) meanings and for future meaningful action in and on the world. It has changed the intellectual/conceptual potential of the meaning-maker, and in this it has changed this individual. That is a result of learning. The second would be to say, interest and partiality operate in quite the same way in learning as they do in representation.

How should principles/practices of assessment deal with that? What is to be assessed? Is it learning or is it conformity to authority? The question of multimodality is, in principle, neutral in this respect, though it does sharply pose the question, 'What is recognised as a sign of learning?' At this point it might be useful to propose a definition of learning:

> Learning is the result of the transformative engagement with an aspect of the world that is the focus of attention by an individual, on the basis of principles brought by them to that engagement; leading to a transformation of the individual's semiotic/conceptual resources.

This provides a general view of *meaning* and *learning*. A (social semiotic) multi-modal approach adds an insistence that meaning is made in a *multiplicity of modes*, always in *ensembles of modes*.

Figure 2.5a and b exemplifies a number of points of an approach to learning and assessment: the role of 'the school', the ceaselessly ongoing nature of semiosis—of meaning-making—and the role of transduction in that.

Figure 2.5b is a page made up (by me) of six small square pieces of paper from a phone notepad. One summer weekend day, the then five-year-old Benjamin had been drawing these images, unbeknown to his parents, who were entertaining friends in the garden. Seeing him laying them out in pairs on the floor in the hallway of the house, his father asked what he was doing. The five-year old said of the first pair, 'The plane is in the air and the bomb is in the air/so they're in the correct order'. Of the second pair he said, 'The boy is in life and the dog is in life/so they're in the correct order'. Of the third pair he said, 'The patterns are in the correct order'.

Some few weeks later, on the ending of the school year, he brought home all his school books. Looking through these, somewhat aimlessly, his father discovered the page, shown in Fig. 2.5a, a page from a school exercise book. The date on the page reveals that this exercise was done some four weeks before the images in Fig. 2.5b.

Figure 2.5a is an exercise in classification—'linking like with like', and when that was completed, spending time left in the lesson in colouring in the shapes—an exercise in control of the pens. My question is about the relation between the two events, separated by several weeks, one done in school as 'work', the other done out of the child's interest, unbidden. Classification connects the two, though in the interval that concept has moved on significantly: 'like' is still connected with 'like', though the notion of 'like' has become more abstract, much more general.

Learning, around the concept of classification, had clearly continued, silently and invisibly, so to speak. At a particular point, 'inner' semiosis ceased momentarily and became external. The conception of 'like' was 'framed' and modally 'fixed' (in the sense of the 'fixing of light' in older forms of photography) in the shape of the six images and in laying them out as pairs on the floor. In Fig. 2.5a, the act of linking 'like' with 'like' was done manually; the manner of holding the pen and of drawing the lines typical of a five-year old is visible in the lines. The act was physical/manual and semiotic/conceptual—as indeed it was in the later instance, though now with a much more general sense of 'like'.

I assume that language was not involved in this at all, at least not overtly, audibly. Language as speech appeared only when the father asked the child what he was doing and the child needed to formulate a response. Learning had obviously continued over the weeks, though where before there would have been the teacher's instruction to link 'like' entities/images by a line, a physical, a visual as well as a semiotic act, now the conceptual work, drawing entities that were 'like' at some remove in abstraction, and ordering them in a layout that showed their conceptual order, was done without speech or writing.

How is learning about generalisation and abstraction to be assessed here? Is it only when speech appears that assessment of the semiotic/conceptual work is possible? My answer is that work produces change and that that change is meaningful. Semiotic work is no exception. Any principles of recognition for assessment will need to include the realisation that wherever work has been done, semiotic work included, meaning has been made, regardless of the mode or the modes in which that happened.

If we were to assess only the linguistic account of the images, the spoken commentary, would we have the 'same' entities available for assessment as the images themselves? The images are actually much 'fuller' and much more precise as indications of just what the child considered as 'like'. In my view, the linguistic account is hugely general compared to the precise and specific images. That means that the verbal account is a reduction of what was available to be assessed and understood in the visual representation.

Again, there is the central issue of recognition: of semiotic and conceptual work in modes other than language, and of learning that takes the school's prompt as the starting point but goes well beyond it.

Sign focuses on issues and resources of representation; concept focuses on inner entities and resources. The individual who has produced new, additional or more potent semiotic resources has achieved an augmentation of capacities for representation; the individual who has produced new conceptual resources has achieved an augmentation of intellectual capacities. In the social semiotic theory that I have sketched here, I take the 'frog spawn' example (but also that of the maps and the classifications) as characteristic of all sign-making, in any mode. I assume that the principles that I have drawn out here apply in all sign-making: signs are always newly made, on the basis of the interest of the maker. A sign newly made is a concept newly made. A concept newly made is a sign of learning.

Recognition, Metrics and Principles of Assessment

From the perspective of a semiotic theory of learning, the following might be said: the *concept/sign* the child has made gives us an insight into his 'stance' in the world, with respect to this specific entity. As a general principle we can take all *concepts/signs* to be precisely that: an indication of the *interest* of the sign-maker in their relation to the specific bit of the world that is at issue; an indication of their experience of the world. Both *concept* and *sign* are shaped by that and give us a sense of the criteria, the principles, the *interest* that led the child to the representations he made. It is a point where we need to think about apt *metrics* for assessing/evaluating what learning had occurred.

Is our interest in learning? This is a strange question to put, though other questions suggest themselves, which makes it somewhat less strange. For instance, is our interest in producing conformity to authority around 'knowledge', or is our interest actually in environments and conditions of learning?

However strange the questions, they shape theories, policies and practices of assessment. The first of the alternative questions goes to the politics of teaching and assessment, to the political and social purposes of education and the second points to a misrecognition in debates about learning. Terms such as 'e-learning', 'mobile learning', 'online learning', 'ubiquitous learning' or life-wide, life-long, formal, informal learning seem to be concerned with environments and conditions of learning rather than with learning itself.

This is not, by any means, to question the significance of these concerns. Quite to the contrary, they point to central issues in relation to potentials for learning. We do need to ask and understand the characteristics of these already taken-for-granted worlds.

From the perspective of multimodality, we need to ask, in regard to something as commonplace now as the BBC website (see Fig. 2.2), what semiotic resources they offer; what social and affective resources are needed to engage with them, whether in everyday communication or as a learner? Rhetorically speaking: what are the characteristics of modal ensembles that most invite, that provide best access to such sites? What is the effect of colour, of images, of genres of image and genres of written elements; what are the effects of layout? What considerations need to be paid to the culturally, intensely diverse environments in which the sites find—or do not find—their audience? In the London component of the museum study that I referred to earlier, it is beginning to become clear that the different composition of the audience—'tourists' broadly speaking, as much as the diverse local population—has real effects on 'reading'. Do 'visitors' have the means for full access and form their own production in response? Questions of modes and the affordances of modes lie very close here. What semiotic/modal resources are needed to be productive in these sites? What 'navigational aids' are needed? In relation to the BBC website, what are the semiotic characteristic of this world? Who prompts this learning? How do we describe what goes on here?

Do we have the theory and the terms to deal with contemporary social environments as communicational environments, never mind as sites of learning? In environments that are intensely multicultural (and multilingual), what rhetorical, communicational and representational responses are apt or adequate?

At this point I wish to introduce the concept of aesthetics. In contemporary market-dominated societies, choice dominates practices, at least ideologically/mythically. Choice is socially shaped as a social process. But choice, being socially shaped, is subject to power in different ways. In that context, style can be seen as the politics of choice. The social valuations of styles are equally and differently shaped by power, so that aesthetics can be seen as the politics of style. If we want to maintain the possibilities of ethical practices of behaviour, we need to recognise that ethics, too, is subject to power, and hence ethics needs to be seen as the politics of value and evaluation.

At this point I have returned to evaluation and assessment. My point is that in societies dominated by the forces of the market in conditions of intense diversity, we cannot attempt to construct a plausible approach to assessment without the consideration of the different aesthetics—the politics of choice and the politics of evaluation—that govern contemporary social life.

Signs of Learning

In a social semiotic theory, signs made outwardly are seen as the best evidence that we can get for understanding the 'inner' processes of learning. The *visitors' maps, the frog spawn examples*, the *classification examples*, are all *signs of learning*.

Here is my final example. It comes from a science classroom; the sign-makers are 13-year-old girls. They have been studying plant cells over four lessons; now their teacher has asked them to prepare a slide of an onion's epidermis and then view it under the microscope. The teacher instructed them to report on what they had done: 'Write what you did' and 'Draw what you have seen'. He gave two further instructions: that they should put the written report at the top of the page, and place the drawing underneath and not to use colour pencils in their drawing. Groups of four girls were working together, each around one microscope, having previously made the one slide. Here are two of their texts:

Apart from the fact that Fig. 2.6 does have the drawing at the top of the page, there are startling differences, especially if we remember that the young women had sat through the same lessons and had prepared and looked at the same slide under the microscope. I have discussed the differences and their significance elsewhere (Kress, 2001, 2003).

It is clear that each student has made different selections from the masses of material the teacher had offered during the lessons, and from the discussions between the girls during their joint work. Each had transformed the material in specific ways. Further, they had not simply 'selected out' and transformed elements, they had also 'moved' material from one semiotic mode (writing or speech) to another (image) in the process of transduction. So, for instance, what had appeared in the mode of writing on a handout sheet ('The cells will look like bricks in a brick-wall') appears in one of the two texts in the mode of image; what had appeared in the mode of speech by one of the girls, in talk around the microscope ('It looks like a wavy weave'), has been transducted to the mode of image (Fig. 2.7).

If we want to get further with the notion of signs of learning, we need to ask more closely about the principles of selection, transformation and transduction that emerge here, arising from their differing interest.

The teacher's instruction to 'Write what you did' is transformed differently: once as the genre of recount (events in chronological order) and once as the genre of procedure (instructions for producing actions in sequence). In these two examples the operation of transformation is clear: material presented by the teacher across the

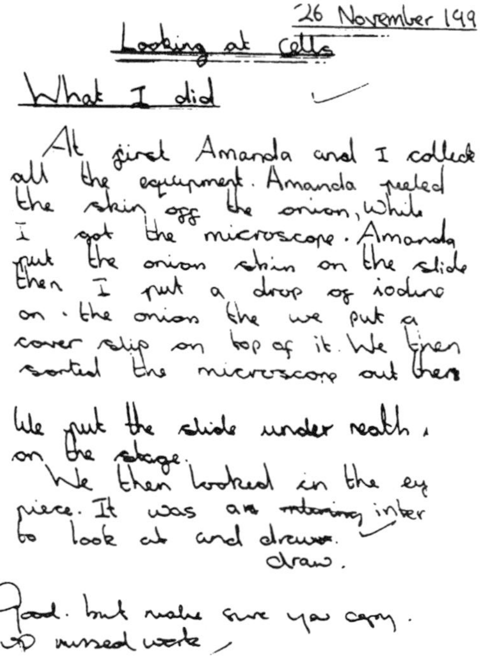
26 November 199
Looking at cells
What I did
At first Amanda and I collect all the equipment. Amanda peeled the skin off the onion, while I got the microscope. Amanda put the onion skin on the slide then I put a drop of iodine on the onion the we put a cover slip on top of it. We then sorted the microscope out then
We put the slide under neath, on the stage.
We then looked in the eye piece. It was an ~~amazing~~ inter to look at and ~~drawn~~. draw.
Good. but make sure you copy up missed work

Fig. 2.6 Onion cell/theory

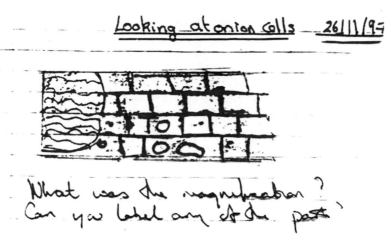

Fig. 2.7 Onion cell/eye-piece

four lessons is taken up and re-presented in relation to each sign-maker's interest. For one girl 'Write what you did' meant 'Report accurately what you actually did'; for the other it meant 'Present a regularised account of what should happen'. Each indicates their sense of what 'being scientific' might mean: in the recount it rests on accurate recounting of all relevant events and actions in the chronological order in which they took place; in the procedure it rests on careful specification of actions in sequence to ensure the replicability of actions.

The images show an interesting difference: the writer of the recount stays close to the handout's statement: 'The cells will look like bricks in a brick-wall'. She treats this as a theoretical statement, and transforms what she saw into a depiction 'predicted' by the theory—'theory tells us that it ought to look like this'. The writer of the procedure stays close to accurate observation, treating that as being essentially 'scientific'. Both drawings are signs of learning: they are precise accounts of the interest of each of the two young women, though resting on different principles. Each has led to distinct notions of 'being scientific'. Each is a sign of the result of the girls' engagement with the lessons and the teacher's demands; from each we get a real sense—I would say *the* real sense—of their learning.

The texts overall—the combination of written genre and image—are precise and complex records of just that. In the one text, the written part suggests that being scientific is to adhere to strictly prescribed practices, while the image suggests that being scientific is to be as accurate as possible in the visual recording of the empirical world. In the other text, the writing suggests that being scientific is about recording as accurately as can be what actions were performed in what sequence, while the image suggests that being scientific is to discover the truth of theory in the messiness of the empirical world. Both are signs of learning of what being scientific is about. In each case we can ask what an apt assessment of learning might consist in—conformity to the authority of the curriculum, or an understanding of the principles that emerge in these signs.

In the 'cells examples' just discussed, writing and image are used to do specific tasks. Writing is used to represent 'what happened—actions and events in sequence, once in the genre of recount and once in the genre of procedure—and image is used to represent what was visually observed in the world. The two modes were used for differential engagement with the world. This might seem obvious, except that on the teacher's handout the look of the cells had been represented using writing, and in the girls' discussion around the microscope what was observed was represented in speech. In other words, there is a choice of what mode to use, and therefore there is a question as to which mode might be better and for what reasons; and further, what the effect of these choices might be on potentials for learning. Choices have been made by each of the young women; and in each case the choices have significant effect on what has been learned—and on what ought to be assessed.

Assessment in a Multimodal, Social Semiotic Theory of Learning: Metrics of Conformity versus Signs of (Principles of) Learning

I have attempted to draw out two strands in an approach to assessment: the need to be clear about a theory of learning as the underpinning of forms of assessment and related to that the need for *principles of recognition of learning*. Here, I briefly restate them.

1. Work produces change; change is meaningful; semiotic work is work and produces meaning.
2. Meaning is made in all modes; learning takes place in all modes.
3. Signs are made in response to *prompts* on the basis of the sign-maker's *interest* in transformative engagement with characteristics of the prompt.
4. The sign made in response to a *prompt* points to the *principles* at work in the sign-maker's engagement with the prompt.
5. Learning is best seen in the frame of a learner's principled transformative engagement with the characteristics of a prior prompt in terms of the learner's interest.
6. Signs of learning constitute apt data for any form of assessment.
7. The question of assessment then becomes a question *either* of attention to *metrics of conformity or* to *principles of semiotic engagement*. As a slogan we can speak of an opposition between *metrics of learning* and *signs of (principles of) learning.*
8. In contemporary environments of communication, as of learning, it is implausible to restrict notions of effective communication to the mode of language alone. Assessment is no exception.

Principles of Recognition of Learning and Forms of Assessment

Multimodality by itself is not a theory of learning, though it does focus on the need to attend to all the modes through which meaning is made and learning happens. Adequate forms of assessment need to address these givens. In systems of assessment that have hitherto focused on the pre-eminence of the linguistic modes of speech and writing as the secure route to understanding of meaning and learning (or of specific canonical modes in other disciplines—numbers, chemical formulae, etc.), this demands a conscious attempt at recognition of meaning-making and learning in all modes involved, in which signs of learning are evident. A theory of learning that aims to be adequate to contemporary forms of communication and engagement with the world, with contemporary views of power and authority by those who are (seen as) learners, and in fact, that wants to be adequate to the facts of human communication, needs to pay close attention to the actions of learners in all environments of learning. These are prerequisites for any serious attempt at assessment of learning. Only what is recognised and accorded full recognition as means and modes for learning can be assessed. What is not recognised will not and cannot be assessed. That leads to severe misrecognition of learners' capacities and actions.

Acknowledgments I wish to thank Roger Kneebone for allowing me to use his image of the operating theatre, and I wish to thank Eva Insulander (2008) for allowing me to use the images of the museum visitor's maps, as well as for her insights on them. I wish to thank Staffan Selander (2008), the Director of the Museum Visitors' Study, for inviting me to participate in that project.

Glossary

Affordance The semiotic potentials and limitations for representation of a mode

Apt, aptness The idea of 'best fit' between what is the meaning to be represented and the form to represent it. An example is a three-year-old child's use of a circle to represent a wheel or the use of the past-tense form—distance in time—to represent social distance, as in 'I wanted to ask you for a small loan'

Attention The focus directed by a participant in a social/semiotic interaction to a specific aspect of the environment of communication

Criterial The factors/features of an object, event or other phenomena that embody the interest of the sign-maker and which, at the moment of representation, capture the essence of that which is to be represented for the sign-maker

Design The arrangement of the means for representation as a text-to-be, which aptly translates the rhetor's interest in the message in a specific communicational event

Engagement The meaning-maker's 'interested', energetic and sustained involvement with a framed segment of the world, which is at issue in an interaction

Environment of learning The (ordered) ensemble of social and semiotic characteristics that constitutes the relevant features of the framed world in which learning takes place

Interpretation The (semiotic) outcome of an engagement with the framed part of the world at issue, as the result of the transformation of the framed world in terms of the meaning-maker's interest and the integration of the resulting sign into the meaning-maker's existent semiotic resources

Interest The 'condensation' at the moment of representation of an individual's (social) history, a sense of who they are in the social environment of communication as well as a sense of the salient features of the environment in which the prompt occurred. These lead to the selection of that aspect of the phenomenon treated as 'criterial' for the purposes of representation

Materiality of mode The recognition that modes are, usually, material/physical and that the materiality is an integral aspect both of affordance and of its semiotic and physiological effects

Metrics of assessment The set of features, based on specific criteria, used to measure the extent to which a response to an evaluation meets the evaluator's expectations

Mode The socially shaped, culturally available material for representation, which exhibits regularities of use as understood by a group

Motivation The assumption that the relation of form and meaning in any sign is not arbitrary but is a motivated expression of the sign-maker's interest in making a transparent sign in which form is apt for the expression of meaning

Multimodality, multimodal The phenomenon of the cultural availability of multiple resources for representation

Navigation The principles used by a reader/visitor for orientation within a (complex) semiotic entity/text in order to both locate material and design, establish and order within the material conforming to the 'navigator's' purposes and interests

Principles of assessment The principles that are brought to bear explicitly or implicitly in the evaluation of a semiotic process, event or object

Principles of recognition of learning The principles that are available or not and/or brought to bear in recognising what learning is, how and where it might happen and how and where it might be represented

Prompt The social and semiotic event, object or other phenomenon that becomes the focus of the attention of a participant in a social event or interaction and leads that participant to a response

Recognition The process whereby some semiotic entity or part of an entity becomes salient, visible and significant in some way to a participant in a social group and its interaction

Rhetoric A view of communication that frames a communicational event to include the initial maker of a representation as a text/message; the resources available for that; the phenomenon that constitutes the thing to be communicated and a sense of the environment of communication in which salient characteristics of the imagined audience are particularly significant

Salience Some feature of a text/message that lends particular prominence to an element of the text/message, whether by positioning or the inherent interest of the element or by intensity of colour, etc.

Semiosis The ceaseless process of meaning-making, usually 'silent', that is, not audible nor visible or sensible in some other way, though occasionally apparent in social interaction

Signs of learning Outwardly made material—visible, tangible, audible—signs, produced in some way as the outcome of an engagement with the world overtly constructed as 'the world to be engaged with in learning' or not constructed in that way but still the object of 'interested attention'

Site of display The material space where a text-as-message is displayed. As such, it functions (also) as the 'medium' whereby a message is disseminated. The site has specific (spatial, temporal or other) aspects that have regularities of meaning that are understood by a social group and have semiotic effects on the message and its audience, for example, a screen, the homepage of a website, an advertising hoarding, the screen of a mobile phone

Sites of learning The actual, material or immaterial social/cultural, site in which learning is to take place, is taking or has taken place, together with the features that have a shaping effect on how learning might take place, such as power, affect, interest as well as physical material conditions of many kinds

Social semiotics A theory of meaning-making and communication that posits that signs are always newly made, that all sign-making is based on the interest of the maker of the sign, who makes signs as the motivated relation of a form which aptly expresses the meaning to be realised

Transduction The process in which meaning expressed in a sign-complex in one mode is 'drawn across' into another mode. In transduction, the entities of the original mode are not present in the 'new' mode, so that meaning has to be newly configured in relation to the affordances of the 'new' mode

Transformation A process of re-ordering the arrangement of entities of a sign-complex into a different sign-complex

References

de Saussure, F. (1983). *Course in general linguistics* (Trans. R. Harris). London: Duckworth.
Insulander, E. (2008). The museum as a semi-formal site for learning. In *Medien Journal, Lernen: Ein zentraler Begriff für die* Kommunikationswissenschaft, 32, Jahr-gang Nr 1/2008.

Jewitt, C., & Kress, G. R. (2001). *Multimodal learing and teaching: The rhetorics of the science classroom*. London: Continuum.

Kress, G. R. (1996). *Before writing: Rethinking the paths to literacy*. London: Routledge.

Kress, G. R. (2001). *Early spelling: Between creativity and convention*. London: Routledge.

Kress, G. R. (2003). *Literacy in the new media age*. London: Routledge/Falmer.

Kress, G. R. (in-press/2009). *Multimodality: A social semiotic approach to communication*. London: Routledge/Falmer.

Kress, G. R., & van Leeuwen, T. (2006). *Reading images: The grammar of graphic design*. London: Routledge Falmer.

Selander, S. (2008). Designs for learning—a theoretical perspective. *Designs for Learning, 1*(1), 6–9.

Chapter 3
Transforming K–12 Assessment: Integrating Accountability Testing, Formative Assessment and Professional Support

Randy Elliot Bennett and Drew H. Gitomer

Introduction

In this chapter, we ask whether advances in cognitive science, psychometrics and technology can transform the accountability paradigm that is currently in place in the United States. Of course, asking this question implies that there are problems with the present enactment of what is known as the *No Child Left Behind* Act, a system that requires each state regularly to test students in specified grades and subject areas against a state-imposed proficiency standard. We begin the chapter by first describing some of the forces that have led to the heightened emphasis on testing, and then articulate some of the fundamental problems with the system as currently implemented.

We then present an assessment-system model that is designed to overcome some of the inherent weaknesses of the present approach. Specifically, we ask whether we can have an assessment system that goes beyond fulfilling a simple accountability function by:

- documenting what students have achieved ('assessment of learning'),
- helping to identify how to plan instruction ('assessment for learning') and
- engaging students and teachers in worthwhile educational experiences in and of themselves ('assessment as learning').

The system we propose is heavily dependent on new technology. However, simply putting current tests on computer will not lead to substantive change in assessment practice. Instead, the system relies on advances in:

- cognitive science and an understanding of how students learn,
- psychometric approaches that attempt to provide richer characterisations of student achievement and
- technologies that allow for the presentation of richer assessment tasks, and for the collection and automated scoring of more complex student responses.

R.E. Bennett (✉)
Educational Testing Service, Princeton, NJ, USA
e-mail: rbennett@ets.org

C. Wyatt-Smith, J.J. Cumming (eds.), *Educational Assessment in the 21st Century*,
DOI 10.1007/978-1-4020-9964-9_3, © Springer Science+Business Media B.V. 2009

We conclude by putting forth the challenges facing the full development and implementation of an assessment system that is intended to support sound educational
practice.

A Brief Overview of the Status of Accountability in the United States

The push for educational accountability has its roots in concerns about the ability
of the educational system to prepare its citizens to meet successfully the challenges
of a global economy. One leg of this argument is that maintaining current living
standards depends upon keeping high-paying jobs at home. Those jobs are created
through business investment, and business investment follows labour pools that are
skilled and productive. However, when a nation's labour pool begins to become less
skilled and productive relative to the pools of other nations, business investment
starts to flow elsewhere, jobs leave, standard of living drops and, in the worst case,
national economic stability is threatened.

The second leg of the argument is that the United States educational system
has not effectively addressed fundamental inequity in access to a quality education.
This unequal access has been primarily defined by race, class and home language.
As the proportion of students who are poor, non-white and/or non-native speakers
of English continues to increase, the need to improve educational quality for all
becomes not only an issue of economic necessity, but also one of moral and democratic principles as well. For a stable democracy to survive, education must be able
to engender an informed and self-sufficient citizenry.

Such arguments are captured in three recent reports:

- *America's Perfect Storm: Three Forces Changing Our Nation's Future* (Kirsch,
  Braun, Yamamoto, & Sum, 2007)
- *Tough Times, Tough Choices: The Report of the New Commission on the Skills
  of the American Workforce* (National Center on Education and the Economy,
  2006)
- *Rising Above The Gathering Storm: Energizing and Employing America for a
  Brighter Economic Future* (Committee on Prospering in the Global Economy of
  the 21st Century, 2007).

These reports generally claim that the United States education system, which is
responsible for producing the skilled and productive labour pools of tomorrow, is
in danger of failing to meet that responsibility. According to the Organisation for
Economic Co-operation and Development's (OECD) Programme for International
Student Assessment (PISA), 15-year olds in the United States performed below the
OECD average in mathematics literacy, science literacy and problem solving (that is,
below the average for the industrialised nations with which the United States com-
petes economically) (Lemke et al., 2004). Upper secondary graduation rates are also
below the OECD average (OECD, 2006). Further, tertiary educational attainment,

meaning the number of years completed beyond secondary school, has slipped from 1st to 7th of the OECD countries. Finally, university graduation rates are below the OECD average.

This skills profile is highly related to socio-economic and language status. *America's Perfect Storm* (Kirsch et al., 2007) makes clear that the fastest growing part of the United States population is coming from families in which English is not the first language. Other studies show that social mobility has decreased dramatically in recent years. Students born into poor and less-educated families have lower likelihoods of moving into higher socio-economic strata than did students of previous generations (Beller & Hout, 2006).

These conditions have raised the call for increased use of assessment as a tool for educational accountability in order to evaluate educational effectiveness and make informed decisions about how to improve the system. Educators and policy makers need mechanisms to identify the competencies, ages, population groups, schools and even the individuals requiring attention.

Assessments, with stakes attached to them, have been viewed as more than information systems. They have been seen as a primary tool with which to focus attention on achievement in specific subject areas and on the achievement of selected population groups. In the United States, those population groups have included ethnic minorities, economically disadvantaged students, students with disabilities and students having limited English proficiency. The focal subject areas have been reading, mathematics and, more recently, science.

In the United States, these assessments are being used to evaluate not only students, but also schools and teachers. Schools can be sanctioned, to the point of being closed, if performance criteria are not satisfied. States and districts are introducing teacher pay-for-performance systems based on student test scores. In reaction to these high-stakes assessments, educational practices are changing, in intended and unintended ways. While there is significant debate about the efficacy of the current assessment system to meet the intended goals of increasing accountability and improving teaching and learning, there is no reason to believe that the emphasis on accountability testing will abate any time soon.

However, we believe there is a fundamental problem with the system as currently implemented. In the United States, the problem is that the above set of circumstances has fashioned an accountability assessment system with at least two salient characteristics. The first characteristic is that there are now significant consequences for students, teachers, school administrators and policy makers. The second characteristic is, paradoxically, very limited educational value. This limited value stems from the fact that our accountability assessments typically reflect a shallow view of proficiency, defined in terms of the skills needed to succeed on relatively short and, too often, quite artificial test items (that is, with little direct connection to real-world contexts).

The enactment of the *No Child Left Behind* Act has resulted in an unprecedented and very direct connection between high stakes assessments and instructional practice. Historically, the disassociation between large-scale assessments and classroom practice was decried, but the current irony is that the influence these tests now have on educational practice has raised even stronger concerns (for example, Abrams, Pedulla, & Madaus, 2003), stemming from a general narrowing of the curriculum, in terms of both the subject areas and the kinds of skills and understandings that are taught. The cognitive models underlying these assessments are long out of date (Shepard, 2000), evidence is still collected primarily through multiple-choice items, and students are characterised too often on only a single proficiency when the nature of domain performance is, arguably, more complex.

Many experts in assessment—as well as instruction—claim that we have quite unintentionally created a system of accountability assessment grounded in an outdated scientific model for conceptualising teaching and measuring proficiency. Further, an entire continuum of supporting products has been developed, including interim (or 'benchmark') assessments, so-called 'formative assessments' and teacher professional development that are emulating—and worse, reinforcing—the less desirable characteristics of those accountability tests.

In essence, the end goal for too many teachers, students and school administrators has become improving performance on the accountability assessment without enough attention being paid to whether students actually learn the deeper curriculum standards those tests are intended to represent.

Designing an Alternative System

The question we are asking at Educational Testing Service is this: Given the press for accountability testing, could we do better? Could we design a *comprehensive system* of assessment that:

- Is based on modern scientific conceptions of domain proficiency and, therefore, causes teachers to think differently about the nature of proficiency, how to teach it and how to assess it?
- Shifts the end goal from improving performance on an unavoidably shallow accountability measure towards developing the deeper skills we'd like students to master?
- Capitalises on new technology to make assessment more relevant, effective and efficient?
- Primarily uses *extended*, open-ended tasks?
- Measures frequently?
- Not only provides formative and interim-progress information, but also accountability information, thereby reducing dependence on the one-time test?

Developing large-scale assessment systems that can support decision making for state and local policy makers, teachers, parents and students has proven to be an elusive goal. Yet, the idea that educational assessment ought better to reflect student learning and afford opportunities to inform instructional practice can be traced back at least 50 years to Cronbach's seminal article 'The two disciplines of scientific psychology' (1957). These ideas continued to evolve with Glaser's (1976) conceptualisation of an *instructional psychology* that would adapt instruction to students' individual knowledge states. Further developments in aligning cognitive theory and psychometric modelling approaches have been summarised by Glaser and Silver (1994); Pellegrino, Baxter, and Glaser (1999); Pellegrino, Chudowsky, and Glaser (2001), the Committee on Programs for Advanced Study of Mathematics and Science in American High Schools and National Research Council (2002), and Wilson (2004).

We are proposing a system that needs to be coherent in two ways (Gitomer & Duschl, 2007). First, assessment systems are *externally coherent* when they are consistent with accepted theories of learning and valued learning outcomes. Second, assessment systems can be considered *internally coherent* to the extent that different components of the assessment system, particularly large-scale and classroom components, share the same underlying views of learners' academic development. The challenge is to design assessment systems that are both internally and externally coherent. Realising such a system is not straightforward and requires a long-term research and development effort. But, if successful, we believe the benefits to students, teachers, schools and the entire educational system would be profound.

There are undoubtedly *many* different ways one could conceptualise a comprehensive system of assessment to improve on current practice. We offer one potential solution that we are pursuing, not because we think it is *the* solution, but because we believe it contains certain core elements that would be integral to any system that endeavoured faithfully to assess important learning objectives summatively at the same time as it encouraged and facilitated good instructional practice.

Our vision entails three closely related systems built upon the same conceptual base. The three systems are:

- Accountability Assessment
- Formative Assessment
- Professional Support.

The Common Conceptual Base

The foundation for all three systems is a common conceptual base that combines curriculum standards with findings from cognitive-scientific research. By cognitive-scientific research, we refer broadly to the multiple fields of inquiry concerned with how students learn (for example, Bransford, Brown, & Cocking, 1999). Of course, calls for assessments driven by theories of learning are not new, so the question is, why have such calls not been heeded?

For one, the sciences of educational measurement and of learning and cognition evolved separately from one another. Attempts to bring the two fields together are relatively recent and have not yet been incorporated into accountability assessment in any significant way. Second, cognitive-scientific research has produced only partial knowledge about the nature of proficiency in specific domains, and we do not yet know how to create practical assessment *systems* that use this partial knowledge effectively. Third, there are practical and economic constraints that have inhibited the development and deployment of such systems. However, sufficient progress has been made on a number of relevant fronts to make the pursuit of a more ambitious vision of assessment a worthwhile endeavour.

The first advance has been in the depth and breadth of our understanding of learning and performance in academic domains. Depending upon the content domain, research offers us one or more of the following: cognitive-scientific principles, competency models and developmental models.

Principles present an important contrast to the outcomes that often characterise curriculum standards. Cognitive-scientific *principles* describe the processes, strategies and knowledge structures important for achieving curriculum standards, and the features of tasks—or more generally, of situations—that call upon those processes, strategies and knowledge structures.

For example, cognitive principles suggest working with multiple representations because information does not come in only one form. Indeed, Sigel (1993) and others have made a compelling case that conceptual competence is, at its core, the ability to understand and navigate between multiple representations. For example, the child who learns to read moves from the direct experience of an object to a picture representation, to a word (for example, 'cat'), to more and more abstract descriptions, all signifying the same concept. Across domains, students need to understand and use representational forms that may include written text, oral description, diagrams and specialised symbol systems, moving easily and flexibly among these different representations.

Cognitive principles also suggest embedding tasks in meaningful contexts, since meaningful contextualisation can engage students and help them link solution strategies to the conditions under which those strategies might best be employed. Cognitive principles suggest integrating component skills because real-world tasks often call for the execution of components in a highly coordinated fashion, and achieving that coordination requires the components to be practiced, and assessed, in an integrated manner.

Fourth, cognitive principles suggest developing component skills to automaticity (Perfetti, 1985). If low-level components—like the ability to decode words—are not automatic, attention must be devoted to them, drawing limited cognitive resources away from higher-level processes, like making meaning from text.

Finally, cognitive principles suggest designing assessment so that it supports— or at least does not conflict with—the social processes integral to learning and performance. At one level, the *sociocultural/situative* perspective focuses on the nature of social interactions and how these interactions influence learning. From this perspective, learning involves the adoption of sociocultural practices, including the practices within particular academic domains. Students of science, for example, not only learn the content of science, but they also develop an 'intellective identity' (Greeno, 2002) as scientists, by becoming acculturated to the tools, practices and discourse of science as a discipline (Bazerman, 1988; Gee, 1999; Hogan, 2007; Lave and Wenger, 1991; Rogoff, 1990; Roseberry, Warren, & Contant, 1992). Similarly, students learn to engage in the practices of writers or mathematicians as they become more accomplished in a domain. This perspective grows out of the work of Vygotsky (1978) and others and posits that learning and the disciplinary practice develop out of social interaction. The second social dimension that needs to be attended to in an assessment design that produces meaningful results is the accommodation of students with a wide range of cultural, linguistic and other characteristics.

Competency models define, from a cognitive perspective, what it means to be skilled in a domain. Ideally, these models not only can tell us the processes, strategies and knowledge structures important for achievement, and the features of tasks that call upon those processes, strategies and knowledge structures, but also how the components of domain proficiency might be organised and how those components work together to facilitate skilled performance. For example, in our work on writing, the competency model is shaped around the interaction of:

- the use of language and literacy skills (skills involved in speaking, reading and writing standard English)
- the use of strategies to manage the writing process (for example, planning, drafting evaluating and revising)
- the use of critical thinking skills (reasoning about content, reasoning about social context).

Assessment is then designed to assess the interplay of these skills using tasks that reflect legitimate writing activity.

Developmental models define, from a cognitive perspective, what it means to progress in a domain. In addition to providing principles and a proposed domain organisation, these models tell us how proficiency develops over time, including how that development is affected by the diverse cultural and linguistic backgrounds that students bring to school.

Together, these cognitive-scientific principles and models help us determine:

- the components of proficiency that should be assessed because they are critical in achieving curriculum standards
- the features of test questions that can be manipulated to distinguish better among students at different proficiency levels, to give diagnostic information, or to give targeted instructional practice
- how to anchor score scales so that test performance can be described in terms that more effectively communicate what students know and can do
- the components of proficiency that should be instructional targets
- how teachers might arrange instruction for maximum effect
- how to better account for cultural and linguistic diversity in assessment.

It is important to note that the nature of most curriculum standards is such that they are not particularly helpful in making such decisions. Current standards are not helpful because they are often 'list-like', rather than coherently grouped; may be overly general so that specifically what to teach may be unclear; or, at the other extreme, are too molecular, encouraging a piecemeal approach to instruction that neglects meaningful integration of components. Thus, in principle, having a modern, cognitive–scientific basis should help us build better assessments in the same way as having an understanding of modern physics helps engineers to build better bridges.

The Accountability System

The accountability system begins with the strong conceptual base described above. Assessments comprised of foundational tasks are administered periodically, with information aggregated over time in order to update proficiency estimates in a dynamic fashion. Timely reports are produced that are customised for particular audiences. Each of these features is described in more detail.

Foundational tasks. Foundational tasks are built upon the conceptual base so that they are demonstrably aligned to curriculum standards *and* to cognitive principles or models. That is, these tasks should be written to target processes, strategies and knowledge structures that are central to the achievement of curriculum standards and proficient performance in the domain. The foundational tasks are the central (but not exclusive) means of measuring student competency.

These foundational tasks generally are intended to:

- require the integration of multiple skills or curriculum standards
- be extended, offering many opportunities to observe student behaviour
- be meaningfully contextualised
- call upon problem-solving skills
- utilise constructed-response formats
- be regarded by teachers as learning events worth teaching towards.

An example of a framework our colleagues have developed for the design of foundational tasks in writing is described in Fig. 3.1.

Periodic accountability assessment. A second characteristic of the accountability system is to employ a series of periodic administrations instead of the model of assessment as a one-time event. In order to assess the intent of curriculum standards faithfully, in terms of both depth and breadth, as well as to provide models of sound educational practice, it is necessary to construct a relatively long test that consists of integrated, cognitively motivated tasks. However, it is impractical to administer such a test at a single point in time. It is also educationally counterproductive to delay assessment feedback until the end of the school year.

Therefore, we divide this hypothetical long test into multiple parts, with each part including one or more foundational task, supplemented by shorter items to test skills that can be appropriately assessed in that latter fashion. Test parts are administered across the school year. Information about students' status and 'formative hypotheses' about achievement are returned after each administration. A final accountability result is derived by aggregating performance over the parts. (How best to accomplish this aggregation is the subject of our continuing research. However, the magnitude of weights assigned to particular assessment tasks and skills may, in part, be a policy

---

The goal is to help students display their writing skills to best advantage by providing multiple opportunities, guidance, and resources for assessments.

Tests and rubrics emphasise the role of critical thinking in writing proficiency.

Each Periodic Accountability Assessment, or PAA, is a project

- Each test is a small-scale project centered on one topic, thereby providing an overall context, purpose and audience for the set of tasks.
- Each test usually focuses on one genre or mode of discourse and the critical-thinking skills and strategies associated with that mode of discourse.
- Short prewriting/inquiry tasks serve as thematically related but psychometrically independent steps in a sequence leading up to and including a full-length essay or similar document.
- The smaller tasks provide measurement of component skills—especially critical-thinking skills—as well as a structure to help students succeed with the larger, integrated task (essay, letter etc.).
- Task formats vary widely (mostly constructed-response, with some selected-response), but all tests include 'writer's checklists' and glossaries of words used in the test.

The project comes with its own resource materials

- To help address varying levels of background knowledge about the PAA's topic, the tests often include short documents that students are required or encouraged to use.
- This approach permits students to engage in greater depth with more substantive topics and meshes with current curricular emphasis on research skills and use of sources.

Tripartite analytic scoring is based on the three-strand competency model

- Strand I (use language and literacy skills):
  - Instead of using multiple-choice items to measure these skills, the approach is to apply a generic Strand I rubric to all written responses across tasks. This rubric focuses on sentence-level features of the students' writing.
- Strand II (use strategies to manage the writing process):
  - A generic Strand II rubric is applied to all written responses of sufficient length in order to measure document-level skills, including organisation, structure, focus and development.
- Strand III: (use critical-thinking skills):
  - Each constructed-response task includes a task-specific Strand III rubric used to evaluate the quality of ideas and reasoning particular to the task. In addition, most of the selected-response tasks measure critical-thinking skills.

Fig. 3.1 Framework for the design of periodic accountability assessments in writing (Source: Paul Deane, Nora Odendahl, Mary Fowles, Doug Baldwin and Tom Quinlan, reproduced with permission of the copyright owner, Educational Testing Service)

decision determined by the test sponsors [for example, state education department staff].)

Periodic administration has multiple benefits. It allows for greater use of tasks worth teaching towards because there is more time for assessment in the aggregate. In addition, the test can cover more effectively the curriculum standards, making for a more valid measure. Because the scores can be progressively accumulated, the accumulated scores should gain in reliability as the year advances; the end-of-year scores should be more reliable than scores from a traditional one-time test, thereby giving a truer picture of student competency; and there should be a greater chance of generating instructionally useful profile information because more information has been systematically assembled than would otherwise be the case. Finally, in contrast to most existing accountability systems, *no single performance is determinative*. Instead, similar to the way in which teachers assign course grades, accountability scores come from multiple pieces of information gathered in a standardised fashion throughout the school year. The more items of information, the less each counts individually, so no student, teacher, school or administrator can be held to one unrepresentative performance.

Timely results. Since accountability administration is periodic, student status with respect to curriculum standards can be updated regularly. That regular updating allows targets for formative assessment to be suggested and at-risk students to be identified while there is still time to take instructional action.

Customised reports. Customised reports will be designed so they are appropriate to the audience, whether student, parent, teacher, head teacher, local administrator or national policy maker. These reports should be available on demand and should suggest actions, not only for students, but also to inform instructional policy development and teacher professional development.

The Formative System

This system is built on a concept of formative assessment as a continuing process in which teachers and students use evidence gathered through formal and informal means, in order to make inferences about student competency and, based on those inferences, take actions intended to achieve learning goals. First, this conception implies that formative assessment encompasses a process aided by some type of instrumentation, formal or not. This instrumentation should be fit for use (that is, suited to instructional decision making). Not all instruments are able to be used effectively in a formative assessment process by the typical teacher because not all instruments are fit for that purpose. Second, the conception depicts formative assessment as a hypothesis-generation-and-testing process, whereby what we observe students doing constitutes evidence for inferences about their competency that, in turn, directs instructional action, as well as the collection and interpretation of further evidence. Third, the conception attempts to focus formative assessment on an underlying competency model, in contrast to focusing it on classroom activities or assessment tasks. Through the competency model, the formative system is linked to the accountability system, as both systems derive from the same conceptual base. The intention is to facilitate student growth, not in the shallow way that many current formative assessments built to improve achievement on multiple-choice or short-answer accountability tests do, but in a deeper fashion that is consistent with cognitive principles and models. Finally, the conception identifies the end purpose of formative assessment as the modification of instruction so that learning of competencies is facilitated.

An important caveat is that while the accountability system may provide information of use to the formative system, the reverse should not occur. That is, performance in the formative system should *not* be used for accountability purposes. This one-way 'firewall' exists for two reasons. First, the formative system is optional and modifiable by design, so students will likely have very different access to formative experiences, making comparability of student results impossible. But more importantly, the formative system is *for* learning, and if students and teachers are to feel comfortable using it for that purpose, they will need to try out problem solutions—and engage in instructional activities—without feeling they are being constantly judged.

The formative system is designed to give students the opportunity to develop target competencies through structured, instructional practice. Teachers may use formative tasks as part of their lesson designs and also may tailor use on the basis of information from the accountability system. For example, information from the periodic accountability assessments may suggest particular student needs.

The formative system is used at the discretion of the teacher and/or school. It is available on demand so that teachers may use it when, and as often as, they need it. The rationale for optional use is in recognition of the fact that teachers are dealing with several mandates already. Our view is that a formative assessment system is likely to be more effective if teachers choose to use it because they believe it will benefit their practice. The challenge will be in creating a system that can justify such a belief.

The aim of the formative system is to give teachers various classroom resources that are instructionally compatible with the accountability system and which they can use in whatever fashion they feel works best. Among these resources would be classroom tasks and focused diagnostic assessment.

Classroom tasks. Classroom tasks are variants of the foundational accountability tasks. They are integrated, extended problem-solving exercises meant to be learning events worth teaching towards. These tasks should be accessible from an online databank, organised by skills required and curriculum level so as to permit out-of-level practice.

Teachers can use these classroom tasks for several purposes. For example, teachers might use them to set practice activities and provide feedback to individual students, or as the basis for peer interaction (for example, students might discuss among themselves the different approaches that could be taken to a task). Finally, teachers might use these tasks as the focus of class discussion so that a particular task, and various ways of responding to it, becomes the object of an extended classroom discourse. These uses of the classroom tasks are intended not only to facilitate student achievement of curriculum standards and development of cognitive proficiencies, but also to facilitate self-reflection and other habits associated with mature practice in a domain. The intention is, as Rick Stiggins has advocated (Stiggins &

Chappuis, 2005), to help students develop ownership of their learning processes and investment in the results.

A brief overview of a classroom formative assessment activity is presented in Fig. 3.2 and in Table 3.1. The activity is designed to help teachers gather evidence about, and facilitate the development of, persuasive writing skills for middle school students. Included are a sample screenshot that introduces the activity (Fig. 3.2) and a description of the series of classroom tasks that comprise the activity (Table 3.1). While an interactive system can be used to administer the tasks and collect student responses, most of these formative tasks can also be administered outside of a technology-based environment.

Diagnostic assessment. The second part of the formative system is diagnostic assessment. Diagnostic assessment is, at the teacher's option, given to students who struggle with certain aspects of performance, either in the accountability system or on classroom tasks. These assessments can be used with students who are at risk of failing, or simply with ones whom the teacher would like to help advance to the next curriculum level. The diagnostic assessment is comprised of elemental items that test component skills in isolation, something for which multiple-choice or short-answer questions might be used very effectively.

The diagnostic assessment helps to suggest instructional targets by attempting to isolate the cause(s) of inadequate performance on the more integrated foundational tasks comprising the accountability system and classroom assessment. For any student who interacts with the formative system, the reports could provide a dynamic synthesis of evidence, accumulated over time, from the accountability system, the classroom tasks (if administered) and the diagnostic assessment (if administered). Multiple sources of evidence can offer more dependable information about students'

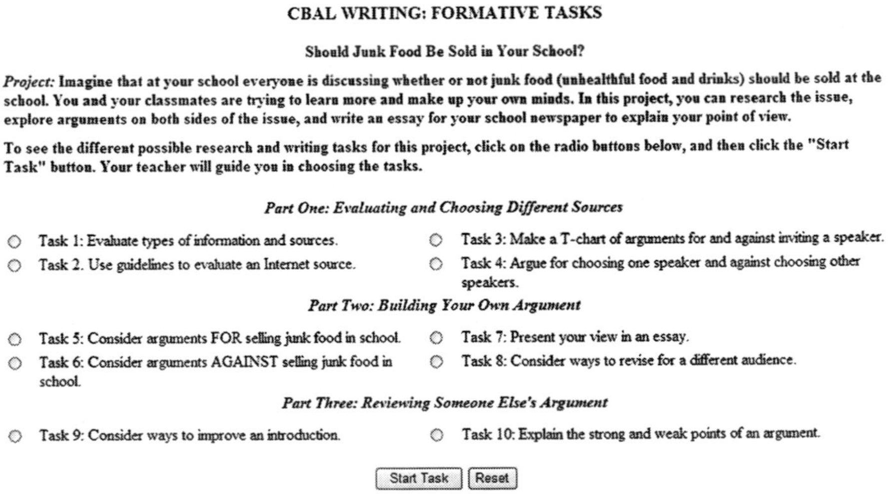

CBAL WRITING: FORMATIVE TASKS

Should Junk Food Be Sold in Your School?

Project: Imagine that at your school everyone is discussing whether or not junk food (unhealthful food and drinks) should be sold at the school. You and your classmates are trying to learn more and make up your own minds. In this project, you can research the issue, explore arguments on both sides of the issue, and write an essay for your school newspaper to explain your point of view.

To see the different possible research and writing tasks for this project, click on the radio buttons below, and then click the "Start Task" button. Your teacher will guide you in choosing the tasks.

Part One: Evaluating and Choosing Different Sources

○ Task 1: Evaluate types of information and sources.   ○ Task 3: Make a T-chart of arguments for and against inviting a speaker.

○ Task 2: Use guidelines to evaluate an Internet source.   ○ Task 4: Argue for choosing one speaker and against choosing other speakers.

Part Two: Building Your Own Argument

○ Task 5: Consider arguments FOR selling junk food in school.   ○ Task 7: Present your view in an essay.

○ Task 6: Consider arguments AGAINST selling junk food in school.   ○ Task 8: Consider ways to revise for a different audience.

Part Three: Reviewing Someone Else's Argument

○ Task 9: Consider ways to improve an introduction.   ○ Task 10: Explain the strong and weak points of an argument.

[Start Task] [Reset]

Fig. 3.2 Formative activity for gathering evidence about, and facilitating the development of, persuasive writing skill (Source: Nora Odendahl, Paul Deane, Mary Fowles and Doug Baldwin, reproduced with permission of the copyright owner, Educational Testing Service)

Table 3.1 Description of tasks comprising a formative activity in persuasive writing

PART I: Tasks 1–3 are short exercises that ask students to apply criteria for evaluating various types of research sources. Then, once students have had the opportunity to work with these criteria, they write a persuasive letter arguing in favour of a particular source (in this case, one of three potential speakers). The aim of this group of tasks is to help students develop their ability to judge sources critically and to articulate those judgments. Moreover, the extended writing task (task 4) gives students an opportunity to write a persuasive piece that is not issue oriented, but instead requires the student to choose from among various alternatives, each with its own pros and cons.

PART II. Tasks 5 and 6 require the student to read about and consider arguments on each side of the general issue (whether junk food should be sold in schools), before writing an essay presenting their own view to a school audience. A follow-up task (task 8) asks students to consider ways in which they revise the essay for a larger audience outside the school. Thus, this group of tasks takes the student through the stages of persuasive writing—considering arguments on both sides of an issue, formulating and presenting one's own position, and demonstrating awareness of appropriate content and tone for different audiences.

Part III. The final two tasks ask the student to take a given text and apply guidelines for writing an introduction and for presenting an argument. These exercises allow students to work with rubrics and examples of persuasive writing in a very focused way.

Source: Nora Odendahl, Paul Deane, Mary Fowles and Doug Baldwin, reproduced with permission of the copyright owner, Educational Testing Service.

strengths and weaknesses than any single source alone. For those students who do interact with the system, it should be possible to provide information to the current teacher, as well as end-of-year formative information to next year's teacher, giving this individual a clearer idea of where to begin instruction than they might otherwise have had.

Professional Support

The final component of our vision is professional support. This component has two goals. The first goal is to help teachers and administrators understand how to use the accountability and formative systems effectively. The second goal is to help develop in teachers a fundamentally different conception of what it means to be proficient in a domain, how to help students achieve proficiency and how to assess it. 'Fundamentally different' implies a conception that is based not only on curriculum standards, but also on cognitive research and on recognition of the need to help students develop more positive attitudes towards, and greater investment in, learning and assessment.

In order to achieve these professional-support goals, there is need to go beyond traditional approaches to teacher in-service training and build more on such ideas as teacher learning communities (McLaughlin & Talbert, 2006). Such communities let interested teachers help one another discover how to use formative assessment best in their own classrooms. We also envision the use of online tools to involve teachers in collaboratively scoring constructed responses to formative system tasks because, through scoring, teachers can develop a shared understanding of what it means to be proficient in a domain.

The Role of Technology

The vision presented assumes a heavy presence of technology. For one, technology can help to make assessment more relevant, since the computer has become a standard tool in the workplace and in higher education. The ability to use the computer for domain-based work is, therefore, becoming a legitimate part of what should be measured (Bennett, 2002). Second, technology can make assessment more informative since process indicators can be captured, as well as final answers, allowing for the possibility of understanding *how* a student arrived at a particular result (Bennett, Persky, Weiss, & Jenkins, 2007). Technology can make assessment more efficient because, in principle, moving information electronically is cheaper and faster than shipping paper.

Of great importance is that technology offers a potential long-term solution for the efficient scoring of complex constructed responses. One of the constraints on the widespread use of constructed-response tasks to date has been the economic expense of human scoring, as well as demands on teachers. To the extent that performances can be scored by computer, this limitation will be obviated. Certain kinds of student responses are already reasonably well handled by automated scoring tools (for example, Shermis & Burstein, 2003; Williamson, Mislevy, & Bejar, 2007), while other kinds of responses still require long-term research and development efforts.

Technology is not a panacea, however, for it can be a curse as well as blessing. If not used thoughtfully, technology can prevent students from demonstrating skill simply because they do not have sufficient familiarity with computers to be able to respond effectively online (Horkay, Bennett, Allen, Kaplan, & Yan, 2006). Technology can narrow the range of skills measured by encouraging exam developers to use only those tasks most amenable to computer delivery. While such tasks may be quite relevant, they might not cover the full range of skills that should be tested. Technology can distort assessment results when automated scoring neglects important aspects of proficiency (Bennett, 2006). Machines do not do a good job, for example, of evaluating the extent to which a student's essay is appropriate for its intended audience. Finally, technology can encourage students and teachers to focus instructional time on questionable activities, like how to write essays that a machine will grade highly, even if the resulting essays are *not* what an experienced examiner would consider well crafted.

What Are the Challenges?

The successful development and implementation of the aforementioned conception is not a given. Among the challenges that we are working to resolve are:

- The aggregation of results across periodic administrations. For example, should results be weighted according to recency of administration, or some other criterion, so as to account better for growth?
- The problem of missed administrations and missing student-performance data in general.
- The dependence of the system and interpretation of student results on specific instructional sequencing within classrooms, schools and districts.
- Issues of test security related to the memorability of extended tasks.
- Ensuring that generalisable claims about students can be made from assessments comprised primarily of extended tasks, which often provide information that is of limited dependability.
- Ensuring the comparability of test forms when different students may be taking different forms and those forms vary in difficulty.
- Ensuring fairness for special populations.
- Making periodic assessment with extended problems affordable.
- Convincing teachers, administrators and policy makers to spend *more* time on assessment because the periodic assessments may, in fact, be longer in the aggregate than was the original end-of-year accountability test.
- Making the accountability assessment a worthwhile instructional experience in and of itself.

Indeed, it is only by making the assessment experience worthwhile in the educational context that we can make a compelling argument for more time and money to be spent in the process of assessment for accountability.

It is our perception that accountability assessment is unlikely to go away. It is too closely bound with the politics of global competition and dissatisfaction with the level of historical accountability by the educational system. However, how we do accountability assessment matters, and it matters a great deal, because educational practice (and learning) is influenced considerably by its design, content and format. We have a range of choices with respect to how we deal with the influence and, indeed, the permanence of accountability assessment. At one end of this range, we can treat accountability assessment as a necessary evil to be minimised and marginalised as best we can. At the other end, we can attempt to rethink assessment comprehensively from the ground up.

Our work is an invitation to a conversation that needs to begin by asking whether we can rethink assessment as a system so that it adequately serves both local learning needs and national policy purposes. That is, can we have an assessment system *of*, *for* and *as* learning? We do *not* know the answer. However, as assessment professionals, we believe we have a moral obligation to do our best to find out.

Theoretical and Methodological Framings

The arguments presented in this chapter build on several disciplines. This supplementary section describes two of those disciplines, cognitive science and psychometric science, and also gives a short glossary of terms.

An Overview of Cognitive Science

Cognitive science comprises the multiple fields concerned with the study of thought and learning. Those fields include psychology, education, anthropology, philosophy, linguistics, computer science, neuroscience and biology. Because it is an interdisciplinary field, cognitive science has no single genesis. Rather, its roots are found in disparate places.

Cognitive science has supplanted behaviourism as the dominant perspective in the study of thought and learning. Behaviourism grew out of the early 20th-century work of Thorndike, Watson and Skinner, which rejected the theoretical need for internal mental processes or states. Behaviourism posited that highly complex performance (that is, behaviour) could be decomposed into simpler, discrete units and that such performance could be understood as the aggregation of those units.

The first cognitive science theories, in contrast, highlighted the importance of hypothetical mental processes and states. These theories focused on how individuals processed information from the environment in order to think, learn and solve problems. These theories hypothesised specific mental processes as well as how knowledge might be organised in supporting acts of human cognition.

Among the theoretical perspectives commonly identified with cognitive scientific research is information processing. The information-processing perspective is commonly traced to the publication in 1967 of Neisser's book, *Cognitive Psychology*, as well as to Newell and Simon's 1972 publication of *Human Problem Solving*. This perspective viewed mental activity in terms similar to the way in which a digital computer represents and processes information. Now, with advances in neuroscience, the biological basis for cognitive processes is becoming much more clearly understood.

Alternative perspectives that include *activity theory* and *situated cognition* do not view cognition as simply a function of mental processes and knowledge that an individual brings to a task. Rather, in these views, cognition is not separated from context and the interactions in which mental activity and learning occur. Cognition is inherently a social activity and learning involves increasingly sophisticated participation in the activities of particular social communities. Major contributions to this perspective are attributed to Vygotsky and Wertsch, and more recently to Lave and Wenger (1991), Scribner, Cole and Greeno.

As cognitive science has matured, the field has recognised the importance of both the information-processing and the situated-cognition/activity theory perspectives. Modern theories of learning, cognition, instruction and assessment integrate these bodies of work into more unified and complete points of view.

An Overview of Psychometric Science

Psychometrics encompasses the theory and methodology of educational and psychological measurement. Its theory and methods essentially attempt to characterise some unobservable attribute of an individual, either in terms of standing on a scale or membership in a category, and the degree of uncertainty associated with that characterisation. The characterisation may be made in relation to a comparison group (that is, norm referenced) or it may be made in relation to some performance standard (that is, criterion-referenced).

The emergence of the field is often traced to the late-19th and early-20th century work of such individuals as Wundt and Fechner in Germany; Galton, Spearman, and Pearson in England; and Binet in France. These individuals developed theories of intelligence, methods for quantifying psychological attributes such as the individual intelligence test and techniques for analysing the meaning of those quantifications, or scores, like the correlation coefficient and factor analysis. In the United States, the work of Thorndike, Yerkes, Thurstone and Brigham, among others, led to creation of the group intelligence, aptitude and achievement tests; the concept of developed ability; and further advances in techniques for analysing test data.

Because many of the field's pioneers were also psychologists—Thorndike, Yerkes, Thurstone and Brigham, to name a few—psychometrics was closely associated with, and influenced by, behaviourism, the dominant psychological perspective for most of the 20th century. That perspective is still quite evident in modern psychometrics, where the specifications for test development are commonly stated in terms of lists of behavioural objectives and test scores are transformations of the sum of the items answered correctly. Both practices fit well with the behaviourist notion that complex performance is the aggregation of discrete bits of knowledge.

Among the dominant methodological theories in psychometrics are classical test theory and item response theory (IRT). Classical test theory is essentially a loose collection of techniques used to analyse test functioning, including but not limited to indices of score reliability, item discrimination and item difficulty. These techniques include many of those generated in the 19th and 20th centuries by Pearson, Spearman, Thurstone and others. Classical test theory is built around the idea that the score an individual attains on a test—the observed score—is a function of that individual's 'true score' and error.

The second half of the 20th century saw the development of IRT and its widespread application. IRT is a unified framework for solving a wide range of theoretical and practical problems in assessment. Those problems include connecting the item responses made by an individual to inferences about their proficiency, summarising the uncertainty inherent in that characterisation at different score levels, putting different forms of a test on a common scale and evaluating item and test functioning.

Most recently, more complex psychometric approaches, including generalisations of IRT, have been created that better capture the multidimensional character typical of cognitive scientific models of cognition and learning.

Glossary

Accountability assessment A standardised, summative examination, or program of examinations, used to hold an entity formally or informally responsible for achievement. That 'entity' could be a learner, as when a school-leaving examination is used to determine whether a student can graduate, or a school, as when league tables are compiled, or the education system as a whole, as when the achievement of different countries is compared.

Formative assessment An ongoing process in which teachers and students use evidence gathered through formal and informal means to make inferences about student competency and, based on those inferences, take actions intended to achieve learning goals.

References

Abrams, L. M., Pedulla, J. J., & Madaus, G. F. (2003). Views from the classroom: Teachers' opinions of statewide testing programs. *Theory into Practice, 42*(1), 8–29.

Bazerman, C. (1988). Shaping written knowledge: The genre and activity of the experimental article in science. Madison: University of Wisconsin Press.

Beller, E., & Hout, M. (2006). Intergenerational social mobility: The United States in comparative perspective. *Opportunity in America, 16*(2), 19–37.

Bennett, R. E. (2002). Inexorable and inevitable: The continuing story of technology and assessment. *Journal of Technology, Learning, and Assessment, 1*(1), Retrieved January 26, 2008, from <www.bc.edu/research/intasc/jtla/journal/v1n1.shtml.

Bennett, R. E. (2006). Moving the field forward: Some thoughts on validity and automated scoring. D. M. In Williamson, R. J. Mislevy, & I. I. Bejar (Eds.), *Automated scoring of complex tasks in computer-based testing* (pp. 403–412). Mahwah, NJ: Erlbaum.

Bennett, R. E., Persky, H., Weiss, A. R., & Jenkins, F. (2007). *Problem solving in technology-rich environments: A report from the NAEP Technology-Based Assessment Project* (NCES 2007–466). Washington, DC: National Center for Education Statistics, United States Department of Education. Retrieved January 26, 2008, from <nces.ed. gov/pubsearch/pubsinfo.asp?pubid=2007466.

Bransford, J., Brown, A., & Cocking, R. (Eds.). (1999). *How people learn: Brain, mind, experience and school*. Washington, DC: National Academies Press.

Committee on Programs for Advanced Study of Mathematics and Science in American High Schools & National Research Council. (2002). J. P. Gollub, M. W. Bertenthal, J. B. Labov, & P. C. Curtis (Eds.), *Learning and understanding: Improving advanced study in mathematics and science in U.S. high schools*. Washington, DC: National Academies Press.

Committee on Prospering in the Global Economy of the 21st Century. (2007). *Rising above the gathering storm: Energizing and employing America for a brighter economic future*. Washington, DC: National Academies Press.

Cronbach, L. J. (1957). The two disciplines of scientific psychology. *American Psychologist, 12*, 671–684.

Gee, J. (1999). *An introduction to discourse analysis: Theory and method*. New York: Routledge.

Gitomer, D. H., & Duschl, R. A. (2007). Establishing multilevel coherence in assessment. In P. A. Moss (Ed.), *Evidence and decision making. The 106th yearbook of the National Society for the Study of Education, Part I* (pp. 288–320). Chicago: National Society for the Study of Education.

Glaser, R. (1976). Components of a psychology of instruction: Toward a science of design. *Review of Educational Research, 46*, 1–24.

Glaser, R., & Silver, E. (1994). Assessment, testing, and instruction: Retrospect and prospect. In L. Darling-Hammond (Ed.), *Review of Research in Education* (Vol. 20, pp. 393–419). Washington, DC: American Educational Research Association.

Greeno, J. G. (2002). Students with competence, authority, and accountability: Affording intellective identities in classrooms. New York: College Board.

Hogan, D. (2007). *Towards 'invisible colleges': Conversation, disciplinarity, and pedagogy in Singapore*. Slide presentation available from Office of Education Research, National Institute of Education, Nanyang Technological University, Singapore.

Horkay, N., Bennett, R. E., Allen, N., Kaplan, B., & Yan, F. (2006). Does it matter if I take my writing test on computer? An empirical study of mode effects in NAEP. *Journal of Technology, Learning and Assessment*, 5(2), Retrieved January 26, 2008, from <escholarship.bc.edu/jtla/vol5/2/

Kirsch, I., Braun, H., Yamamoto, K., & Sum, A. (2007). *America's perfect storm: Three forces changing our nation's future*. Princeton, NJ: Educational Testing Service.

Lave, J., & Wenger, E. (1991). *Situated learning: Legitimate peripheral participation*. Cambridge, UK: Cambridge University Press.

Lemke, M., Sen, A., Pahlke, E., Partelow, L., Miller, D., & Williams, T., et al. (2004). *International outcomes of learning in mathematics literacy and problem solving: PISA 2003 results from the U.S. perspective* (NCES 2005–003). Washington, DC: United States Department of Education, National Center for Education Statistics.

McLaughlin, M., & Talbert, J. E. (2006). *Building school-based teacher learning communities: Professional strategies to improve student achievement*. New York: Teachers College Press.

National Center on Education and the Economy. (2006). *Tough times, tough choices: The report of the New Commission on the Skills of the American Workforce*. Washington, DC: Author.

Newell, A., & Simon, H. A. (1972). *Human problem solving*. Englewood Cliffs, NJ: Prentice-hall.

Organisation for Economic Co-operation and Development. (2006). *OECD Education at a glance 2006: OECD briefing note for the United States*. Retrieved January 26, 2008, from <www.oecd.org/dataoecd/51/20/37392850.pdf>

Pellegrino, J. W., Baxter, G. P., & Glaser, R. (1999). Addressing the 'two disciplines' problem: Linking theories of cognition and learning with assessment and instructional practice. In A. Iran-Nejad & P. D. Pearson (Eds.), *Review of Research in Education* (Vol. 24, pp. 307–353). Washington, DC: American Educational Research Association.

Pellegrino, J. W., Chudowsky, N., & Glaser, R. (Eds.). (2001). *Knowing what students know: The science and design of educational assessment*. Washington, DC: National Academies Press.

Perfetti, C. A. (1985). *Reading ability*. New York: Oxford University Press.

Rogoff, B. (1990). *Apprenticeship in thinking: Cognitive development in social context*. New York: Oxford University Press.

Roseberry, A., Warren, B., & Contant, F. (1992). Appropriating scientific discourse: Findings from language minority classrooms. *The Journal of the Learning Sciences, 2*, 61–94.

Shepard, L. A. (2000). The role of assessment in a learning culture. *Educational Researcher, 29*(7), 4–14.

Shermis, M. D., & Burstein, J. C. (2003). *Automated essay scoring: A cross-disciplinary perspective*. Hillsdale, NJ: Lawrence Erlbaum Associates.

Sigel, I. (1993). The centrality of a distancing model for the development of representation competence. In R. Cocking & K. A. Renninger (Eds.), *The development and meaning of psychological distance* (pp. 141–158). Mahwah, NJ: Lawrence Erlbaum Associates.

Stiggins, R., & Chappuis, J. (2005). Using student-involved classroom assessment to close achievement gaps. *Theory Into Practice*. Retrieved January 26, 2008, from <findarticles.com/p/articles/mi_m0NQM/is_1_44/ai_n13807464>

Vygotsky, L. S. (1978). *Mind in society*. Cambridge, MA: Harvard University Press.

Williamson, D. M., Mislevy, R. J., & Bejar, I. I. (Eds.). (2007). *Automated scoring of complex tasks in computer-based testing*. Mahwah, NJ: Lawrence Erlbaum Associates.

Wilson, M. (Ed.). (2004). *Towards coherence between classroom assessment and accountability*. Chicago, IL: National Society for the Study of Education.

Chapter 4
Assessment Issues and New Technologies: ePortfolio Possibilities

Glenn Finger and Romina Jamieson-Proctor

Introduction: ICT and Assessment in the 21st Century

During the past three decades, we have witnessed dynamic technological changes that have been accompanied by considerable policy developments and initiatives by governments and education systems. For the purposes of this chapter, the technological developments focused on are specifically those related to information and communication technologies (ICT). A comprehensive definition of ICT is adopted here to include not only personal computers, but also allows for consideration of a wider range of new and emerging technologies that can be used for information and communication purposes, such as the Internet, mobile phones, digital cameras, digital video recorders, learning objects, personal digital assistants (PDAs), interactive whiteboards, wireless and networking technologies, podcasts, mp3 players, virtual reality and voice over Internet protocol (VoIP).

These ICT technological developments have coincided with the emergence of a language that positions thinking about teaching, learning and the role of assessment in the 21st century. For example, in shaping the next phase of technology use in education in the United Kingdom, there have been calls for educators to 'fully exploit the power of technology to provide a 21st Century education that reaches and benefits all learners and enable the UK to compete globally' (Becta, 2007a, p. 2). Elsewhere, in the United States, a coalition of leading education, business and technology organisations formulated the reports *Learning for the 21st Century* (Partnership for 21st Century Skills, 2003) and *Assessment of 21st Century Skills: The Current Landscape* (Partnership for 21st Century Skills, 2007). The latter report asks the question, 'How can we best prepare students to succeed in the 21st century?' There are concerns that there is now a 'profound gap between the knowledge and skills most students acquire in school and those required in today's 21st Century communities and technology-infused workplaces' (Partnership for

G. Finger (✉)
School of Educ & Professional Studies, Griffith University, Gold Coast Campus, QLD 4222, Australia
e-mail: g.finger@griffith.edu.au

C. Wyatt-Smith, J.J. Cumming (eds.), *Educational Assessment in the 21st Century*, DOI 10.1007/978-1-4020-9964-9_4, © Springer Science+Business Media B.V. 2009

21st Century Skills, 2007, p. 4). Furthermore, this raises another critical question, 'How do we measure 21st-century learning?' (Partnership for 21st Century Skills, 2007, p. 4)

Similarly, in Australia, the government has portrayed its vision of the central importance of ICT in the 21st century through its strategic action plans, such as *Learning for the Knowledge Society: An education and training action plan for the information economy* (Education Network Australia, 2000) and *Learning in an Online World: Online Content Strategy* (Department of Education, Training and Youth Affairs (DETYA), 2000). Subsequent strategy statements have built upon those strategic documents and recognised the importance of online content (Ministerial Council for Education, Employment, Training and Youth Affairs (MCEETYA), 2003), pedagogy (MCEETYA, 2005a) and leadership (MCEETYA, 2006), which collectively reflect 'a national vision for improving education and training outcomes for all Australians through the ubiquitous use of information and communications technology (ICT)' (MCEETYA, 2005b, p. 1). The expectation is that ICT can and will transform pedagogies by empowering teachers to 'use planning tools to connect learning programs with curriculum assessment and reporting frameworks' (MCEETYA, 2005a, p. 7). Therefore, there has been the recognition of the important interface of ICT and assessment:

> Significant changes have occurred in education and the use of information and communication technologies (ICT) . . . These reflect inter-related developments in . . . school reform, curriculum, pedagogy and assessment.
>
> (MCEETYA, 2005b, p. 3)

As schools adopt learning management systems (LMSs), local area networks (LANs), learning management content systems (LMCSs) and virtual learning environments (VLEs), it has become apparent that those digital systems, by themselves, have been unable to interact successfully with other digital services, resulting in the emergence of managed learning environments (MLEs). The next likely phase is digital ecosystems conceptualised as learning platforms that keep learning central, enable interoperability and form a foundation for ongoing development through use of new technologies and increased capabilities of educators to use ICT for curriculum, pedagogy and assessment (Ingvarson & Gaffney, 2008). Digital ecosystems might include student administration, LAN (requiring teacher and student logins and passwords), VLE, content repository, community links, utilise Web 2.0 (social networking) technologies and have student assessment and achievement as integral to the platform.

This chapter specifically aims to contribute insights into the possibilities provided by ICT for new ways of assessing learning in the 21st century and highlights some of the implications and issues of using ICT in assessment. Specifically, the chapter provides examples of the use of ICT for assessment, where ICT is the focus, where the content is the focus, where ICT is used as a data-collection tool, as a recording, analysis and communication tool, as a plagiarism detector and used for ePortfolio purposes. In particular, ePortfolio possibilities are discussed, including the potential of Web 2.0 technologies to enable innovative approaches to the assessment of students' lifelong and life-wide learning.

Assessment and ICT: Technological Pedagogical Content Knowledge for Educators

Both assessment and ICT hold challenges for many teachers. While well-designed assessment can enhance students' learning effectiveness, and *all* teachers should be 'assessment literate' and capable of using assessment to inform instructional practice (Campbell & Collins, 2007), these expectations are not matched by studies of teachers' assessment knowledge (Brookhart, 2001; Campbell & Evans, 2000). Studies dating back as far as 50 years ago have provided similar concerns about inadequate teacher preparation courses in assessment (Mayo, 1967; Noll, 1955). Assessment literacy is an important component of a teacher's pedagogical content knowledge (PCK) (Wang, Wang, & Huang, 2008). PCK was proposed by Schulman (1987) as the 'special amalgam of content and pedagogy that is uniquely the province of teachers, their own special form of understanding' (p. 8).

Similarly, in addition to the importance of teachers' assessment literacy, there have been growing expectations for teachers to add ICT literacy to their PCK repertoire, resulting in an interface between assessment literacy and ICT literacy as new technologies provide opportunities for new approaches to assessment. Teachers are gaining access to a range of ICT tools that allow them to not only work online to construct test items, correct test papers and record scores using web-based, database and communications technologies, but also afford opportunities for assessment practices that utilise hypermedia, including audio, video and even virtual or dynamic images (Wang et al., 2008, p. 4). Technological pedagogical content knowledge (TPCK) has been proposed to describe this new knowledge set required by teachers, in order to allow them to effectively capitalise on ICT (AACTE Committee on Innovation and Technology, 2008).

That conceptualisation highlights not only the importance of pedagogical knowledge (knowing how to teach) and content knowledge (knowing what to teach), which teachers need in order to effectively teach and assess students, but also technological knowledge in order to effectively harness the affordances ICT can bring to teaching and assessment in the 21st century. Various education systems have developed expectations or standards for teachers that already go some way towards identifying TPCK, though this might not be explicitly articulated.

For example, the International Society for Technology Education (ISTE, 2007a, 2007b) considers assessment and evaluation as essential conditions for students to be able to effectively leverage technology for learning. It refers to the use of ICT in terms of assessment both *of* learning and *for* learning. In terms of expectations for teachers, the *ISTE NETS for Teachers (NETS·T)* (ISTE, 2000) identifies the fundamental concepts, knowledge, skills and attitudes that teachers need in order to apply technology in educational settings. In relation to assessment and evaluation, the expectations are that:

Teachers apply technology to facilitate a variety of effective assessment and evaluation strategies.

A. apply technology in assessing student learning of subject matter using a variety of assessment techniques.
B. use technology resources to collect and analyse data, interpret results, and communicate findings to improve instructional practice and maximize student learning.
C. apply multiple methods of evaluation to determine students' appropriate use of technology resources for learning, communication, and productivity.

(ISTE, 2000, p. 9)

Thus, international standards explicitly expect teachers to have technological knowledge (TK) and to be able to 'apply technology' and 'use technology' for assessment and evaluation purposes (TPCK). However, the interface between TK and PCK presents new challenges in assessing student learning, including challenging traditional models of assessment that were generally confined to pencil and paper. Many of today's students are immersed in rich technological environments outside of formal schooling. They increasingly access information and communicate using mobile devices and online in a networked, multimedia, hypertextual, digital world. The activities provided by these online spaces are becoming increasingly important in the development of identity and are a repository for an individual's life experiences and a reflection of their growth and development over time. In the past, it might have been sufficient for teachers to understand how to design paper and pencil, or oral assessments, but now teachers need to embrace the affordances and implications of ICT for assessment as well. The question that now needs to be addressed is, 'How might ICT be used for assessment purposes?'

Possible Uses of ICT for Assessment

ICT can assist assessment through ICT-based assessment, ePortfolios, Performance and Assessment (PANDA) data and software packages that can be used for screening, target setting and assessment purposes (Becta, 2004). In addition to providing an efficient means for data collection, manipulation and reporting, the use of ICT for assessment is being progressively introduced, whereby students are expected to interact with on-screen tests using computers to enable effective data collection and data access, which is then used to inform learning and teaching (Becta, 2004). ICT obviously makes the collection and analysis of assessment data efficient and effective, but we would argue that limiting of the use of the technology for these purposes does not harness its full assessment potential.

The ways in which ICT might be used for assessment are dependent upon how the role of ICT in teaching and learning is perceived and what types of assessment are required (Bitter & Legacy, 2006; Bitter & Pierson, 2005). For example, the focus of assessment might be the ICT itself as reflected in the aim of the recently introduced National ICT Literacy Test in Australian schools (MCEETYA, 2007). Unfortunately, while this form of assessment might answer questions related to *whether or not* students can use ICT tools proficiently, it is limited in its provision of evidence about student learning, particularly in terms of *how* students are able to use ICT for learning in a range of curriculum contexts, and for the development of creative, complex and critical thinking.

ICT, when used for assessment purposes as a data-collection tool, recording, analysis and communication tool, and as a plagiarism detector (Bitter & Pierson, 2005), offers advantages afforded by ICT largely by making the assessment process more efficient, particularly in terms of large-scale assessment of students, where the focus is on assessment for mastery of skills and content (Forcier & Descy, 2002, pp. 300–301). In discussing additional ways in which ICT can be used for assessment, Bitter and Legacy (2006, pp. 208–217) provide examples where ICT tools are integrated into assessment practices, while Finger, Russell, Jamieson-Proctor, and Russell (2007) suggest that ICT software can be categorised according to the function it serves, such as ICT-assisted instruction for online tutorials, simulation, instructional games, problem solving, integrated learning systems (ILSs) and ICT assistant tools (see also Newby, Stepich, Lehman, & Russell, 2006) or support tools (see Roblyer, 2006) for word processing, presentation software, spreadsheets, databases, material generators, data collection and analysis tools, graphics tools, planning and organising tools, research and reference tools and content area tools (Finger et al., 2007, pp. 174–177). Drawing upon these categorisations, the following summary provides examples of the use of ICT for assessment where ICT is the focus, where the content is the focus, where ICT is used as a data collection tool, where ICT is used as a recording, analysis and communication tool, where ICT is utilised as a plagiarism detector and is used for ePortfolio purposes.

ICT as the Focus

This has been evident in large national, state or district studies, often involving online surveys to collect data related to ICT performance indicators, such as the number of computers, time spent by students using computers and, more recently, emphasis has been on obtaining data about student ICT skills and competencies. Examples include the *iSkills* (Educational Testing Service, 2008a— see <www.ets.org/ictliteracy>) and *NETS Online Technology Assessment* (ISTE, 2007c—see <www.iste.org/resources/asmt/msiste>). In Australia, the *MCEETYA National Assessment Program—ICT Literacy Years 6 & 10 Report 2005* (MCEETYA, 2007) obtained ICT literacy data about Year 6 and Year 10 students and, interestingly, indicated among its conclusions that:

> One should not assume that students are uniformly becoming adept because they use ICT so widely in their daily lives. The results of the assessment survey suggest that students use ICT in a relatively limited way and this is reflected in the overall level of ICT literacy.

Communication with peers and using the Internet to look up information are frequent applications but there is much less frequent use of applications that involve creating, analysing or transforming information.

(MCEETYA, 2007, p. xiv)

Content as the Focus

Where content is the focus, ICT is seen as a tool for instructional delivery, communication or information searching and delivery, and student learning is measured on mastery of content objectives. For these purposes, strategies for assessment with ICT need to be designed in ways consistent with quality assessment principles. Examples include the design and use of ICT programs for planning, assessment, recording and reporting of student achievement, such as *Assessment Management Solutions* (Excelsior Software, 2008—see <www.gradebook.com>), collaborative Internet projects such as *ThinkQuest* (Oracle Education Foundation, 2008—see <www.thinkquest.org>), the use of learning objects, such as those developed by The Le@rning Federation (Curriculum Corporation, 2008—see <www.thelearningfederation.edu.au>), LMSs such as Blackboard, LAMS and online assessment rubrics, for example, *Kathy Schrock's Teacher Helpers: Assessment and Rubric Information* (Discovery Education, 2008—see <school.discovery.com/schrockguide/assess.html>).

ICT as a Data-Collection Tool

Numerous examples exist whereby ICT can be used to develop tests, such as computer-based tests, computer adaptive tests and test-creation applications. These applications usually have the function to collate and archive results. Examples include:

- Computer-based tests, which are often computer-based versions of traditional paper-based tests. Essay grading software tends to be limited in its ability to assess creativity or organisation of writing; for example, *Intelligent Essay Assessor* (Pearson Education, 2008a—see <www.knowledge-technologies.com/prodIEA.shtml>).
- Computer adaptive tests, which are able to change their form in response to the input from the student being tested; for example, *GRE®—Graduate Record Examinations®* (Educational Testing Service, 2008b—see <www.gre.com>).
- Test-creation applications are available whereby teachers can create their own online quizzes, exams and tests, and access banks of tests and test items already created; for example, *Test banks: Rubistar* (Altec at University of Kansas, 2008—see <rubistar.4teachers.org>); FunBrain's Quiz lab.com (Pearson Education, 2008b—see <www.FunBrain.com>); QUIA (QUIA Corporation, 2008—see <www.quia.com>); and WebAssign (North Carolina State University, 2007—see <www.webassign.net>).

ICT as a Recording, Analysis and Communication Tool

For assessment applications in which ICT is used as a recording, analysis and communication tool, ICT is used to assist teachers with quantitative and qualitative record keeping. In addition, ICT can enable the generation of reporting to various audiences to portray student learning. Examples include:

- Quantitative record keeping. Through the use of spreadsheet software, ICT enables formulae for statistical calculations, analysis and graphical representation. Applications can be used for attendance, calculating grades from scores, and web-based grade book management systems can allow teachers to manage grades online, including emailing students their results; for example, *ThinkWave Educator* (Thinkwave Inc., 2007—see <www.thinkwave.com>).
- Qualitative record keeping. Qualitative information such as observations and anecdotal records can be created, stored and accessed digitally.

Technology as a Plagiarism Detector

Major challenges and issues relate to the social, legal and ethical issues of online assessment. Educators are being presented with issues of academic integrity and academic misconduct, often related to plagiarism, which have tended to increase due to students' easy access to online content. ICT applications and processes have been developed to detect plagiarism; for example, *TurnItIn Digital Assessment Suite* (TurnItIn, 2008—see <www.turnitin.com>) and *SafeAssign* (Blackboard, 2007—see <www.safeassign.com>). The implication for schools and school systems is the need to develop and revise policies to cover new problems created by ICT related to plagiarism, and ICT itself is providing some of the preventive and detection solutions to these challenges.

ePortfolio Assessment

We argue that ePortfolios provide an extremely powerful means for developing stories of deep learning through an increased range of evidence such as text, audio, narration and digital video when compared with the more limited paper-based forms of assessment evidence. A more comprehensive discussion and the possibilities of ePortfolios are provided later in this chapter.

We contend that it is important to select and design the assessment based upon an educationally justifiable rationale for the use of ICT. In relation to TPCK, a central issue is that teachers require substantive knowledge of assessment, TPK to use the new technologies and PCK. This seems unlikely to be the case in many settings. For example, in the United Kingdom, Ofsted (2005) reported that students' ICT was not systematically assessed and that in many cases teachers were too easily impressed with mediocre application of ICT by pupils. Disturbingly, even where ICT work was assessed, pupils generally received insufficient feedback on how they could improve their work, and in many schools teachers did not evaluate how well pupils applied and used their ICT skills across the curriculum (Ofsted, 2005). Interestingly, the methodological aspect in relation to the use of ICT to support assessment that seemed most to capture people's imagination was the use of computer-based item banks (Matters, 2006).

Due to the increasing use of student performance data within a high-stakes accountability environment, in relation to methodological perspectives, it is important to consider carefully the conduct, analysis and interpretation of the data (Matters, 2006). This is a contested territory that requires careful consideration of the purpose of the assessment that ICT is enabling, the ways in which the data might be interpreted and the ways in which the data might be used. An ethical perspective is required which 'encompasses the social and political components of data use' (Matters, 2006, p. 52) and, therefore, interplays with the methodological and strategic perspectives, such as fairness in assessment, appropriate data use and anticipating the consequences of the use of data (Matters, 2006).

Consequently, ICT use for assessment purposes needs to be guided by principles of quality assessment and the ways in which assessment can assist learning, rather than being a means for inappropriate methodological, strategic and ethical approaches to data collection, analysis and interpretation. Connectedness and responsiveness is a hallmark of quality assessment and should take 'account of students' interests, capabilities and repertoires of practice, both inside and outside schooling, including the actual and virtual communities in which students live' (Wyatt-Smith, Cumming, & Elkins, 2005, p. 278). However, being online without an intentional purpose will not necessarily result in meaningful learning, and the current generation of learners is learning to use the World Wide Web as an electronic encyclopaedia from which they copy others' ideas instead of learning to create and represent their own unique ideas (Jonassen, 2000). That is, if teachers and students use the new ICT-enabled resources in largely traditional tasks, this might 'provide an incremental advantage over existing practices' (Grabe & Grabe, 2004, p. 237). Rather, alternative approaches should be implemented by educators that offer a 'transformational advantage' (Grabe & Grabe, 2004, p. 237), whereby the Internet can provide tools for communication, inquiry and construction (Bruce & Levin, 1997).

With access to new and emerging technologies, and with the skills to use those technologies, students will be able to produce work that demonstrates their knowledge and understanding in ways that many might find difficult to imagine (Forcier & Descy, 2002). New possibilities for assessment have become available through online or eLearning environments. An extensive range of online tools is now available, such as email, bulletin boards, discussion forums, blogs, wikis, chat rooms, instant messaging and videoconferencing. Most higher education institutions and an increasing number of schools have adopted course management systems such as Blackboard™, which provide an environment for online learning and assessment. In particular, Web 2.0 technologies, often referred to as social networking technologies, have enabled cyber-collaboration whereby many users located in diverse settings can interact synchronously and asynchronously. The implications for educators are how to capitalise upon the use of these technologies for assessing student learning in a networked, digital world.

ePortfolio Approaches

Portfolios have been used for a variety of purposes for some time and have usually been perceived as being a collection of student work, both formative and summative in nature. Traditional portfolios might be described as a work-in-progress that contain a collection of physical artefacts which reflect a student's development and progress over time, with the final product and portfolio evidence presented as a paper copy for assessment (Barrett, 2005). In theorising portfolio approaches, Barrett (2004, 2005) notes the limitations of a portfolio approach, which foregrounds the collection of evidence and consequently recommends that a more effective approach needs to be underpinned by assessment *for* learning, is to emphasise reflection and its importance in promoting deep learning, as displayed in Fig. 4.1.

ePortfolios, also known as digital portfolios or electronic portfolios, tend to be a collection of authentic and more diverse evidence than the traditional portfolios, drawn from a larger archive representing what a person or organisation has learned over time, upon which the person or organisation has reflected, and has been designed for presentation to one or more audiences for a particular rhetorical purpose (Barrett, 2005). The ePortfolio process, involving collecting, selecting, reflecting, directing and celebrating, can be enhanced through the use of ICT, through the use of multimedia, hypermedia and eLearning architecture to enable archiving, linking and thinking, storytelling, collaborating and publishing, as displayed in Fig. 4.2. ICT extends the ability over largely linear, paper-based portfolios

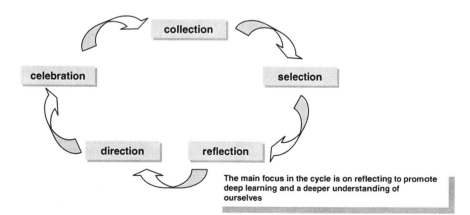

Fig. 4.1 Reflective portfolio process—emphasis is on *reflection* (Source: adapted from Barrett, 2005)

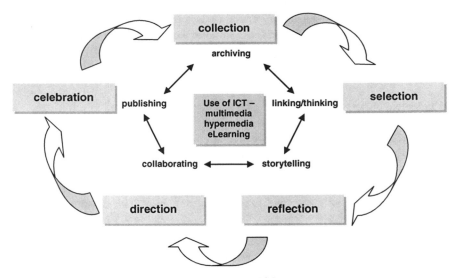

Fig. 4.2 Enhanced ePortfolio process enabled through ICT

to communicate digital stories of learning through ePortfolios using video, audio, graphics and text in a web-based, digital, hypertextual portfolio.

In higher education, three types of academic portfolios have become prominent, namely:

Student learning portfolios—these are purposeful collections of examples of student work annotated (ideally) with students' reflective commentary.

Teaching portfolios—these consist of course syllabi, assignments, student work and other artefacts, collected by practising or aspiring teachers with the intention of fostering self-reflection and peer review of teaching.

Institutional portfolios—these contain examples of [an] institution's activities, programs and initiatives, each expressing an element of reflection and self-assessment. (Ketcheson, 2001, p. 84)

Similarly, in school settings, interest is being taken in ePortfolio approaches, and a recent study of existing practices by Bussitil-Reynaud et al. (2006) identified four types of ePortfolio being used in schools in the United Kingdom, namely:

Transition ePortfolios—relevant administrative and educational information about the learner is transferred from one institution to another as a learner progresses.

Assessment ePortfolios—information and evidence about work undertaken by learners and achievements for assessing or matching against specified criteria is collected and managed.

Presentation ePortfolios—learners select and present evidence of personal information or achievements;

Learning ePortfolios—the learner develops a broader, more general resource that can support whatever the individual wants to do and that could form the basis of any of the previous portfolios if desired (Bussitil-Reynaud et al., 2006, cited in Becta, 2007b, p. 31).

Central to any of these ePortfolio approaches is the aim of enabling learning stories and reflections by students to emerge through the use of their own voice. This approach could be described as a meta-narrative that reflects a 'story' of learning. The 'stories' encourage learners to connect their formal study with their life experiences, including their personal use of new technologies and, therefore, provide a means for connectedness and relevance, which is a feature of quality assessment (Wyatt-Smith et al., 2005). We know that stories are distinguished from silences and there are narratives that assist to provide representations of reality and representations of culture (Preskill, 1998). Bourdieu (1991) refers to teachers' stories as cultural capital, as they provide them with their knowledge, ideas, attitudes and values (Hatch, 2004), and Preskill (1998) categorises the cultural capital into the narratives of social criticism, apprenticeship, reflective practice, journey and hope.

The narrative of reflective practice is also evident in the narrative of journey, 'for without reflection, growth and change cannot occur' (Hatch, 2004, p. 117). The narrative of reflective practice becomes important in student learning: What worked well? What do I need to know? What have I learned? Where have I been? Where do I want to go? Who am I? Who do I want to become? ePortfolios are becoming increasingly used as assessment and presentation portfolios in ways in which learners are required to design and create an ePortfolio to portray a personal story of deep learning, reflecting the metaphor of 'story' and 'journey' (Paulson & Paulson, 1994; Preskill, 1998). Clearly, ePortfolios can take various forms and be guided by different purposes and audiences. Tolley (2008) believes that 'this is where we are at with e-Portfolios—many different opinions and for different purposes.' (p. 2)

ePortfolios: Assessment for Learning and Assessment of Learning

While there are many instances in the assessment literature of the notion that assessment *for* learning and assessment *of* learning are dichotomous, the two are different not merely dichotomous (Matters, 2006). Matters indicates that the term 'assessment for learning', originally used by the Assessment Reform Group (2002) in the United Kingdom, highlighted the value of assessment to enhance learning compared with assessment *of* learning. In highlighting the extensive debate surrounding the terms assessment *of* and assessment *for* learning, Matters parodies Churchill's well-known statement made during World War II, by stating that 'Never in the field of educational assessment was so much written by so many about so few prepositions' (Matters, 2006, p. 25). However, when formulating the use of ePortfolios for assessment purposes, we must first ask, 'What kind of assessment do we require?' (Barrett, 2006). As summarised in Table 4.1, we provide a summary of Barrett's main ideas in relation to ePortfolios used for assessment *of* learning and for assessment *for* learning.

Table 4.1 ePortfolios—assessment *of* learning and assessment *for* learning

Portfolios used for assessment *of* learning	Portfolios that support assessment *for* learning
Purpose of portfolio is prescribed by institution	Purpose of portfolio agreed upon with learner
Artefacts mandated by institution to determine outcomes of instruction	Artefacts selected by learner to tell the story of their learning
Portfolio usually developed at the end of a class, term or program—time limited	Portfolio maintained on an ongoing basis throughout the class, term or program—time flexible
Portfolio and/or artefacts usually 'scored' based on a rubric and quantitative data is collected for external audiences	Portfolio and artefacts reviewed with learner and used to provide feedback to improve learning
Portfolio is usually structured around a set of outcomes, goals or standards	Portfolio organisation is determined by learner or negotiated with mentor/advisor/teacher
Sometimes used to make high-stakes decisions	Rarely used for high-stakes decisions
Summative—what has been learned to date? (past to present)	Formative—what are the learning needs in the future? (present to future)
Requires extrinsic motivation	Fosters intrinsic motivation—engages the learner
Audience: external—little choice	Audience: learner, family, friends—learner can choose

Source: Adapted from Barrett, 2006.

Early attempts to develop ePortfolios tended to use ICT applications that were often published on CD and, in some instances, if the file size permitted, were uploaded to the Internet. Examples included Microsoft Office documents, Apple iLife06 (iDVD containing photos and video and published on a DVD) and webpage editors such as Dreamweaver and Microsoft FrontPage to create webpage repositories for information and a way to link to other static documents such as portable document format (PDF) files and .jpg format photos. New possibilities are now available for designing web-based ePortfolios using Web 2.0 tools such as blogs and wikispaces, and Open Source Portfolios, such as OSP and Elgg. They offer both creators and audiences more flexibility and access options, are able to be integrated with formal coursework and offer opportunities for peer review and group collaboration through employing Web 2.0 technologies (Zhang, Olfman, & Ractman, 2007), which are explored in the following section.

ePortfolios and Web 2.0 Technologies

Beyond the formal schooling experiences of students, there has been a proliferation in more recent times of social networking, evidenced by the high levels of engagement with texting (text messaging via mobile phone), iPhones, MSN, MySpace, FlickR, Facebook and YouTube, and numerous other social networking sites that enable blogging and wikis. The entry to Internet communication and publishing is minimal when compared with paper-based publishing. Information exchange in

Web 1.0 tended to be characterised by the webpage with hyperlinks, while Web 2.0 technologies enable linking and exchanging information, data and communication over the web (Kelly, 2007). To illustrate, Really Simple Syndication (RSS) publishes updated content (for example, news headlines and podcasts) in a standardised format, allowing web users to subscribe to regularly published RSS feeds on websites in an automated manner.

Central to the concept of Web 2.0 is that it involves connections and collaborations between people, and connections between ideas and hypermedia. Therefore, Web 2.0 companies design the social aspect of the application into the architecture (Kelly, 2007) and, unlike economic theory, whereby the increasing use of a resource results in a depreciation of its value, the more that a resource is used in the Web 2.0 environment, the greater the value it aggregates (Bricklin, 2000, cited in Kelly). Thus, social software can 'take advantage of and cultivate collective knowledge' (Kelly, 2007, p. 2). Connectivism attempts to account for learning in a digital age, where knowledge is growing exponentially, where new information is being acquired and reconstituted or remixed, and where know-how and know-what is being supplemented by know-where (Siemens, 2004). Consequently, there is a distinction between Web 1.0, which is usually represented by traditional static web pages, and Web 2.0, which is represented by server-side software that is more interactive and is sometimes called the 'Participatory Web' based on an architecture for interaction (Barrett, 2006). Thomas Friedman, in his revised version of *The World is Flat*, 'changed his fourth "flattener" from "Open-Sourcing" (Self-Organizing Collaborative Communities) to "Uploading" (Online Communities, Open Source, Blogging, Wikipedia and social networks)' (Barrett, 2006, p. 5).

From her review of Web 2.0 developments and possibilities, Barrett (2006) revised her earlier work on ePortfolios to conceptualise what she refers to as ePortfolio 2.0, and this is summarised in Table 4.2.

Table 4.2 ePortfolios 1.0 and ePortfolios 2.0

ePortfolios 1.0	ePortfolios 2.0
Hierarchical, designed	Networked, emergent
Metaphor: Portfolio as checklist	Metaphor: Portfolio as story
Data-driven	Learner-driven
Focus on standardisation	Focus on individuality, creativity
Feedback from authority figures	Feedback from community of learners
Large, complex systems	Small pieces, loosely joined—'Mash-ups'
Web-based form	Blog and wiki
Positivist	Constructivist, connectivist
Accountability-driven	Learning-focused
Proprietary	Open standards
Digital paper (text & and images)	Digital story (multimedia)
Local storage (hard drives, CD)	Network storage (lifetime personal web space)

Source: Adapted from Barrett, 2006, p. 7.

In terms of the TK and subsequent TPCK demands on teachers, ePortfolio 2.0 requires new knowledge and understandings of social networking technologies and their implications (for example, legal and ethical uses, plagiarism, copyright and digital rights management), the challenges of lack of control over access and content, interoperability, contemporary theories of learning, such as social constructivism and connectivism, and new approaches to assessment, such as the metaphor of ePortfolio as story, rather than as a checklist. Students can be expected to be motivated by and want more attractive technology options built into their formal course experience, including multimedia and collaborative tools (Zhang et al., 2007).

ePortfolio 2.0, used within a paradigm of assessment *for* learning, has the potential to truly engage learners, as students are motivated to use online social networking sites, enabling students to perceive their ePortfolios as an 'academic MySpace' (Barrett, 2006, p. 8). This opens up possibilities for learning to be mediated by interaction with others, of collaborative learning and what Wenger ([70] 1998, [71] 2001) describes as a 'community of practice'. With Web 2.0 tools, student work can be posted and feedback invited (for example, through blogging), collaboration invited (for example, through wikis and Google.docs) and, if necessary, authorship can be tracked, for accountability. The increasing popularity of these kinds of websites have been observed by Zhang et al. (2007), who subscribed to the MSN Group *PhD students* for 6 months and found that about 10 new members joined the group each week. Furthermore, they investigated the site statistics reports of *Phinished.org* and found that an average of 200 000 pages are requested per month. However, while commercial learning environment systems such as Blackboard™ and Open Source such as Moodle provide discussion forums, blogs and wiki support, a key criticism is that those tools are limited to the students, instructor and teaching assistants, and collaborative content needs to be able to connect to course materials and ePortfolio systems in the online, networked digital world of the student outside formal education (Zhang et al., 2007).

An alternative model is proposed by Cohn and Hibbitts (2004), who suggest that 'rather than limit people to the e-portfolio model, why not develop a model providing a personal Web space for everyone, for their lifetimes and beyond?' (p. 1). They refer to this as the Lifetime Personal Web Space (LPWS), which could store searchable content (personal, business, social and educational) that was important in a user's past and will be accessible for future use, as well as for use in current projects. They indicate that the virtual structure of the LPWS could consist of multiple cells with flexible entry points, allowing internal cells and connections to external web-based courses, mentors, peer reviewers and libraries. The primary user of the LPWS would decide what sections were public or private, and it would be available anywhere, anytime. Similarly, Tolley (2008) proposes the *Universal ePortfolio* and identifies that the 'prime directives' for any ePortfolio must be:

1. **Portable.** It cannot be located in any one institution or embedded within a proprietary Virtual Learning Environment (VLE).
2. **Personal.** It is 'owned' by the user and is customisable to the user's age, stage and style.

3. **Generic.** It is not modelled on any particular curriculum delivery system or content.
4. **Web 2.0.** It should be compliant with all generic formats within the application.
5. **MIS-free.** It is not 'hard-wired' to any institution's MIS infrastructure.
6. **'Light'.** It is not a permanent repository of all of a user's files, rather a 'transit camp'.
7. **Life-long.** Ownership must be maintainable as a continuity, ages '5–95'.
8. **Life-wide.** It is capable of being used by all ages and abilities through a wide range of assistive templates.
9. **Accessible.** It must recognise common standards of accessibility in terms of both outputs and inputs.
10. **Credible**. Evidence of any summative assessment must be linked to a secure repository; that is, the awarding body or a central MIAP/Minerva archive. (Tolley, 2008, pp. 5–6)

This provides directions for educators in capitalising upon new technologies to enable rich evidence to demonstrate evidence for the assessment of life-long and life-wide learning. A key issue for educators is how to create sustainable communities of practice based on building and supporting learning communities around ePortfolios (Evans & Powell, 2007). Models, such as the *learning landscape* model, have been proposed to help students see learning as more than just a narrow course or program but, rather, for students to view learning in ways that incorporate experience from a variety of contexts through social networking, whereby 'Learning with computers is not about programming or drill and practice, nor about multimedia, nor about fast updating or cost-efficiency—it is all about humans sharing ideas' (Tosh, Werdmuller, Chen, & Haywood, 2006, p. 7). The *learning landscape* acts as a focus for students when building their ePortfolios using Web 2.0 tools so that they are encouraged to link the various components that comprise the ePortfolio in order to maximise its usefulness for life-long and life-wide learning. Ownership of the ePortfolio resides with the user rather than an educational institution or teacher, and takes advantage of online communities of learners to create powerful social learning environments.

Conclusion

This chapter commences by acknowledging the implications of the rapid technological changes and expectations of teaching and learning in the 21st century. ICT now enables the potential for new approaches to assessing learning to be realised, and accompanying this, there are new challenges and expectations for teachers. Technological knowledge (TK) is now an important expectation for teachers. The conceptualisation of technological pedagogical content knowledge (TPCK) is useful in highlighting TK as an additional consideration to PCK conceptualised by Schulman (1987). We argue that there is an interface between ICT and assessment.

This chapter provides a synthesis of the purposes of ICT use for assessment where ICT is the focus, where the content is the focus, where ICT is used as a data-collection tool, as a recording, analysis and communication tool, as a plagiarism detector and used for ePortfolio purposes. Subsequently, ePortfolio approaches enabled by ICT are analysed, and possibilities of ePortfolios enhanced by Web 2.0 technologies are presented and discussed. Our concluding advice is that educators need a strong understanding of how students are learning in the 21st century in order to inform their creation and selection of powerful approaches that use the affordances of ICT to assess students and provide a diverse range of evidence of the students' learning journey.

References

AACTE Committee on Innovation and Technology. (2008). *The handbook of technological pedagogical content knowledge (TPCK) for educators.* Hinsdale, NJ: Lawrence Erlbaum Associates.

Assessment Reform Group. (2002). *Assessment for learning.* Retrieved May 23, 2008, from <www.qca.org.uk/7659.html>

Altec at University of Kansas. (2008). *Rubistar.* Retrieved May 23, 2008, from <rubistar. 4teachers.org>

Barrett, H. (2004). *Electronic portfolios as digital stories of deep learning.* Retrieved May 23, 2008, from <electronicportfolios.org/digistory/epstory.html>

Barrett, H. (2005). *White paper researching electronic portfolios and learner engagement.* Retrieved May 23, 2008, from <www.electronicportfolios.org/reflect/whitepaper.pdf>

Barrett, H. (2006). *Authentic assessment with electronic portfolios using common software and Web 2.0 tools.* Retrieved May 23, 2008, from <electronicportfolios.org/web20.html>

Becta. (2004). *Assessment and ICT: Essential guides for school governors.* Retrieved May 23, 2008, from <foi.becta.org.uk/content_files/corporate/resources/foi/archived_publications/ essential_guides_assessment_ict.pdf>

Becta. (2007a). *Harnessing technology learning in the 21st century. Call to action.* Retrieved May 23, 2008, from <publications.becta.org.uk/display.cfm?resID=33995&page=1835>

Becta. (2007b). *Harnessing technology review 2007: Progress and impact of technology in education.* Retrieved May 23, 2008, from <publications.becta.org.uk/display.cfm?resID=33979>

Bitter, G. G., & Legacy, J. M. (2006). *Using technology in the classroom: Brief edition.* Boston: Pearson Education.

Bitter, G. G., & Pierson, M. E. (2005). *Using technology in the classroom* (6th ed.). Boston: Pearson Education.

Blackboard. (2007). *SafeAssign.* Retrieved May 23, 2008, from <www.safeassign.com>

Bourdieu, P. (1991). *Language and symbolic power.* Cambridge: Polity Press.

Bricklin, D. (2000). The cornucopia of the commons. Cited in Kelly, M. (2007). *E-portfolios and Web 2.0.* Retrieved May 23, 2008, from <www.education.ed.ac.uk/e-learning/ gallery/kelly_eportfolios.pdf>

Brookhart, S. M. (2001). *The 'standards' and classroom assessment research.* Paper presented at the annual meeting of the American Association of Colleges of Teacher Education, Dallas, Texas.

Bruce, B., & Levin, J. (1997). Educational Technology: Media for inquiry, communication, construction and expression. *Journal of Educational Computing Research, 17*(1), 79–102.

Bussitil-Reynaud, G., Winkley, J., Roads, M., Burke, P., Jeram, K., & Hammond, J., et al. (2006). Report for Becta scoping and evaluating e-Portfolios. April, 2006, Coventry: Becta. Cited in Becta. (2007). *Harnessing technology review 2007: Progress and impact of technology in education.* Retrieved May 23, 2008, from <publications.becta.org.uk/display.cfm?resID=33979>

Campbell, C., & Collins, V. L. (2007). Identifying essential topics in general and special education introductory assessment textbooks. *Educational measurement, issues and practice, 26*(1), 9–18.

Campbell, C., & Evans, J. A. (2000). Investigation of preservice teachers' classroom practices during student teaching. *Journal of Educational Research, 93*(6), 350–355.

Curriculum Corporation. (2008). *The Le@rning Federation*. Retrieved January 26, 2008, from <www.thelearningfederation.edu.au>

Cohn, E. R., & Hibbitts, B. J. (2004). Beyond the electronic port6folio: A lifetime personal webspace. *Educause Quarterly, 27*(4), Retrieved May 23, 2008, from <www.educause.edu/apps/eq/eqm04/eqm0441.asp?print_yes>

Discovery Education. (2008). *Kathy Schrock's teacher helpers: Assessment and rubric information*. Retrieved May 23, 2008, from <school.discovery.com/schrockguide/assess.html>

Department of Education Training and Youth Affairs (DETYA). (2000). *Learning for the knowledge society: An education and training action plan for the information economy*. Canberra: J.S. McMillan Printing Group. Retrieved May 23, 2008, from <www.dest.gov.au/NR/rdonlyres/585FDC77-350A-44A8-9352-59D5A91AE604/4503/learning.pdf.

Education Network Australia (EdNA). (2000). *Learning in an online world: The school action plan for the information economy*. Retrieved May 23, 2008, from <www.edna.edu.au/edna/webdav/site/myjahiasite/shared/00_learning_onlineworld.pdf>

Excelsior Software. (2008). *Assessment management solutions*. Retrieved May 23, 2008, from <www.gradebook.com>

Educational Testing Service. (2008a). *iSkills*™. Retrieved May 23, 2008, from <www.ets.org/ictliteracy>

Educational Testing Service. (2008b). *GRE®—Graduate Record Examinations®*. Retrieved May 23, 2008, from <www.gre.com>

Evans, M. A., & Powell, A. (2007). Conceptual and practical issues related to the design for and sustainability of communities of practice: The case of e-portfolio use in preservice teacher training. *Technology, Pedagogy and Education, 16*(2), 199–214.

Finger, G., Russell, G., Jamieson-Proctor, R., & Russell, N. (2007). *Transforming learning with ICT: Making IT happen*. Frenchs Forest NSW: Pearson Education Australia.

Forcier, R. C., & Descy, D. E. (2002). *The computer as an educational tool: Productivity and problem solving* (3rd ed.). Columbus, OH: Merrill Prentice Hall.

Grabe, M., & Grabe, C. (2004). *Integrating technology for meaningful learning* (4th ed.). New York: Houghton Mifflin.

Hatch, S. (2004). Narratives: How teachers' stories connect us, support us, encourage us and enable us as teachers. In Bill Rogers (Ed.), *How to manage children's challenging behaviour*. London: Paul Chapman Publishing.

Ingvarson, D., & Gaffney, M. (2008). Developing and sustaining the digital education ecosystem: The value and possibilities of online environments for student learning. In M. Lee, & M. Gaffney (Eds.), *Leading a digital school: Principles and practice*. Victoria, Australia: ACER Press.

International Society for Technology in Education (ISTE). (2000). *ISTE National Educational Technology Standards (NETS) and Performance Indicators for Teachers*. Retrieved November 12, 2007, from <cnets.iste.org/teachers/pdf/page09.pdf.

International Society for Technology in Education (ISTE). (2007a). *National Educational Technology Standards for Students: The next generation*. Retrieved November 12, 2007, from <www.iste.org/inhouse/nets/cnets/students/pdf/NETS_for_Students_2007.pdf>

International Society for Technology in Education. (2007b). *Essential conditions—Necessary conditions to effectively leverage technology for learning*. Retrieved November 12, 2007, from <www.iste.org/inhouse/nets/cnets/students/pdf/NETS-S_Essential_Conditions.pdf>

International Society for Technology in Education. (2007c). *NETS Online Technology Assessment*. Retrieved May 23, 2008, from <www.iste.org/resources/asmt/msiste>

Jonassen, D. (2000). *Computers as mindtools for schools engaging critical thinking* (2nd ed.). Columbus, OH: Merrill Prentice Hall.

Kelly, M. (2007). *E-portfolios and Web 2.0*. Retrieved May 23, 2008, from <www.education.ed.ac.uk/e-learning/gallery/kelly_eportfolios.pdf>

Ketcheson, K. A. (2001). Public accountability and reporting: What should be the public part of accreditation? In J. L. Ratcliff, E. S. Lubinescu, & M. A. Gaffney (Eds.), *How accreditation influences assessment* (pp. 83–93). San Francisco: Jossey-Bass.

Matters, G. N. (2006). Using data to support learning: Students, schools, systems. *Australian Education Review, 49*. Melbourne: Australian Council for Educational Research.

Mayo, S. T. (1967). Pre-service preparation of teachers in educational measurement. Final report. Chicago, IL: Loyola University.

Ministerial Council for Education, Employment, Training and Youth Affairs (MCEETYA). (2003). *Learning in an online world: Online content strategy*. Retrieved May 23, 2008, from <icttaskforce.edna.edu.au/icttaskforce/webdav/site/icttaskforcesite/users/root/public/online _content_strategy.pdf>

Ministerial Council for Education, Employment, Training and Youth Affairs (MCEETYA). (2005a). *Learning in an online world: Pedagogy strategy*. Retrieved May 23, 2008, from <www.mceetya.edu.au/verve/_resources/pedagogy_strategy_file.pdf>

Ministerial Council for Education, Employment, Training and Youth Affairs (MCEETYA). (2005b). *Contemporary learning. Learning in an online world: the school action plan for the information economy*. Retrieved May 23, 2008, from <www.mceetya.edu.au/ verve/_resources/Contemp_Learning_Final.pdf>

Ministerial Council for Education Employment, Training and Youth Affairs (MCEETYA). (2006). *Learning in an online world: Leadership strategy*. Retrieved May 23, 2008, from <www.mceetya.edu.au/verve/_resources/Leadership_Strategy.pdf>

Ministerial Council for Education, Employment, Training and Youth Affairs (MCEETYA). (2007). *MCEETYA National Assessment Program—ICT Literacy Years 6 & 10 Report 2005*. Retrieved May 23, 2008, from <www.curriculum.edu.au/verve/_resources/NAP_ICTL _2005_Years_6_and_10_Report.pdf>

North Carolina State University. (2007). *WebAssign*. Retrieved May 23, 2008, from <www. webassign.net>

Newby, T., Stepich, D., Lehman, J., & Russell, J. (2006). *Educational technology for teaching and learning* (3rd ed.). Upper Saddle River, NJ: Pearson Merrill Prentice Hall.

Noll, V. H. (1955). Requirements in educational measurement for prospective teachers. *School and Society, 82*, 88–90.

Oracle Education Foundation. (2008). *ThinkQuest*. Retrieved May 23, 2008, from <www. thinkquest.org>

Ofsted. (2005). *Embedding ICT in schools—A dual evaluation exercise*. Ofsted, December 2005, HMI 2391. London: author.

Partnership for 21st Century Skills. (2003). *Learning for the 21st century*. Retrieved May 23, 2008, from <www.21stcenturyskills.org/index.php?option=com_content&task=view&id=29 &Itemid=42>

Partnership for 21st Century Skills. (2007). *Assessment of 21st century skills: The current landscape*. Retrieved May 23, 2008, from <www.21stcenturyskills.org/index.php?option=com _content&task=view&id=131&Itemid=103>

Paulson, F. L., & Paulson, P. (1994). Assessing portfolios using the constructivist paradigm. In R. Fogarty (Ed.). (1996). *Student portfolios*. Palatine: IRI Skylight Training & Publishing.

Pearson Education. (2008a). *Intelligent essay assessor*. Retrieved May 23, 2008, from <www.knowledge-technologies.com/prodIEA.shtml>

Pearson Education. (2008b). *FunBrain's quiz lab.com*. Retrieved May 23, 2008, from <www.FunBrain.com>

Preskill, S. (1998). Narratives of teaching and the quest for the second self. *Journal of Teacher Education, 49*(5), 344–357.

QUIA Corporation. (2008). *QUIA Where learning takes you*. Retrieved January 26, 2008, from <www.quia.com>

Roblyer, M. D. (2006). *Integrating educational technology into teaching* (4th ed.). Upper Saddle River, NJ: Pearson Merrill Prentice Hall.

Schulman, L. S. (1987). Knowledge and teaching: Foundations of the new reform. *Harvard Educational Review, 57,* 1–22.

Siemens, G. (2004). *Connectivism: A learning theory for the digital age.* Elearnspace, Winnipeg, Canada. Retrieved May 23, 2008, from <www.elearnspace.org/Articles/connectivism.htm>

ThinkWave Inc. (2007). *ThinkWave educator.* Retrieved May 23, 2008, from <www.thinkwave.com>

Tolley, R. (2008). *A universal e-Portfolio?* Paper presented at the *iLearning Forum 2008,* 4–5 February, 2008, Palais des Congrés de Paris, Paris.

Tosh, D., Werdmuller, B., Chen, H., & Haywood, J. (2006). The learning landscape: A conceptual framework for e-portfolios. In A. Jafari, & C. Kaufman (Eds.), *Handbook of research on ePortfolios.* Hershey, PA: Idea Group.

TurnItIn. (2008). *Digital Assessment Suite.* Retrieved May 23, 2008, from <www.turnitin.com>

Wang, T., Wang, K., & Huang, S. (2008). Designing a web-based assessment environment for improving pre-service teacher assessment literacy. *Computers & Education, 51*(1), 448–462.

Wenger, E. (1998). *Communities of practice: Learning, meaning, and identity.* Cambridge, UK: Cambridge University Press.

Wenger, E. (2001). *Supporting communities of practice: A survey of community-oriented technologies.* Retrieved May 23, 2008, from <www.ewenger.com/tech/.

Wyatt-Smith, C. M., Cumming, J. J., & Elkins, J. (2005). Redesigning assessment. In D. Pendergast, & N. Bahr (Eds.), *Teaching middle years: Rethinking curriculum, pedagogy and assessment.* Crows Nest NSW: Allen & Unwin.

Zhang, S. X., Olfman, L., & Ractman, P. (2007). Designing ePortfolio 2.0: Integrating and coordinating Web 2.0 services with ePortfolio systems for enhancing users' learning. *Journal of Information Systems Education.* Retrieved May 23, 2008, from <findarticles.com/p/articles/mi_qa4041/is_s00707/ai_n19511581>

Chapter 5
Towards Theorising Assessment as Critical Inquiry

Claire Wyatt-Smith and Stephanie Gunn

Introduction

Throughout the past two decades assessment has operated on two fronts. First has been the continuing interest in large-scale, standardised testing, which affords governments and countries data for accountability and reporting purposes. Second has been the increasing interest in assessment within a learning culture (Shepard, 2000). Broadly speaking, this has concentrated on formative assessment for improving learning and has generated a proliferation of phrases seeking to highlight vital connections between assessment and learning (for example, 'assessment for/as learning'). Each of these fronts can be understood as giving priority to particular assessment activities and contexts. In the case of standardised testing, usually undertaken to generate data for systems' purposes, the context is necessarily controlled, with variables such as time and place fixed and regulated. Priority is given to common conditions for taking the same test, for example. Where assessment for learning occurs, there is more scope for a range of assessment opportunities, and usually the teacher can tailor these for individual students and circumstances. Assessment opportunities can extend, for example, to include feedback from others, with tasks being completed over an extended time and, at least in part, outside the classroom. Against this background, we seek to progress the argument that there is a need to take theorising assessment practices across a range of assessment contexts into the 21st century. To this end, we propose a framework of assessment as critical inquiry and discuss its application in an Australian study. The framework is prompted by the lack of a general theoretical position that connects assessment to 'meaning making' (Delandshere, 2002), including concepts of knowledge, learning and language. It serves to raise a suite of issues around the nature of quality assessment, the factors that underpin and motivate how assessment is developed and enacted, how the option of teacher assessment for summative purposes might be adopted with confidence, and how we understand, interpret and use the evidentiary base that assessment practices call forth, in system and local school contexts.

C. Wyatt-Smith (✉)
Faculty of Education, Mt Gravatt campus, Griffith University, 176 Messines Ridge Road, Mt Gravatt QLD 4122, Australia
e-mail: c.wyatt-smith@griffith.edu.au

C. Wyatt-Smith, J.J. Cumming (eds.), *Educational Assessment in the 21st Century*,
DOI 10.1007/978-1-4020-9964-9_5, © Springer Science+Business Media B.V. 2009

In contributing to current debates about the nature and purposes of assessment, the chapter is written in three parts: first, it presents three main issues of direct relevance to the present educational context in Australia. These set the scene for part two, which presents the framework of assessment as critical inquiry within an assessment, teaching and learning nexus, the aim being to generate new conversations about the factors shaping how assessment is planned for, and implemented, with evidence interpreted and given value. The third part considers the framework in relation to what is known already, and possible education and assessment futures.

Part One: Setting the Scene

The development of this chapter has been motivated by consideration of three main issues. First is the relationship between students' social backgrounds and their performances on tests, as evidenced in international comparisons provided by the PISA[1] data. Second is the predisposition in some education settings in Australia to conflate socio-economic disadvantage with educational disadvantage, with underperformance in schooling being accounted for in terms of the expected, inevitable influence of students' social backgrounds. The third is the all-too-obvious observation that, currently in Australia, standardised testing continues to gain strength in public policy priorities, with policy firming around the necessary contribution of large-scale external testing for public accountability and credible reporting.

In relation to the first issue, analyses of the PISA data have consistently concluded that, overall, Australian school students perform at high standards in comparison with that of other countries. In relation to subgroups of students, however, the data show a key nexus between social backgrounds and educational performance in the country. The report of the steering committee for the Council for the Australian Federation (Dawkins, 2007) addressed the PISA data as it relates to equity in Australian school education. The writers made the useful distinction between results that show high quality and those that show low equity. They indicated that, in the case of reading, 'disadvantaged students in Australia do better than those in Germany but they are significantly behind their counterparts in Finland and Canada' (Dawkins, 2007, p. 11). In elaborating, they stated that:

> Australia's results in reading are high-quality but are low-equity. The challenge for Australia is to match the performances of countries like Finland and Canada (and Japan, Korea and Hong Kong-China) which are high-quality and high-equity. (p. 11)

While there may be some who would wish to discount this use of the data as reliant on a limited data sample, it is not easy to dismiss the following:

> Domestic evidence shows that Australia has not been making any progress on this [improving the balance between equity and quality] front. Data from the 1975 survey of literacy and

---

[1] PISA—the results from the Programme for International Assessment undertaken by the Organisation for Economic Cooperation and Development (OECD, 2004, 2006).

numeracy levels of Australian students, and subsequent Longitudinal Surveys of Australian Youth (LSAY), show that differences in social background had as much impact on differences in educational achievement in 1998 as they did in 1975. This should be of concern to all Australian governments as well as to the Catholic and independent school sectors.

(Dawkins, 2007, p. 11)

In the extract above, the clear challenge is to strive to re-balance quality and equity in educational outcomes, the aim being to achieve high quality and high equity. Moreover, the clear message is that the responsibility for redressing the balance should fall to all governments and sectors.

The second main issue is the dangerous predisposition to conflate socio-economic disadvantage with educational disadvantage. Teacher expectations are key in this mix. There is ample research evidence suggesting that teachers' assumptions about students' backgrounds and their communities are carried forward to classroom practice, impacting on the learning opportunities provided to students. A study that explored literacy practices in and out of schools in low socio-economic urban communities in Queensland, Australia (Freebody, Ludwig, & Gunn, 1995), for example, showed how teacher expectations were lowered in accordance with what they knew about students' social backgrounds. It was found that sites of poverty offered cognitively less demanding opportunities to learn and to demonstrate achievement. Similarly, a study of teacher judgment practices (Wyatt-Smith & Castleton, 2005) showed that some teachers adjusted their sense of standards with what they knew of the community surrounding the school, and more specifically, with the socio-economic status of the area, as well as their reported knowledge of individual students. The potentially more serious insight, provided by teachers informally, was their reported perception that relative to the weight of influence that socio-economic variables can have on achievement in schooling, specifically, poverty and family contexts, their influence—their agency as teachers—can be relatively weak. This sense of the inevitable power of social backgrounds to determine schooling outcomes is a serious concern for those working towards improvement of teaching and assessment practices.

The third issue is the public policy priority given to education, and more specifically to accountability and standards. There can be no doubt about the Australian federal government's commitment to monitoring performance, primarily through assessment of all students at particular year levels, and to public reporting of external assessments of students in state and national testing programs. What we are yet to see is how teachers respond to these moves as they face the competing demands in their classrooms. On the one hand, there are the imperatives to develop and implement assessments that have high 'site validity'.[2] Characteristic of such assessments

---

[2] Validity refers to what is assessed and how well this corresponds with the behaviour or construct that it is intended to assess (Harlen, 2004). In the case of 'site validity' it involves assessments that intend to assess the range of skills and knowledges that have been made available to learners in the classroom context or site. High 'system validity' involves assessments that intend to assess an often narrower range of skills and knowledges, deemed essential by the particular government body or system.

are the teachers' efforts in establishing connections between in-school and out-of-school knowledges, ensuring that school activities are relevant to the demands of contexts outside schooling (Cumming & Wyatt-Smith, 2001). On the other hand, as McClay (2002) highlighted, there is increasing downward pressure to rehearse standardised testing conditions, to make students 'test-savvy' and to demonstrate quality assurance. These pressures can lead the teacher to adopt narrow forms of assessment that are likely to have high system validity.

Against the backdrop of these three issues, we propose a way of thinking about assessment as critical inquiry that connects assessment to concepts of knowledge, learning and language. This move towards an expanded theorising of assessment and meaning making opens a way of thinking about assessment as a key element in leveraging educational improvement. The proposition on offer is that the challenges mentioned above, namely to re-balance equity and quality in education outcomes and to ensure that teacher agency can affect real improvements, call for a considerably expanded understanding of assessment, how it is enacted in particular contexts and its dynamics with learning and teaching. In this chapter we propose that assessment be understood as not only being aligned with learning and teaching, but that it also be foregrounded—'front-ended'—in designing learning and teaching, with a sharp focus on quality task design.

Foundational to the proposal is that assessment needs to be understood as generating an evidentiary basis for teacher and system decision making and action. The latter centres on quality and how learning is occurring; how learning can be improved and how standards—when central to classroom practice—can serve the best interests of systems, school communities, teachers and students. Linked here, as well, is the understanding that assessment events are inevitably social and cultural in nature: reflective of a nest of assumptions, often implicit, about knowledge and what counts as valued knowledge; about the relationship between learning, teaching and assessment; about teacher judgment practices and understandings about the relationship between literate capabilities and curricular knowledges. At issue, therefore, are the dynamics of how classroom assessment occurs—the shaping factors—and the urgent need to better understand these, if we are to improve outcomes for all students and especially those most at educational risk.

Part Two: Proposing a Framework for Enacting Assessment as Critical Inquiry

Delandshere's (2002) notion of 'assessment as inquiry' highlights how 'the call for change in assessment follows an almost unanimous recognition of the limitations of current measurement theory and practice' (p. 1461). In responding to Delandshere's call and to Sadler's (1989, 1998) orientation towards student empowerment that focuses on standards, discussed later in this chapter, a four-part framework is proposed for enacting assessment as critical inquiry within a teaching, learning and assessment nexus. Essentially, the proposition put forward is that, when assessment is understood as critical inquiry, the practices and processes of assessing—social and cultural acts of doing assessment in actual contexts—can be considered in relation to four main lenses:

1. conceptions of *knowledge* including the nature of the knowledge domains and the related capabilities to be assessed
2. conceptions about the alignment of *assessment, learning and teaching* and how teachers enact their conceptions in practice
3. *teacher judgment* practices, especially as these relate to standards, moderation opportunities, requirements of assessment tasks and expectations of quality performance
4. the *curriculum literacies*[3] required to participate in and contribute to knowledge domains, including those represented in formal curriculum.

Each of the four elements shown above can be thought of as a lens that enables particular characteristics of enacted assessment to come to the fore. Collectively, the set of four lenses works to reveal what is at play in how student achievement is evaluated and therefore valued. These lenses are interrelated and interdependent, each informing the other, and are taken as the desirable considerations and conditions for realising quality assessment. These mutually informing lenses work to align curriculum and assessment with the potential to inform ongoing pedagogical work. Focusing the dynamic interaction of these four elements is task design. The pedagogical outcome of the framework is desired learnings, which should articulate into improved outcomes for students, particularly those at educational disadvantage. The focus is on identifying and examining the suite of conceptions, values and assumptions at play in decisions about ways of doing assessment. In this way the framework has clear implications for identifying and examining the practices used to establish how quality is judged and reported. As suggested earlier, the framework is prompted by the lack of a general theoretical position that connects assessment to meaning making (Delandshere, 2002), including concepts of knowledge, learning, language and context.

In what follows, these four lenses are discussed as separate components of a framework for enacting assessment as critical inquiry. In practice, the lenses, as a complementary set, are understood as interrelated and mutually informing. The framework is necessarily a construct and has been developed as a way to map and explore the complexities inherent in curricular pedagogic-assessment practices in diverse pedagogic and geographic contexts. It builds on research insights from already published work (Wyatt-Smith & Bridges, 2006) in assessment, some of which have been incorporated into practice and policy. For example, the chapter draws upon an evaluation study (Wyatt-Smith & Bridges, 2008) that investigated the impact of the alignment of inclusive assessment, pedagogy and curriculum on

---

[3] 'Curriculum literacies' refers to the discipline-specific literacy demands that students meet in completing set tasks, these typically remaining implicit in teaching, learning and assessment practices (Cumming et al., 1998; Wyatt-Smith & Cumming, 2001). Refer to 'Lens 4: Curriculum literacies' later in this chapter for further detail.

students in the middle phase of schooling in Queensland, Australia. This evaluation study was part of a larger Queensland government initiative (federally funded), which aimed to increase teachers' knowledge, understanding and professional skills development in literacy and numeracy assessment, curriculum planning and teaching instruction for their school contexts. The aim was to support the development of teachers' professional capacity to assess and teach explicitly curriculum literacies and numeracies, in order to respond to the needs of educationally disadvantaged students and provide opportunities for teachers and schools to work together and model effective assessment practices and approaches. The initiative, among others (for example, Lincoln & Neville, 2006), put into practice some of the components of the framework that are the focus of this chapter and, by doing so, acknowledged that optimum outcomes for teachers and students rely upon effective communication and strong connections across theory, research and practice.

Lens 1: Knowledges

This lens brings to the fore the conceptions of knowledge and the assumptions made about the nature of valued knowledge and learning that inevitably underpin acts of assessment. When coming to grips with conceptions of knowledge, Freebody (2006) emphasises the need to consider 'what schooling is for, and about what kinds of futures individuals and communities can expect to be put on offer through schooling' (p. 2). This includes consideration of 'the distinctive logical and content structures of particular bodies of human knowledge and understanding', or the epistemological domain (p. 8), along with the connection of 'learning with the social, cultural, and economic elements of the surrounding community and "the world" outside the classroom', or pragmatic domain of curriculum (p. 15).

Despite the influence of such undergirding conceptions and assumptions, their operation in and influence over what comes to count as assessment evidence is rarely acknowledged. More than a decade ago, Gill (1993) observed that '[a]mong the many and various articles and books on the quality and direction of American education, one searches in vain for an in-depth discussion of how knowing takes place, of who knowers are, and of what can be known' (p. 1). Drawing on this observation, Delandshere (2002, p. 1462) asserted:

> Until we come to grips with, or at least frame the issue of, knowledge and knowing in ways that can guide education practices (including assessment), the enterprise of education runs the risk of being fruitless and counterproductive. In its current state, assessment appears to be a process of collecting data about phenomena or constructs that we have not adequately defined, to answer questions that we have not articulated, and on the basis of which we draw inferences about the quality of the education system.

Essentially, Delandshere's argument is that there is some urgency in reconnecting assessment and, more generally, educational practices to theoretical considerations as a means of clarifying assumptions made about what counts as valued knowledge, and therefore what should be provided for students in the name of quality teaching and learning. These two related matters raise a suite of issues around how knowledges, and more specifically curricular knowledges, are conceptualised and how different conceptualisations lead to quite different assessment possibilities for students to demonstrate what they know and can do.

In drawing on the work of James (1998), Harlen (2004) concurs with Deland-shere's assertion of the importance of a clearly defined and articulated domain of knowledge as the basis for teaching and assessment:

> The argument is that an assessment cannot require the use of the knowledge and skills or other constructs that are supposedly assessed unless there is clear definition of the domain being assessed, and evidence that in the assessment process the intended skills and knowledge are used by the learners (p. 25).

While interrogation of what counts as valued knowledge was outside the scope of the Wyatt-Smith and Bridges (2008) study, the researchers worked from the premise that knowing the learning domain and relevant syllabus materials are foundational to planning and effective practice. While this may seem to be self-evident in good practice, within a period of reform and change, time to reflect critically on the knowledge demands of units of work is often felt by teachers to be an academic luxury when faced with the challenges of daily operation. Participating teachers were supported in collaborative networks of schools. Further, they were provided with additional time dedicated to focused and critical planning for learning and assessment. This is reflected in the following observation:

> ... so there's a much better knowledge of the syllabus, at least in terms of the units—the two units that we developed and other needs that we might have had like making things authentic ... planning process ... [has] ... been a very genuine learning process for everybody ...
> (Wyatt-Smith & Bridges, 2008, Appendix 1, p. 44)

A key observation from the study was the need for time to be committed to teachers' working with domain knowledge. This was beneficial not only in planning for learning and teaching, but also in regard to teacher knowledge of the assessment demands that students faced in completing set activities. While the role of the teacher as designer of in-class assessment tasks was not new, most had not extended this role to writing up the assessment criteria and standards related to the tasks. By critically interrogating task demands through the application of assessment criteria and standards (see Glossary), teachers were asked to question what they were assessing in classroom tasks, this focus extending to the knowledge and skill requirements of syllabus materials, as well as literacy and numeracy capabilities. Participating teachers were asked to develop standards specifications that were locally relevant, all the while critically reflecting on issues such as task complexity and knowledge demands.

Additionally, the participating teachers in the study were asked to interrogate and verify the suitability of their assumptions about students' prior knowledges and capabilities as these related to curriculum, literacy and numeracy. Such assumptions are not readily brought to the surface, and the teachers reported that they had limited experience in this type of critical reflection. However, with support, they reviewed earlier assumptions about student readiness to proceed and how these assumptions could impact upon student engagement and achievement. This part of the teachers' work also extended to deconstructing the demands of the task so as to focus on realistically attainable goals. In these ways, teachers reflected critically upon the implicit knowledge they brought to curriculum planning. Awareness was raised in terms of the students' prior knowledge; the physical and cultural resources of the community in which the school was located, and how this could inform efforts to connect students' in-school learning with their out-of-school learning.

While the impact of the critical pedagogy movement has been felt at the intellectual or 'inside the head' level, participating teachers had limited experience in subjecting their own classroom practice to examination, either by themselves or with others. In this study, they were asked to discuss and evaluate their understanding that, as social beings, teachers' bring their personal, sociocultural backgrounds to classroom interactions. One intention of these discussions was to question the conventional ways of thinking about 'difference' in terms of student backgrounds and knowledges and to confront latent connections across difference, social class and performance expectations. A related intention was for the teachers to consider what they actually knew and how they knew about the varied learning experiences their students brought through the school gate.

Teachers from different sites and sectors came together around syllabus and other policy materials to focus on their curricular choices. One outcome of this exercise was greater knowledge of assessment task design, as this relates to intellectual rigour, and a greater awareness of students' prior knowledge as a factor impacting upon academic engagement and ultimate success. Consider, for example, the segment below:

> ... probably the biggest learning for a lot of our teachers was the scope of the task that they were asking their kids to do and just understanding the burrowing down, drilling down of that was what the biggest learning I think for a lot of our teachers, what they were asking for their kids to do, from the beginning was just miles too big, we were trying to achieve too much and for some of our teachers that was the biggest learning they had, the expectations that they had, their awareness of what the kids knew before ...
>
> (Wyatt-Smtih & Bridges, 2008, Appendix 1, p. 45)

Similarly, in a current study investigating standards-driven reform in the middle years of schooling in Queensland, Australia,[4] one teacher clearly articulated the potential impact of the opportunity to reflect on issues relating to domain knowledge, the design and complexity of assessment tasks and the relationship of this to actual classroom practice. In the following extract, the teacher emphasises how consideration of the centrally developed assessment task was expected to have a beneficial effect on classroom practice in science.

> ... So those discussions they had [about the assessment task] and they came to that same conclusion that in their class, the textbook that they were using didn't require students to do that [higher order thinking], it actually didn't value writing and thinking ... so they actually started questioning the programs that they were using that were restricting them in the way that they allowed their students to answer their work [in assessment tasks], and were in fact

---

[4] See <http://www.griffith.edu.au/education/faculty-education/research/research-projects/investigating-standards-driven-reform-in-assessment-in-the-middle-years-of-schooling>.

deciding that they were going to change the way that they did a lot of the work in class and get students to have different ways of showing their thinking. So that was a massive, for me, pedagogical leap that will make a difference down the track ... and we're looking long-term, two or three years down the track, to an improvement in student outcomes as a result of it.

The above comment points to the direct carry-forward of domain knowledge to the teacher's design of assessment tasks. More specifically, it highlights the teacher's realisation of how assessment can open up (and close down) opportunities for students to demonstrate what they know and can do. More than this, the comment points to the need for teachers to be able to critique the breadth and depth of learning that students should engage in, and how this articulates with suitably demanding assessment opportunities. In this case, it was the assessment that challenged the teacher to rethink the pedagogy—'a massive pedagogical leap'—expected to flow on to improved outcomes.

In summary, the first lens of the framework highlights a need to understand the relationship between curricula; the sociocultural contexts of members of the classroom; and the knowledges and capabilities to be assessed. This leads to further examination of a second lens of the framework for assessment as critical inquiry—the relationship between assessment, learning and teaching.

Lens 2: Linking Assessment, Learning and Teaching

In the past two decades, studies of assessment have shown increasing interest in how classroom assessment can be used to improve the learning experiences and outcomes of students. More specifically, the emphasis in educational assessment reform has increasingly been on meaningful, contextualised and purposeful activity that focuses on demonstrations of what students know and can achieve, rather than on students' shortfalls in knowledge and failure to achieve (Cumming & Maxwell, 1999; Gipps, 1994). Essentially, assessment has been reframed in relation to its role in a learning culture (Shepard, 2000).

In the study referred to earlier (Wyatt-Smith & Bridges, 2008), the key to reshaping teachers' conceptualisations of assessment was the issue of 'front-ending' assessment. The underpinning belief was that being explicit about assessment expectations would have a focusing effect on pedagogy, facilitating deeper student learning. Front-ending assessment was a process whereby the planned, culminating tasks for assessment were critically analysed to identify the explicit knowledges that needed to be built into the unit planning and learning opportunities. This conceptualisation of assessment as a driver for curriculum design has been used in other contexts (for example, Harris, McNeill, Lizotte, Marx, & Krajcik, 2006).

Specifically, in the Wyatt-Smith and Bridges (2008) study, the notion of front-ending assessment was applied by middle schooling teachers across curriculum domains such as mathematics, literacy, science and studies of society and environment (SOSE) as well as in units designed as integrated or cross-disciplinary studies. The teachers employed this notion to place the unit assessment task/s at the heart of planning. Planning teams critically evaluated the proposed formative and summative tasks when planning the unit. This evaluative process required deconstruction of the knowledges, curriculum literacies, numeracy demands and potential blockers for students at educational risk. This extended to consideration of resourcing require-ments, both human and material, and how these related to student engagement in and completion of set tasks.

The strategy of front-ending helped teachers to align learning and assessment through the systematic analysis of the assessment demands of tasks. The desired effect was for an improvement in students' engagement and academic success. Therefore, by 'drawing attention to the interactivity of their assessment, teaching and learning, [participating] teachers saw that teaching and learning became fused with assessment—both formative and summative—as a dynamic process of engaged inquiry' (Wyatt-Smith & Bridges, 2008, p. 47). Further, as shown below, teachers reported their own shifts away from traditional understandings of assessment as an end-point activity, with assessment only coming into focus after teaching and learning has been completed.

> So basically once you have the assessment firmly in place the pedagogy become really clear because your pedagogy has to support that—that sort of quality assessment task ... that was a bit of a shift from what's usually done, usually assessment is that thing that you attach on the end of the unit whereas as opposed to sort of being the driver which it has now become.
>
> (Wyatt-Smith & Bridges, 2008, Appendix 1, p. 48)

Fundamental and productive changes in learning and teaching practice resulted from critical reflection on the assessment evidence to be collected, with this reflection occurring before teaching began. Professional conversations focusing on assessment as evidence-based practice occurred at the stage of task design, with teachers inter-rogating the quality and demands of the assessment they were developing relative to the standards they planned to use in judging quality. Through such a focus on assessment expectations and quality task design prior to commencing the unit of work, the teachers reported that they developed a language for talking about qual-ity in the classroom and gained confidence in the feedback they gave the students. Additionally, the teachers reported that in many cases the employment of statements of assessment criteria and standards as teaching tools assisted students to take own-ership of the learning process and work more independently. Many reported that such statements or scoring guides supported students to have a clear and shared understanding of task expectations:

> ... I think to a certain extent that we've empowered students in the learning process because there's not secret teacher's business anymore in terms of what the expectations are, that students are becoming very au fait with the criteria and being able to apply them in their own work.
>
> (Wyatt-Smith & Bridges, 2008, Appendix 1, p. 61)

Sadler's (1989, 1998) work on formative assessment provided a model for a teaching–learning–assessment nexus that shows how improvement follows when students are inducted into assessment knowledge and expertise. This is taken to include knowl-edge of standards and how to use them for improvement purposes. From Sadler's formative assessment position, the teacher's ethical practice and hence, authority as master, follows a guild model, with students taking on the role of apprentices. For this to be realised in practice, the teacher must possess, first, a concept of quality appropriate to the task and the student group; second, an ability to judge the student's work in relation to that concept and a desire to induct student-apprentices into the appraisal process; and third, a history of evaluative decision making developed over time. Moreover, it depends on a critical ability and willingness to facilitate students' transition from feedback to self-monitoring. For this to occur, the teacher must already possess the knowledge of what constitutes quality and must value opportunities for sharing this knowledge. Stiggins (2004) has similarly highlighted the importance of student involvement in assessment practices, suggesting that maximum learning comes from productive interactions between teachers and students, with both sharing the responsibility for making learning and assessment effective. Sadler (1998) in particular argued that 'if teacher-supplied feedback is to give way to self assessment and self monitoring, some of what the teacher brings to the assessment act must itself become part of the curriculum for the student, not an accidental or inconsequential adjunct to it' (p. 82).

While the use of stated assessment criteria and standards to facilitate teacher and student conversations about quality and learning has been common practice in the senior years of schooling in Queensland, Australia, this has not been routine practice for teachers in the early years of school (years 1–10). In recognising this, Wyatt-Smith (2008) developed a set of reflective questions that explored a number of features for consideration when developing quality-assessment opportunities. These included questions about the following features: (1) alignment; (2) intellectual challenges and engagement; (3) assessment scope and demand; (4) language used to communicate the task; (5) literate capabilities involved in doing and completing the task; (6) performance contexts; (7) knowing what is expected both during and on completion of the task; (8) student self-assessment for improvement; and (9) intended purposes of assessment information. In part, this was motivated by an interest in enabling teachers to probe for themselves the demands of assessments that they developed for classroom use. More specifically, the questions enabled teachers to focus on 'front-ending', whereby the planned, culminating tasks for assessment were critically analysed to identify the explicit skills and knowledges that needed to be built into the unit planning and learning opportunities.

This leads to the third lens regarding the fundamental elements that need to be in place to ensure confidence in teacher judgment practices within the assessment, teaching and learning nexus.

Lens 3: Teacher Judgment Linked to Standards and Moderation Opportunities

Central to the proposal for a critical-inquiry approach to assessment is the understanding that teacher judgment is taken to be nested within a range of decision making relating to curriculum frameworks, assessment practices, the school–community interface and individual student learning needs and goals, as suggested earlier. Beyond this is the principle that the teacher and students are active in gathering information about and reflecting on learning and performance over time. Generally speaking, there is support for this position in the field of educational assessment research. Sadler (1998) argued that there is strong support for the view that stated standards can be productive in informing not only judgment, but also teaching and learning. As mentioned earlier, he advocated that the teacher's role extend to development of students' evaluative experience by involving them in applying standards to their own work. For Sadler, standards and improvement were directly connected. Working from a similar stance, Stigler and Hiebert (1997) presented the cautionary note that 'A focus on standards and accountability that ignores the processes of teaching and learning in classrooms will not provide the direction that teachers need in their quest to improve' (p. 19–20). Even though judgment is a routine part of each teacher's work, it is difficult to subject it to scrutiny, even by the individual teacher concerned, unless scaffolded opportunities are provided to do so (Phelps, 1989). Studies of teacher judgment have shown that individual teachers carry with them not only evaluative experience, but also, more specifically, their own judgment policies that typically remain private, though they work to shape in powerful ways the processes by which judgments of quality are reached (Wyatt-Smith & Castleton, 2005). Moreover, operating within these policies can be evaluation practices that are as much tied to recollected observations of in-class learning and behaviours as to the qualities of the piece to be assessed.

A way forward is to recognise that *teacher judgment,* in conjunction with *clearly specified standards* and *opportunities for moderation,* are a linchpin of a robust assessment culture in schooling. The study reported by Wyatt-Smith and Bridges (2008) aimed to support sustained professional conversations around matters including planning for assessment; how assessment activities are designed; how evidence is collected, interpreted and recorded; what contexts are suitable for undertaking particular assessment activities; and what standards are in place to assist teachers in assessing quality. Such conversations were seen as enabling judgment practices to be de-privatised and judgments made defensible. In effect, these ongoing professional conversations started at the stage of task design and continued throughout the assessment, teaching and learning cycle. This can be achieved when judgment practices involve a process of matching work samples to stated assessment standards, with attention focusing on the features or qualities of performance as these were evidenced in the work. Teacher judgment can therefore be understood as evidence based, with standards playing a useful function in informing, substantiating and making judgments defensible. In distinguishing this practice of standards-referenced assessment from judgments relying on direct inter-student comparison as the basis for judgment, Sadler (1987) stated:

> The primary function of educational standards is to enable statements about a student's quality of performance or degree of achievement to be made without reference to the achievement of other students, which conceivably could be either all poor or all excellent. In addition, fixed standards enable long-term changes in a phenomenon to be detected. (p. 196)

Several writers (Harlen, 2005; Sadler, 1989; Wyatt-Smith, Castleton, & Ryan, 2004) have emphasised how common standards provide external reference points for informing judgment and are pivotal in achieving comparability and confidence in teacher judgments. Further, opportunities for teachers to integrate 'judgments of students' responses to the various modes with those of other teachers' judgments are essential (Wilson, 2004, p. 11). Such opportunities for sustained professional conversations to support teacher judgment are defined as 'social or consensus moderation' and described as a 'form of quality assurance for delivering comparability in evidence-based judgments of student achievement' (Maxwell, 2007, p. 2). Maxwell highlighted two functions of moderation, namely quality assurance and comparability. The former he linked with the status of the assessment as high (or low) and comparability with common standards:

- *Quality assurance* refers to methods for establishing confidence in the quality of procedures and outcomes. Confidence is seen as a matter of degree with more stringent quality assurance and greater confidence required for high-stakes assessment.
- *Comparability* 'requires assessment against common characteristics or criteria, such as provided by a subject syllabus or other frame of reference' and 'requires consistency in the application of common standards so that all achievements given the same grade or level of achievement have reached the same standard' (Maxwell, 2007, p. 2).

Here, social moderation is considered key to standards-referenced teacher judgment, whereby the frames of reference (standards, scoring guidelines, assessment criteria, etc.) are defined and disseminated to allow for common interpretation (Maxwell, 2007). This calls for clear recognition of the social nature of moderation, whereby teachers interact with one another, sharing judgments of student work samples. Such sharing is an act that necessarily involves an openness to making available information about interpretations of the standards; disclosures that may otherwise remain private and unarticulated.

In order to achieve high reliability while preserving validity, it is important for teacher assessors to develop common understandings of stated standards and reach 'similar recognition of performances that demonstrate those standards' (Maxwell, 2001, p. 6). This is especially the case where standards are written as verbal descriptors and as such remain open to interpretation. Sadler (1989) argued that exemplars or samples of student work provide concrete referents that can be used to illustrate standards that otherwise remain abstract mental constructs. He made the point that the stated standards and exemplars work together to show different ways of satisfying the requirements of say, an A or C standard. Smith's (1989)[5] study of standards in senior English curriculum in Queensland, Australia (years 11 and 12 as the final 2 years of schooling) showed the utility of exemplars in the form of student work samples, together with an accompanying commentary, in illustrating standards and how they apply at particular levels. In particular, Smith showed how the commentary could make available insights into the teacher's cognitive processes in combining

---

[5] Smith—now writing as Wyatt-Smith.

or *trading-off* strengths and limitations of the work relative to the required characteristics of the standards at various levels. In short, annotated exemplars and commentaries can show the processes of formulating an overall or on-balance judgment. In the absence of such materials and, in particular, the commentaries, the treatment of compensatory factors and the complex features of teacher judgment necessarily remain unarticulated. More specifically, a final grade recorded on a student piece of work bears no trace of, or resemblance to, the complex decision making involved in arriving at a grading decision.

While standards and commentaries such as those discussed can serve to make clear expectations of quality, they do not necessarily account fully for the factors that shape teacher judgment. In a large-scale Australian study of teacher judgment in middle schooling, Cooksey, Freebody, and Wyatt-Smith (2007) reported high levels of variability in teachers' notions of quality and also unearthed the range of factors that shape how judgments are reached. While this study pointed to the need for the promulgation of stated standards to include exemplars, it also opened a vital space for consideration of social moderation as focal in quality-assurance processes at local and systemic levels. Specifically, it suggests how social moderation can act as a context or social space for teachers to make available for scrutiny to themselves and others the bases of their judgment practices and their use of standards in those practices. It is in this context that the legitimacy of the mix of factors impacting judgment can be opened for scrutiny.

Several conditions for successful implementation of social moderation have been described in the literature (for example, Daugherty, 1997; Harlen, 2005; Matters, 2006; Maxwell, 2006; Wilmut, 2005; Wilson, 2004). These include the development of quality assessment tasks; an element of commonality among assessments such as responding to a common set of assessment tasks, standards or criteria; provision of guidelines and procedures; acknowledgement of the various referents upon which teachers draw in the judgment process (for example, teachers' personal knowledge of students and context); establishment of 'social' protocols (for example, working collaboratively, negotiation and trust); and the need for professional development in moderation processes and expectations. While moderation is one part of a robust assessment culture, it is an essential element for maintaining teacher and public confidence in a standards-referenced assessment model. An ongoing challenge in securing such confidence is, of course, the vital and continuing work of inducting the teaching profession, including successive generations of graduates, into the underpinning understandings about standards-referenced assessment and related moderation.

Lens 4: Curriculum Literacies

This fourth lens draws on a new conceptualisation of the literacy–curriculum interface that emerged from a national study of the literacy demands of curriculum in senior schooling (Cumming, Wyatt-Smith, Ryan, & Doig, 1998). For the purpose of the study, literacy was defined as including reading, writing, listening, speaking, viewing and critical thinking and was recognised as a major determinant of success in education. The literacy demands of assessment were also viewed as providing 'a filter for or enabler of student success in all areas' (Wyatt-Smith & Cumming, 2003, p. 48). Hence, while the study focused on literacy demands of the curriculum, the interactions with assessment were also a focus. Based on the finding that cross-curricular literacy was mainly treated as a generic skill with minor adaptation for different subject areas, the researchers developed the term 'curriculum literacies', where 'curriculum' is deliberately used as a noun, rather than the adjectival 'curri cular', to demonstrate that this conjunction represents the interface between a specific curriculum and its literacies, rather than literacies related to curriculum in a generic sense, or a single literacy that can be spread homogeneously across the curriculum' (Wyatt-Smith & Cumming, 2003, p. 50). Building on this work, Wyatt-Smith and Cumming (2003) argued the need to explore the coherence of literacy demands that students encounter in managing their learning in different contexts, and for the need to incorporate these demands explicitly in instruction and assessment. Their reconceptualisation of curriculum literacies challenges current constructs of assessment and calls for the domains of assessment to be expanded to include both curriculum knowledge and epistemological domains that take account of diverse ways of working with and in semiotic systems. In a framework of assessment as critical inquiry, curriculum literacies are therefore central. It is this lens that focuses attention on the success (or failure) of systems, as well as pedagogical and assessment practices, to enable students to gain increasing control of this combination of curricular and literate knowledges and the ability to use these productively. As Wyatt-Smith and Cumming (2003) explain:

> Our recurrent theme is that to be successful, students need to be able to identify and engage with these curriculum literacies within each subject, not just for learning, but also for successful negotiation of assessment within each subject . . . Overall student academic success in meeting expected appropriate demonstrations of performance will depend very much on how well the student can manage to understand, participate in and respond to the created intersection of the curriculum-literate environment. (pp. 49–50)

Cumming et al. (1998) found that 'an assumption prevails that students have acquired the abilities to meet the literacy demands of post-compulsory curriculum during their earlier years of schooling' (p. 10). Further, there were apparent assumptions that students could develop an understanding of the meta-language of a subject without explicit instruction, with the gap for assessment tasks appearing to be even greater. The study confirmed the key role of ongoing teacher assessment in checking how students are managing the cognitive demands and pace of curriculum delivery, including student understandings of specific subject terminology or the meta-language of the subject. Moreover, it was found that 'many students appeared not to have a clear understanding of expected performance standards and to be working "in the dark" as to the nature of a quality performance' (Wyatt-Smith & Cumming, 2003, p. 53). The study highlighted the need to make the features of quality performance, framed by curriculum literacies, more explicit. Given this, assessment requirements need to be written in student-friendly terms while maintaining the meta-language of the subject. However, the researchers concluded that the provision of student-friendly guidelines, while a necessary condition, was not sufficient of itself. They reported a clear need for teachers 'to assist students to understand those expectations so that they can use such knowledge to self-assess and monitor learning over time' (p. 54). The researchers concluded that the literacy environment of school curriculum places highly complex demands on students and reiterated that:

> Some students succeed in negotiating these, apparently drawing on resources other than those that teachers provide. Others may spend their compulsory years [of schooling] in an environment that is essentially conducted in a foreign language in which they never gain sufficient proficiency. And students need to be fluent, to negotiate the even more demanding literacy-bound assessment requirements successfully.
> ... the role and nature of the curriculum-literacies that are in-built in assessment activities, and which impact upon the students' performances, should be more explicit ... Assumptions of students' curriculum literacies is not sufficient. These need to be incorporated in direct instruction.
>
> (Wyatt-Smith & Cumming, 2003, p. 58)

This conceptualisation of curriculum literacies has been played out in both policy and practice. First, the Queensland government literacy initiative, titled 'Literacy the Key to Learning: Framework for Action 2006–2008' (Department of Education and the Arts, 2006) focuses on actions to address identified challenges in improving literacy outcomes for all students in the state. The framework reflects the state's commitment to social justice and recognition of the diverse abilities, cultural backgrounds and life circumstances of the students it is serving, and places as central to the framework the notion of curriculum literacies, stating that 'effective learning entails developing the literacy capabilities needed to learn in the curriculum' (p. 1). Second, in the Queensland teacher capacity-building initiative discussed earlier, participating teachers were asked to examine notions of literacy in refocusing curriculum and assessment planning. Essential to the process was the strong recognition that teachers needed to teach explicitly the literacy demands of assessment requirements and to provide a meta-language for students to use in furthering their own understandings of the literacy demands of the tasks. While many had a 'broad' understanding of the literacy demands of their curriculum area/s, a critical unpacking of these demands when designing assessment tasks was not a routine, familiar practice. Clearly, teachers needed a firm understanding of the nature of subject-specific literacy demands within their own subjects to ensure continuity of literacy demands and expectations placed on students. Teachers reported that the focus on curriculum literacies had enabled direct links to be made between curriculum literacies, teaching and assessment expectations in curriculum areas (that is, Key Learning Areas—KLAs) and that such work proved to be invaluable for ongoing teacher learning and ultimately student outcomes:

> We found focusing on the curriculum literacies increased teacher awareness of the curriculum literacies within the KLA, but it made some teachers more comfortable with teaching literacies within their KLA ... sometimes there has been resistance to that, and the students were able to see clearly the links and the purposes of the activities and the programs that we were doing.
>
> (Wyatt-Smith & Bridges, 2008, p. 49)

Interestingly, there is the mention here of the student being able to see clearly the links and purposes of activities and the programs. Such seeing resulted from teachers themselves attending in their pedagogy and assessment to ways of connecting curricular knowledge and language usage.

Part Three: Lessons Learned and Challenges in Shaping Education Futures

Assessment policy and practice in schooling are currently being challenged to review the nature of the knowledges and skills being assessed. In addition, opening for review is the optimum range of contexts and conditions for collecting assessment information about how students work with and reconstitute knowledges. These two related questions raise a suite of issues around how curricular knowledges are conceptualised and how different conceptualisations lead to quite different assessment possibilities for students to demonstrate what they know and can do.

The assessment-as-inquiry framework proposed in this chapter is underpinned by reconfigured relations of assessment to knowledge domains, to learning and to language. As part of this move towards theorising assessment in relation to meaning making, we suggest that the teacher's claim to expertise may be tied primarily to how they promote both quality learning and the qualities of learners so that learning will increasingly be about creating a kind of person, dispositions and orientations to the world and to ways of working with and reconstituting knowledge as problem-solvers and collaborators. The reality is that while many teachers have initiated their own professional conversations around assessment practice, both within their school and at district level, it is also fair to say that many teachers experience a sense of isolation as they go about their work as assessors, having no sustained opportunities for such sharing. A related observation is that the provision and proliferation of standards in themselves do not secure reliable judgments in which teachers and the community can have confidence. There is a clear and pressing need to support teacher dialogue around the issues of assessment and judgment, including standard setting, and how to make available for students useful information about expectations of quality.

This chapter has opened up some of the complexities that can be considered when critically inquiring into educational assessment. It has proposed a framework in order to realise the interactivity of assessment and related foundational elements for quality learning. At one level the framework represents an attempt to see educational assessment in terms of its connectedness to issues of meaning: knowing, learning, teaching and language. At another level, it is a provocation to reconsider the divergent assessment priorities and goals of various education stakeholders, both nationally and internationally, and the pressure on some to follow short-term imperatives of appearing to be delivering improved results. Deep learning and improvement take time, however. They also involve new conversations around what is to be valued both in classroom-based and system assessment policies and practices. The challenge for the educational community is to be supportive of those assessment initiatives that focus on providing support for the long-term professional development necessary to effect change and deliver improved outcomes. As teachers know only too well, assessment procedures, of themselves, do not necessarily lead to improvement. Instead, teachers' professional knowledge and judgment practices are central, if we are serious about improving learning and student engagement for all.

Glossary

Criterion A distinguishing property or characteristic of any thing, by which its quality can be judged or estimated, or by which a decision or classification may be made (Sadler, 1987, p. 164). (From the Greek *kriterion*, 'a means for judging').

Literate capabilities Refers to reading, writing, viewing, speaking and critical thinking, as well as text production online, using written, visual and auditory channels of communication. The term extends connections made across everyday social practices, young people's literate activities and learning inside and outside schooling, and the critical, evaluative stances they may adopt.

Policy materials Documents that outline a course of action or a program of actions developed by the governing educational authority. The term is inclusive of official curriculum materials that prescribe a course of study and related assessment requirements.

Sectors The various educational authorities governing schools. For example, in Queensland, Australia, there are three main sectors: state (public), Catholic and independent (private).

Site A place where educational activity is occurring, usually a school.

Standard A definite level of excellence or attainment, or a definite degree of any quality viewed as a prescribed object of endeavour or as the recognised measure of what is adequate for some purpose, so established by authority, custom or consensus (Sadler, 1987, p. 164). (From the Roman *estendre*, 'to extend').

Syllabus A document that outlines course objectives, prescribed learning, resource materials and assessment requirements. It specifies the course of study and refers to the content or subject matter of an individual subject as well as required resources. Syllabi are usually developed (and at times mandated) by a governing educational authority.

Task An assessment activity undertaken by students to provide information on what students know, understand and are able to do. Tasks can be written for a range of modes.

Teacher judgment Involves teachers assessing and awarding a grade to student work. It involves considering the qualities of performance evidenced in the work being assessed.

References

Cooksey, R. W., Freebody, P., & Wyatt-Smith, C. M. (2007). Assessment as judgment-in-context: Analysing how teachers evaluate students' writing. *Educational Research and Evaluation, 13*(5), 401–434.

Cumming, J. J., & Maxwell, G. (1999). Contexualising authentic assessment. *Assessment in Education: Principles, Policy and Practice, 6*(2), 177–194.

Cumming, J. J., & Wyatt-Smith, C. M. (2001). *Literacy and curriculum: Success in senior schooling*. Melbourne: ACER.

Cumming, J. J., Wyatt-Smith, C. M., Ryan, J., & Doig, S. M. 1998. *The literacy-curriculum interface: The literacy demands of the curriculum in post-compulsory schooling*. Final Report. Brisbane: Centre for Literacy Education Research, Griffith University, and Department of Employment, Education, Training and Youth Affairs.

Daugherty, R. (1997). Consistency in teachers' assessments: Defining the problem, finding the answers. *British Journal of Curriculum and Assessment, 8*(1), 32–38.

Dawkins, P. (2007). *Federalist paper 2: The future of schooling in Australia*. Victoria, Australia: The Council for The Australian Federation.

Department of Education and the Arts. (2006). *Literacy the key to learning: Framework for action 2006–2008*. Queensland: Author.

Delandshere, G. (2002). Assessment as inquiry. *Teachers' College Record, 104*(7), 1461–1484.

Freebody, P. (2006). *Knowledge, skill and disposition in the organisation of senior schooling*. A discussion paper prepared for the Queensland Studies Authority. Queensland, Australia: Queensland Studies Authority.

Freebody, P., Ludwig, C. M., & Gunn, S. (1995). *Everyday literacy practices in and out of schools in low socio-economic urban communities*. Canberra: Commonwealth Department of Employment, Education and Training.

Gill, J. H. (1993). *Learning to learn: Towards a philosophy of education*. Atlantic Highlands, NJ: Humanities Press.

Gipps, C. (1994). *Beyond testing: Towards a theory of educational assessment*. London: Falmer.

Harlen, W. 2004. *Can assessment by teachers be a dependable option for summative purposes?* Paper presented at General Teaching Council for England Conference, 29 November, 2004, London.

Harlen, W. (2005). Teachers summative practices and assessment for learning tensions and synergies. *The Curriculum Journal, 16*(2), 207–223.

Harris, C. J., McNeill, K. L., Lizotte, D. J., Marx, R. W., & Krajcik, J. (2006). *Usable assessments for teaching science content and inquiry standards*. Peers Matter, Washington, D.C: National Science Teachers Association.

James, M. (1998). *Using assessment for school improvement*. Oxford: Heinemann Educational.

Lincoln, M., & Neville, M. 2006. *Middle phase of learning cluster project 2006: Final report*. Retrieved July 30, 2008, from <http://education.qld.gov.au/curriculum/middle/docs/mpl-cluster-final.pdf>.

Matters, G. (2006). *Assessment approaches in Queensland senior science syllabuses*. A report to the Queensland Studies Authority. Brisbane: ACER.

Maxwell, G. (2001). *Moderation of assessments in vocational education and training*. Queensland: Department of Employment and Training.

Maxwell, G. 2006. *Quality management of school-based assessments: Moderation of teacher judgments*. Paper presented at the 32nd IAEA Conference, Singapore.

Maxwell, G. (2007). *Implications for moderation of proposed changes to senior secondary school syllabuses*. Paper commissioned by the Queensland Studies Authority. Brisbane: Queensland Studies Authority.

McClay, J. K. (2002). Hidden 'treasure': New genres, new media and the teaching of writing. *English in Education, 36*(1), 46–55.

Organisation for Economic Co-operation and Development (OECD). (2004). *Learning for tomorrow's world: First results from Programme for International Student Assessment 2003*. Paris: Author.

Organisation for Economic Co-operation and Development (OECD). (2006). *PISA 2006: Science competencies for tomorrow's world*.

Phelps, L. (1989). Images of student writing: the deep structure of teacher response. In C. M. Anson (Ed.), *Writing and response: Theory, practice, and research*. Urbana, IL: NCTE.

Sadler, D. R. (1987). Specifying and promulgating achievement standards. *Oxford Review of Education, 13*, 191–209.

Sadler, D. R. (1989). Formative assessment and the design of instructional systems. *Instructional Science, 18*, 119–144.

Sadler, D. R. (1998). Formative assessment: Revisiting the territory. *Assessment in Education, 5*(1), 77–85.

Shepard, L. A. (2000). *The role of assessment in a learning culture*. Presidential address, American Educational Research Association, New Orleans, April 2000.

Smith, C. M. (1989). *A study of standards specifications in English*. Unpublished masters thesis. Brisbane: University of Queensland.

Stiggins, R. (2004). New assessment beliefs for a new school mission. *Phi Delta Kappan, 86*(1), 22–28.

Stigler, J. W., & Hiebert, J. (1997). Understanding and improving classroom mathematics instruction: An overview of the TIMSS video study. *Phi Delta Kappan, 78*(1), 14–21.

Wilmut, J. (2005). *Experiences of summative teacher assessment in the UK*. A review conducted for the Qualifications and Curriculum Authority. London: Qualifications and Curriculum Authority.

Wilson, M. (Ed.). (2004). Towards coherence between classroom assessment and accountability. In *The 103rd Yearbook of the National Society for the Study of Education Part 2*. Chicago: Chicago University Press.

Wyatt-Smith, C. M. 2008. *Developing quality assessment opportunities*. In C.M. Wyatt-Smith & S. Bridges, *Meeting in the middle—Assessment, pedagogy, learning and students at educational disadvantage*. Evaluation for The Literacy and Numeracy in the Middle Years of School Initiative Strand A. Retrieved August 8, 2008, from <http://education.qld.gov.au/literacy/docs/deewr-myp-final-report.pdf>.

Wyatt-Smith, C. M., & Bridges, S. 2006. *Assessment for learning: An Australian study in middle schooling*. International association for Educational Assessment, Singapore, 2006. Retrieved July 30, 2008, from <http://www.iaea2006.seab.gov.sg/conference/download/papers/Assessment%20for%20learning%20-%20An%20Australian%20study%20in%20middle%20schooling.pdf>.

Wyatt-Smith, C. M., & Bridges, S. 2008. *Meeting in the middle—Assessment, pedagogy, learning and students at educational disadvantage*. Evaluation for The Literacy and Numeracy in the Middle Years of Schooling Initiative Strand A. Retrieved July 30, 2008, from <http://education.qld.gov.au/literacy/docs/deewr-myp-final-report.pdf>.

Wyatt-Smith, C., & Castleton, G. (2005). Examining how teachers judge student writing: An Australian case study. *Journal of Curriculum Studies, 37*(2), 131–154.

Wyatt-Smith, C. M., & Cumming, J. J. (2003). Curriculum literacies: Expanding domains of assessment. *Assessment in Education: Principles, policy and practice, 10*(1), 47–59.

Wyatt-Smith, C. M., & Cumming, J. J. (Special Issue Editors) (2001). Examining the literacy-curriculum relationship. *A special edition of Linguistics and Education, 11*(3), 295–312.

Wyatt-Smith, C., Castleton, G., & Ryan, J. (2004). New research methodologies for researching new literacies. *International Journal of Learning, 11*, 421–429.

Wyatt-Smith, C. M., Cumming, J., & Elkins, J. (2005). Redesigning assessment. In D. Pendergast & N. Bahr (Eds.), *Teaching middle years*. Crows Nest, NSW: Allen & Unwin.

Part II
Building Social Capital: Difference, Diversity and Social Inclusion

Chapter 6
Fairness in Assessment

Caroline Gipps and Gordon Stobart

Introduction

Fairness is a concept for which definitions are important, since it is often interpreted in too narrow and technical a way. We set fairness within a social context and look at what this means in relation to different groups and cultures. Similarly, we are using *educational assessment* in a more inclusive way than is often the case; we include tests, examinations, teachers' judgments or evaluations ('assessment' in the United Kingdom) of student performance. We then explore *bias* in measurement and how it relates to validity, as well as the broader concept of *equity*. Finally, three examples of approaches to ensure fairness are given.

We argue that 21st-century assessment will need to take ever more account of the social contexts of assessment and to continue the movement away from seeing fairness simply as a technical concern with test construction. Fairness in assessment involves both what precedes an assessment (for example, access and resources) and its consequences (for example, interpretations of results and impact) as well as aspects of the assessment design itself.

Fairness

How would we tell whether a test is fair for different groups (male/female; socially/advantaged/disadvantaged; ethnic groupings)? The dilemma is that different groups will have different qualities and experiences, so fairness in assessment cannot be judged in terms of equal scores or outcomes.

Differences in performance on a test may be due to differing access to learning, or because the test is biased in favour of one group. Wood (1987) described these different aspects of fairness as the opportunity to acquire talent (access issues) and the opportunity to show talent to good effect (fairness in the assessment).

In our view, fairness in assessment cannot be considered in isolation from access issues in the curriculum and the educational opportunities offered to the students:

C. Gipps (✉)
Vice-Chancellor, University of Wolverhampton, Wulfruna Street, Wolverhampton WV1 1LY
e-mail: c.gipps@wlv.ac.uk

C. Wyatt-Smith, J.J. Cumming (eds.), *Educational Assessment in the 21st Century*,
DOI 10.1007/978-1-4020-9964-9_6, © Springer Science+Business Media B.V. 2009

fairness in access opportunities both to schooling and to the curriculum provide the 'level playing field' that must precede a genuinely fair assessment situation.

Fairness and Equity

We use the term 'equity' interchangeably with 'fairness'. *Equity* is defined in the *Chambers Concise Dictionary* (1992) as 'moral justice'. Equity does not imply equality of outcome and does not presume identical experiences for all—both of these are seen to be unrealistic, but it asserts that assessment practice and interpretation of results need to be fair and just for all groups.

For example, it is possible to have similar outcomes for two groups and yet to see this as unfair to one of them, which may have been disadvantaged in terms of access to the curriculum. Conversely, it is possible to have unequal group outcomes that may be seen as fair. An example would be where there are group differences in the application to learning and preparation, where each had similar resources and opportunities.

Equity is also a quasi-legal term. The legal meaning of *equity* is 'the spirit of justice' and, building on the work of Walter Secada (1989), we see it as a qualitative concern for what is just. 'Equity attempts to look at the justice of a given state of affairs, a justice that goes beyond acting in agreed upon ways and seeks to look at the justice of the arrangements leading up to and resulting from those actions' (p. 81).

The implication is that equity is not the same as equality. Equity represents the judgment about whether equality, be it in the form of opportunity and/or of outcomes, achieves just ('fair') results. Looking for equality requires essentially a quantitative approach to differences between groups, while equity goes beyond this and looks at the justice of the arrangements prior to the assessment.

The approach we take includes these broader issues and, therefore, owes more to sociocultural theory than to measurement theory. Sociocultural research and theory builds on Vygotsky's work, in which it is used as a specific term embodying the roles of social interaction and cultural context in learning and identity formation (Cobb, 1994; Penuel & Wertsch, 1995.) Although assessment is a key player in the learner's formation of identity (Gipps, 1999), we do not focus on that aspect of sociocultural approaches to assessment in this chapter. Rather, we take a view of assessment that places it in social, cultural and political contexts: assessment is a socially embedded activity that can only be fully understood by taking account of the social and cultural contexts within which it operates, alongside the technical characteristics.

A Brief History of Assessment and 'Fairness'

There is a significant history of assessment being used for fairness and equity purposes. This stems from the belief that testing is fairer than selection by patronage or birth, since all sit the same test under the same conditions. This, as we shall show, is a very restricted view of fairness.

Selection

Selection has probably been the most pervasive role of assessment over the years (Glaser & Silver, 1994). Assessment for selection, which later became linked with certification, illustrates well the power and control aspects of assessment as well as its role in cultural and social reproduction.

Examinations were first developed in China under the Han dynasty (206 BC to AD 220) in order to select candidates for government service. The Jesuits introduced competitive examinations into their schools in the 17th century, possibly influenced by Jesuit travellers' experience in China. It was not until the late 18th century and early 19th century that examinations developed in northern Europe—in Prussia and then in France and England—again, in order to select candidates for government positions.

In Europe, as the industrial capitalist economy flourished, there was an increasing need for trained middle-class workers. Access to the professions had been determined, before the 19th century, by family history and patronage rather than by academic achievement or ability. In the 19th century this picture began to change. The economy required more individuals in the professions and in managerial positions. Society, therefore, needed to encourage a wider range of individuals to take on these roles. This was the first time that upward mobility became a practical proposition on a wide scale. Of course, there had to be some way of selecting those who were deemed suitable for training, as well as certifying those who were deemed to be competent, and examinations were used as the tool. The appeal of examinations was that they were the same for everyone who took them, though, of course, this was generally restricted to educated males. Thus, although the exams limited nepotism and corruption, they could not eliminate the advantages afforded by gender, social status and wealth. In Britain, in the case of the Civil Service exams, for example, it was still almost exclusively those who had received an appropriate fee-paying education who were able to pass.

Assessment for selection has also been a key theme *within* school systems. In the United Kingdom and elsewhere, intelligence testing has historically played a central role both in identifying those considered able enough for an academic secondary education and selecting out of the system those with special educational needs deemed more suitable for 'special' schools, an approach enshrined in the 1944 *Education Act* in the United Kingdom (Sutherland, 1996). The validity of intelligence (IQ) tests as a fair means of selection has come under increasing scrutiny (Gardner & Cowan, 2005). It is now widely recognised that IQ tests are culturally based and biased in favour of individuals from the dominant culture. Therefore, the sociocultural critique of intelligence testing is that it obscures the perpetuation of social inequalities because it legitimates them (Gould, 1996; Hanson, 1993).

Equity was also a driving force behind the development of 'objective' tests. By 'objective' we are referring to multiple-choice tests and others that require no judgment in scoring. From their post-World War I origins onwards, the development of objective tests for sorting and selecting students was seen, particularly in the United States, as a scientific, even progressive, activity (Stoskopf, 2008; Ryan, 2008). The growth of such testing has grown exponentially in the United States (Madaus &

Raczek, 1996) and its efficiency as a method of mass assessment has increasing appeal around the world. Such tests have highly replicable and reliable scoring—hence the 'objective' label. This appeal has often obscured the limited validity of such tests and the subjective nature of item writing, selection of material and formulation of answer choices.

Of longer pedigree is the more open-ended ('constructed response') tradition of written examinations, though the critique is in many ways similar (Broadfoot, 1979). There may be added concern that examinations, with their demands for culturally dependent forms of response (for example, the argumentative essay), may penalise those from more disadvantaged or culturally different backgrounds as there may be a mismatch between the language and culture of the home and the school. As a result, examinations may offer a less-than-fair assessment, and furthermore, because of their role in certification, they may institutionalise and legitimate social stratification (Stobart, 2008).

To summarise, although external examinations, IQ testing and objective testing were seen originally as equitable tools for selection and certification purposes, a sociocultural critique calls this into question. Assessment, in its various forms, has a determining role to play in cultural reproduction and social stratification. The discussion of fairness in this chapter needs, therefore, to be set against this background.

Developments in Assessment and Their Relationship to 'Fairness'

There have been considerable developments in the nature and conceptualisation of assessment over the past 50 years. These have often been the result of the changing purposes for which assessment has been used. One example is the use of testing for accountability purposes, particularly the use of targets based on the results of high-stakes testing such as the *No Child Left Behind* testing program in the United States (Stobart, 2008). Such programs raise the issue of fairness in large-scale testing, which we address later in the chapter.

The second example (which has received increasing emphasis) is the use of assessment to contribute to the learning process, in general terms called 'educational assessment'. It is to fairness issues in this approach that we now turn.

The Move to Educational Assessment

Building on the critiques of IQ testing, and developments in understanding of how learning takes place, researchers—mostly in the United States at first—began to conceptualise different types of, and approaches to, assessment, usually with an educational purpose rather than an 'organisational' one such as selection.

In the development of educational assessment, the work of Glaser was critical. His 1963 article on criterion-referenced testing was a watershed in the development of a new type of assessment, which moved away from classical testing based on psychometric theory. Glaser (1963) made the point that norm-referenced testing developed from psychometric work that focused on aptitude, selection and prediction. Educational assessment, by contrast, aimed to devise tests that look at the individual as an individual, rather than in relation to other individuals, and to use measurement to identify strengths and weaknesses individuals might have, so as to aid their educational progress. The development of this criterion-based approach, rather than one based on norms, was not driven by fairness but can be seen as a fairer approach.

New developments—performance assessment, 'authentic' assessment, portfolio assessment and so forth—were part of a move to design assessment that supports learning and provides more detailed information about students (Wolf, Bixby, Glenn, & Gardner, 1991). We can see this, also, as a shift towards 'an opening up' of traditional assessment, an approach that can itself be seen as a fairness issue.

However, focus on an assessment approach on its own is not sufficient for a discussion of fairness. Consideration must still be given to students' opportunity to learn (Linn, 1993), the knowledge and language demands of the task (Baker & O'Neil, 1994) and the criteria used for scoring (Linn, Baker, & Dunbar, 1991). Clearly, as with traditional forms of assessment, questions of fairness arise in the selection of tasks and in the grading of responses. Furthermore, the more informal and open-ended such assessment becomes, the greater the reliance on the judgment of the teacher/assessor. The strength of classroom assessments is that a broader range can be assessed than in a timed examination, increasing validity, while reliability may benefit from repeated assessments. A threat to reliability, however, may come from any bias in the teacher's judgment, either in the form of negative stereotyping or a 'halo' effect for favoured students. These may themselves reflect cultural attitudes about, for example, gender.

What we do know is that a broadening of assessment approaches will offer students alternative opportunities to demonstrate achievement if they are disadvantaged by any one particular assessment in a classroom or program. According to Linn (1992), '[m]ultiple indicators are essential so that those who are disadvantaged on one assessment have an opportunity to offer alternative evidence of their expertise' (p. 44).

Fairness and Validity

Our claim that fairness should be seen within a sociocultural frame rather than as a technical exercise mirrors, a shift that has taken place in developments around the concept of validity. In this section we claim that fairness should be embedded within validity arguments rather than treated as a separate and often 'add-on' concept. This is because current validity theorising incorporates concerns about fairness and bias, and reflects similar understandings of the social basis of assessment.

At the heart of the reformulation of validity is the move from treating it as a *fixed property* of an assessment to seeing it as *process* that investigates an assessment in terms of both the construct being assessed (how effectively it sampled the target domain) and, crucially, the inferences and actions based on the results. The 1999 United States *Standards for educational and psychological testing*[1] takes this approach:

> Validity refers to the degree to which evidence and theory support the interpretations of test scores entailed by proposed uses of tests. Validity is, therefore, the most fundamental consideration in developing and evaluating tests. (p. 9)

The importance of this for considerations of fairness and bias is that we cannot declare a test to be unfair or biased until we know what the purpose of the testing was and how the results were interpreted. Our argument that fairness is a sociocultural issue, rather than simply a technical one, is the same as the argument advanced for this understanding of validity. Validity is not simply the way in which a test functions, but depends on what it is used for and the interpretation and social consequences of the results. This was recognised by Samuel Messick in his seminal 1989 chapter:

> For a fully unified view of validity, it must also be recognised that the appropriateness, meaningfulness and usefulness of score-based inferences depend as well on the social consequences of the testing. Therefore, social values cannot be ignored in considerations of validity. (p. 19)

Incorporating Fairness Concerns into Validity Arguments

An essential part of validity is the concern with whether the inferences made from the results of an assessment are fair to all those who were assessed. If a test has sampled a domain in a way that benefits a particular group, then its validity is reduced, since the inferences drawn from the results may be misleading. As we have already seen, this is the error of assuming that a test is 'fair' because candidates sat the same test at the same time—without consideration of whether some candidates were privileged in terms of preparation for it. This may then be further compounded by the privileged candidates' interpretation of their performance in terms of merit and natural ability, so that their success can then be put down to merit rather than privilege—a Victorian line of reasoning that is still with us today (Stobart, 2008). Equity concerns about what precedes an assessment are therefore a part of the validation of the assessment. Validity enquiry must also involve construct validity and the interpretation and consequences of the results.

We provide three examples of validity enquiries that focus on fairness: large-scale assessments, test construction and teachers' assessments of their students.

---

[1] AERA, APA, & NCME (1999). *Standards for educational and psychological testing*. Washington, D.C.: AERA. Michael Kane's definitive chapter on validity in the 4th edition of *Educational measurement* (2006) takes a similar approach.

Example 1: Fairness in Large-Scale Multicultural Assessments

This example emphasises the role of construct validity by looking at the assumptions made about what is assessed. We take the position that there is no cultural neutrality in assessment or in the selection of what is to be assessed, and attempts to portray any assessment as 'acultural' are a mistake. Cumming (2000) observes that 'Acultural knowledge has definite cultural roots. This is knowledge that is privileged in our standards and testing procedures' (p. 4). She goes on to raise two key questions, which link with those in Table 6.1:

1. When setting standards and test content, are we really sure this is the knowledge we need?
2. Are we really privileging certain knowledges to maintain a dominant culture and in doing so ensuring perpetuation of ourselves, as people who have succeeded in the formal educational culture to date?

These concerns are central to fairness and validity. This line of reasoning has implications both for what is sampled in an assessment and how we interpret the results if we know some groups have been disadvantaged in both access and preparation. These are summarised in Table 6.1.

In every country, there will be examples of groups being disadvantaged in terms of access and preparation. For example, Meier (2000) has reported that in South Africa the teacher–learner ratio was 1:40 for black learners compared to 1:21 for whites. This was compounded by a shortage of qualified teachers in mathematics and science, which meant that many schools for black students did not even offer these subjects, even though they were part of the official curriculum. Mwachihi and Mbithi (2000) reported how in Kenya the introduction of 'cost sharing' has

Table 6.1 Access, curriculum and assessment questions in relation to equity and validity

Access questions	Curricular questions	Assessment questions
Who gets taught and by whom?	Whose knowledge is taught?	What knowledge is assessed and equated with achievement?
Are there differences in the resources available for different groups?	Why is it taught in a particular way to this particular group?	Are the form, content and mode of assessment appropriate for different groups and individuals?
What is incorporated from the cultures of those attending?	How do we enable the histories and cultures of people of colour, and of women, to be taught in responsible and responsive ways? (Apple, 1989)	Is this range of cultural knowledge reflected in definitions of achievement? How does cultural knowledge mediate individuals' responses to assessment in ways which alter the construct being assessed? (Gipps & Murphy, 1994)

Source: Stobart, 2005.

meant that schools now have to fund the purchase of books and other materials, leaving schools in poorer areas without adequate resources. This has been exacerbated by the introduction of a more complex, centrally devised curriculum that is deemed irrelevant to regional needs. In the United States, inequalities in access and preparation have been addressed through highly controversial 'affirmative action' approaches in which disadvantaged, but lower-scoring, students were given priority. This has been increasingly subject to legal challenge. This has been mirrored in England by prestigious universities such as Bristol offering admission to students in state schools in preference to some students from private schools, who may have had similar or better grades. There has been a considerable media backlash, stoked by parents who have paid for their children's education and who now see themselves as disadvantaged. In China, the disadvantages for rural minority groups have been recognised by setting differential pass standards on its Higher Education Entrance Examination (Zhao, 2000).

These examples illustrate how the validity concerns about how the results are interpreted meld with fairness concerns about what has gone on before the assessment itself and how results should be interpreted and acted upon.

Example 2: Fairness in Test Development

Equity concerns with access and preparation overlap with test development, even though fairness in test development has often been reduced to statistical consideration of bias in test items. Our argument is that simply seeking to minimise item bias is insufficient; tests take place in a social context and this needs consideration.

However, seeking to create tests that are as fair as possible to different groups is a necessary part of the process. The risk is that it may lead to a concern with presentational features rather than with which constructs are being sampled and how. This restricted view of bias is captured in the fairness section of *Standards for educational and psychological testing* (AERA, APA, & NCME, 1999):

> A full consideration of fairness would explore the many functions of testing in relation to its many goals, including the broad goal of achieving equality of opportunity in our society... The *Standards* cannot hope to deal adequately with all these broad issues... Rather the focus of the *Standards* is on those aspects of tests, testing and test use that are the customary responsibilities of those who make, use and interpret tests. (p. 73)

This is also reflected in the six Educational Testing Service (ETS) International Principles for Fairness Review of Assessments (2004):

Principle 1.	Treat people with respect in test materials.
Principle-2	Minimise the effects of construct-irrelevant knowledge or skills.
Principle-3	Avoid material that is unnecessarily controversial, inflammatory, offensive, or upsetting.
Principle-4	Use appropriate terminology to refer to people.
Principle-5	Avoid stereotypes.
Principle-6	Represent diversity in depictions of people.

Source: ETS, 2004.

In relation to validity, these are seeking to avoid what Messick (1989) called 'construct irrelevant variance', features that are likely to interfere with the assessment of a construct; in this case by distracting or upsetting a candidate or drawing on something culturally unfamiliar. We now look at some of the issues that have to be addressed within this more restricted approach to bias.

Test Bias

A test is biased if 'two individuals with equal ability (in the subject being tested) but from different groups do not have the same probability of success' (Shepard, Camilli, & Averill, 1981).

A cause of bias in a test could be that it was designed by one cultural group to reflect their own experience, and thus disadvantages test takers from other cultural groups, an accusation levelled at IQ tests. Thus, bias may be due to the content matter in a test, or lack of clarity in instructions, which leads to differential responses from different groups. Bias may also be due to scoring systems that do not credit appropriate or correct responses that are more typical of one group than the other.

Gould (1996) provides us with an extreme historical example of questions asked of newly arrived non-English speaking immigrants:

> Crisco is: patent medicine, disinfectant, toothpaste, food product;
> Christy Mathewson is famous as a: writer, artist, baseball player, comedian.

They also had to respond to verbal instructions such as:

> When I say 'go' make a figure 1 in the space which is in the circle but not in the triangle or square, and also make a figure 2 in the space which is in the triangle and circle but not in the square. Go.
>
>   (Gould, 1996, p. 230)

If we wish students to do well in tests/exams, we need to think about assessment that elicits an individual's best performance (after Nuttall, 1987). This may involve tasks that are concrete and within the experience of the student (an equal-access issue), presented clearly (the student must understand what is required of them if they are to perform well), relevant to the current concerns of the student (to engender motivation and engagement), and in conditions that are not threatening (to reduce stress and enhance performance) (Gipps, 1994).

We are now well aware that the form of assessment can differentially affect results for different groups. In England, there has been far more analysis of this in relation to gender than to ethnicity. We know that during compulsory schooling (up to 16 years) girls are likely to outperform boys on tasks that involve open-ended writing, particularly when this involves personal response. Even within multiple-choice tests, traditionally seen as favouring boys, there are differential response patterns. In the United States, Carlton (2000) has shown that in such tests, females perform better than males, matched for ability, on questions in which the content is a narrative or is in a humanities field and when the content deals with human relationships. As the context of an item grows longer the relative performance of females also improves. Males outperform females on questions relating to science, technical matters, sports, war or diplomacy. We also know that where examinations have a coursework (or essay) element, the performance of girls is likely to be more consistent, though the effect this has on final grades in English school-leaving exams has often been overstated (Elwood, 1995).

We know less about other aspects of the form of assessment, particularly in relation to ethnicity. For example, oral assessment plays little part in the examination system in England outside examining languages. Does the emphasis on written response disadvantage groups who place more emphasis on oral communication in their culture?

The existence of group differences in average performance on tests is often taken to imply that the tests are biased, the assumption being that one group is not inherently less able than the other. However, as we have argued, the two groups may well have been subject to different environmental experiences or unequal access to the curriculum. This difference will be reflected in group test scores, but the test is not, strictly speaking, biased.

One of the key statistical measures for identifying potential item bias in multiple-choice tests is the use of differential item functioning (DIF):

> A statistical measure related to fairness should be used, whenever sample sizes permit, as an empirical check on the fairness of questions. Statistical measures based on the way matched people in different groups perform on each test question, called differential item functioning or DIF, are preferred. DIF occurs when people in different groups perform in substantially different ways on a test question, even though they have very similar scores on the test. If DIF data are available, tests should be assembled following rules that keep DIF low.
>
> (ETS, 2004, p. 11)

While the intention with DIF is laudable, we have reservations about how this may undermine construct validity. The requirement should be to select assessment content *that accurately reflects the construct*, even if it produces gender/ethnic group differences, and to avoid content that is not relevant to the construct and that could affect such differences. This again takes us beyond a technical exercise to broader considerations in which different interests need to be recognised. It should also be noted there is nothing equivalent to DIF to guide construction of other forms of assessment, apart from professional judgment and examination of overall grades for different groups.

Example 3: The Fairness and Validity of Teachers' Informal Evaluations/Assessments

Fairness in assessment in the informal setting of the classroom can be both more difficult—because there are many complex issues for the teacher to consider— and more possible, since a range of assessment approaches is possible. It is more feasible for the teacher to offer, in the informal assessment setting, a range of assessment tasks and modes, an approach that supports fairness as we argued above. It is also more feasible to provide the situation that can elicit an individual's best performance, since it is under the teacher's control.

Referring back to our introductory espousal of a sociocultural stance, a crucial aspect of this approach to assessment includes allowing students the tools to help them show what they can do, and arguably the most important tool is the teacher. In classroom-based assessment, there is opportunity for teacher and students to clarify/discuss the objective being assessed, how it might be assessed and what counts as success or mastery. Such an approach brings the student into a more active role in the learning process and helps to build self-evaluation and meta-cognitive skills and is thus good learning practice (Black & Wiliam, 2006; Edwards, 2005; Pryor & Crossouard, 2008). Through this, students from a range of backgrounds also have the chance to have their strengths and understandings recognised. This undeniably places demands on the teacher, and staff development may be required to ensure that the teacher is open to such new interpretations and, indeed, relationships. Thus, the developing corpus of work on sociocultural approaches to assessment has implications for fairness, although these implications have not been explicitly addressed.

However, teachers' informal assessment is, to a certain extent justifiably, perceived as being unreliable and biased (Harlen, 2004). This is often to do with lack of clarity, and variability, in standards or criteria. It is possible to improve the consistency of teachers' assessments through: providing clear criteria, training teachers to assess against these, and supporting the process with moderation of judgments via discussion (ARG, 2006).

It is also possible that teachers' cultural values could lead to bias in the assessment. These may themselves reflect cultural attitudes about, for example, gender, with research showing that in the United Kingdom noisy young boys are more likely to be marked down by teachers (Harlen, 2004). Baker & O'Neil (1994) also showed how the use of portfolios, regarded by their advocates as a progressive move towards authentic assessment, were viewed by some minority groups in the United States as a white, middle-class activity which disadvantaged those with fewer resources and opportunities.

In relation to the curriculum offered and opportunity to learn, there is another inconvenient fact: teacher expectation can affect the curriculum and learning experiences offered to children. There is clear evidence that teachers offer a different curriculum to children for whom they hold low and high expectations (Harlen, 2004; Tizard, Blatchford, Burke, Farquhar, & Plewis, 1988; Troman, 1988). This is pertinent to the equal-access issue.

Conclusion

Fairness is both essential and elusive. It is the appeal to fairness that has made educational 'measurement' a pivotal part of most cultures. We have argued that different groups being allowed to sit, and be judged by, the same test is a simplistic view. Fairness needs to be linked to equality of opportunity, which includes access to similar resources and curricular opportunities. The more familiar, and narrower, discussion of bias in testing is only a small part of this.

The challenge for 21st-century assessment is to broaden our views of fairness to take fuller account of social and cultural contexts. The temptation, however, is to back away from the larger social issues because they are difficult, and to concentrate on the assessment itself, for example, in relation to bias. Just as the theorising of validity has moved from it being a property of a test to a process based on how the results are interpreted, we can envisage a move to the discussion of fairness focusing on the inferences made about the results and the impact of these. So we move away from talking about a biased test to talking about interpreting the results in a way that is fair to all the groups taking the assessment. The debates around positive discrimination and allowing for disadvantage would be a part of this.

We will never achieve fair assessment, but we can make it fairer: The best defence against inequitable assessment is openness. Openness about design, constructs and scoring and grading will bring out into the open the values and biases of the test design process, offer an opportunity for debate about cultural and social influences and open up the relationship between assessor and learner. These developments are possible, but they do require political will.

References

AERA, APA, & NCME (American Educational Research Association, American Psychological Association, & National Council on Measurement in Education). (1999). *Standards for educational and psychological testing*. American Educational Research Association: Washington, DC: AERA.

Apple, M. W. (1989). How equality has been redefined in the Conservative restoration. In W. Secada (Ed.), *Equity and Education*. New York: Falmer Press.

Assessment Reform Group (ARG). (2006). *The role of teachers in the assessment of learning*. Assessment Reform Group pamphlet. See also ARG website at <www.assessment-reform-group-org>.

Baker, E., & O'Neil, H. (1994). Performance assessment and equity: A view from the USA. *Assessment in Education, 1*(1), 11–26.

Black, P., & Wiliam, D. (2006). Developing a theory of formative assessment. In J. Gardner (Ed.), *Assessment and learning* (pp. 81–100). London: Sage.

Broadfoot, P. (1979). *Assessment, schools and society*. London: Methuen.

Carlton, S. T. (2000). *Contextual factors in group differences in assessment*. Paper presented at 26th IAEA Conference, Jerusalem.

Cobb, P. (1994). Where is the mind? *Educational Researcher, 23*(7), 13–20.

Cumming, J. (2000). *After DIF, What culture remains?* 26th IAEA Conference, Jerusalem.

Edwards, A. (2005). Let's get beyond community and practice: The many meanings of learning by participating. *The Curriculum Journal, 16*(1), 49–65.

Elwood, J. (1995). Undermining gender stereotypes: Examination and coursework performance in the UK at 16. *Assessment in Education, 2*(3), 283–303.

Educational Testing Service (ETS). (2004). *ETS International principles for fairness review of assessments*. Princeton NJ: Author.

Gardner, J., & Cowan, P. (2005). The fallibility of high stakes '11-Plus' testing in Northern Ireland. *Assessment in Education: Principles, Policy and Practice, 12*, 145–165.

Gipps, C. (1994). *Beyond testing, towards a theory of educational assessment*. London: Falmer Press.

Gipps, C. (1999). Sociocultural aspects of assessment. *Review of Research in Education, 24*, 357–392.

Gipps, C., & Murphy, P. (1994). *A fair test? Assessment, achievement and equity*. Buckingham: Open University Press.

Glaser, R. (1963). Instructional technology and the measurement of learning outcomes: Some questions. *American Psychologist, 18*, 519–521.

Glaser, R., & Silver, E. (1994). Assessment, testing, and instruction: Retrospect and prospect. In L. Darling-Hammond (Ed.), *Review of research in education* (pp. 393–419). Washington, DC: American Educational Research Association.

Gould, S. J. (1996). *The mismeasure of man*. New York: Norton.

Hanson, F. A. (1993). *Testing: Social consequences of the examined life*. Berkeley: University of California Press.

Harlen, W. (2004). *A systematic review of the evidence of reliability and validity of assessment teachers use for summative purposes*. In *Research evidence in education library* Issue 3, London: EPPI-Centre, Social Science Research Unit, Institute of Education. Retrieved April 4, 2007, from http://eppi.ioe.ac.uk/EPPIWeb/home.aspx?page=/reel/review_groups/assessment/review_three.htm.

Linn, M. C. (1992). Gender differences in educational achievement. In J. Pfleiderer (Ed.), *Sex equity in educational opportunity, achievement and testing*. Princeton, NJ: Educational Testing Service.

Linn, R. L. (1993). Educational assessment: Expanded expectations and challenges. *Educational Evaluation and Policy Analysis, 15*, 1.

Linn, R. L., Baker, E., & Dunbar, S. (1991). Complex, performance based assessment: Expectations and validation criteria. *Educational Researcher, 20*(8), 15–21.

Madaus, G. F., & Raczek, A. E. (1996). The extent and growth of educational testing in the United States: 1956–1994. In H. Goldstein (Ed.), *Assessment: Problems, developments and statistical issues*. Chichester: John Wiley & Sons.

Meier, C. (2000). The influence of educational opportunities on assessment results in a multicultural South Africa, Paper presented at the 26th IAEA Conference, Jerusalem.

Messick, S. (1989). Validity. In R. L. Linn (Ed.), *Educational measurement* (3rd ed., pp. 13–103). New York, NY: American Council on Education and Macmillan.

Mwachihi, J. M., & Mbithi, M. J. 2000. Assessment and equity assurance in the Kenyan multicultural background, Paper presented at 26th IAEA Conference, Jerusalem.

Nuttall, D. (1987). The validity of assessments. *European Journal of Psychology of Education, 11*(2), 109–118.

Penuel, W., & Wertsch, J. (1995). Vygotsky and identity formation: A sociocultural approach. *Educational Psychologist, 30*(2), 83–92.

Pryor, J., & Crossouard, B. (2008). A socio-cultural theorisation of formative assessment. *Oxford Review of Education 2007, 34*(1), 1–20.

Ryan, A. M. (2008). *From child study to efficiency: The use of testing in the Chicago public schools, 1899 to 1928*. Paper presented at the American Research Association's Annual Meeting, New York.

Secada, W. G. (1989). Educational equity versus equality of education: An alternative conception. In W. G. Secada (Ed.), *Equity and education*. New York: Falmer Press.

Shepard, L., Camilli, G., & Averill, M. (1981). Comparison of procedures for detecting test item bias with both internal and external ability criteria. *Journal of Educational Statistics, 6*, 317–375.

Stobart, G. (2008). *Testing times: The uses and abuses of assessment*. London & New York: Routledge.

Stobart, G. (2005). Fairness in multicultural assessment systems. *Assessment in Education, 12*(3), 275–287.

Stoskopf, A. (2008). Sowing grain and cultivating roses: IQ testing and educational reform in the Boston public schools, 1910–1932. Paper presented at the American Research Association's Annual Meeting, New York.

Sutherland, G. (1996). Assessment: Some historical perspectives. In H. Goldstein (Ed.), *Assessment: Problems, developments and statistical issues*. Chichester: John Wiley.

Tizard, B., Blatchford, P., Burke, J., Farquhar, C., & Plewis, I. (1988). *Young children at school in the inner city*. Hove: Lawrence Erlbaum Associates.

Troman, G. (1988). Getting it right: Selection and setting in a 9–13 middle school. *British Journal of Sociology of Education, 9*(4), 402–422.

Wolf, D., Bixby, J., Glenn, J., & Gardner, H. (1991). To use their minds well: Investigating new forms of student assessment. *Review of Research in Education, 17*, 31–74.

Wood, R. (1987). *Measurement and assessment in education and psychology*. London: Falmer Press.

Zhao, H. (2000). *The minority nationality related issues in China public examinations*. Paper presented at the 26th IAEA Conference, Jerusalem.

Chapter 7
Assessment, Gender and In/Equity

Susan M. Brookhart

Introduction

This chapter examines how males and females perform on different types of assessment tasks and in different disciplines. The focus is on assessment tasks that indicate students' levels of achievement in the academic disciplines taught in school: reading/language arts, mathematics, science and social studies. The population of interest is school-aged children. Three sections develop a line of inquiry based on questions. First, are there gender differences in achievement? If so, what might they mean? And does the assessment process itself contribute to creating them? The approach taken here is to examine large-scale national and international studies of achievement, using, when possible, standardised measures of effect sizes. This book presents international perspectives on student achievement, and thus this chapter aims to report gender issues across national borders. It relies on studies where achievement outcomes were measured with different assessments. Standardised measures are required in order to make valid comparisons from country to country and from assessment to assessment. Classroom processes, including classroom assessment, are the most important aspects of schooling, and the classroom is the source of achievement measured by standardised tests. However, studies of classroom assessments were not used in this review because of the chapter's purpose. The theoretical and methodological discussions at the end of the chapter describe in detail the methodological choices.

Are There Gender Differences in Achievement?

In a discussion of assessment and gender, the first and obvious question that must be dealt with is: Does student achievement differ by gender? If the answer to that question is no, then follow-up questions become moot. If the answer is yes, then it is

S.M. Brookhart (✉)
Duquesne University, Helena, MT, USA
e-mail: susanbrookhart@bresnan.net

C. Wyatt-Smith, J.J. Cumming (eds.), *Educational Assessment in the 21st Century*,
DOI 10.1007/978-1-4020-9964-9_7, © Springer Science+Business Media B.V. 2009

important to describe the differences and ask how educators and others have interpreted their meaning. This chapter begins with a brief review of studies investigating gender differences in achievement on standardised tests.

Reading and Language Arts

The Organisation for Economic Co-operation and Development (OECD) began its Programme for International Student Assessment (PISA) in 1997, in an effort to collect internationally comparable information about student performance and related student, family and institutional factors that could inform policy making. The first PISA survey assessment was conducted in 2000. There was another PISA survey in 2003, and one in 2006. The 2006 survey included data from 30 OECD member countries and 27 partner countries.

Gender differences in reading have been evident in all three PISA surveys (OECD, 2007). In the 2006 PISA survey, gender differences in reading, favouring females, existed in every country. These differences were between 20 and 57 points, averaging 38 points. The overall standard deviation in reading is 99, so the effect sizes of these differences are between 0.20 and 0.58, averaging 0.38, which puts them in the 'small-' to 'medium-effect-size' range (Cohen, 1988). The difference was found in every country surveyed. The 2006 PISA reading data from the United States were not used in the analysis because of an error in printing the reading test booklets, so there were 56 countries with reading data and 56 countries with a gender gap in reading, favouring girls.

In the United States, the National Assessment of Educational Progress (NAEP) is the only nationally representative, ongoing study of student achievement. NAEP measures reading comprehension by asking students to read passages and answer questions about what they have read. NAEP data, like the PISA data internationally, find a consistent gender gap in reading, favouring girls. Klecker (2006) analysed NAEP reading data for the public school samples from 1992, 1994, 1998, 2002 and 2003. Effect sizes were small in 4th grade (0.13–0.27) and small to moderate in 8th grade (0.27–0.43) and 12th grade (0.22–0.44). The 2007 NAEP data (Institute of Education Sciences, 2007) also show females outscoring males in reading by 7 points (effect size of approximately 0.20) in 4th grade and by 10 points (effect size of approximately 0.29) in 8th grade, continuing the same pattern.

Lietz (2006) studied gender differences in reading across English and non-English speaking countries. Her stated research purpose was to use modern statistical techniques (meta-analysis and hierarchical linear modelling) to address the question of gender differences in reading in order to address conflicting reports in the literature, much of which reported that girls out-performed boys in reading, but some of which did not. Her meta-analysis included 139 effect sizes from various studies of secondary school reading achievement between 1970 and 2003, including the International Association for the Evaluation of Educational Achievement (IEA) Reading Comprehension Study (1970–1971) and Reading Literacy Study (1990–1991), PISA 2000, NAEP 1992–2003, a number of national studies in Australia over the period 1975–2002 and other published studies. The overall grand mean was an effect size of 0.19, a small effect that meant girls outscored boys overall. Gender differences were most pronounced in PISA, followed by the Australian assessment programs and NAEP. The effect for gender held whether English was the language of test administration or not, and the effect for gender did not increase or decrease with age. There was also some unexplained variance, which meant the predictors used did not completely explain differences in effect sizes among the studies.

Mathematics

The literature on gender differences in mathematics is more variable than findings about gender differences in reading and language arts. Many authors report that boys perform better than girls in mathematics, and cite some literature to support that in literature reviews preceding their own studies of the matter. However, differences between the genders on mathematics achievement are small, when they do exist, are not consistent among countries and often are washed out with between-country differences. Thus, the cultural argument—that differences in performance when they exist are most likely due to differences in curriculum, instruction, opportunity to learn, and cultural, political or social factors—is easily supported for mathematics.

In the 2006 PISA survey in mathematics, there were smaller gender differences than in reading, favouring males. Males outperformed females in some countries, but not by much, with an average 11-point difference (effect size 0.12). In Qatar, however, females outperformed males in mathematics (OECD, 2007). Based on previous PISA research, the OECD used a cultural and economic argument to explain the differences, most notably that the tendency of males to outscore females in mathematics is mitigated by the tendency for females to attend higher performing school programs (OECD, 2007, p. 324).

This conclusion (about the effect of school program) is reinforced by a comparison made in PISA 2003, when PISA also measured student performance in problem solving, reported in *Problem Solving For Tomorrow's World: First Measures of Cross-curricular Competencies* from PISA 2003 (OECD, 2004). This suggested that males and females perform roughly equally in analytical reasoning skills, which also form one component of mathematics tasks. The gender differences in mathematics appeared to correspond to the contexts in which tasks are embedded at school, rather than to the underlying mathematical reasoning skills.

Beller and Gafni (1996) compared the performance of 9- and 13-year olds in 14 and 20 countries, respectively, on the mathematics and science portions of the second International Assessment of Educational Progress, with data collected in 1991. Consistent with other studies reviewed, they found effect sizes (corrected for attenuation due to unreliability) of 0.05 and 0.12 for 9- and 13-year olds, respectively, for mathematics overall performance and 0.17 and 0.30 for 9- and 13-year olds, respectively, for science overall performance. The same trends were found within countries, but with some differences in the magnitude of the differences.

Ethington (1990) analysed data from the 1981–1982 Second International Mathematics Study (SIMS). She used median polishing, an exploratory data analysis method that does not require a priori hypotheses. Largest differences in medians were associated with country. The effects of gender were small and went both ways. The largest gender effect favouring females was an expectation of 1.5 percentage point better score on fractions, and the largest effect favouring males was an expectation of 1.5 percentage point better score on geometry. However, there were interaction effects between country and gender; for example, there was more of an effect against girls in France and in favour of girls in Thailand.

Science

In addition to reading and mathematics, PISA 2006 also studied science performance. In the combined science scale, most of the 57 countries (30 OECD and 27 partner countries) had no significant differences. Among the 14 that did show significant differences, only four of those differences had an effect size of 0.20 (a 'small' effect) or greater, three countries favouring females (Jordan, Qatar and Thailand) and one favouring males (Chile). Similarly, there were not many countries with gender differences on a 'general interest in science' scale, and those differences were mixed (some favouring boys and some girls). OECD (2007, p. 163) concluded that there were no entrenched performance differences by gender, but there were gender differences in attitudes towards science, and these differences varied by country.

For example, in many countries there were differences favouring girls on scales measuring 'identifying scientific issues' and 'level of concern for environmental issues' and differences favouring boys on 'self-confidence in science'. Other scales measuring science attitudes produced mixed results for gender. Looking across attitude scales, PISA 2006 identified countries in which males had higher average scores on at least five attitude scales: Germany, Iceland, Japan, Korea, the Netherlands, the United Kingdom, Chinese Taipei, Hong Kong-China and Macao-China—although in Iceland, Germany and the Netherlands, females also had at least one higher-than-average attitude scale ('concern for environmental issues' or 'responsibility for sustainable development') than males, as well. Even though there were few differences in science achievement, gender differences in science attitudes were of concern because of their potential effects on future education and career choices.

Multiple Subjects

Some studies have looked at gender differences across subjects. This section reviews results from just a few. The selection of studies is intended to be illustrative, not exhaustive. Like the PISA project, these studies have assessed achievement in school subjects by school-aged students.

Nowell and Hedges (1998) looked at seven surveys of 12th-grade student achievement in the United States from 1960 through to 1992, plus the 1971–1994 National

Assessment of Educational Progress, in multiple subjects (reading, mathematics, science and writing in all surveys including NAEP, plus vocabulary and perceptual speed subtests in some of the other surveys). An important feature of their study is that they examined differences in means, variances and extreme scores. Differences in means and variances were small, while differences in extreme scores were sometimes substantial. Writing produced the largest mean differences (moderate effect sizes of 0.48–0.61, favouring females). Females also outperformed males in reading (small effect sizes of 0.00–0.30). Males outperformed females, on average, in science (small-to-moderate effect sizes, 0.22–0.51) and mathematics (mostly small effects, and a few moderate, 0.09–0.40).

Nowell and Hedges (1998) also did a trend analysis and concluded that the gender differences have not changed significantly over time, with the exception of NAEP science scores and non-NAEP mathematics scores, both in the direction of closing the gender gap somewhat. Nowell and Hedges also analysed variances; in almost all samples, males' performance was more variable than females. They also analysed the proportions of males and females in the extremes of score distributions and found that males were over-represented in the upper tails of score distributions for mathematics, science and survey composite scales. Females were over-represented in the upper ends of reading, vocabulary and perceptual speed, but to a lesser degree than was the case for males in mathematics, science and composites.

Sammons (1995) used hierarchical linear modelling to study gender, ethnic and socio-economic differences in student achievement on Britain's 'School Matters' student cohort, which followed students over the period 1980–1984 as they progressed through public examinations in years 3, 5 and 6 (transfer to secondary school), and then checked their performance on the General Certificate of Secondary Education in 1989 (GCSE, for year 11 students). The statistical modelling technique allowed the effects of background characteristics to be estimated as net effects, with other background and school membership characteristics controlled. Gender differences (favouring girls) were found in reading but not in mathematics in year 3, and in both reading and mathematics (favouring girls in both subjects, although the mathematics effect was smaller) for year 5, and gender helped predict mathematics progress (but not reading progress) between these years. However, socio-economic effects were larger than gender effects. By the time of GCSE, in year 11, gender effects still favoured girls but socio-economic effects were still stronger than gender effects. Sammons (1995) noted that the junior school tests were not multiple choice and that the GCSE included course work.

DeLisle, Smith, and Jules (2005) studied primary school achievement as measured by the 2004 national examinations for standard 1 (7–8-year olds) and standard 3 (9–10-year olds) and by the 2003 Secondary Entrance Assessment (11–12-year olds) in Trinidad and Tobago. They found that girls had an advantage across all assessments at different grade levels on both language and mathematics, but the gap was very small in mathematics—not of practical significance—and decreased at higher-grade levels. Girls had larger advantages in language arts and creative writing, some of which DeLisle et al. (2005) judged to be practically significant. Girls' advantage in language arts was most evident for pupils in lower-ability groups, higher-grade levels and rural educational districts. In answer to their title question, 'Which males and females are most at risk and on what?' therefore, they pointed out that not all boys but rather boys who were doing poorly at school overall and who lived in rural areas in Trinidad and Tobago were the at-risk students.

In the United States, many high school students take one of two voluntary college admission tests (the ACT® and the SAT®) to include with their college applications. While this results in a self-selected sample, interest in potential gender differences on these tests runs high because of the potential implications for students' college admission and future study.

The ACT® test covers English, mathematics, reading and science, and reports a composite score. For the ACT®, the popular belief had been that boys outscored girls (male ACT® composite average was about 0.2 points higher than females for 1999–2004; ACT, 2005). ACT's (2005) analysis of two states that had adopted the ACT as part of required state assessment for all students showed that the male score advantage was a result of self-selection. The gap changed directions (to a 0.1- and 0.2-point advantage for the girls in the two states, respectively) for the states in which all students took the ACT®. These score differentials are tiny and, ACT (2005) concluded, not of practical significance.

Coley (2001) wrote an analysis of gender and racial/ethnic differences in achievement for Educational Testing Service, publisher of the SAT®. He found that black college-bound seniors were the only group in which girls scored higher than boys on the SAT® I Verbal Test. On the SAT® I Mathematics Test, boys in all racial/ethnic groups scored higher than girls. More girls than boys took Advanced Placement (AP) exams; these are challenging exams that can earn students course credit in college, typically by scoring a 3 or better on a 5-point scale. Among students who scored in this range, there were few differences in the percentage of males and females on the AP Literature and Composition Examination. However, a higher percentage of boys than girls scored in this range on the AP Biology or AP Calculus AB Examination.

Conclusions Across Subjects

The results of these studies suggest that the answer to the question, 'Are there gender differences in achievement?' is 'Yes and no'. There does appear to be a rather robust 'gender gap', favouring girls, in language arts in most countries, with effect sizes reported in the small-to-medium range. However, in other subjects, there may or may not be differences, depending on the country. Gender differences in achievement tend to be small in comparison with socio-economic differences, with racial/ethnic differences in some countries, and with differences between countries. Some countries, for example, have gender differences favouring boys in mathematics, and some do not.

A notable point from the PISA study is that patterns of variability are more dramatic than mean differences. There was more variation in gender gap size between schools in any one country than between countries. Also, within-country variance was greater than between-country variance (OECD, 2007). This means that, whatever differences were apparent in aggregated data, individual boys and girls, and individual schools, may be very different from the average. This also means that, even where gender differences exist, gender explains at most a small part of student performance.

What Do Gender Differences in Achievement Mean?

Having established that there are gender differences at least in language arts achievement, the next logical question is what those differences mean. Is there a 'gender gap' sizable enough to be of practical significance? What causes this gap? Can results be altered by changes in policy or educational program?

What Are the Different Stances on This Issue?

Interpreting whether the gender gap is of practical significance, and, if so, what to do about it, reflects the interpreter's theoretical stance in philosophy, sociology, psychology, economics and politics. The two basic divisions are between 'nature' and 'nurture' stances, the former privileging biological differences as explanations and the latter privileging culture, upbringing, education and experience (Francis & Skelton, 2005).

What Is the Author's Bias with Regard to the Meaning of Gender Differences in Achievement?

'Nature' and 'nurture' are not mutually exclusive, and I do not believe that biological or cultural differences are necessarily 'bad', either. Various cultures have developed to make sense of the world and life in it. No true experimental manipulations can be done—researchers cannot 'assign' students to cultures or genders. However, a gender effect across cultures is more supportive of biologically based explanations, whereas variation in gender effects between cultures is more supportive of culture- and experience-based explanations.

For the purpose of interpreting assessment results, it is important to consider what constructs the assessments were designed to measure. I subscribe to the view that true learning implies the ability to use knowledge. Thus, I find evidence from the PISA assessments more persuasive than, for example, basic skills tests, because PISA took a 'literacy' approach to the constructs measured by the assessments. Reading literacy was defined in PISA as understanding and using written material in order to develop one's knowledge and potential. Similarly, PISA measured mathematical literacy as the ability to analyse, reason and communicate as they solve mathematical problems. Scientific literacy, a focus for PISA 2006, was measured as the ability to understand and use science concepts and to think scientifically about evidence (OECD, 2007).

Two other points about my approach combine both assessment and methodological concerns. As an educator, I believe that relative comparisons ('Who outscored whom?') are less important than change over time ('What progress is being made?'). I also believe that relative comparisons are less important than descriptions of performance capabilities: the answer to the question 'Who is better, boys or girls?' is less important than the answer to 'What can boys and girls do now?' and 'What else could they be expected to do next?' Relative comparisons are not as useful for making instructional improvements as information about progress and performance.

These theoretical and methodological stances contribute to the discussion in this chapter. Another reader might draw somewhat different conclusions from the same studies.

How Can Knowledge of Gender Differences in Achievement Help Inform the Assessment Process?

Francis and Skelton (2005) pointed out that different countries have responded to the 'gender gap' news with different levels of alarm, and with different educational policies. Australia and the United Kingdom, for example, reacted with policy documents about gender equity that were concerned in particular with the 'underachievement' of boys. Australia, especially, has been noted for its strong policy documents arguing for the education of boys in 1997 (*Gender Equity: A framework for Australia's schools*) and 2002 (*Boys: Getting it right. Report into the Inquiry of Education of Boys*).

In the United States, however, the 2001 *No Child Left Behind* legislation has focused on equity among groups based on ethnicity, socio-economic status, student-disability status and English-proficiency status. Schools must report student achievement data disaggregated according to these groups, but not gender.

Some researchers have intentionally addressed issues of interpretation in their research questions, study designs and discussion of results. Robertson (2005) presented results of a series of international surveys and the Scottish Assessment of Achievement Programme (AAP) that showed a small but statistically significant gender gap in mathematics, favouring boys especially in some sub-domains. In 1988, girls were better at whole-number arithmetic but boys were better at measurement, area, and some other sub-domains, depending on age. By the early 1990s and continuing to 2000, differences had disappeared. Robertson (2005) interpreted this closing of the gap in terms of government and school policy changes.

Duffy, Gunther, and Walters (1997) examined gender differences in mathematical problem solving, and interpreted their results as supporting the socialisation or 'nurture' (as opposed to the biological or 'nature') explanation. They measured attitudes towards mathematics as well as problem solving. They found a complex relationship between gender and mathematics: there were no systematic gender differences on one test (GAUSS) but there were on another (CTBS), overall and among the top 10 per cent in ability. Content experts, however, rated the GAUSS questions as being more abstract and difficult. Attitudes predicted performance on testing at one occasion but not at another. The authors reasoned that, if biological differences were the explanation for mathematics performance difference, there would have been gender differences in performance on both tests.

Another study took a developmental approach. DeFraine, Van Damme, and Onghena (2007) studied the relationship between academic self-concept and achievement in Dutch, in Flemish students (Flanders is the Dutch-speaking part of Belgium). Changes in self-concept and achievement were not related, although there was a positive relation between self-concept and achievement. In secondary school self-concept declined, faster for girls than boys, and achievement rose for girls but dipped and then rose for boys. Achievement was high overall in Flemish-speaking schools in Flanders. These developmental changes are more congruent with a sociological than a biological explanation because they are situated in students' educational experiences.

What Is Known About Gender Differences in Assessment Development?

This section focuses on whether assessments themselves—differences in assessment design, development, administration and use—could be responsible for observed gender differences. Some studies have attempted to address aspects of assessment hypothesised to explain part of the gender gap. These have mostly focused on questions of assessment format, usually with the hypothesis that girls will do better on performance assessment and problem-solving tasks (variously theorised to be because of their more interactive nature or because of their language components) than on traditionally formatted tests and basic skills questions. Willingham and Cole (1997) and their contributing authors published a landmark review of these issues. The literature they reviewed did not make a compelling case that any of the assessment aspects studied provided major explanations for gender differences. The results of more recent studies have not changed that conclusion.

Efforts to Remove Gender Bias During Assessment Development

Professional standards for test developers require that they try to prevent differences by gender and any other categories that should be irrelevant to the construct to be measured. For example, in the United States the *Code of Fair Testing Practices in Education* (Joint Committee on Testing Practices, 2004) states that test developers should 'obtain and provide evidence on the performance of test takers of diverse subgroups, making significant efforts to obtain sample sizes that are adequate for subgroup analyses. Evaluate the evidence to ensure that differences in performance are related to the skills being assessed'.

In the *Standards for Educational and Psychological Testing* (American Educational Research Association, American Psychological Association, & National Council on Measurement in Education, 1999), Section "Test Administration and Test-Takers' Behaviour" is devoted to 'Fairness in Testing and Test Use'. The introduction to the section points out that there are many definitions of 'fairness' in testing, including lack of bias, equitable treatment in test administration, equality of outcomes and opportunity to learn. Bias, on the other hand, refers to 'construct-irrelevant components that result in systematically lower or higher scores for identifiable groups of examinees' (p. 76). To use an extreme hypothetical example to illustrate, if in some country girls were allowed to go to school but boys were not, and gender differences in achievement were noted, that would not be 'fair' in the sense that girls and boys did not have equal opportunity to learn, but it would not necessarily mean the test was biased. The test might be measuring real differences in achievement in a valid manner.

At the item-development stage in test construction, sensitivity reviews typically have panels of experts to review item content. Items that are offensive or that conceptually seem to favour one group over another are edited or discarded. At the pilot testing stage, empirical data are reviewed for evidence of construct-irrelevant bias. The term 'differential item functioning' (DIF) analysis is used for methods that statistically compare performance between reference and focal groups of students. DIF methods hold achievement constant; for instance, a gender DIF analysis would compare performance on a given item between boys and girls at the same achievement level. Many statistical methods are available to study DIF. There are methods by which to evaluate DIF for both multiple-choice or other right/wrong items and for multi-point items or tasks. DIF analysis is used routinely in the preparation of large-scale tests. Sometimes, validity evidence offered for tests also includes studies designed to test for differential prediction; for example, if a test score was a better predictor of grades or other future achievement scores for girls than for boys.

Therefore, the reader should not expect this section to find major assessment effects that are large enough to explain gender differences in achievement. Standard procedures require reviews, conceptually at the item development and review stage and empirically at the pilot-testing stage, that are designed to prevent construct-irrelevant gender differences in assessment items or tasks.

The following sections summarise what is known about gender differences in various aspects of the assessment process. Readers who would like more detail should consult Willingham and Cole's (1997) book-length review of this topic.

Choice of Construct and Test Content

Content of multiple-choice items. Can the content of multiple-choice items affect girls' and boys' performance differently? Bridgeman and Schmitt (1997) reviewed exploratory studies of gender DIF conducted before such analyses became a routine part of test development. They concluded that these early DIF studies supported the finding that items with content about human relationships or aesthetics/philosophy were differentially easier for females and that items with science-related content and specialised terminology were differentially easier for males. In mathematics, algebra items were differentially easier for females and geometry items were differentially easier for males. Abstract, pure mathematics problems were differentially easier for females, and mathematics word problems were differentially easier for males. As an example of the use of specialised terminology, Bridgeman and Schmitt (1997) used an item from one of the studies they reviewed (Curley & Schmitt, 1993, cited in Bridgeman & Schmitt, 1997). The analogy 'vortex:water::' with the correct answer choice 'tornado:air' was differentially more difficult for females. Changing the item stem to 'whirlpool:water::' removed the gender DIF and also made the item easier overall.

Because current practice specifies the routine use of DIF analyses in test development, DIF analyses conducted now with operational tests would not find much in the way of gender differences. Potentially biased items are discarded before test forms are finalised. In addition, analyses at the item level are instructive, but not the whole picture. Total test (or subtest) scores rely on sets of items that represent the construct of interest in a balanced manner.

Content of essay prompts. Perhaps test items that require students to write could have more of an effect than multiple-choice items. Can the content of essay prompts affect girls' and boys' performance differently? Breland and Lee (2007) studied gender differences in scores from the computer-based Test of English as a Foreign Language (TOEFL®-CBT) essay prompts from 1998 to 2000. A total of 87 different essay prompts were studied. While many of the prompts had significant gender DIF, none of the effect sizes were large enough to be characterised as having an important group effect. The mean effect size across prompts was –0.13, favouring girls.

Bridgeman and Schmitt (1997) studied gender differences in performance on the 1993 and 1994 Advanced Placement (AP) U.S. History and Biology Examinations in the United States. They found mean gender differences on some but not all of the essay questions (absolute value of effect sizes ranged from 0.00 to 0.21), although the differences were smaller than for the multiple-choice questions on the same exams. In U.S. History, what differences there were favoured girls in 1993 and boys in 1994, while in biology, they favoured boys in both years. Identifying the content of specific essay prompts that contributed to gender differences in AP examination performance is difficult, however, because students are allowed some choice about which essay they answer. Unlike DIF analyses, analyses of mean differences do not control for the achievement level of the students on the construct of interest, so if the essay prompts were each answered by somewhat different students, comparison is problematic. Bridgeman and Schmitt (1997) concluded by pointing out that in this situation, the optimal solution is to make sure to offer balanced choices for students.

Types of Assessment Items and Tasks

Can the format of an assessment affect girls' and boys' performance differently? This question has been studied in several ways. Some researchers have examined gender differences between multiple-choice and constructed-response test items. Others have examined gender differences between tests and performance assessments.

Multiple-choice versus constructed-response items. Willingham and Cole (1997) reviewed studies testing for format effects between multiple-choice and constructed-response test items. Constructed-response test items ask students to formulate their own answer to a test question; multiple-choice items ask students to select an answer from a list of options. Neither of these formats is an extended-performance assessment task. Willingham and Cole (1997) reviewed 12 studies that looked at whether multiple-choice and constructed-response test items measured the same construct and whether format differences were associated with gender differences. None of the studies that looked for gender differences by format found them, and most of the studies that looked for construct differences did not find them, either. They concluded (Willingham & Cole, 1997, p. 276) that available evidence did not support the hypothesis that multiple-choice format per se was a significant source of gender differences in test results.

More recently, DeMars (1998) studied performance on the mathematics and science sections of the state of Michigan's High School Proficiency Test in the United States. DeMars was interested in whether gender differences would appear between the two item formats used on the test: multiple-choice and constructed-response. There was no gender-by-format interaction on the mathematics test, and only a small interaction in science. When scores from only the top five per cent of students were used for analysis, males scored higher on the multiple-choice sections and females on the constructed-response sections (except for one form of the mathematics test, males still outscored females on the constructed-response section, but by a smaller margin than for the multiple-choice section). However, these differences were small, and in summary, DeMars (1998) did not judge any of the differences found to be of practical significance.

Tests versus performance assessments. If format-of-test items do not contribute to gender differences, what about tests versus more extended performance assessments? Performance assessments require observation and judgment of students' processes as they do tasks, and/or observation of products students create. Performance assessments take place over extended periods of time, are often complex and employ a degree of student choice.

Cox (2000) studied gender and urban/rural differences on student performance in the 1992 dataset of Common Assessment Tasks (CATs) for the Victorian Certificate of Education in Australia. There were four CATs: two were long-term performance assessments and two were more traditional examinations, one multiple-choice and one short-answer. Each CAT measured six subjects within mathematics curriculum for year 12 students (for example, space and number). For most subjects, girls outperformed boys on the two long-term performance assessments, and boys outperformed girls on the examinations. The hypothesis that girls are better with language was advanced as an explanation. The performance tasks required written work. In addition, the performance tasks allowed for drafts to be shared with teachers, and the authors hypothesised that girls might be more willing to submit to feedback and pay attention to it. For the authors of the study, the urban/rural effect was equally troubling (city students had an advantage over rural students for many of the subjects and tasks).

Woodfield, Earl-Novell, and Solomon (2005) studied students at Sussex University in the United Kingdom, from first-year and last-year students in cohorts graduating in 1999, 2000 and 2001. They compared scores on two modes (course work versus examination) of assessment data from course work in a variety of different disciplines, in a mixed model analysis of variance (ANOVA) with gender as the between-groups factor. Results indicated that female students did outperform male students, but by about the same amount on both course-work assignments and examinations. The population of interest in this study was undergraduate students, not school-aged children. However, year 12 students and first-year undergraduates are very close in age. Woodfield and her colleagues' results are therefore of interest here because they used a sample from another country and obtained different results than did the Cox (2000) study.

Test Administration and Test-Takers' Behaviour

Bridgeman and Schmitt (1997) reviewed studies in several categories related to the conditions of testing and the behavioural responses of test takers. Time, time pressures and speededness of tests have been studied with respect to gender differences. Their review of these studies led Bridgeman and Schmitt (1997, p. 206) to conclude that 'at least on academic reasoning tests, time limits do not appear to be an important consideration in explaining gender differences in test scores'. Studies of student guessing and omitting answers similarly failed to find gender-related effects. In addition, studies of the effects of changing answers failed to find differential gender effects on performance. That is, there were no differences between boys and girls in score gains or losses resulting from changing answers. Thus, it does not appear that gender differences in achievement are explained by test administration factors or differential test-taking behaviours.

Test anxiety is another area in which gender effects have been hypothesised. Hembree (1988) did a meta-analysis of 562 studies of test anxiety and its relationship to performance. He found that test anxiety and performance were significantly related at Grade 3 and above. Across grades, girls exhibited higher mean test anxiety than boys, but their higher test anxiety did not appear to translate into a difference in performance. Again, cultural transmission seems to fit better as a hypothesis for test anxiety effects than a biological explanation.

Scoring of Items

Rater effects. Do rater effects explain gender differences in achievement on performance tasks? Bridgeman and Schmitt (1997) pointed out that while machine-scoring is blind to student characteristics, there could be rater effects associated with gender or other student characteristics for hand-scored responses. In fact, this has been a classic question in the literature, based on a study (Goldberg, 1968) that suggested female raters were prejudiced against female students. Swim, Borgida, Maruyama, and Myers (1989) did a meta-analysis of 119 studies of gender effects among raters to investigate this stereotype. They found little evidence that raters evaluate females differently than they do males. Most of the mean effects they tested were not significantly different from zero, and where effects were found the effect size was very small. There was no main effect overall, for example, for gender of person rated; however, studies that did find differences were more likely to find those differences favoured males. Similarly, there was no interaction effect of gender of rater by gender of person rated; however, male raters exhibited more variability in ratings than did female raters.

Rubrics. Performance assessments are often scored with rubrics, which assign performance-quality levels under various criteria. The performance levels defined for rubrics should be written to index levels of achievement on the construct that a particular performance assessment is designed to tap. Therefore, asking whether the content of rubrics explains gender differences in achievement is not, strictly speaking, asking a question about construct-irrelevant variance. Nevertheless, at least one study did just that.

Wang and Lane (1996) studied differential item functioning on 33 mathematical thinking and reasoning items on the QUASAR Cognitive Assessment Instrument (QCAI), in the United States. Only two items were of concern. On one, girls with low mean total-test scores outperformed boys matched for total test score. On the second, girls with high mean total-test scores performed less well than boys matched for total-test score. The authors speculated that the second item's DIF may have appeared because it was on the same test form as the first. The first item read (Wang & Lane, 1996, p. 193): 'Jerome, Elliott, and Arturo took turns driving home from a trip. Arturo drove 80 miles more than Elliott. Elliott drove twice as many as Jerome. Jerome drove 50 miles'. The task was to write three mathematical questions that could be answered by this scenario, and/or with additional information provided in the student's response. The scoring rubric was based on the number, not the complexity, of the questions. Post-hoc analysis showed that girls wrote more questions than boys. Eighty-two per cent of girls wrote at least one question, compared with 76 per cent of boys. However, 60 per cent of boys, compared with 54 per cent of girls, wrote more complex questions. Therefore, a scoring rubric that took into account the complexity of the questions students wrote might have resulted in no differential item functioning by gender. The rubric encodes the intended construct into the score levels; the decision whether to score complexity as well as number should be based on the definition of problem solving used to represent the construct.

Summary and Conclusion

This chapter begins with the question as to whether gender differences in achievement do exist and, if so, where. There do appear to be gender differences in achievement in language arts that, while variable across countries and cultures, do favour girls. Differences in mathematics and science are more variable. Where they exist, they are more likely to favour boys, but not always. This chapter presents evidence for those differences, based on the most recent PISA international comparison study and supported with corroborating findings from other studies.

The chapter then explores two different questions about the meaning of gender differences. First, the more general question of meaning, namely 'Are gender differences biologically or culturally based?' It appears that explanations for gender inequities that exist in some places are found in studies of culture, economics/politics and environment. Second, a more specific question addressed whether aspects of the assessment process itself might explain gender differences in achievement. Assessments seem to be able to indicate the issue, but in the main they are not the reason for differential performance by gender. While the conclusions that are drawn from an assessment should be informed by what is known about gender differences, it appears that what is known so far supports sociological, as opposed to biological or measurement-based, causal hypotheses.

Future research, then, will ask questions about achievement gaps in various countries, cultures and educational systems. Because gender equity at the item level will continue to be a quality-control issue in standardised test development, future research will look for explanations of gender differences in social, cultural and educational influences. Studies of policies that have brought equity—their operations, effects and unintended consequences—will join more theoretical studies to attempt to explain not only cause, but also solution strategies, for gender equity in achievement.

Challenges this future research will encounter include, first and foremost, the chicken-and-egg nature of questions about causes and influences of gender differences in achievement. Are differences a result of cultural and educational patterns or a cause of them, or both? Another challenge for future research is the relative importance of gender differences, which are mostly small, compared with economic and cultural differences in achievement. Given limited resources, studying gender differences might (and maybe should) give ground to studies of economic and cultural patterns in achievement, which may be more amenable to change.

Theoretical and Methodological Framings

The Quantitative Approach Taken in This Chapter

Studies used as evidence to answer this chapter's question 'Are there gender differences in achievement?' were large-scale studies, implementing national or international comparisons, using standardised tests. Effect sizes were the preferred statistics for reporting, where available. Following is the rationale for these choices.

Since the book presents international perspectives on student achievement, this chapter discusses gender issues in achievement across national borders. Standardised tests are less context-bound than classroom assessments or tests developed by researchers for particular evaluations or studies. While standardised test results depend on student opportunity to learn, they also depend on opportunity to learn in the general sense, not in the specific sense of a classroom test, where opportunity to demonstrate knowledge of particular concepts and skills taught in the short term are more important. Standardised tests usually measure large-grain constructs like 'reading comprehension' or 'mathematics problem solving', rather than the ability to do one certain kind of reading or mathematics, as taught by one particular curriculum or group of teachers.

Effect sizes report research results in standardised terms. Because the aim is to answer a question about whether gender differences exist, it is important to standardise the comparisons between male and female students. Any differences reported should not be an artefact of the scale for the particular test given, or the number of students in the sample (as long as sample sizes were reasonable), or the number of items on the test, and so on. The 'effect size' used in this chapter is the standardised mean difference, sometimes called 'Cohen's d'. It is sometimes defined as the difference between mean performance of an experimental and control group, divided by the standard deviation of the control group. In this way it reports group differences in standard deviation units, which allows comparisons about the size of group differences from study to study, no matter what scale the outcome measure (in this case, an achievement test) used. In this chapter, differences between male and female students, as opposed to experimental and control group means, are compared, using usually a pooled standard deviation, to allow comparisons of gender differences across studies. For example, if girls outscored boys in language arts by 0.15 standard deviations on the achievement test used in one study and by 0.30 standard deviations on the achievement test used in another study, it is proper to conclude that the first difference is small and the second difference is moderately sized and larger than the first. These methodological choices are made to remove issues of tests and scaling as much as possible from the discussion, to allow concentration on the question of gender differences.

Glossary

Constructed-response format items Test questions for which the student responds with their own ideas (writing, drawing, working problems) instead of selecting from among prescribed choices

Differential item functioning (DIF) analysis Study of whether examinees of the same ability, but from two different groups, perform differently on a test item

Effect size While an effect size can be any of several standardised measures of the size of a result, in this chapter the effect size used is the difference between two groups' performance on an assessment expressed in standard deviation units.

Hierarchical linear modelling A method of analysis that takes into account the nested nature of data (for example, students within classrooms and classrooms within schools)

Median polishing A method of analysis to examine differences among factors, similar to analysis of variance but comparing medians for each factor rather than means

Meta-analysis A quantitative method for synthesising the results of a set of studies on a given topic by describing the distribution of effect sizes, and sometimes by analysing differences in effect sizes related to study characteristics

Multiple-choice format items Test questions for which the student selects from among prescribed choices instead of responding with their own ideas

Performance assessments Assessment tasks that require students to carry out a process or produce a product, and associated scoring schemes that require observation and judgment of the quality of that process or product

Rubrics A set of rules to evaluate the quality of a student performance, typically by specifying levels of quality according to a set of criteria for the performance

Speededness The degree to which the speed of an examinee's responses contributes to their score on a test

References

American Educational Research, Association American Psychological Association, & National Council on Measurement in Education. (1999). *Standards for educational and psychological testing*. Washington, DC: Authors.

ACT Inc. (2005). *Gender fairness using the ACT*. Retrieved May 5, 2008, from: <www.act.org/path/policy/pdf/gender.pdf>.

Beller, M., & Gafni, N. (1996). The 1991 International Assessment of Educational Progress in mathematics and sciences: The gender differences perspective. *Journal of Educational Psychology, 88*, 365–377.

Breland, H., & Lee, Y.-W. (2007). Investigating uniform and non-uniform gender DIF in computer-based ESL writing assessment. *Applied Measurement in Education, 20*, 377–403.

Bridgeman, B., & Schmitt, A. (1997). Fairness issues in test development and administration. In W. W. Willingham, & N. S. Cole (Eds.), *Gender and fair assessment*. Mahwah, NJ: Erlbaum.

Cohen, J. (1988). *Statistical power analysis for the behavioral sciences* (2nd ed.). Hillsdale, NJ: Lawrence Erlbaum.

Coley, R. J. (2001). *Differences in the gender gap: Comparisons across racial/ethnic groups in education and work*. Princeton, NJ: Educational Testing Service.

Cox, P. (2000). Regional and gender differences in mathematics achievement. *Journal of Research in Rural Education, 16*, 22–29.

Curley, W. E., & Schmitt, A. P. (1993). Revising SAT-Verbal items to eliminate differential item functioning (CB Rep. No. 93-2; ETS RR-93-61). New York: College Entrance Examination Board.

DeFraine, B., Van Damme, J., & Onghena, P. (2007). A longitudinal analysis of gender differences in academic self-concept and language achievement: A multivariate multilevel latent growth approach. *Contemporary Educational Psychology, 32*, 132–150.

DeLisle, J., Smith, P., & Jules, V. (2005). Which males or females are most at risk and on what? An analysis of gender differentials within the primary school system of Trinidad and Tobago. *Educational Studies, 31*, 393–418.

DeMars, C. (1998). Gender differences in mathematics and science on a high school proficiency exam: The role of response format. *Applied Measurement in Education, 11*, 279–299.

Duffy, J., Gunther, G., & Walters, L. (1997). Gender and mathematical problem solving. *Sex Roles, 37*, 477–494.

Ethington, C. (1990). Gender differences in mathematics: An international perspective. *Journal for Research in Mathematics Education, 21*, 74–80.

Francis, B., & Skelton, C. (2005). *Reassessing gender and achievement: Questioning contemporary key debates.* London: Routledge.

Goldberg, P. (1968). Are women prejudiced against women? *Transaction, 5*, 28–30.

Hembree, R. (1988). Correlates, causes, effects, and treatment of test anxiety. *Review of Educational Research, 58*, 47–77.

Institute of Education Sciences, United States Department of Education. (2007). *National Assessment of Educational Progress at Grades 4 and 8: Reading 2007. NCES Report No. 2007-496.* Retrieved May 1, 2008, from <nces.ed.gov/nationsreportcard/pdf/main2007/2007496.pdf>.

Joint Committee on Testing Practices. (2004). *Code of fair testing practices in education (Revised).* Washington, DC: Author.

Klecker, B. M. (2006). The gender gap in NAEP fourth-, eighth-, and twelfth-grade reading scores across years. *Reading Improvement, 43*, 50–56.

Lietz, P. (2006). A meta-analysis of gender differences in reading achievement at the secondary school level. *Studies in Educational Evaluation, 32*, 317–344.

Nowell, A., & Hedges, L. (1998). Trends in gender differences in academic achievement from 1960 to 1994: An analysis of differences in mean, variance, and extreme scores. *Sex Roles, 39*, 21–43.

Organisation for Econonic Co-operation and Development (OECD). (2004). *Problem Solving for Tomorrow's World—First measures of cross-curricular competencies from PISA 2003.* Paris: Author.

Organisation for Economic Co-operation and Development (OECD). (2007). *PISA 2006: Science competencies for tomorrow's world. Volume 1: Analysis.* Paris: Author.

Robertson, I. (2005). Issues related to curriculum, policy, and gender raised by national and international surveys of achievement in mathematics. *Assessment in Education, 12*, 217–236.

Sammons, P. (1995). Gender, ethnic and socio-economic differences in attainment and progress: A longitudinal analysis of student achievement over 9 years. *British Educational Research Journal, 21*, 465–485.

Swim, J., Borgida, E., Maruyama, G., & Myers, D. G. (1989). Joan McKay versus John McKay: Do gender stereotypes bias evaluations? *Psychological Bulletin, 105*, 409–429.

Wang, N., & Lane, S. (1996). Detection of gender-related differential item functioning in a mathematics performance assessment. *Applied Measurement in Education, 9*, 175–199.

Willingham, W. W., & Cole, N. S. (1997). *Gender and fair assessment.* Mahwah, NJ: Erlbaum.

Woodfield, R., Earl-Novell, S., & Solomon, L. (2005). Gender and mode of assessment at university: Should we assume female students are better suited to coursework and males to unseen examinations? *Assessment and Evaluation in Higher Education, 30*, 35–50.

Chapter 8
Assessment, Disability, Student Engagement and Responses to Intervention

Deb Keen and Michael Arthur-Kelly

Introduction

Assessment is central to the provision of meaningful and productive learning experiences for all students. The majority of students in today's classroom benefit from core instruction; however, for a small percentage of students with a disability, learning requires more intensive instruction. It is this cohort of learners that we consider in this chapter. While the needs of these learners are diverse, they have in common some teaching and learning challenges that have direct implications for assessment practices. We consider three major challenges:

- the various learning priorities for students in need of intensive instruction, and how to maximise the connection between current and targeted skills and knowledge;
- how to measure change through skill or knowledge acquisition when the rate and magnitude of change may be achieved in small increments; and
- how to determine whether change that does occur is attributable to our teaching, and what to do when teaching is not effective in achieving change.

In the absence of this information, there is a serious risk that instruction will be less than effective, will lack social validity and that learners will fail to make progress and achieve positive learning outcomes. Within the context of a cycle typical of intensive instruction, we examine how assessment can play a key role in enhancing and facilitating teaching and learning in the classroom by addressing these three major challenges. We also review the practical challenges that teachers in regular classrooms face in utilising systematic assessment and programming strategies to meet the needs of all the students in their classrooms.

D. Keen (✉)
Faculty of Education Executive, Mt Gravatt campus, Griffith University, 176 Messines
Ridge Road, Mt Gravatt, QLD 4122, Australia
e-mail: d.keen@griffith.edu.au

C. Wyatt-Smith, J.J. Cumming (eds.), *Educational Assessment in the 21st Century*,
DOI 10.1007/978-1-4020-9964-9_8, © Springer Science+Business Media B.V. 2009

Conceptual Background and Framing of Assessment

An examination of the literature on the education of students with disabilities reveals a relatively brief history that had its roots in the selective provision of services to those deemed 'educable' (Foreman, 2008). Determinations of whether those with a disability could benefit from education were made through a classification system that used standardised assessments of intelligence to identify individuals as being educable, trainable or custodial (Foreman, 2008). While not an entitlement, those classified as educable, and a few of those considered trainable, received some educational provision.

Assessment played an important role in this categorical, deficit-based approach to the education of students with a disability. Assessments were used to identify and categorise students and to inform student placement decisions that led to the education of selected students in specialised and mostly segregated settings. Reliance on a limited range of standardised assessments often failed to identify the learning potential of this population, with those deemed 'custodial' receiving relatively few learning opportunities when compared with the non-disabled population.

Current educational provision demonstrates a significant shift away from these earlier approaches and is characterised by a more inclusive, functional, strengths-based approach. Education is now an entitlement for children with disabilities in many countries, and students with a disability have been increasingly included in mainstream education settings. In Australia, for example, just 9 per cent of children with a disability and aged 5–14 years are being educated in special schools (Australian Institute of Health and Welfare, 2006).

While increasing numbers of students with disabilities have been included in regular education settings, it has been acknowledged that many of these students may need special provisions to support their learning. Assessment has been central to these provisions, by informing decisions about allocation of limited resources. Questions regarding eligibility for additional support and the degree of support (resources) needed are vexing and continue to challenge most educational systems. Various classification schemes have been devised, some with the sole purpose of determining funding support. Others have provided a conceptual framework to guide planning and decision making on the types and levels of support that might be needed to enable individuals with disabilities to participate in daily life across a range of contexts and environments (Foreman, Bourke, Mishra, & Frost, 2001; Thompson et al., 2002). Classification systems based on levels of support have been developed. For example, Sigafoos and Arthur (2005) identify four levels: intermittent (support as needed or short-term); limited (consistent, but time-limited); extensive (regular, daily and long-term in at least some environments); and pervasive (high-intensity, across all environments).

In the educational context, and drawing on the notion of intensity level of support, helps in consideration of the differing educational needs of students with disabilities in order for learning to take place. The concept of varying levels of instruction for students with disabilities was described by Salvia, Ysseldyke, and Bolt (2007). They suggested that the majority of students benefit fromcore instruction, while some require enhanced instruction and a few need intensive instruction. Figure 8.1 provides a visual representation of how a small percentage of students may require individualised and intensive levels of instruction in addition to the class-wide instruction typically provided for their peers. Moving along the continuum of instructional intensity, from least to most intense, small group or modified one-on-one programs of instruction may be required by some students (see Duker, Didden, & Sigafoos, 2004). The percentage of students who may require particular levels of instruction is illustrative, although data from the Australian Institute of Health and Welfare (AIHW) have been used as a guide to inform the design of Fig. 8.1.

According to the AIHW (2006), 8.3 per cent of all Australian children have an identified disability. Of this group, 9 per cent of children aged 5–14 years are educated in special schools and 4.3 per cent have a severe or profound core-activity limitation.[1] Furthermore, 63 per cent of children with disabilities experience difficulty at school such as intellectual or learning difficulties. These data are based on a definition of disability, adopted by the Australian Bureau of Statistics, whereby a person has at least one of 17 limitations, restrictions or impairments, which has lasted or is likely to last for at least six months. Information about core-activity limitations and schooling restrictions is then sought from those meeting the criteria for disability. A person could be classified as having a disability but may or may not experience core-activity limitations or schooling restrictions. This approach is consistent with the International Classification of Functioning, Disability and Health (ICF), developed by the World Health Organization in 2001, which takes into account: body functions and structures; activities people do and the life areas in which they participate; and factors in their environment that affect these experiences.

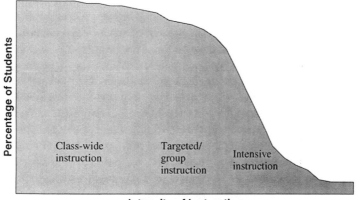

Intensity of Instruction

Fig. 8.1 Percentage of students requiring differing levels of intensity of instruction

[1] Core-activity limitation refers to the need for personal assistance with, or difficulty with, or use of aids or equipment for, self-care, mobility and communication. Ratings range from profound limitation whereby an individual always needs assistance from another person to perform a core activity through to mild limitation, where there is some difficulty in performing core activities or no difficulty when aids or equipment are used.

As we discuss shortly, the need for more intensive instruction is not determined by the presence or absence of a disability, but by the learner's response to instruction. It is likely that a percentage of those children with a disability as defined above, in addition to children without disabilities (those with learning, social and emotional difficulties, for example) will be in need of more intensive instruction. There is, however, no automatic link between disability and the need for more intensive instruction. The intensity of instruction must be viewed as a continuum along which students may move in either direction over time as their needs change. The number of students requiring a particular level of instruction varies across schools, districts and regions.

This concept of instructional intensity can assist us in examining, in a more holistic way, the role and purpose of assessment for students with disabilities. In this chapter we concentrate on assessment as it relates to those students who require more individualised and intensive instruction than the majority of students who continue to participate in and benefit from class-wide instruction. It is this group of students who can most challenge our assessment practices, perhaps as a function of the extremity of their needs, or conversely, their antipathy to our instructional efforts. We review assessment practices of relevance for all learners, with an emphasis on strategies that are critical to the meaningful inclusion of students with disabilities in regular classrooms. As a frame to this discussion, we focus on the concepts of student engagement and response to intervention.

Student Engagement

One of the first issues that often surfaces when considering the inclusion of students who require more intensive instruction is how effectively to engage these students in classroom-based learning. The broader issue of school engagement has been of increasing interest to educators as schools grapple with problems of retention/dropout, motivation and academic achievement (Alexander, Entwisle, & Horsey, 1997; Mahoney & Cairns, 1997). School engagement has been identified as one of the best predictors for positive student outcomes (Logan, Bakeman, & Keefe, 1997). This is of particular relevance to students with developmental disabilities, who have been found to spend less time actively engaged with adults and peers, and in mastery-level engagement with materials than children without disabilities (McWilliam & Bailey, 1995). Low levels of engagement and limited opportunities to learn and practise skills can have serious consequences for a child's development (Hart & Risley, 1995).

There appears to be agreement in the literature about the importance of engaging students in the learning experience but less agreement about how engagement can be best defined and subsequently assessed. For example, some argue that engagement is best determined by observing the degree to which a child is participating in, or involved with, an activity or other people (Massey & Wheeler, 2000; Watanabe & Sturmey, 2003). Others suggest that engagement involves factors both internal (for example, temperament, diagnosis) and external (environment) to the student. In assessing whether a student is engaged, advocates of this approach argue that both the focus and level of engagement must be considered (de Kruif & McWilliam, 1999; McWilliam & Bailey, 1992).

This is an important issue in the development and implementation of effective assessment practices, illustrated through the findings of pilot research recently conducted by the first author.

The study involved six students aged 3–5 years who attended an early intervention program for individuals with autism. The students were videotaped receiving intensive instruction from their teachers. Two students and two teachers were involved in each session of approximately 10 minutes duration. The videotapes were then coded for child engagement, based on a definition drawn from the research of Bevill, Gast, Maguire, and Vail (2001). The mean level of engagement for the six students ranged from 24 to 68 per cent, while engagement during individual sessions ranged from 20 to 92 per cent. Although there were some relatively low levels of engagement, the engagement levels fluctuated widely across sessions for most of the students. For example, one student displayed engagement levels ranging from 50 to 90 per cent, while another student's engagement levels ranged from 30 to 53 per cent and yet another from 33 to 63 per cent.

These preliminary data highlight the potential risks for students with a disability in achieving learning outcomes when disengaged from the learning process. The data also bring to light the need for continuous assessment of the investment being made by students in their own learning. Information from this type of assessment can inform teaching in numerous ways, including the selection of learning materials to motivate and stimulate the learner, and the choice of instructional procedures to engage or re-engage a student.

An Illustrative Case Study

Trent is a 9-year-old student who has been identified as functioning on the autism spectrum. Trent is fully enrolled and involved in the life of his Year 4 classroom, and he has educational goals related to his needs in the social and communication domains. His teacher employs a technique known as 'functional assessment' to map when Trent is most involved with his peers (for example, in highly structured peer-tutoring activities), and conversely, when episodes of mild anti-social behaviour occur. By collecting data on the time of day, the learning domain, demonstrated social behaviour and so on, the teacher is able to effectively and systematically increase Trent's engaged participation and reduces the possibility of disruptive outbursts that may be a problem for Trent and the whole class. A focus on his abilities, therefore, implicitly guides the prevention of problems.

Response to Intervention

The concept of 'Response to Intervention' (RTI) was introduced in the United States as part of the revisions to the Individuals with Disabilities Education Act (IDEA, 2004). As mentioned earlier in this chapter, decisions about the provision of educational support to students with disabilities were historically based on classification systems that relied on the use of standardised assessments. RTI was developed as an alternative means of providing early intervention to all children at risk of school failure (Fuchs & Fuchs, 2006). RTI involves regularly monitoring change in a student's level or rate of learning through dynamic assessment. This allows for a more individualised and flexible approach to assessment because interest is centred on improvement in student performance that is linked to instruction. Curriculum-based assessment (CBA) is arguably one of the most effective ways to monitor student responsiveness to instruction and is discussed in more detail below.

Curriculum-Based Assessment

Assessment can and should provide critical links between educational resources, curriculum, pedagogy and outcomes, for students with and without disabilities alike. CBA, in its simplest form, is the dynamic process of evaluating the efficacy of these links at the individual student level. Effective CBA can establish whether functional relationships exist between the skills and knowledge learnt and the teaching instruction and resources used to achieve these outcomes (Arthur-Kelly, 2008). Additionally, the relevance or meaning of what is learned must be addressed. According to Reschly and Ysseldyke (2002) 'The single greatest challenge in current practice is demonstration that students with disabilities and those who are at risk actually benefit from the educational programs, services, and interventions they receive' (p. 6). It may seem surprising that we make this point. The rationale lies in historical patterns of assessment in special education that have focused on identification and service provision, rather than meaningful educational programming. For example, in the past, students who were assessed within certain parameters of intellectual functioning were typically placed in specialised, often segregated classes with peers who had similar diagnoses (see Foreman, 2008). It is now generally agreed that assessment and intervention are best focused on maximising the individual learning outcomes achieved by the student, from a strengths perspective. Specifically, rather than perhaps allowing arbitrary identification on the basis of deficits, and a resultant setting or placement to determine what type of curriculum is introduced, how instruction will be delivered, and so on, a contemporary approach starts with two simple questions:

- What can the student do now? (existing skills, knowledge and attitudes)
- What do they need to master? (targeted instructional objectives)

Figure 8.2 suggests a continuum of three levels that can be considered when identifying the assessment processes and outcomes that are relevant to a particular student.

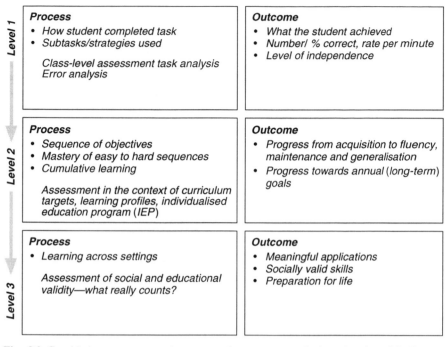

Level 1

Process	Outcome
• How student completed task • Subtasks/strategies used Class-level assessment task analysis Error analysis	• What the student achieved • Number/ % correct, rate per minute • Level of independence

Level 2

Process	Outcome
• Sequence of objectives • Mastery of easy to hard sequences • Cumulative learning Assessment in the context of curriculum targets, learning profiles, individualised education program (IEP)	• Progress from acquisition to fluency, maintenance and generalisation • Progress towards annual (long-term) goals

Level 3

Process	Outcome
• Learning across settings Assessment of social and educational validity—what really counts?	• Meaningful applications • Socially valid skills • Preparation for life

Fig. 8.2 Considering processes and outcomes in assessment: A three-tiered model (Source: Foreman, 2008, reproduced with the permission of Cengage Learning Australia Pty Ltd.)

Level 3 asks the 'big-picture' questions: Where is this person heading in relation to life-long learning? How can they best be supported in the challenge to enhance their engagement with their curriculum and use their skills and knowledge across settings, situations and time? Typically, such decisions are made using an Individual Educational Plan (IEP), a process and a document that is mandated in some countries, such as the United States, and simply recommended in others like Australia (Arthur-Kelly, 2008). In the past, a critical assessment decision was related to the curriculum focus, and more particularly, whether the student would participate in the regular curriculum (on offer to students without disabilities), or some form of vocational, life-skills or functional curriculum. Recent developments in many countries, emphasising or requiring the inclusion of all students in the regular curriculum, have changed this situation, albeit with a raft of perceived challenges and benefits (see Agran, Alper, & Wehmeyer, 2002; Agran, Cavin, Wehmeyer, & Palmer, 2006).

At level 2, the question of how students are learning and progressing towards their planned outcomes is assessed in the context of annual goals. Using the IEP as a framework, all members of the educational support team identify existing challenges and positive strategies for linking objectives and levels of learning. Without doubt, enhancing and supporting student learning and performance through the acquisition of skill and knowledge and on to fluency, maintenance and generalisation, represent core business for educators, regardless of whether students have an identified disability or learning difficulty.

For the purposes of our discussion, level 1 in Fig. 8.2 describes the daily class-room assessment, programming and teaching protocol that are the central theme of this chapter. Curriculum-based assessment, or class-level teaching and testing, represents the core component of effective practice that is the daily work of all teachers. Put simply, CBA is the minute-by-minute, lesson-by-lesson diagnosis of instructional need that teachers achieve whenever they check work samples, question students, conduct a running record as a student reads to them or assist in the development of items for portfolios (Wiig, Larson, & Olson, 2004). There are several defining features of CBA (Jones, Southern, & Brigham, 1998). First, it is classroom based, in contrast to the imposition of another person conducting an isolated testing event away from the instructional environment. Attention is necessarily paid to the curriculum on offer in the classroom. Second, it is dynamic, because the data that is produced is ongoing and ties in directly to the establishment of targeted learning outcomes and instructional strategies. Finally, CBA allows the teacher to quickly adjust instruction when errors or problems in learning are encountered. The focus on formative assessment and cumulative learning at one's own speed means that it is impossible to project with any accuracy where an individual will be functioning in a time frame in relation to the larger corpus of key learning outcomes in the syllabus. Rather, progress is based on mastery of content in small, cumulative steps. The teacher using CBA is interested in both the learning process (and more especially, where successes and challenges lie for the individual) and the progressive outcomes that contribute to the attainment of long-term objectives. In terms of the learning process, individual assistance may be required in either the task-analysed steps in an instructional sequence, or the cognitive strategies employed by the learner. Instructional adaptation and differentiation for individual students on the basis of these assessment data is one of the most valuable aspects of this classroom-level approach.

The benefits of CBA, for students, especially from a motivational perspective, are considerable. Few would argue that the opportunity to celebrate authentic success, achieved at a speed that meets the needs of the individual, has huge potential as an impetus to future learning. For students with disabilities, who may have had a history of failure in the past, the opportunity to ignite curiosity, increased independence, engagement and self-actualisation represent central educational goals. By reducing errors and increasing success on a given task, confidence and achievability are enhanced. However, like any approach, there are also some practical constraints, the most critical of which centres on the range and intensity of demands made on the teacher. In order to design and deliver effective instruction, and track student achievement in response to that instruction, a great deal of time and commitment is required.

It is now appropriate to explore the link between assessment, planning and instruction. How can a teacher embed curriculum-based data into instructional planning and delivery? What variables need to be considered in order to maximise learning outcomes for all students in the diverse classroom, including those with high instructional needs?

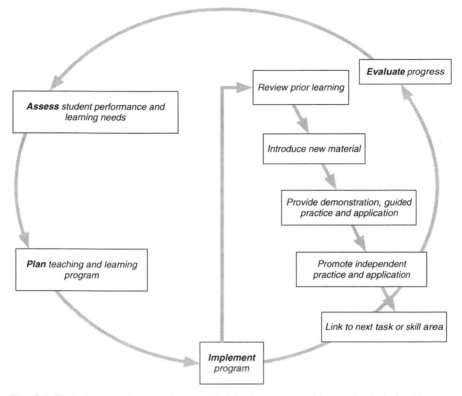

Fig. 8.3 Typical instructional cycle embedded in the process of instructional design (Source: Foreman, 2008, reproduced with the permission of Cengage Learning Australia Pty Ltd.)

Effective Planning and Instruction

One of the defining features of modern instructional design is the inherently dynamic flow of events that informs daily classroom practice. In contrast to the fairly disparate assessment, placement and intervention practices of the past, contemporary approaches emphasise a seamless and synergistic focus on quality teaching and learning practices. Student and teacher variables are part of the interplay that is contemporary pedagogy (Ellis, Worthington, & Larkin, 2006).

With this in mind, Fig. 8.3 embeds a typical instructional cycle within the larger process of instructional design. The macro-cycle emphasises the way in which assessment, planning, instruction and evaluation continuously inform each other. Effective teachers are rigorous in their efforts to use assessment data to plan and set learning goals, address these goals and evaluate progress. Effective teaching is a dynamic art form, constantly changing to address student needs and maximise learning. Importantly, the focus of such an approach is on what students can do and the outcomes they achieve as a result of educational intervention, rather than serving to point to any deficits in their skills or knowledge.

Interestingly, the process of authentic assessment that has emerged in the past decade means that teachers use a wide range of techniques to gauge student performance, and consequently, they collect information from a raft of data sources (for example, see Szarkowicz, 2006 in relation to early childhood assessment). Such data are critically related to the type of skill or ability that is assessed. For many children with and without disabilities, this may mean performance on traditionally accepted core academic or key learning areas; for example, work samples in creative art, group and individual performances in drama, or pencil-and-paper tests in mathematics. However, it is also possible and appropriate to identify different means to assess functional domains for students with additional needs. A little later, we provide a case study of a student with very high and complex support needs who participates in the regular classroom. Assessment of this girl's needs and abilities centred on her level of alertness and responsiveness as a dependent variable or skill that was to be targeted through the teaching program. It is very possible, then, especially in the diverse inclusive classroom, that teachers will be assessing quite distinct and different types of learner performance, and programming to address such differentiated needs (Dempsey & Arthur-Kelly, 2007; Keeffe & Carrington, 2006).

Within Fig. 8.3, we have embedded a typical but by no means universal instructional cycle. Based on the extant data relating to effective instruction, the importance of reviewing previous learning, priming new learnings, supporting and scaffolding learning and linking to subsequent learning outcomes are underlined in this schema (Arthur-Kelly, 2008). For the purposes of discussion here, the salient point is that effective teachers embed into their teaching a dynamic review of how their students are progressing. One of the precepts of special education has been the importance of interrupting a failure set, progressing success in small steps and motivating individuals who may have experienced a history of rejection or discouragement in learning. By collecting meaningful data and interpreting them from a mastery perspective before proceeding to new, more complex skills, teachers are seeking to maximise achievement and reduce frustration in their students.

As we noted earlier, this generic instructional design and cycle find application in the educational planning and support of students across the spectrum of needs. In the box below, an illustrative case study for a young student with very high learning needs is presented. Note the way in which the arbitrary phases of assessment–planning–instruction–evaluation are continually linked in daily practice.

An Illustrative Case Study

Background

Sophie attends her age-appropriate class in the local school and has a range of challenges, including profound intellectual disability, no control of her limbs and quite limited sight (for distance) due to retinal degeneration and stigmatism. Sophie relies on others to meet al.l of her basic daily needs. She also has a great smile, especially when familiar people come into view, and the ability to move her mouth to activate a tilt switch mounted on her standing frame and wheelchair.

Assessment

At the regular case conference, convened twice-yearly by the school's learning support team, the central long-term goals agreed upon for the individual education plan involved increasing the level and quality of responsive involvement in learning activities and participation by Sophie in meaningful interactions with those around her (family members, peers, teachers, aides and relevant others). To address this need, a form of observational data collection known as 'behaviour state assessment' was planned with the intention of understanding Sophie's existing level of alertness and noting events and conditions that improved her levels of involvement with others (see Foreman, Arthur-Kelly, Pascoe, & Smyth King, 2004 for details). Observers (in this case, the teacher aide/paraprofessional) made a judgment every minute about whether Sophie was awake and actively alert, dazed, asleep and so on. Notes were also made about the communication opportunities available at the time, the type of syllabus area being covered in the class, and Sophie's positioning and social grouping.

Planning

The curriculum that is most relevant for Sophie is the human one: how to connect with and sustain communications with valued others. Although a little different to traditional areas such as maths and English, planning in a curriculum-based assessment approach centres around the most important learning domains for the individual student and matches goals to current functioning and future needs. In the case of Sophie, several teaching goals were identified in light of the assessment data collected:

- planned increases in length of class time during which Sophie was awake and actively alert, with decreases in dazed state
- increased range of communication partners and changes in the cueing behaviours of these partners
- stronger provision of binary choices that require a selection by Sophie via her mouth-activated tilt switch (for example, 'Would you like chips/yes/no? or fruit/yes/no?').

Instruction

A range of structured and incidental learning opportunities was planned to address the above goals for Sophie and those engaging with her. Specifically, it was important that learning activities were brief, interesting and relevant to the sensory abilities in which Sophie was strongest, including tactile, olfactory and limited visual modalities. The most helpful strategy was direct cueing for communication during small group tasks in several learning areas including music and art. Of most interest is the priority that was given to partner behaviour as part of the instructional design: how teachers, aides and others delivered information and responded to Sophie's efforts was a key determinant of instructional success.

Evaluation

This is perhaps the most vital and challenging aspect of the curriculum-based model. Data on Sophie's progress, her communication partners and learning/engagement opportunities are constantly critiqued with reference to the learning goals, and the program is modified as necessary.

Specific changes have included:

- more professional development for staff on correctly providing meaningful choices and delivering cues for communication that engage Sophie
- reducing the duration of the target lessons in which Sophie is encouraged to visually track peers and other partners in close proximity
- increasing the range of affect indicators that demonstrate engagement and alertness (for example, slight smile, facial flicker).

For students with such complex and high support needs, ongoing data plays a central role in maximising daily learning outcomes (just like any other child!).

Issues, Challenges and Future Research Directions in Assessment

The history of assessment for students with disabilities has been driven by a particular agenda related to the perceived purpose of assessment. That is, assessment has been linked to decision-making processes around eligibility for particular educational and support services, access to resources and placement in regular or specialised settings. Inclusive practices that have been embraced in many countries throughout the world have brought with them a decline in the need to gather assessment data to inform decisions about placements in specialised settings. In any economy, however, the resources available to assist students with additional support needs will always be limited. Ways to allocate these resources equitably are likely to be the centre of ongoing debate and the quest for assessment tools that can provide information about support needs and eligibility for service to inform this debate is also likely to continue.

We have discussed how some children, with and without disabilities, fail to respond to classroom-wide instruction as the primary mode of educational delivery and require more intensive instruction in order for optimal learning to occur.

For students who require more intensive instruction, we have argued that the primary purpose of assessment should be to provide information about the relationship between skills and knowledge learnt, and the teaching instruction and resources used to achieve these outcomes. In considering this issue, it is helpful to return to the quote from Reschly and Ysseldyke (2002) cited earlier in the chapter. They contended that one of the greatest challenges in current practice is to demonstrate that students with disabilities benefit from the programs they receive. We have outlined how effective assessment can play a key role in meeting this challenge but the adoption of a comprehensive assessment approach that is focused on individual needs, as described in this chapter, requires a shift in thinking. This shift involves moving beyond assessment as a means of categorising students with disabilities and allocating limited resources, to understanding assessment as a process that is integral to planning, teaching and evaluation.

Furthermore, a shift is required not only in our thinking but also in our practice. Salvia et al. (2007) have likened the need that students may have for different levels of instruction in the classroom to the need for primary, secondary and tertiary levels of intervention for challenging behaviours described in the positive behaviour support literature. Primary interventions are those implemented at a school-wide and classroom-wide level from which most students benefit. When effective school-wide interventions are implemented, the number of students needing more intensive levels of intervention is reduced. Classroom instruction can be viewed in the same way, emphasising the implementation of effective classroom-wide instruction as a fundamental first step to achieving the best learning outcomes possible for students with disabilities. This approach is elaborated in the RTI literature. RTI, discussed earlier in this chapter, has been gaining favour in some regions as a means of identifying children with learning disabilities and providing early intervention for children at risk for school failure (for example, Fuchs & Fuchs, 2006).

In this chapter, we focus on assessment processes related to students who require more intensive levels of intervention, but there is a need for all teachers to master and use a data-based (curriculum-based) approach to teaching and learning programs in order to achieve effective practices at all levels of intervention. This has implications for both pre-service and in-service training for teachers and for learning specialists in the way they work with teachers in response to the needs of students with disabilities, and just as importantly, the time priorities allotted to this task. In a comprehensive and timely investigation led by Tony Shaddock, the Australian Department of Education, Science and Training (DEST) recently published a report entitled *Improving the learning outcomes of students with disabilities in the early, middle and post compulsory years of schooling* (2007). In one part of the research that informed this report, 294 Australian teachers in regular schools were invited to indicate the types of adaptations they made for students with disabilities in their classrooms. While the participants were moderately supportive of such inclusion, especially in relation to social outcomes for their students, it was stated that '... a very significant stress for most teachers is their perceived lack of time for preparing for and responding to the diverse needs of the students in their mainstream classes' (DEST, 2007, xiv).

CBA, in its pure form, profiles the individual student against the syllabus on offer in the classroom. Students do not find themselves compared with each other, but rather, their skills and knowledge are assessed in terms of their previous learning and the established objectives for the next lesson.

The practical challenges in tracking student progress and identifying individual needs in the typically diverse heterogeneous classroom are immense. The simple opportunity to reach each child, evaluate their learning and plan for new content (or revise not-yet-mastered content) is, arguably, impossible considering that one teacher may be responsible for up to 30 students.

This obstacle can be addressed in a variety of ways. Grouping students of similar ability and teaching/testing on this basis may prove effective. It may also be appropriate to use individualised assessment with a select group of students (for example, higher-ability and lower-ability students), although this runs counter to the inclusive and individualised emphasis of CBA.

At a systemic level, such as teacher preparation, it may take some time to convince senior educators that the type of accountability and sequenced progression of skills and knowledge reflected in CBA is the mandate of every teacher. The relics of the debate on whole-language instruction, in relation to a concern for learning experience rather than learning outcomes, may still resonate in some faculty, thus inhibiting a commitment to the importance of assessment that is both dynamic and personalised.

In sum, then, future research could focus on identifying:

- the factors that facilitate and mitigate against teachers' use of curriculum-based approaches to assessment and programming in diverse classrooms
- models of staff development that enhance teachers' skills and knowledge in individualising and differentiating assessment, planning, instruction and evaluation
- the nature of the relationship between student abilities, teacher behaviours, levels of engagement and responses to intervention in modern classrooms.

Conclusion

This chapter reviews best practice in assessment for students with disabilities attending schools in the 21st century. By focusing on the individual needs of children regardless of the educational setting that supports them, our intention has been to describe the constant features of instructional design as recommended in the research literature.

Using a series of case studies, attention was paid to:

- seamless transitions across curriculum, pedagogy and learning outcomes in relation to assessment and programming for individuals
- the cyclical nature of the intervention process comprising assessment, planning teaching and evaluation
- the central role of instructional data in modifying teaching and learning programs.

We conclude by calling for more systematic research into the learning outcomes achieved by students with disabilities in regular classrooms. Ideally, it would be helpful to gather data on student learning outcomes as a function of critical variables such as teacher preparation, instructional methodologies employed, socio-economic and other context differences and so on. There are very little Australasian data of this kind available. Such information would be especially helpful if it reflected a longitudinal focus and covered the range of schooling years. There are also relatively little data to fill the evidence-to-practice divide. Evidence to practice is the translation of empirically proven strategies into everyday situations. There appears to be a dearth of such analyses in the Australasian context. The literature on co-operative learning, for example (with some eminent exceptions, such as the work of Gillies & Ashman, 2000), is almost entirely based on United States educational data. What factors may influence especially the efficacy or otherwise of the various co-operative learning methodologies when utilised in other regions of the world? Are there barriers or facilitating factors in practice that are unique to a region? More information is required to answer this question for many instructional methodologies. The DEST (2007) report is a welcome step in the right direction for Australia, with several critical findings that inform this ongoing research-to-practice agenda in the wider international context. Perhaps most importantly, these data underlined the complexity of the modern educational environment and the need to find ways more directly to link educational supports for teachers and schools with measurable improvements in student learning and performance.

Theoretical and Methodological Framings

Curriculum-Based Assessment

The central theoretical orientation for CBA is applied behaviour analysis, which has its roots in psychological and educational traditions underpinned by the principles of respondent (or classical) and operant conditioning. Respondent conditioning, initially described by Ivan Pavlov, involves the pairing of stimuli so that an unconditioned stimulus elicits a response. Pavlov's example involved the reflexive response of a dog to salivate at the sight of food. He then paired food with the sound of a bell until the bell elicited salivation in the absence of food. Operant conditioning principles move beyond the classical conditioning of reflexive responses to involve behaviours generally considered voluntary. Operant principles were first described by B. F. Skinner and are best understood by considering the three-term contingency (or ABC) model (Skinner, 1953). This model depicts a functional relationship between antecedents (A), behaviours (B) and consequences (C), whereby in any situation (A), the probability of a behaviour occurring (B) is determined by its history of consequences (C). For example, a driver approaching a stop sign (A) applies the brakes and comes to a stop (B) to prevent an accident (C).

The behaviour analyst is interested in establishing and verifying these functional relationships by defining behaviours that are observable and measurable. Behaviour may then be influenced by acting on the antecedents and/or consequences that are functionally related to that behaviour. There are many ways in which this can be done, and which draw on a rich behavioural literature (Alberto & Troutman, 2006).

In addition to the principles outlined above, there has been a growing interest in the importance of context on the practice of applied behaviour analysis and CBA. The ecological model put forward by Urie Bronfenbrenner provides one example of the kinds of contextual factors that may be influential from a developmental perspective (Bronfenbrenner, 1979, 1986; Bronfenbrenner & Morris, 1998). Bronfenbrenner's model conceptualises the child as central, with surrounding contextual layers that nestle within each other like a set of Russian dolls (Bronfenbrenner, 1979). The layer closest to the child is the microsystem, which includes not only the child's family but also school and peers. Moving outwards, there are the mesosystem (interrelationships between settings in which the child participates), exosystem (settings in which the child is not directly involved but is affected by indirectly), macrosystem (society and culture) and chronosystem (accounting for the dynamic nature of contexts over time).

Thus, gathering systematic data from a range of sources, the CBA practitioner attempts to capture an understanding of what students can presently do and their subsequent instructional requirements. Using task-analytic principles, a clear sequence of intended student learning outcomes is identified, and progress mapped against this sequence. In this sense, CBA is deconstructionist, in that it seeks to order learning, and behaviourist in its reliance on hard evidence that learning has taken place. For a teacher adopting a CBA approach, the relevance of contextual factors is particularly evident when considering conditions that may affect the strength or nature of the functional relationship between the components of the ABC model. This may include environmental factors (for example, classroom, teacher and peers) that impact on a child's motivation to learn and the effectiveness of objects, events or activities selected as reinforcers. An understanding that these factors may influence behaviour and therefore the outcome of any assessment is seen as central to the effective use of assessment data to modify teaching practices and learning outcomes.

Inclusion

Inclusion is both a philosophy and a course of action that finds expression in education and community supports for people with and without disabilities. In terms of ideas about how to engage with other people, inclusion infers that all people have the right to the same life opportunities and bring something unique to the world and their community. Consequently, genuine acceptance of the right to participate and celebration of human difference are two beliefs that underpin the inclusion approach.

As a strategy, inclusion is the opportunity to participate fully in experiences with others regardless of the fact that you may have a disability. A benchmark question might be: What happens for same-aged peers without a disability? What school do they attend and what opportunities are afforded them? Even when such basic equal opportunities are provided, inclusion may not really be in evidence.

For example, a child who has a severe physical disability can be accommodated physically in her or his local neighbourhood school through the use of ramps, lifts and so on. However, the child's human ecology may not be welcoming. Peers may ignore and teachers may stigmatise her or him. This is not inclusive practice.

Inclusion, therefore, underlines the central dignity of social membership and acceptance despite the presence of differing needs and circumstances. Inclusive practices can be considered a function of interpersonal, physical, curricular, instructional and many other forms of adjustment and support in human contexts.

Glossary

Assessment In an educational context, the collection of any form(s) of information that allows educators to identify current skills and knowledge and map new directions for intended learning outcomes to be achieved by students. Assessment may be formative or ongoing (during instruction), as well as summative (at the end of a unit of work or series of lessons)

Authentic assessment The collection of information about student learning from a rich range of sources, including, importantly, the individual. Portfolios, checklists, work samples, diaries, permanent products, pencil-and-paper tests, observations and other forms of assessment may shed light on what the student knows or is able to demonstrate, and the direction(s) required in one's learning program

Intervention The systematic delivery of a planned series of strategies to address learning objectives and improve educational outcomes

Engagement The degree to which a student is observed to connect meaningfully with the curriculum and with those around them

References

Agran, M., Alper, S., & Wehmeyer, M. (2002). Access to the general curriculum for students with significant disabilities: What it means to teachers. *Education and Training in Mental Retardation and Developmental Disabilities, 37*, 123–133.

Agran, M., Cavin, M., Wehmeyer, M., & Palmer, S. (2006). Participation of students with moderate to severe disabilities in the general curriculum: The effects of the Self-Determined Model of Instruction. *Research & Practice for Persons with Severe Disabilities, 31*, 230–241.

Australian Institute of Health and Welfare (AIHW). (2006). *Disability updates: Children with disabilities* (Bulletin No. 42. AIHW cat. no. AUS 19). Canberra: Author.

Alberto, P. A., & Troutman, A. C. (2006). *Applied behavior analysis for teachers* (7th ed.). Upper Saddle River, NJ: Pearson.

Alexander, K., Entwisle, D., & Horsey, C. (1997). From first grade forward: Early foundations of high school dropout. *Sociology of Education, 70*, 87–107.

Arthur-Kelly, M. (2008). Planning effective teaching strategies. In P. Foreman (Ed.), *Inclusion in action* (2nd ed., pp. 164–197). Melbourne: Thomson.

Bevill, A., Gast, D., Maguire, A., & Vail, C. (2001). Increasing engagement of preschoolers with disabilities through correspondence training and picture cues. *Journal of Early Intervention*, *24*, 129–145.

Bronfenbrenner, U. (1979). *The ecology of human development: Experiments by nature and design*. Cambridge, MA: Harvard University Press.

Bronfenbrenner, U. (1986). Ecology of the family as a context for human development: Research perspectives. *Developmental Psychology, 22*, 723–742.

Bronfenbrenner, U., & Morris, P. (1998). The ecology of developmental processes. In W. Damon, & R. Lerner (Eds.), *Handbook of child psychology* (Vol. 1, pp. 993–1028). New York: John Wiley & Sons.

de Kruif, R., & McWilliam, R. A. (1999). Multivariate relationships among developmental age, global engagement, and observed child engagement. *Early Childhood Research Quarterly*, *14*, 515–536.

Dempsey, I., & Arthur-Kelly, M. (2007). *Maximising learning outcomes in diverse classrooms*. Melbourne: Thomson Learning.

Department of Education Science and Training (DEST). (2007). Improving the learning outcomes of students with disabilities in the early, middle and post compulsory years of schooling. Canberra: Australian Government Printer.

Duker, P., Didden, R., & Sigafoos, J. (2004). *One-to-one training: Instructional procedures for learners with developmental disabilities*. Austin, TX: Pro-Ed.

Ellis, E. S., Worthington, L. A., & Larkin, M. J. (2006). *Executive summary of the research synthesis on effective teaching principles and the design of quality tools for educators*. Retrieved November 30, 2007, from <Idea.uoregon.edu/~ncite/documents/techrep/tech06.html>

Foreman, P. (Ed.). (2008). *Inclusion in action* (2nd ed.). Melbourne: Thomson.

Foreman, P., Bourke, S., Mishra, G., & Frost, R. (2001). Assessing the support needs of children with a disability in regular classes. *International Journal of Disability,* Development and Education, *48*, 239–252.

Foreman, P., Arthur-Kelly, M., Pascoe, S., & Smyth King, B. (2004). Evaluating the educational experiences of students with profound and multiple disabilities in inclusive and segregated classroom settings: An Australian perspective. *Research and Practice for Persons with Severe Disabilities*, *29*, 183–193.

Fuchs, D., & Fuchs, L. S. (2006). Introduction to response to intervention: What, why, and how valid is it? *Reading Research Quarterly*, *41*, 93–99.

Gillies, R., & Ashman, A. (2000). The effects of cooperative learning on students with learning difficulties in the lower elementary school. *The Journal of Special Education*, *34*, 19–27.

Hart, B., & Risley, T. R. (1995). Meaningful differences in the everyday experience of young American children. Baltimore: Paul H. Brookes.

IDEA (2004). *Individuals with Disabilities Education Improvement Act of 2004*, Pub. L. 108–466.

Jones, E. D., Southern, W. T., & Brigham, F. J. (1998). Curriculum-based assessment: Testing what is taught and teaching what is tested. *Intervention in School and Clinic*, *33*, 239–49.

Keeffe, M., & Carrington, S. (2006). *Schools and diversity*. Sydney: Pearson.

Logan, K. R., Bakeman, R., & Keefe, E. G. (1997). Effects of instructional variables of engaged behavior of students with disabilities in general education classrooms. *Exceptional Children*, *63*, 481–497.

Mahoney, J., & Cairns, R. (1997). Do extracurricular activities protect against early school dropout? *Developmental Psychology*, *33*, 241–253.

Massey, N. G., & Wheeler, J. J. (2000). Acquisition and generalization of activity schedules and their effects on task engagement in a young child with autism in an inclusive pre-school classroom. *Education and Training in Mental Retardation and Developmental Disabilities*, *35*, 326–335.

McWilliam, R. A., & Bailey, D. B. (1992). Promoting engagement and mastery. In D. B. Bailey, & M. Wolery (Eds.), *Teaching infants and preschoolers with disabilities* (2nd ed., pp. 230–255). New York: Macmillan.

McWilliam, R. A., & Bailey, D. B. (1995). Effects of classroom social structure and disability on engagement. *Topics in Early Childhood Special Education*, *15*, 123–147.

Reschly, D. J., & Ysseldyke, J. E. (2002). Paradigm shift: The past is not the future. In A. Thomas, & J. Grimes (Eds.), *Best practices in school psychology IV* (pp. 3–20). Bethesda, MD: National Association of School Psychologists.

Salvia, J., Ysseldyke, J. E., & Bolt, S. (2007). *Assessment in special and inclusive education* (10th ed.). Boston: Houghton Miflin.

Sigafoos, J., & Arthur, M. (2005). Educating students with high support needs. In A. Ashman, & J. Elkins (Eds.), *Educating children with diverse abilities* (2nd ed., pp. 435–463). Frenchs Forest, NSW: Pearson Education Australia.

Skinner, B. F. (1953). *Science and human behavior*. New York: Macmillan.

Szarkowicz, D. (2006). *Observations and reflections in childhood*. Melbourne: Thomson.

Thompson, J. R., Hughes, C., Schalock, R. L., Silverman, W., Tasse, M. J., & Bryant, B., et al. (2002). Integrating supports in assessment and planning. *Mental Retardation*, *40*, 390–405.

Watanabe, M., & Sturmey, P. (2003). The effect of choice-making opportunities during activity schedules on task engagement of adults with autism. *Journal of Autism and Developmental Disorders*, *33*, 535–539.

Wiig, E. H., Larson, V., & Olson, J. (2004). *S-Maps: Rubrics for curriculum-based assessment and intervention: For grades K-12*. Wisconsin: Thinking Publications.

Chapter 9
Assessment Challenges, the Law and the Future

J. Joy Cumming

Introduction

This chapter takes a legal perspective on educational assessment issues, examining court responses to challenges to educational assessment in the jurisdictions of Australia, the United States of America (United States) and England. To date, the predominant focus of legal challenges in education has been regarding either education for children with special needs, or allegations of negligence resulting in physical or emotional injury. However, throughout the jurisdictions considered, challenges on assessment-focused grounds have included discrimination in assessment and testing, allegations of inappropriate assessment and/or failure to provide appropriate educational instruction as a result of errors in assessment. The chapter explains briefly the nature of law in the jurisdictions considered, including legislation and case law. Since laws in these jurisdictions are based in the doctrine of precedent (MacAdam & Pyke 1998), this chapter cannot provide a definitive statement of the status of law on assessment—it changes with each new judgment. The chapter does not comment on the desirability or adequacy of education laws in the jurisdictions considered, nor is the discussion exhaustive as to issues that have arisen in relation to educational assessment. The purpose of this chapter is twofold: namely to demonstrate the various ways in which educational assessment matters may end up in the courts and the approaches the courts have taken and to consider the directions legal issues for educational assessment may take in the 21st century.

In many nations, policy agendas promoting educational accountability have led to an increase in legislation with implications for educational assessment. Immediate

J.J. Cumming (✉)
Faculty of Education, Mt Gravatt campus, Griffith University, 176 Messines Ridge Road,
Mt Gravatt QLD 4122, Australia
e-mail: j.cumming@griffith.edu.au

C. Wyatt-Smith, J.J. Cumming (eds.), *Educational Assessment in the 21st Century*,
DOI 10.1007/978-1-4020-9964-9_9, © Springer Science+Business Media B.V. 2009

to mind is the *No Child Left Behind* legislation in the United States,[1] where educational progress is specifically targeted through states' assessment performance. In Australia, similar federal legislation, the *Schools Assistance Act 2004*, specifies areas of assessment and school reporting frameworks.[2]

Legislation applies not just to student assessment but also to schools, for example, the publication of 'league tables' specified in *The Education (School Information) (England) Regulations 2002*. Thus, it is timely to examine how the courts countenance arguments regarding educational assessment.

Setting the Context for the Chapter

The Western Legal System and Black-Letter Law

This discussion is situated within two legal contexts. First, the statute, or legislative law (law made by government) and case law (judgments by the courts) discussions are situated within Western legal systems and jurisdictions that have evolved from the English legal system, instituted in many nations colonised by England. In a Western legal system, parliament enacts legislation on a range of matters. However, when disputes arise, courts, which should be independent of government, interpret legislation and make judgment about its application, or develop law from equity principles, known as the common law. Court reasoning sets precedents, with precedents having superiority according to court hierarchy. In Australia, the High Court is the superior court, and lower courts must follow the reasoning, or precedent, of High Court decisions.

Many European and Asian jurisdictions have civil or codified law systems. Codified laws also exist in Western legal systems; for example, criminal law, where a code may specify both offences and penalties.[3] Under a codified criminal law, the role of the courts is to determine whether the evidence is sufficient to demonstrate that an individual has committed an alleged crime, not to decide whether an action is criminal.

The legal system is an interpretative system. The law is not 'right' or 'wrong'. Judges explore legislation to examine intent, ambiguity and clarify meaning. Given the interpretative nature of the law, it is not possible to state definitively how the courts will respond to different claims in different contexts and in different times.

The second context for this chapter is the approach taken to discuss the law. As in all fields of research endeavour, legal researchers hold different theoretical stances when considering the law, including feminist perspectives, socio-legal perspectives,

---

[1] The Strengthening and Improvement of Elementary and Secondary Schools 2002 amendments to the *Elementary and Secondary Education Act of 1965*, commonly known as 'No Child Left Behind Act' (NCLB).

[2] *Schools Assistance (Learning Together—Achievement Through Choice And Opportunity) Act 2004* ss 15, 36.

[3] *Criminal Code Act (Qld) 1899; Homicide Act 1957* (England & Wales); various state laws in the United States, such as Ohio Criminal Procedures under *General Provisions Title 29*.

critical perspectives and so on. The chapter is written from the perspective of black-letter law:

> [f]undamental legal principles that have been accepted as part of the common law or are embodied in legislation.
>
> (Nygh & Butt, 1998, p. 53)

Black-letter law analyses legislation and case law to identify the legal principles that have been used by the court and legislators, or have developed through court judgments to resolve disputes—here, for matters involving educational assessment. This approach does not challenge the court findings but seeks to present an overview of issues that have arisen in educational assessment, the degree to which the courts have been willing to entertain such challenges and the judgments and bases for reasoning, that have emerged, especially in the contexts of Australian, United States and English law.

Fields of Law and Necessary Elements for Success in a Legal Challenge

Establishing a Cause of Law

Law in the Western legal system is often discussed in terms of fields of law such as contract, tort, real and personal property, equity (including trusts), criminal, administrative, family, company and constitutional law. Education law is not seen as a distinctive legal field in itself, although with the growing quantity of legislation and litigation in this area, and the need to situate legal issues in complex educational environments, it has been argued that such recognition is due (Mawdsley & Cumming, 2008b/in-press).

Educational assessment matters usually arise under tort law and administrative law, although they may arise in any field. For example, in Fiji, an employee of the Ministry of Education (Exams) was found guilty, under criminal law, of stealing and selling examination papers and was sentenced to imprisonment, not because of the small sum of money involved, but for undermining the integrity of the examination system.[4]

However, the issues discussed here relate to the appropriate professional conduct of assessment, arising in the main under discrimination or constitutional law, tort and administrative law. Through the common law, each of these fields has established necessary elements for a case to be heard and proven, with judgment in favour of the person bringing the complaint; that is, the plaintiff. The first hurdle faced by an individual who wishes to take legal action about an issue is that they must be able to find a cause of action the court is willing to consider. An issue that in social

---

[4] *Vereivalu v The State* [2004] FJHC 154.

terms appears wrongful, harmful or morally unjust may not be so in law and may be rejected by the courts as beyond their jurisdiction.

Tort law, encompassing professional negligence, is a basis of many legal challenges in education. The most obvious are claims regarding physical injury to a student, with alleged negligence by staff in their professional responsibilities or duty of care to keep the child safe. A successful claim under tort law of negligence requires the plaintiff to satisfy several elements, established in common law in the English case *Donohue v Stevenson*[5] that:

- a duty of care was owed by the defendant to the plaintiff
- the duty of care was not met either by act or omission
- the plaintiff suffered foreseeable damage (injury or loss) as a result of the breach.

Further, the plaintiff must establish that a legal remedy can address the alleged damage, either an award of damages (financial) or an injunction that requires the defendant to do, or not to do, a disputed activity. A causal link from the negligent act or omission to the claimed damage must be established, a high barrier for education and assessment matters.

Educational assessment challenges have also arisen under administrative law, when it is alleged that appropriate policy or procedures have not been followed or natural justice has been denied, with a plaintiff often asserting an *individual* right. The status of individual rights varies across jurisdictions. In the United States, the Amendments to the *Constitution* grant individual rights that frequently form the basis of educational legal challenges, and administrative and due-process issues are therefore usually mounted under constitutional law. In Australia, similar individual rights have not been granted through the *Constitution*. England, without a written constitution, has, as part of the European Union (EU), more recently incorporated the European *Convention on Human Rights* into its framework through legislation such as the *Human Rights Act 1998* (UK). More broadly, however, general principles of natural justice such as the right to a fair hearing and to present one's case against allegations are regarded as essential in countries with a Western legal system and which operate under rule of law.

While individual rights may not be constitutionally driven, government legislation provides rights in certain circumstances. The anti-discrimination legislation enacted in many nations, at both federal and state levels, is an important example of legislated rights, with such legislation often incorporating or informing education provision.[6] Anti-discrimination legislation also demonstrates how government-made law evolves to reflect developing social mores of the time—mores established

---

[5] *Donohue v Stevenson* [1932] AC 562.

[6] Australian examples, at state level: *Anti-Discrimination Act 1977* (NSW), at federal level: *Racial Discrimination Act 1975* (Cth), *Sex Discrimination Act 1984* (Cth), *Disability Discrimination Act 1992* (Cth), *Age Discrimination Act 2004* (Cth); United Kingdom: *Disability Discrimination Act 1995*; United States (federal level) Section 504 of the *Rehabilitation Act of 1973*, *Americans With Disabilities Act of 1990*, *Individuals With Disabilities Education Act* (IDEA).

in common law through the actions of the courts before legislation is established, but which then pressure governments to adopt the same social stance.

Educational assessment challenges have occurred under a number of other fields of law such as contract, property and, a recent development, privacy law. In contract law, one party offers to provide a product or service and the other provides 'consideration' in exchange for the service, usually, but not always, money. If either side does not meet the contracted terms, then they may be liable for breach of contract and ordered by the court to fulfil the contract or pay restitution. In the United States, a high school diploma has been found to be a student's *property*,[7] and hence inappropriate educational actions that deny a student's rights to such property may be actionable. However, challenges in this area are usually mounted, and successful, under other causes of action, particularly due process under constitutional law (the 14th Amendment). In the United States, a parent of a student challenged a teacher's practice of students peer-assessing other student's work and then students calling out their grades in class as embarrassing for her children and a violation of the 14th Amendment and the *Family Education Rights and Privacy Act of 1974* (FERPA).[8] The point at issue was whether such grades were education records, protected under FERPA.[9] While this challenge was eventually unsuccessful, it demonstrates that privacy law issues may arise more in the future for assessment matters.

This brief overview of fields of law demonstrates that the courts and parties have many parameters to consider in educational law challenges. A further consideration is how a court reaches a determination. While the burden of proof necessary to convict a person of a criminal offence is 'beyond all reasonable doubt', a different standard applies in the common law areas previously discussed, the balance of probabilities—whether it is more likely than not that an event and consequences of the event occurred. Further, the balance of probabilities in some jurisdictions is considered on a sliding scale, often referred to as the *Briginshaw*[10] standard, according to the severity of the issue examined. If the consequence of a judgment is that a person could lose their work and livelihood, such a decision would require a higher standard of proof than if the consequence were a small fine.

Law and education law are complex. The educational assessment cases discussed here focus either on external examinations, including standardised procedures and public examinations and related technical matters, or appropriate diagnosis of student learning disabilities and needs, again through the use of appropriate standardised procedures. Few, if any, challenges have occurred about teacher judgment

---

[7] *Debra P. v Turlington*, 474 F. Supp. 244 (M.D. Fla. 1979).

[8] No. 99-5130, *Falvo v Owasso Independent School District No. 1-011*.

[9] Originally unsuccessful, the mother appealed, with the Court of Appeals ruling the grades were protected 'education records' under FERPA, maintained by the students as 'agents' of the school, although violation of the 14th Amendment had not been established. The School District appealed to the Supreme Court and was successful. The decision was reversed and such grades were held not to constitute education records until at least they were in 'the teacher's hands' (*Owasso Independent School Dist. No. 1011 v Falvo* 534 U.S. 426 (2002)).

[10] Based on the judgment in *Briginshaw v Briginshaw* [1938] HCA 34.

of student achievement in class, despite the large quantity of such assessment in both daily classroom instruction and high-stakes certification procedures. However, such assessment is rarely a singular and defining event that could be shown as leading to damage to a student or class, or remediable in time by a court response. Before the discussion proceeds to specific assessment issues, the overall philosophy informing the courts' response to educational challenges is worth noting.

The General Approach of Courts to Challenges of an Educational, Not Physical, Nature

Historically, courts prefer to avoid involvement in disputes against schools and statutory authorities, argued on policy grounds (Hopkins, 1996; Cumming, 2000) that allowing such actions to be considered in court would mean court involvement in implementation of public (education) policy;[11] or courts setting professional standards, which they are not qualified to do. Arguments include concern for the potential social impact of such legal cases, such as the fear of opening the 'floodgates' to educational negligence claims with financial implications for education resources,[12] or that such challenges could lead to overcautious and defensive teaching,[13] and deter good students from entering the teaching profession. While these concerns may appear to be overcautious and not based on legal grounds, they do of course reflect social reality. The fear of allegations of physical or sexual abuse has led many teachers to be very conservative in making any physical contact with students (Cumming & Mawdsley, 2008/in-press), with such fear even argued to have led to a decrease in the number of male teachers in classrooms (Sachs & Mellor, 2005). Any successful legal assessment challenge will have an impact on school or teacher behaviour.

However, such policy arguments do not transfer to the 21st century, when policy directions are towards accountability and professional responsibility of schools and teachers for students' educational progress. While courts argued previously that they could not be the creators or arbiters of professional standards for teachers, governments and the teaching profession have been rushing to establish such standards over the past decade through policy or legislation. For example, proposed amendments to the *Elementary and Secondary Education Act of 1965* (ESEA) may set professional standards for teachers in the United States, while in England 'performance standards' were introduced in September 2007,[14] linked through legislation to teachers'

---

[11] Wade J in *London Borough of Southwark v Williams* [1971] Ch at 750.

[12] *X v Bedfordshire CC* (1995) 2 AC 633.

[13] *Phelps v London Borough of Hillingdon* [1998] ELR 38.

[14] See, for example, Training and Development Agency for Schools London. (2007). *Professional standards for teachers. Core*; Training and Development Agency for Schools London. (2007). *Professional standards for teachers. Qualified teacher status, Q11*. Retrieved September 23, 2007, from <http://www.tda.govuk/teachers/professionalstandards.aspx>.

pay.[15] Such standards define professional expectations with respect to assessment proficiency or assessment-related components.

In the common law, in the mid-20th century, courts in England established the *Bolam* test as the appropriate standard of a professional; a professional has behaved appropriately if he/she has acted in accordance with a practice accepted as proper by a responsible body of professionals in that area of expertise.[16] The *Bolam* standard is now incorporated in Australian legislation, for example, in the Civil Liability Acts of Queensland, New South Wales, Tasmania and Western Australia:

> S 22 Standard of care for professionals
> A professional does not breach a duty arising from the provision of a professional service if it is established that the professional acted in a way that (at the time the service was provided) was widely accepted by peer professional opinion by a significant number of respected practitioners in the field as competent professional practice.[17]

These policy and legislative directions from Australia, the United States and England erode previous court arguments that appropriate professional teaching standards cannot be identified for use in the courts. Inevitably, professional responsibilities for appropriate and quality assessment practices by teachers and schools will underpin legal challenges in the future.

The previous discussion has provided an overview of the legal systems being considered, fields of law under which a claim may be made, the burdens for plaintiffs, and the court response. The following discussion focuses on significant areas of legal challenge that have already occurred in relation to educational assessment. I look at challenges that have occurred under discrimination law, alleged by individuals or by those who perceive systemic discrimination against themselves as part of a group of students or student cohort and challenges under professional negligence. From these cases, an important issue regarding assessment law is emerging through all of these areas of challenge—the growing engagement of the courts in matters of test validity. While this issue cannot be elaborated fulsomely in this chapter, it is worthy of specific discussion as a space to watch.

Legal Challenges in Educational Assessment

Discrimination Law and Discrimination

Most education systems have legislation that provides for provision of appropriate education for children with special needs. Identification of special needs usually requires an assessment of some form, most often through a classroom teacher referring a student for assessment. Alternatively, parents may seek specialist assessment

---

[15] The Education (School Teacher Performance Management) (England) Regulations 2006.

[16] *Bolam v Friern Hospital Management Committee* [1957] 2 All ER 118.

[17] *Civil Liability Act 2003* (Qld); see also, for example, s 22 *Civil Liability Act 2002* (Tasmania); s 50 *Civil Liability Act 2002* (New South Wales).

of their child if they feel the child has special learning needs. Challenges about appropriate or inappropriate assessment arise in Australia and England most often under anti-discrimination law or negligence, and in the United States under due process (rights) or special education legislation.

Our education and court systems are most comfortable dealing with complaints raised by individuals who belong to a class with special attributes, usually delineated in legislation, such as gender, special needs, learning or physical disability, or language or cultural diversity. Discrimination can occur either through direct or indirect action. Examples of discrimination are most obvious for students with special needs, such as a visual impairment. It would be unreasonable to expect that a student with visual impairment could 'read' a standard printed test and demonstrate their knowledge to the same extent as a sighted student (Cumming & Dickson, 2007, p. 205). In general, legislation in the jurisdictions considered here requires that appropriate adjustments should be made in assessments for students with special learning needs. In Australia, the *Disability Standards for Education 2005* (Cth), state that

> [m]easures that the education provider may implement to enable the student to participate in the learning experiences (including the assessment and certification requirements) of the course or program, and any relevant supplementary course or program, on the same basis as a student without a disability, include measures ensuring that:
> ... the assessment and certification requirements for the course or program are appropriate to the needs of the student and accessible to him or her; and ...
> (f) the assessment procedures and methodologies for the course or program are adapted to enable the student to demonstrate the knowledge, skills or competencies being assessed.[18]

In the United States, section 504 of the *Rehabilitation Act of 1973* prohibits discrimination on the basis of disability in programs that receive federal financial support. The section notes that eligibility requires both initial and continuing evaluations, and the use of test and other evaluation materials

> ... selected and administered so as to best ensure that, when a test is administered to a student with impaired sensory, manual, or speaking skills, the test results accurately reflect the student's aptitude or achievement level or whatever other factor the test purports to measure, rather than reflecting the student's impaired sensory, manual, or speaking skills (except where those skills are the factors that the test purports to measure).[19]

Legal challenges in the United States on behalf of individual students with special needs are most plentiful under the *Individuals with Disabilities Education Act* (IDEA), which provides for appropriate assessment and free educational provision for all students, with parents frequently alleging that such assessment was not undertaken or that free and appropriate provision did not occur as a result of the assessment.

Developing policy and legislation to enforce appropriate assessment for more sensitive areas of difference, such as cultural diversity, is more difficult. In England, expectations that 'access' to assessments will be suited to individual needs across

---

[18] *Disability Standards for Education 2005* (Cth), formulated under the *Disability Discrimination Act 1992* (Cth).
[19] *Rehabilitation Act of 1973* (US) s 504 [84.35(3)].

many dimensions of diversity are the most inclusively stated, such as for the Key Stage examinations in England

> It is not possible to provide specific rules governing the use of adaptations because of the wide range of children's needs and circumstances. Teachers should use their knowledge of individual children in deciding which adaptations to make, bearing in mind the nature and level of support that these children receive as part of the normal classroom practice.[20]

In general, if assessment practice can be shown to be discriminatory to a student or group of students, then the courts will find for the students. Such challenges can be avoided by ensuring that appropriate forms of assessments are available. The approach in England places great emphasis on school administration staff or teacher professional knowledge and skills to devise a range of assessment modes and forms to suit the needs of all students. No specific challenges on these grounds have been noted in England to date, but clearly, the ground has been laid for students to challenge whether assessments have been sufficiently sensitive to their circumstances.

In Australia, few legal challenges regarding assessment and discrimination in school assessment have occurred or been successful. Usually such matters are addressed through policy and administrative procedures and rarely reach courts or tribunals. One interesting case from Australia involved a student sitting for the Higher School Certificate examinations in Australia. The student, who was identified as having attention deficit hyperactivity disorder, had argued for extra examination time. He was offered a break in his examination, which he and his medical support argued was contraindicative to assisting his performance.[21] However, following policy, a practice writing activity had demonstrated that he could achieve an average standard of results within the set time frame. The student's argument was that he was hampered from being able to demonstrate superior performance through such examinations. The student was unsuccessful in his legal challenge (seeking an injunction that he be allowed extra time) as policy had been followed. This case is interesting for educators for two reasons: it demonstrates that adherence to policy is an effective way to remove the risk of successful legal action by students over assessment regardless of 'educational' fairness of the outcome; it also demonstrates that in the area of student diversity, assessment authorities have difficulty in considering students who may be both disabled and intellectually advanced. The legal standard is to enable students to demonstrate achievement to the norm, but not to consider how to enable high achievement.

Another interesting Australian case occurred when a student argued that group assessments were extremely difficult for him, given his medical condition of schizophrenia and emotional problems such as oversensitivity to his peers.[22] Evidence was

---

[20] Qualifications and Curriculum Authority (QCA), *Assessment and Reporting Arrangements (ARAs) (Key Stage 1)* [5.9], [5.8]. Retrieved November 16, 2006, from <http://www.qca.org.uk/eara/21.asp>.

[21] *BI* [2000] NSWSC 921, [34].

[22] *Reyes-Gonzalez v NSW TAFE Commission* [2003] NSWADT 22 (Unreported, Ireland J, Members Silva and Strickland, 3 February 2003) (*'Reyes-Gonzalez'*).

provided that when the student worked alone he could attain adequate standards. However, the educational institution argued that capacity to work in a team and interpersonal skills were essential learning outcomes of the course and the group assessments were essential.

Systemic Discrimination and Assessment

Outside individual challenges, major discrimination-based challenges have been launched against education authorities regarding changes in examination and certification policies. One underlying principle is that all students should have had the 'opportunity to learn' what is being assessed and adequate of notice about changes to assessment (Cumming, 2008/in-press).

The opportunity to learn challenge in the United States that has received most attention is the initial 1979 Florida challenge, *Debra P. v Turlington*, and subsequent appeals.[23] The challenge was by groups of students including 'all present and future twelfth grade public school students in the State of Florida who have failed or who hereafter fail the SSAT II (The Florida Student State Assessment Test, Part II)' and 'all present and future twelfth grade black public school students in the State of Florida who have failed or who hereafter fail the SSAT II'.[24] They challenged, under the 14th Amendment (equal protection and due process), a 1978 amendment to the *Educational Accountability Act of 1976* (Florida, US) that required students to pass a functional literacy test (the SSAT-II) in order to receive a high school diploma, to be enacted for the 1978–1979 school year. A core issue was the notice given to prepare for the changed requirements, including the provision of adequate information to teachers, given that the legislation provided just over a year to prepare for the change. The initial judgment found that a 4–6-year period was necessary for such a change to be implemented, and provided an injunction against the introduction of the new certification requirement for 4 years, confirmed on the naturally consequential appeal by the authority.

Discrimination challenges can highlight a variety of assessment issues. In another Australian challenge, a 9-year-old, gifted girl, M was denied accelerated admission to public high school.[25] The girl sought discrimination on the basis of age. Admission had been denied, in part, it was claimed, because M had not met all of the assessment standards for primary school. However, requisite levels of achievement in order to progress to high school are not explicitly stated. The student was unsuccessful but was successful in appeal to the state supreme court, with that outcome

---

[23] *Debra P. v Turlington*, 474 F. Supp. 244 (M.D. Fla. 1979); aff'd in part and rev'd in part, *Debra P. v Turlington* 644 F. 2d 397 (5th Cir. 1981); rem'd , *Debra P. v Turlington* 564 F. Supp. 177 (M.D. Fla. 1983); aff'd , *Debra P. v Turlington* 730 F. 2d 1405 (11th Cir. 1984).

[24] *Debra P. v. Turlington*, 644 F. 2d 397 (5th Cir.1981), 401.

[25] *MalaxEtxebarria on behalf of MalaxEtxebarria v State of Queensland* [2006] QADT 14, Malaxetxebarria v State of Queensland [2006] QSC 286 (4 October 2006), Malaxetxebarria v State of Queensland [2007] QCA 132.

in turn overturned by a government appeal to the appeals court. The series of cases provide informative reasoning for readers who wish to understand more about how the law operates to settle matters of dispute. While initial cases are determined on matters of fact and the evidence, appeals can generally only occur on matters of law, not matters of fact, unless fresh evidence is available. While the first challenge in the anti-discrimination tribunal was being heard, M had enrolled in a private high school and demonstrated achievement success at that level, essentially demonstrating that those assessment 'requirements' had been met. In the appeal by M, it was argued that these should have been considered. The Supreme Court agreed, returning the case for reconsideration by the tribunal. The government appeal argued that the information had not been provided to the authority, that therefore a claim of discrimination could not be found, as the 'fresh evidence' was not known at that time. The Court of Appeal held that:

> the judge hearing the initial appeal from the Tribunal erred, because of the imprecision in defining the decision constituting the alleged act of discrimination, in concluding that the reporting of the child's performance in the first semester of 2004 was a relevant consideration.[26]

Therefore, discrimination was not found and the government's decision was supported. This case demonstrates the extent to which statutory authorities will defend their decisions in the courts on grounds of law, while educators are left pondering the educational consequences for such legal outcomes.

Fortunately or unfortunately, in Australia, many challenges are settled out of court. Governments often decide that it is less expensive and potentially less damaging and likely to lead to the establishment of precedents, to settle claims by students and parents rather than to pursue matters through expensive court processes. In New South Wales, the Anti-Discrimination Tribunal had found three counts of discrimination and detriment for a child, Rhys, with motor dyspraxia, including that the school failed to provide access to the school counsellor for a full assessment, and that this was denial of a benefit to the detriment of the child.[27] The government appealed the decision, but the case was settled out of court.

This case provides an example of the significance of the role of the classroom teacher, and school leaders, in recognising that a child may need special assessments and referral. In Rhys' case, a student with a complex range of both learning abilities and disabilities, the teacher had perceived him as 'lazy and unmotivated'.[28]

---

[26] *Malaxetxebarria v State of Queensland* [2007] QCA 132, [6].

[27] Ibid. [303]. An important component of this decision is an expectation that observation of Chinchen's difficulty in interacting with school work in some contexts should have led a 'reasonable' teacher to consider that there was a problem, cf *Sluggett v Flinders University of South Australia* [2003] FCAFC 27, where in a university context, it was found the university had not acted discriminatorily in addressing a student's difficulties, as the student had not made the difficulties known to the university, and it would not be a reasonable expectation that an observer would know the nature of the disabilities.

[28] Ibid. [48].

This is not an uncommon statement in such cases. While the challenge by Rhys occurred under discrimination law, most often such challenges regarding failure to diagnose, or misdiagnosis, occur through tort or negligence law. These are best examined through consideration of the extensive United States and England case law in the area.

Professional Negligence and Assessment

The most common area in which legal challenges in assessment have occurred to date is the diagnosis and placement of students in educational programs. These cases also provide the case-law principles likely to underpin future assessment claims of a more general nature.

In the United States, the courts have consistently refused to countenance educational negligence (malpractice) claims, for the policy reasons discussed. Several historical allegations regarding misdiagnosis and educational placement, with serious consequences for individuals, have occurred but without relief from the courts. In one of the historically noted cases of 30 years ago, *Peter W*,[29] where the courts first used the policy arguments, the allegation was not just that a school and authority had failed to diagnose and provide appropriate remedial education for Peter during his schooling, but also that the assessment of his school achievements and the awarding of a high school graduation certificate indicated that Peter had made satisfactory progress when he was several grade levels below in his work, argued as 'intentional misrepresentation'. On graduation, Peter lacked the essential skills needed to undertake employment. The court found that the plaintiff had not established an acceptable cause of action as it was grounded in educational malpractice and, further, for the allegation of 'intentional misrepresentation', it had not been established that the family had relied on the advice regarding Peter's achievement, provided by the assessment reports, to their detriment. Similar cases in the United States in the 1970s and 1980s have had the same result.[30]

In another case in the United States, Hoffman, assessed on entry to kindergarten by a clinical psychologist 'in the school system',[31] was educated for over 10 years in a class for children with retarded mental development. Retesting at this point indicated he was not mentally retarded. The psychologist had originally recommended that he be retested within 2 years, as testing may have been influenced by a speech defect. This had not been undertaken as standardised achievement tests confirmed Hoffman's limited reading and mathematical skills. Hoffman was initially successful in his case and awarded substantial damages of US $750,000 by a jury, affirmed

---

[29] *Peter W. v San Francisco Unified Sch. Dist.*, 60 Cal. App. 3d 814, 131 Cal. Rptr. 854, Cal. App. 1976.

[30] *Donohue v Copiague Union Free School Dist.* 391 N. E. 2d 1352; Donohue v Copiague Union Free School Dist. 391 N. E. 2d, 1979; *Hoffman v Board of Ed. of City of New York* 400 N. E. 2d 317, 1979.

[31] *Hoffman v Board of Ed. of City of New York* 400 N. E. 2d 317, 1979, 318.

at appeal with damages reduced to US $500,000. However, the Appeal Court of New York reversed the decision and awards, restating the case as 'educational malpractice, against the professional judgment of the board of education' which would require the court 'to substitute its judgment for the professional judgment of the board of education as to the type of psychometric devices to be used and the frequency with which such tests are to be given'.[32]

A case treated differently from others in the United States was *Snow v State* (*'Snow'*).[33] Snow, who was deaf, was assessed as mentally retarded by a psychologist using an inappropriate intelligence test and was institutionalised from 1965 to 1974. He suffered permanent mental damage, his capacity to learn to communicate was affected and the state had failed to undertake further follow-up testing despite recommendations that such should occur. Snow's challenge was successful—but because it was treated by the courts as medical negligence, not educational. The courts in the United States still hold that they will not hear educational malpractice claims. However, given the previous commentary on the development of professional standards for teachers, this stance may be wobbly (Mawdsley & Cumming, 2008a/in-press).

In England, similar challenges to those in the United States have occurred, with the finding in *Phelps v Hillingdon London Borough Council* (*'Phelps'*)[34] establishing that the English courts take a contrary view to the courts of the United States and will consider educational negligence claims. *Phelps* followed similar cases, *X v Bedfordshire*,[35] involving similar circumstances to those in the United States: alleged failure to refer for assessment and identification of special needs (*E, Christmas*) and alleged inappropriate placement in a special needs program (*Keating*). Without discussing the many legal parameters considered in these cases, a central argument considered by the courts was whether school authorities and schools had a duty of care to educate children and whether failure to exercise this duty could lead to a claim of negligence.

Lord Browne-Wilkinson's judgment that a more general claim in the tort of negligence on educational grounds including inappropriate assessment or failure to assess could be available under appropriate circumstances, has been revisited in many subsequent cases.

> The question therefore is whether the headmaster of any school, whether private or public, or a teaching adviser is under a duty to his pupils to exercise skill and care in advising on their educational needs? It is accepted that a school and the teachers at the school are under a duty to safeguard the physical well-being of the pupil ... But there is no case where a school or teacher has been held liable for negligent advice relating to the educational needs of a pupil. ...

---

[32] Ibid., 319–320.

[33] *Snow v State* 98 A. D. 2d 442, 1983, aff'd 475 N. E. 2d 454 (N.Y. 1984).

[34] [2001] 2 AC 619.

[35] *X and others (minors) v Bedfordshire County Council; M (a minor) and another v Newham London Borough Council and others; E (a minor) v Dorset County Council; and other appeals* [1995] 3 All ER 353, 363.

In my judgment a school which accepts a pupil assumes responsibility not only for his physical well-being but also for his educational needs. The education of the pupil is the very purpose for which the child goes to the school. The head teacher, being responsible for the school, himself comes under a duty of care to exercise the reasonable skills of a headmaster in relation to such educational needs. If it comes to the attention of the headmaster that a pupil is under-performing, he does owe a duty to take such steps as a reasonable teacher would consider appropriate to try to deal with such underperformance.[36]

In *Phelps*, a young girl after leaving school established that her school had failed to diagnose and address her dyslexia. She had been assessed at school for her evident literacy problems, which were diagnosed as having an emotional basis, with the school's opinion that she 'lacked motivation and did not try'.[37] In 2007, Phelps was awarded damages of £45 651.50 against the Local Education Authority. Despite the relative small cost of the damages awarded versus the cost of further legal action, the decision was naturally appealed by the authority on a number of legal grounds and the appeal upheld. However, Phelps appealed further with success, heard with a number of similar cases by the House of Lords. An important comment in the appeal judgment was reference to dyslexia as a 'congenital' condition. In a sense, the decision in *Phelps*, while characterised by the English courts as a claim in educational negligence, parallels the United States court decision in *Snow*, with medical overtones. More importantly for assessment issues for classroom teachers and all students, the judgment in *Phelps* noted that:

the question which arises, and cannot be shirked, is whether teachers owe duties of care to *all* their pupils in respect of the way they discharge their teaching responsibilities. . . . I can see no escape from the conclusion that teachers do, indeed, owe such duties. . . . If a teacher carelessly teaches the wrong syllabus for an external examination, and provable financial loss follows, why should there be no liability? Denial of the existence of a cause of action is seldom, if ever, the appropriate response to fear of its abuse.[38]

Since *Phelps*, many similar cases have been heard, perhaps justifying the court fears that such judgments will open the floodgates to claims. However, many of these cases are turning on points of law, in particular, whether cases are being filed within the statutes of limitations from the time at which the plaintiff became 'aware', or 'knew' of their status or 'injury', or whether such limitation periods should be disregarded on legal grounds.[39]

---

[36] Ibid., 353, 395–6.

[37] *Phelps and The Mayor and Burgesses London Borough of Hillingdon* [1998] ELR 38, [1999] 1 All ER 421; upheld [2000] 4 All ER 504; *Phelps v London Borough of Hillingdon; Anderton v Clwyd County Council; Jarvis v Hampshire County Council; Re G (a minor)* [2000] 4 All ER 504, *Jarvis v Hampshire County Council* [2000] 2 FCR 310.

[38] *Phelps v London Borough of Hillingdon; Anderton v Clwyd County Council; Jarvis v Hampshire County Council; Re G (a minor)* [2000] 4 All ER 504, *Jarvis v Hampshire County Council* [2000] 2 FCR 310, 530.

[39] See, for example, *Rowe v (1) Kingston-Upon-Hull City Council (2) Essex County Council* [2003] EWCA Civ 1281; *Adams v Bracknell Forest Borough Council* [2004] 3 WLR 89; *Richard Smith and Liverpool City Council, Hampshire County Council, Knowsley Metropolitan Borough*

A recent case in England presents the quandary for educators and the courts previously noted in Australian cases dealing with assessment issues for students with a disability but the potential for high achievement. *Skipper*[40] argued negligence due to failure to refer for appropriate diagnosis of learning difficulties, specifically dyslexia, and that appropriate diagnosis would have led to appropriate treatment within the year. The student was, however, very capable in other areas. Negligence was claimed against the school's educational psychologist in 1994 and 1997 for failing to diagnose dyslexia, although this did apparently occur in 1997.[41] The damages claimed included humiliation for, among other matters, 'the persistent attitude of the teachers that she was lazy and could do better if she tried' and, 'the lost gain', loss of *better* grades in GCSEs and A levels, and career opportunities,[42] particularly the loss of options for a professional career and salary.[43] While the school allowed more time in examinations, the Examinations Board did not allow extra time for her GCSE and A-level examinations.[44] The original challenge was struck out for lack of prospects of success due to the judge's view that the claimant would not have been able to prove loss.[45] On appeal, the case was allowed to proceed; further outcomes are not known at the time of writing.

Professional Negligence, Assessment and the General Classroom Teacher

The cases discussed previously have involved individual challenges, by students with special needs, under either discrimination or negligence law. Clearly at this point in time, the United States courts will not sanction claims of educational negligence in assessment against classroom teachers. In England, the dicta of the courts in the judgments that have been discussed allow the potential for such cases to be heard, if the elements of negligence can be established. Establishing these elements for a whole classroom is more difficult, as it is necessary to show that all students suffered a detriment due to a teacher's negligence, and further that a remedy can be established.

No such cases have been identified in English law. However, two settled cases in Australia show that care is needed and the legal potential exists. In these cases, the negligence was not so much in the teachers' assessment practices but the apparent failure to teach the appropriate curriculum for external examinations for certification

---

Council [2006] EWHC 743 (QB); *Marr v Mayor and Burgesses of The London Borough of Lambeth & Ors* [2006] EWHC 1175 (QB).

[40] *Skipper v Calderdale Metropolitan Borough Council, The Governors of Crossley Heath School* [2006] EWCA Civ 238.

[41] Ibid., [3].

[42] Ibid., [4].

[43] Ibid., [16].

[44] Ibid., [9].

[45] Ibid., [5].

purposes. A class of students from a New South Wales' secondary school alleged negligence when their Higher School Certificate (HSC) English examination results fell in the lowest 20 per cent of outcomes in the state, in contrast with the results for their other subjects, which were in the top 20 per cent (Williams, 1996). It was reported that the teacher had failed to teach a significant component of the curriculum with resulting limitations on students' capacity to achieve in their examination. The case, and another similar case, was reportedly settled out of court (Tronc, 1999). However, the cases highlight the implications of Lord Browne-Wilkinson's assertion that all teachers could be held responsible for professional classroom practices, including assessment.

Professional Negligence and Testing Development and Administration

Test developers are well aware of the legal consequences of errors in test development and administration. Reported multi-million dollar settlements have occurred.[46] The dramatic increase in the United States of standardised testing under the *No Child Left Behind Act* (2002) has led to fairly regular reports of failures in test scoring. These failures have affected large numbers of students (and teachers undertaking proficiency tests), often preventing them from attaining the university of their choice, having impact on their employability, or in the worst instances, requiring students to undertake summer studies unnecessarily and to resit examinations.

Similar problems have arisen with limited frequency in Australia but have occurred; for example, loss of HSC papers in New South Wales, misrecording of results of the GAMSAT. In England, errors in setting, distributing or scoring examinations have been reported.[47] As the number of mandated tests increases and professional test-development resources are stretched, the likelihood of errors increases. Not only will students be affected, but with increased emphasis on publication of various 'league tables', schools could end up misreported to the authorities and to the public, with serious consequences for reputation and funding. If the increase in such testing continues, the legal professional may reap the most benefit.

---

[46] See, for example: Winerip, M. (2006). Standardized tests face a crisis over standards, *The New York Times* March 22, 2006: 'Pearson admitted that it had incorrectly scored thousands of the College Board's SAT tests. The Educational Testing Service agreed to pay $11.1 million to settle a class-action suit brought on behalf of 4, 100 people who were told that they had failed a teacher licensing test when they had actually passed. And in New York, new seventh- and eighth-grade tests developed by McGraw-Hill included several questions from practice tests that were mistakenly used again on the real tests.'; *The Sun*, Baltimore, Md.; welcome to the *Russo v NCS Pearson*, Inc. SAT settlement website <http://www.fairtest.org/3-million-settlement-sat-scoring-error> at 8 April 2008.

[47] Lightfoot, L. (2002). Head teachers demand exam board's closure 1 June 2002, *The Telegraph*; Hall, M, Exam chaos as computer error wipes out records. 19 May 2002, *The Telegraph*.

The Courts and Validity

Many of the assessment misdiagnosis cases rest on the use of inappropriate tests with the student being assessed. These have been considered under professional negligence matters. However, despite the reticence of courts to enter into discussions about educational policy and government decision making, on a number of occasions, the courts have considered technical issues of validity of testing to inform decisions.[48] Such considerations normally occur when the matter has high stakes, and aligned with either discrimination allegations or allegations of failure to provide due process.

In the first appeal for *Debra P.* in 1981, the court, while affirming lack of due process for the graduating class, reversed a lower-court finding that the test to be introduced was appropriate for use.[49] The appeal court considered that test validity had not been established and ordered further 'factual findings' as to 'whether the test covered material actually studied in the classrooms of the state',[50] termed 'curricular' validity,[51] or as the Court more succinctly put it, 'if Florida is teaching what it is testing',[52] in order to allow the test to be reintroduced.[53] The validity hearing by the District Court in Florida was reported in 1984.[54]

A program of surveys and observations of classrooms was established, interviews conducted with a range of stakeholders and instructional material was examined. The court had heard testimony from different experts, with experts for the defendant, Dr James Popham and Dr Robert Gagne, concluding that the SSAT-II was instructionally valid, while experts for the plaintiffs, including Dr Robert Linn, argued both limitations to the work undertaken to establish the validity as well as the sufficiency of the exposure of the students to the material for the test to be fair.[55]

The judgment in this final review of *Debra P.* shows the distinction between the level of proof needed to satisfy the courts regarding the validity of a test versus the expectations of educational professionals.

> ... in large part, this Court has been called upon to settle not only a legal argument but also a professional dispute. At times, the distinction between these two spheres has blurred. The

---

[48] *Gulino v New York State Education Department* [2006] USCA2 305; 460 F. 3d. 361, provides extensive and recent discussion of test-validation requirements for employment-related tests, in this case with respect to teacher certification testing. The case is interesting for the background provided on the different legal expectations of validity for content-related tests versus predictive/construct-related tests. Most education tests are defined as content-related.

[49] *Debra P. v Turlington* 644 F. 2d 397 (5th Cir. 1981), 400.

[50] Ibid., 402.

[51] Ibid., 400. See also, *GI Forum et al. v Texas Education Agency et al.,* 87 F. Supp. 2d 667 (W. D. Tex. 2000), 672. Following the arguments of opportunity to learn in *Debra P.*, if the curricular validity of a test can be established for an existing student population, this may reduce the time needed before its introduction.

[52] *Debra P. v. Turlington* 564 F. Supp. 177 (D.C.Fla. 1983), 179.

[53] *Debra P. v Turlington* 730 F. 2d 1405 (11th Cir. 1984), 1409.

[54] Ibid.

[55] See *Debra P. v Turlington* 564 F. Supp. 177 (M.D. Fla. 1983), 181–182.

experts for both sides spoke in terms of 'fairness', 'adequacy' and 'sufficiency'. Yet, these terms are not necessarily synonymous with constitutionality ... any judicial decision on this issue 'will reflect only the minimum standards essential to fairness under our legal system. Policymakers must meet, but are not limited to, the minimum standards pursuing the goal of educational equity for students' ... In other words, even though the defendants might have implemented a much more equitable program, their actions might still pass constitutional muster.[56]

Test validity was also considered by the court in *Anderson v Banks*,[57] a case on similar grounds at the same time as *Debra P*. The court noted that:

> ... in light of the strong language in Debra P., the Court has no choice but to conclude that the ... District has not sustained its burden. ... 'fundamental fairness requires that the state be put to test on the issue of whether the students were tested on material they were or were not taught' ... The Court can only conclude that where the award of a diploma depends on the outcome of a test, the burden is on the school authorities to show that the test covered only material actually taught.[58]

About the same time, in another United States case, an argument was made by plaintiffs that a test should have separate validation for 'handicapped students'.[59] However, the case was determined on a different point of law and the courts avoided the issue of such validation.

More recently, in *G.I. Forum v Texas Education Agency* ('*G.I. Forum*'),[60] a case that has prompted considerable debate and academic writing (see, for example, McNeil, 2000; Saucedo, 2000; Ward, 2000), the court considered the validity of a test that formed part of high school graduation requirements. The test was found to be a valid measure of student mastery of expected skills and knowledge, that is, to have 'curricular' validity,[61] although the outcomes for students through the implementation of the requirement for higher test scores for high school graduation, the focus of the legal challenge, led to a prima facie finding of 'significant adverse impact' on Latino and African-American students.[62] However, the public purpose was found by the court to override this impact. It is interesting to see a case judgment in which a judge has had to summarise matters such as Rasch item analysis and consider the appropriateness of 'cut scores' to determine student passing grades,[63]

---

[56] Ibid., para. 183.

[57] *Anderson v Banks* 20 F. Supp. 472 (SD Ga. 1981).

[58] Ibid., 509.

[59] *Brookhart v Illinois State Board of Education* [1983] USCA7 1; 697 F. 2d. 179, [20]. In this case, the school authority was ordered to graduate a number of plaintiffs who had met all graduation requirements apart from the test but met other requirements, on the basis that they had not been given adequate notice, given that they would need more time to meet requirements than 'normal' students, and the time lapse since leaving school meant it was unrealistic to expect the students to return for additional classes, [37]–[38]. The legal argument was lack of due process leading to denial of a property right (the graduation diploma).

[60] *GI Forum et al. v Texas Education Agency et al.*, 87 F. Supp. 2d 667 (W. D. Tex. 2000).

[61] Ibid., 682.

[62] Ibid., 679.

[63] Ibid., 680.

although, as the judge noted, the court was not asked to 'rule on the wisdom of standardized examinations'.[64] In *GI Forum*, the court took cognisance that 'current prevailing standards for the proper use of educational testing recommend that high-stakes decisions ... should not be made on the basis of a single test score'[65] (AERA, APA, NCME, 1999, Standard 13.6). The court noted that the Texas graduation requirements for students had three components, of which the standardised test was only one. The issue was whether this met multiple sources or graduation hinged on the Texas Assessment of Academic Skills (TAAS) tests. Given the other graduation requirements and the fact that the students could undertake the TAAS nine times before graduation, the court found that, therefore, graduation did not hinge on a single test score or a single test administration.[66]

Assessment Challenges, the Law and the Future

This discussion of the variety of areas in which educational assessment has been challenged in the courts highlights where the courts have been and the directions they have taken. The discussion is not exhaustive of topics, case law or findings. However, it does serve to show the many ways in which educational assessment may come under scrutiny.

Despite some of the recent outcomes in the English courts, the judgments tend to show that plaintiffs have a high burden of proof to establish failure to follow due process, discrimination or negligence. From this perspective, the weight of decisions tends to favour schools and authorities. In general, in law, authorities, schools and teachers do not need to be fearful about floodgates of educational assessment claims if policies are clear and care is taken to consider the educational needs and opportunities of all students. While legal challenges will clearly continue, sufficient guidance is available to educators about the standards necessary to avert successful claims. Similarly, test developers and authorities need to maintain vigilance in test preparation and administration or face very expensive litigation consequences.

However, consideration of the case law to date, and the directions that are being followed, in conjunction with the increasing dependence on student achievement data for accountability purposes, provide insight into some new areas where challenges might emerge or flourish more strongly in the 21st century.

First, the imposition of testing for school certification purposes has the courts considering the nature of tests more carefully. An area of litigation yet to reach jurisdictions outside the United States to the same degree as in the United States has been public delving into the validity of various forms of assessment or examination, both with the match to intent and the match to different sectors of the student population.

---

[64] Ibid., 669–670.
[65] Ibid., 674–675.
[66] Ibid., 675.

While the matter has been avoided in the courts to date, Baker and Linn (2002) have argued that standardised tests should be validated both for students whose language is not English and with special populations—to ensure 'the test reflects the student's knowledge and skills but not the specific disability' (pp. 21–22). Given the growing recognition of the impact of culture on knowledge and learning, assumptions that validity established within a dominant cultural group is valid for all may not hold up in courts of law (Mawdsley & Cumming, 2004). We can also expect more court challenges about the adequacy or inadequacy of provision of alternate modes of assessment (not just accommodations) to assess student achievement, given that legislation that requires alternative forms and the extent to which compliance has not yet been achieved. In the United States, many education systems are walking a tight timeline in the development of alternative forms of assessment to meet legislated guidelines. Furthermore, what are the consequences of the current policies, practices and legal interpretations for those children who are both learning enabled and disabled? Will the educational or the legal system adjust to meet their needs first?

Genuinely different forms of assessment, including classroom assessments, need to be developed, challenging prior technical definitions as to what constitutes validity and reliability, and creating forms of assessment that truly address the complexity of each student—in terms of learning abilities, language and cultural backgrounds. Expectations that 'standardised' procedures will have to become more genuinely accommodating and non-standardised will grow with the increasing expectation of individual rights in all jurisdictions, not just the United States. In England, the European Convention is having an impact on the rights of individuals. In Australia, some states (and a territory) have implemented or are considering Charters of Rights and Responsibilities for individuals. Educators will need to be aware of these contexts. It is true to say that, at present, education and the courts deal with diversity in terms of special needs or educational difference as categories that deviate from, to make a critical observation, a hypothetical norm. However, returning to the original statement that the courts can be active to make law that reflects changing equity values in society, the courts may eventually be convinced that current practices do not reflect equitable practice in fact.

Second, in conjunction with this direction towards strengthened expectations of individual rights, governments, schools and authorities may have to stop assuming that student assessment data are available without constraint for their use. Individuals, even young children, may start to claim rights under privacy legislation. Consider the current circumstances. In most jurisdictions, universities would not provide student achievement data to parents without the student's authority, even for students not of legal age. In schools in Australia, high-school graduation certification and achievement data are provided to a student directly, not to parents, even though many students are not of legal age. In many European countries, many students in senior schooling are of legal age, and schools have to deal with the students directly. There is no legal impediment to a younger child seeking to have their data kept confidential and not used for purposes without their permission. An authority may be able to prevail legally by arguing that provision of achievement information to parents or guardians is in the child's best interests.[67] However, this would not give the school or authority automatic access to use the achievement data for other purposes such as school rankings. In Norway, in 2004, the government sought to introduce a new framework testing to be used to provide information about the quality of schools. The change invoked considerable controversy, not just about the purpose, but also with respect to the quality of the tests to be used. The students' union advocated a boycott of the tests and by the second year of implementation, 2005, between 36 and 45 per cent of high school students in upper secondary school boycotted the tests in mathematics, reading and English writing (Tveit, 2008, personal communication). The Norwegian testing reform became a political agenda at the next election, a change in government led to a year's moratorium on the testing, and consultation with stakeholders, with students through their union having considerable input, to improve the framework and purpose of the new curriculum and assessment policies (Hølleland, 2007), with new tests proposed only for 5th and 8th grades from 2007. (See Chapter 12 for a more thorough discussion of this reform.) In the 21st century, we may see increased expectations by students (and their parents) that they will be involved in assessment policy decisions and not be treated as compliant robots enacting the latest assessment policy agenda. In the United States, challenges are increasingly mounted within states, by students and parents, about what are seen as excessive and educationally inappropriate assessment regimes[68] and are continuing by the states against federal regimes that are seen as being without established educational merit.[69] Participant stakeholders have already started to use the courts, albeit mostly unsuccessfully to date, to try to establish a voice in educational assessment policies.

Third, the more education systems and schools promise, even without the boundaries of contract law, the higher the expectations that parents and students will hold for the learning outcomes the students will achieve in school. Parents and students will therefore expect to see evidence that both a range of outcomes has been achieved by the student and teaching and assessment focuses address a range of outcomes. The narrowness of the current accountability regimes is constantly criticised. However, little criticism has yet occurred regarding the lack of other forms of evidence of student achievement. What student or parent in the jurisdictions considered here would currently believe that they have adequate information

---

[67] While Australia does not have individual rights, it is a signatory to the United Nations *Convention on the Rights of the Child 1989*, which establishes rights for children in education. The underlying principle of the convention is that acts have to be in the 'best interests' of the child (Article 3.1). The convention has been incorporated in various legislations in Australia. England, as part of the United Kingdom, of Great Britain and Northern Ireland, is also a signatory; however, the United States is not.

[68] See, for example, Bowie, L. (2007). Graduation exams test states' will—groups challenge new standards to earn a high school diploma. October 7, 2007.

[69] Walsh, M. (2008). Full Appeals Court to reconsider ruling that revived NCLB suit. *Education Week*, May 1, 2008. Retrieved May 6, 2008, from <www.edweek.org/ew/articles/2008/05/07/36conn.h27.html?tmp=2025380746>.

about student progress in developing critical thinking, personal resilience, problem-solving, or life-long learning skills? However, these are all proposed as key learning goals of schooling. Will parents and students start to challenge for *more* assessment to be addressed at these areas? What field of law might they use: administrative law claiming that outcomes are not being met? Contract law if fees are being paid? Tort law for negligent omission of important educational outcomes? This possibility is a stretch, but if the real stakeholders in education exert for more power, who knows what the future will bring?

Areas that currently are the domain of courts can be removed from the courts by specific legislation. Some areas of contention are dealt with initially in many jurisdictions through the use of tribunals. In Australia and England, alternative dispute resolution is increasing in use, and not all disputes head to the courts. It may be that if education challenges in law increase, nations will introduce an arbiter, an education ombudsman, as the first port of call to resolve disputes. Many would consider this a desirable direction for future education law and a way to reduce court involvement with its incumbent significant time delays and costs, that '[q]uick, efficient and cost effective public law remedies at the time are surely better than post mortems long after the event' (Booth, 1998, p. 3).

This chapter has only been able to consider some of the areas, and outcomes, in which legal issues and challenges have arisen with respect to educational assessment. What is certain is that current policy agendas and the increased frequency and public nature of assessment and accountability, in conjunction with growing expectation, with or without constitutional support, of individual rights will heighten awareness of legal implications of educational assessment with a subsequent increase in challenges. In addition, a discussion of legal issues for teacher performance assessment and determination of pay has not even begun.

References

American Educational Research Association (AERA), American Psychological Association (APA), & National Council on Measurement in Education (NCME). (1999). *The standards for educational and psychological testing*. Washington, DC: AERA.

Baker, E., & Linn, R. (2002). *Validity issues for accountability systems*. Los Angeles: NCRESST.

Booth, C. (1998). Foreword. *The Liverpool Law Review, 20*(1), 1–3.

Cumming, J. J. (2000). *Establishing a professional standard for teachers' duty of care*. Proceedings of the Australian and New Zealand Education Law Annual Conference, Adelaide, 12–14 July.

Cumming, J. J. (2008). Legal and educational perspectives of equity in assessment. *Assessment in Education: Principles, Policy and Procedures, 15*(2), 123–135.

Cumming, J. J., & Dickson, E. A. (2007). Equity in assessment: Discrimination and disability issues from an Australian legal perspective. *Education and the Law, 19*(3–4), 201–221.

Cumming, J. J., & Mawdsley, R. D. (2008). Student searches in Australia: A consideration of roles, responsibilities and rights of students, school staff and police. *Australia and New Zealand Journal of Law and Education, 13*(1), 49–70.

Hølleland, H. (2007). Nasjonale prøver og kvalitetsutvikling i skolen. In S. Tveit (Ed.), *Elevvurdering i skolen—grunnlag for kulturendring* (pp. 29–44). Oslo: Universitetsforlaget.

Hopkins, A. (1996). Liability for careless teaching: Should Australians follow the Americans or the British? *Journal of Educational Administration, 34*(4), 39–59.

MacAdam, A., & Pyke, J. (1998). *Judicial reasoning and the doctrine of precedent in Australia.* Sydney: Butterworths.

Mawdsley, R. D., & Cumming, J. J. (2004). High stakes testing and the demand for school district accountability: A dilemma for special education students in the United States and Australia. *Australia and New Zealand Journal of Law and Education, 9*(2), 19–36.

Mawdsley, R. D., & Cumming, J. J. (2008a). Educational malpractice and setting damages for ineffective teaching: A comparison of legal principles in the U. S., England and Australia. *Education and the Law, 20*(1), 25–46.

Mawdsley, R. D., & Cumming, J. J. (2008b). The origins and development of education law as a separate field of law in the United States and Australia. *Australia and New Zealand Journal of Law and Education, 13*(2), 7–20.

McNeil, L. M. (2000). Sameness, bureaucracy, and the myth of educational equity: The TAAS system of testing in Texas public schools. *Hispanic Journal of Behavioral Sciences, 22*(4), 508–523.

Nygh, P. E., & Butt, P. (1998). *Butterworths concise Australian legal dictionary.* Sydney: Butterworths.

Sachs, J., & Mellor, L. (2005). Child panic', risk and child protection: An examination of policies from New South Wales and Queensland. *Journal of Education Policy, 20*, 125–140.

Saucedo, L. M. (2000). The legal issues surrounding the TAAS case. *Hispanic Journal of Behavioral Sciences, 22*(4), 411–422.

Tronc, K. (1999). Educational malpractice. *Australian Professional Liability—Education, 20*, 303.

Ward, C. A. (2000). *GI Forum v Texas Education Agency*: Implications for state assessment programs. *Applied Measurement in Education, 13*(4), 419–426.

Williams, P. (1996). Suing for negligent teaching: An Australian perspective. *Journal of Law and Education, 25*(2), 281–306.

Part III
Assessment in a Context: Geography, Policy and Practice

Chapter 10
Teachers' Use of Assessment Data

Patrick Griffin

> ... *it was important* ... *to say* ... *that a test signals where to*
> *start intervention and not the end point of instruction* ... *the*
> *idea of Evidence Based Teaching is very important and I*
> *complement you on highlighting the idea and your emphasis*
> *of obtaining appropriate resources to implement effective use.*
> Robert Glaser (personal communication, 28 June 2007)

Developmental Learning Framework

The emphasis has to be on development, and teachers need to be clear about the difference between deficit and developmental learning approaches. Clinical and deficit approaches sometimes focus on the things that people cannot do and hence develop a 'fix-it' approach. 'It is a myth that intervention is only needed for the struggling student' (Tayler, 2007, p. 4). Developmental models not only build on and scaffold existing knowledge bases of every student, but they also have to be clinical in that they focus on readiness to learn and follow a generic thesis of developing the student. They ought not entertain a deficit thesis of focusing on and emphasising 'cures' for learning deficits. In order to become a specialist in developmental learning, teachers need to have expertise in developmental assessment because it is integral to the formulation of personalised learning plans. How often have we heard the teacher say 'we start where the student is at'? It is impressive rhetoric but unless teachers are capable of monitoring learning and identifying where both the student and the teacher are 'at' on developmental pathways, and targeting intervention, it is likely that the rhetoric may be realised only serendipitously. This chapter examines an overall approach to the use of assessment data to inform teaching intervention decisions and then illustrates the possible results that can be achieved.

In a developmental framework there is a need to break the link between whole-class teaching and instructional intervention. Teachers have to focus on 'individual developmental and personalised learning' for every student. When teachers pursue a developmental model, their theory of action and psychology of instruction needs to

P. Griffin (✉)
Melbourne Graduate School of Education, The University of Melbourne,
Parkville VIC 3010, Australia
e-mail: p.griffin@unimelb.edu.au

C. Wyatt-Smith, J.J. Cumming (eds.), *Educational Assessment in the 21st Century*,
DOI 10.1007/978-1-4020-9964-9_10, © Springer Science+Business Media B.V. 2009

focus on theorists who have promoted and given substance to developmental learning. Being able to identify the 'Vygotsky zone of proximal development (ZPD)' is fundamental to the identification of where a teacher would intervene to improve individual student development (or 'where the student is at'). Teachers need to be able to recognise and use the evidence to implement and monitor within the Vygotsky approach. Which developmental theory underpins the work is negotiable, but choosing a developmental theoretical basis is an important aspect of all forms of teacher education (both pre-service and in-service) if teaching for individual developmental learning is to be realised.

It is also evident that when a developmental model of learning is implemented, the teacher has to reorganise the classroom and manipulate the learning environment to meet the needs of students. Manipulation of the learning environment is an important skill, and the way in which a teacher links classroom management, intervention strategies and resources used to facilitate learning is always a challenge. The strategies need to be guided by a developmental framework of student learning.

Changing the Paradigm: Assessing 'What' and 'How Well' in Learning

The topic 'assessment' still conjures images of tests. Tests conjure ideas of standardised measures of literacy and numeracy and 'easy-to-measure' disciplines. Standardised measures conjure normative interpretations, labelling, ranking and deviations; there is a widespread belief that ease of measurement dictates assessment and that the hard-to-measure subjects are ignored. Assessment and measurement are in turn seen as reducing learning and curriculum to what is easy to measure. In fact, nothing is too hard to measure. As Thurstone (1959) said, 'If it exists it can be measured and if it can't be measured is doesn't exist'. It all depends on how measurement is defined.

It is not necessarily true that only easy areas are measured. A slight reconceptualisation of measurement can allow assessment to focus on difficult areas to measure and help link learning to targeted intervention. Educational measurement typically demands technical skills, and its specialists are generally engaged in large-scale testing programs at systemic, national and international levels. Assessment, on the other hand, requires a different but overlapping set of skills and is linked more generally to teaching and intervention, although measurement can and should be conceptually at least underpinning the assessment. Too often at the school level, or in teacher education, measurement or technical aspects of assessment are seen as encroaching on discipline areas of curriculum. It is often regarded as a subdomain of curriculum. Of course, assessment is a part of curriculum, but it needs explicit treatment and the development of the relevant skills base.

Griffin & Nix (1990) defined assessment as the process of observing, interpreting and making decisions about learning and intervention, whereas measurement was regarded as the process of assigning numbers to observations. Neither of these is curriculum. *It is only when the numbers have a meaningful interpretation that measurement and assessment begin to merge and they build a link to curriculum.* The bodies of knowledge for measurement and assessment are different but overlapping. What a psychometrician does is not what a classroom teacher does, but the logic and framework that a psychometrician works with can be used to inform classroom practice and, where it is, the teacher is offered a more rigorous approach to personalised and clinical approaches to intervention.

In a curriculum framework, teachers are taught to identify what is wrong, mostly using test items or assessment tasks (rich or otherwise) to identify what the students cannot do and then to concentrate on fixing, or curing, the problem. The focus on fixing deficits is the 'norm'. The motive looks like 'fix the weak and let the strong learn on their own' (Stanovich, 1986). This leads to the situation in the classroom where one group of students struggles to learn things far beyond its learning readiness, another group is coasting ahead of the 'pack' and the rest of the class is being taught as a homogeneous group.

It is possible to turn it around and engage every student at their point of readiness to learn. A shift towards developmental-learning outcomes demands both a change in thinking about curriculum and developmental learning, and the method for implementing change across multiple levels of student learning.

The first step, assessment, monitors what a student needs to learn. It is not always possible, and certainly not necessary, to assess everything that all students need to learn, but assessing a good sample of the attitudes, skills and knowledge is important. Hence, there is no need to list all the discrete skills as a definitive litany of mandatory achievements that must all be demonstrated. The attitudes, skills and knowledge that students acquire are not isolated, discrete entities. They are best learned when they are conceptualised and introduced as sets of cohesive and interrelated skills, attitudes and knowledge that build to a developmental continuum.

Test Construction and Developmental Progressions

Good tests and good assessments have a psychometric basis, in that they attempt to measure a specific developmental pathway that psychometricians call a 'variable' (or construct). Sometimes a test or assessment task might attempt to measure a small set of variables; teachers need to know and understand the nature of the underlying variable. Addressing or teaching to the underpinning construct is important because it takes away any focus on each of the individual test items.

Embretson and Reise (2000) showed that the overall test developmental variable is made up of three parts. These were the underlying developmental progression, or 'latent' variable, the items that point to the developmental progression, or 'manifest', variables and the error associated with each of the test items. Each individual item can measure a range of things, some of which are related to the latent developmental progression, but they each measure 'other things' as well; the extent to which these 'other things' influence the measure is related to the reliability of the test. The extent to which the items relate *as a set* to the developmental progression emphasises the validity of the test and of the interpretation of the construct. A test instrument is constructed to measure student ability on a developmental progression (or, technically, a latent construct), not on the individual items. In this sense the nature of the item selection for the test is, while not unimportant provided that the item set is sampled from the appropriate domain, designed to measure a specific trait. Figure 10.1 shows the relationship between the latent construct (developmental progression), the test items and the error terms, or 'noise', in the measurement of the construct.

Embretson and Reise (2000) also showed that the test items represented separate ideas that built into the developmental construct. It is the construct or the progression that mattered, not the specific choice of items. The items are replaceable, provided that the 'bigger idea' or the developmental progression can remain the main basis of the assessment and understanding of the student development. The items might be represented as 'little ideas' all contributing to the measure of the 'bigger idea' embedded in the progression. At the same time, each test item is measuring other things as well. The tendency to measure or reflect the influence of other things is known as 'measurement error'. The danger in focusing on the 'little ideas' (or teaching to the test) may mean that the process is unable to see the 'forest for the trees'.

It is possible that some items may have different properties in different schools or in different curricula. If this is the case it is identified using a process called 'differential item function analysis' (Adams & Khoo, 1995). When measurement

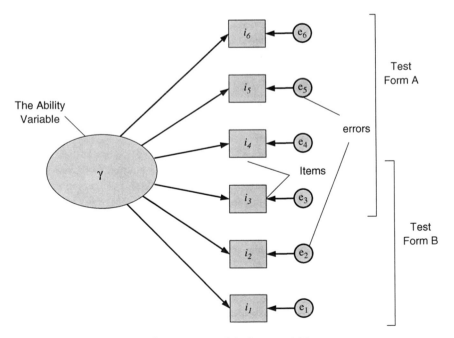

Fig. 10.1 Relationship between items, errors and the latent variable

specialists identify this effect, the offending items are usually excluded from the test intended to measure a common construct across different student samples. In classroom tests it is possible to identify this effect with a little analysis, but the detail is beyond the scope of this chapter. It is generally the case that the standardised test used in high-stakes programs have been through this evaluation process and offending items have been removed. The sample of items left still measure the same underpinning construct but the absence of some topics often raised the ire of content-focused assessment specialists.

It is also important to remember that a test is one way to observe student behaviour in order to make an inference about their ability and their location on a developmental progression. It is just one form of evidence and generally needs to be considered along with other information that the teacher might have. Once the developmental progression is described the teacher can use it, the test data and other evidence to make decisions about the student's level of development.

Perhaps the greatest weakness of the reports linked to high-stakes accountability testing programs is not the lack of consistency across schools, but the failure to explicate the nature of the underlying variable. The reports too often have focused on individual items and encouraged this approach to interpretation. We often see media discussions of individual items illustrating student deficits and ignoring the overall picture of development or level of competence.

The competence levels are related directly to the definition of criterion-referenced interpretation of data. Glaser (1963, 1981, 1990) first defined criterion-referenced performance and development in terms of the tasks performed. However, this definition lost the idea of multiple tasks that form a cohesive and developmental continuum, and the misinterpretation of the concept in the 1970s led to the distortion of the concept. Glaser later clarified criterion referencing as 'the development of procedures whereby assessments of proficiency could be referred to stages along progressions of increasing competence' (1981, p. 935, emphasis added).

The words 'stages along progressions of increasing competence' are important in test design and calibration. However, criterion referencing is a means for interpretation rather than a means for test design, and *criterion-referenced interpretation* is the correct term rather than criterion-referenced testing. Criterion-referenced interpretation is also an excellent framework within which to use item response modelling such as the Rasch model (Rasch, 1960; Wright & Stone, 1979). Glaser's word 'stages' can cause concern because some interpret 'stages' as a strict hierarchical step. In fact, the stages are artificial divisions on a continuum. The thresholds between contiguous levels are arbitrary; a person can theoretically be placed on the continuum within each 'stage'. Progression on a continuum is *not* monotonic and individuals will make progress, but it is almost always mixed with regression depending on the context of observation.

Performance in a competency model is dependent on context. A person's performance depends on the demands made by the context and the personal factors at work at the time of the observations. These variations are generally interpreted as measurement errors, but we know that there are a range of issues that affect performance. If the test fails to engage the student, the performance will be reduced. If the student is not interested, is ill, unmotivated or in general disinterested, it will not accurately measure ability. Therefore, any use of a score to identify a level or stage is influenced by both the personal factor and issues arising from the instrument itself. Hence, the use of the term 'stage' does not imply a fixed description of a performance, but one that is indicative of a phase of development and different instruments or different circumstances, all of which may change this measurement. The variation in the measures is generally called 'measurement error'. In this way, we can argue that the use of levels is more likely to capture the description of the person's competence than a single number or score. It is educationally more meaningful (for teachers' use) to use levels or stages of competence than a score or a number.

Variable Mapping

There are ways to use the data constructively, however. Combining the ideas of criterion-referenced interpretation with item response modelling directly links a measure of the position of a person or an item on a variable (a variable map, as shown in Fig. 10.2) to an interpretation of what a student, or groups of students, can do, rather than focusing on a score or the performance relative to a percentage or a group. It also orients the use of the test data towards substantive interpretation of the measurement than does a score or grade. The combined set of procedures gives meaning to test scores and helps to establish the meaning and interpretation of the latent variable. As such, it has important implications for the validity of the variable and helps to focus attention on the 'bigger picture', rather than the collection of little ideas represented by the items. The little ideas represented by the items are defined by the cognitive skills that are required to get the right answer to each of the items. The process of identifying these skills is called a 'skills audit'.

It can be seen from Fig. 10.2 that test items tend to group or cluster together at different points along an underlying dimension or scale. Once the clusters are identified, the next task is to determine whether the items within these clusters can be interpreted as having something in common. Figure 10.2 exaggerates the idea of clustering to assist in explaining the point. Each item is reviewed for the skills involved in responding correctly. The process requires an understanding or empathy with 'how the students think' when they are responding to the items. Experienced teachers are very good at this task and those dealing with mathematics or science instruction can readily identify the levels within the test from a skills audit of individual items.

The variable map in Fig. 10.2 shows that items are grouped according to similar levels of difficulty. Students are represented by X; items are represented by the circle with the item number embedded, and the interpretation of the skills involved in the item clusters is represented by the text on the right of the figure. The levels are differentiated using the horizontal lines. In this example five levels are shown, but the number of levels depends on the clusters and separation of the items on the latent variable represented by the vertical arrow. Given that the ability of the students is approximately matched to the difficulty of the items at each level, and the items and

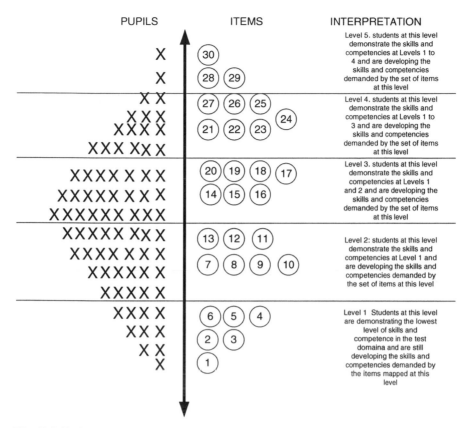

Fig. 10.2 Typical variable map interpretation

students are mapped onto the same scale, the students can also be grouped within the same 'ability'/'difficulty' range as the items that have similar difficulty levels. This grouping of items (and students) identifies a kind of 'transition point' (indicated by the horizontal line), where an increase of item difficulty is associated with a change in the kind of cognitive skill required to achieve a correct answer.

When the person's ability and the item's difficulty are equal, the odds of success are 50/50. Hence, in Fig. 10.2, the students represented by the Xs adjacent to the cluster of items have about a 50/50 chance of being able to solve the items in the adjacent cluster of items, less than 50/50 chance of solving the items above their level and a better than 50/50 chance of solving the items below their level. It is also possible to describe their level of ability by identifying the cognitive skills in the items at each level or cluster. If the student were to improve a little, they would have a better-than-even (50/50) chance of succeeding on items in the adjacent group, and it could be argued that the main task of a teacher is to increase the odds of success in each of these competency levels to a level greater than 50/50. It is also a clear identification of where the student is 'ready to learn' and will learn with assistance more readily than they would learn alone. This level where intervention is best targeted has the same interpretation as the ZPD (Griffin, 2007).

Improvement through intervention at the ZPD can take the student close to, and perhaps past, the transition point between clusters of items; the students are beginning to exhibit a change in cognitive skill. This is, in turn, defined by the set of cognitive skills demanded by the group or cluster of items. Curriculum and teaching specialist panels (or teachers) need to undertake the content analysis of the skills/competencies required to succeed on the set of items. A change in the required cognitive skill level could be directly translated into an implication for a change in teaching, and so discussions with curriculum specialists would be needed to identify the kind of instruction needed to help the student progress on the variable or construct. A summary description of these skills can then be assigned to each item and the student.

The item grouping can be justified on statistical and conceptual grounds if the items have behaved in a cohesive manner that enables an interpretation of a variable underpinning the test. This item behaviour is sometimes described as a Rasch-like manner because it is also a requirement of the Rasch model analysis. Labelling the skills is based on conceptual rather than statistical grounds. If the items within a group do not suggest a meaningful and unifying set of skills or competencies, the set may need to be 'adjusted' to make the interpretation clearer; that is, some items may need to be omitted because, despite statistically appropriate qualities, they may not be conceptually relevant to the underlying construct or to identifiable and comprehensible levels within the construct. This is a more powerful reason for omitting items from a test than a misfit analysis. Under these circumstances, they might not belong in the test at all. These procedures can, at times, also identify gaps in the item set. These approaches have been explained in detail by Griffin (1998). The labelling or clustering interpretation is not just a list of the skills for each of the items included in the cluster. Identifying and naming the level description involves a similar process to that used in interpreting a factor in a factor analysis. In Fig. 10.1, it is the description of the construct, or the 'big idea', underpinning the set of items in the cluster. This is a generalisation of the level description, treating the items in the cluster as a sample of all possible items that could represent this level of development.

There is a further advantage to this procedure. If the content analysis 'back translates' to match or closely approximate the original hypothesised construct used to design and construct the test, it can also be used as evidence of the construct validity. When this is linked to the index of item separation there are two pieces of evidence for the construct validity of the test (see Wright & Masters, 1983; Griffin & Nix, 1990). The technique of 'levels' has been used sparingly but has emerged in several international studies, including the PISA and Southern and Eastern African Consortium for Monitoring Educational Quality studies (Murimba et al., 2002). Greaney and others used the procedure in their report on the Pakistan *Education For All* project (Greaney, Khandker, & Alam, 1990), in which they cited Griffin and Forwood's (1990) application of this strategy in adult literacy. More recently, Murimba et al. (2002) illustrated the competency levels identified in the SACMEQ tests across 15 southern African countries.

From a curriculum point of view, the clustering and labelling enable teachers to identify where targeted intervention is warranted for individuals. Systems can use aggregated data on distributions across levels for the identification of priority areas at which to thrust resources. It is a more efficient approach than that which focuses on individual items and encourages 'washback' based on item-level skills or 'little ideas'. However, recall that the skills embedded in the items represent only a sample of the population of possible skills that make up the developmental progression. The skills used in the test might only be used because they are relatively easy to obtain in large-scale testing programs. When teachers use this test information, they need to be encouraged to supplement with other observations.

The Fundamental Role of Assessment

In any assessment, it is only possible to use directly observable behaviour because these act as pointers, or indicators, to an underpinning generalised learning. Humans can only provide evidence in the form of what they *write, make, do* and *say* (Griffin, 1997), and it is from these four observable actions that all learning is inferred. This is the basic and fundamental role of *assessment*—to help interpret observations and infer learning. The more skills are observed, the more accurately generalised learning can be inferred. Hence, there is a need to document the discrete observable skills and find a way to blend them into cohesive evidence sets so that strategic intervention can be a part of teaching and learning. The range and quality of the data (records of observed skills) enable the inference of a developmental progression, and this enables a *generalisation* to be made that can be independent of the specific set of discrete skills observed. Generalisation helps to identify where scaffolded intervention can occur (Vygotsky, 1986) for every student—high achievers as well as the lower achievers—and this is the basis of developmental learning. It eschews deficit thinking.

Of course, every student is different and no one follows a generalised pattern exactly, but it is possible to identify the typical *generalised* developmental path. It gives the teacher a framework within which to work, but it never replaces the judgment of the teacher about where to start, how to proceed or how to teach. Rather, it becomes the framework within which teaching decisions can be made (Griffin, 2007). The developmental progression is therefore an organising framework for communication, reporting and scaffolded intervention purposes. It is not a measure of performance. It is not a score, not a grade and not an assessment instrument.

Formative Assessment and the Role of Professional Learning Teams

In the context of assessment and learning as outlined in the preceding discussion, formative assessment has to be an identification of the appropriate level of development for a scaffolded intervention by the teacher, in order to facilitate a student's progress. It is not the identification of a weakness, lack of skill or error. This is an important point in making maximum use of formative assessment. It is also not true that any form of continuous assessment is formative. Unless they are linked to a developmental progression, practices called 'formative assessment' can be relatively useless and can even be detrimental to student learning.

Formative decisions based on developmental assessment also define the *intervention* role of a teacher. It is a truism that students learning at different levels on a developmental progression need different teaching strategies. Formative assessment in a developmental model focuses on the level of readiness to learn, not the errors, deficits or flaws. Where this is not recognised, it is possible for the teacher to fall into the trap of teaching to a test and, while this might improve a test score, it does not necessarily improve ability or generalised development. (For example, coaching for an intelligence test may improve the IQ score, but not the person's intelligence.) Once a student's level of development is identified, the teacher's decision making shifts from *what* the student needs to learn to *how* the student can best learn at that level (ZPD). This involves the teacher in making decisions about what *intervention strategy* is best for that student at the generalised level of development or *readiness to learn*. When confronted by a range of students at differing levels of development and with differing learning needs and styles, the teacher may need to use a range of teaching strategies even with small groups of students. Practical experience suggests that students can be grouped by levels of development, and a teacher does not have to individualise every aspect of teaching and learning, but classroom management is affected.

Because there will inevitably be a range of possible intervention strategies, just as there are students at different levels of development, *resources* needed for each level also have to be identified, and teachers working alone often need support. Discussion, monitoring and evaluation by the teachers targeting instructional strategies help to clarify and spread the accountability between teachers within schools. There is evidence linking formative use of assessment from standardised tests to the improvement of student learning outcomes through critical and collaborative analysis and discussion of data (for example, Phillips, McNaughton, & MacDonald, 2004; Halverson, Grigg, Prichett, & Thomas, 2005). Evidence-based problem analysis focusing on teacher activities and student achievement is an effective form of professional development that links assessment data directly to teaching, using the evidence for discussion in professional learning teams (PLTs) (Hawley & Valli, 1999). Teachers need to discuss with their colleagues their materials and interventions for each student or group of students.

In addition to monitoring student developmental learning, teachers need a process with which to analyse the data, link them to their own teaching and test the links using evidence in PLTs. The role of these teams is important to the improvement of student learning. Teachers need the opportunity to test their understanding of the data, to propose their strategy and resource allocation and to have their colleagues examine these interpretations and strategies from a critical perspective. When this is done in teams for each learning sequence for the students at different levels on the continuum, real professional development occurs, accountability to peers is inbuilt and teachers get reinforcement from their peers. The students are the eventual winners.

If data are used this way, it is imperative that teachers understand their own practice and how it relates to student achievement. Critical and collaborative discussions where teachers test their theories about these links in PLTs are an important vehicle for doing just that. Discussion and analysis as a component of professional development have been shown to improve teaching and student achievement (Timperley & Robinson, 2001) and are an effective form of professional development in comparison to traditional workshop models (Hawley & Valli, 1999). Worthwhile and significant change in teaching practice can occur when teachers are engaged in examining their own theories of practice (Bransford, Derry, Berliner, & Hammermass, 2005; Hawley & Valli, 1999; Richardson, 1990).

It is of course important for teachers to reflect critically on their own practice individually, but doing so collaboratively has been linked to improved student achievement (Ladson-Billings & Gomez, 2001; Phillips et al., 2004) and changed teacher perceptions (Timperley & Robinson, 2001). Collaborations in PLTs enable teachers to have access to a greater number and divergence of theories against which to test their theories, particularly if the community draws on differing expertise, but it can be a slow and painful process (Ladson-Billings & Gomez, 2001). It does, however, instil a peer approach to accountability within the team and enables each teacher to draw on the expertise and experience of their colleagues. Learning teams of teachers and school leaders, policy makers and researchers can accelerate learning, but the collaborations are only effective if they involve rigorous examinations of teaching and learning, rather than comfortable collaborations in which ideas are simply shared (Ball & Cohen, 1999; Robinson & Lai, 2006).

Having and using the assessment tools, however, are insufficient conditions for teachers to inform their teaching (Halverson et al., 2005). Using standardised assessments formatively also requires the tests to have sufficient diagnostic capacity for teachers to monitor students' learning developmentally. Teachers need to be able to access and interpret assessment data at both the group and individual levels. The diagnostic, clinical or formative capacity of the test must be linked to the identification of the latent variable (the developmental progression). Test scores and item-level (right/wrong) data can be detrimental to formative use of tests. Unless the test items act as a cohesive set and allow the levels of clusters of items to identify underpinning skills, the diagnostic information is minimised and perhaps even counterproductive. When the items act as a cohesive set, they allow an underlying variable to be recognised and used in a formative process.

Different interventions need different *resources* to be identified, acquired, used and evaluated. It may be that the same resource can be used for different levels of development; it may be that the same level of development and the same skill acquisition needs different resources for different students with different learning needs. Matching resources and intervention strategies to student readiness and learning styles is a complex professional skill and one that needs well-developed classroom management skills and resource use. They are professional decisions that teachers make when faced with students at different developmental levels, and with differing developmental needs and differing learning styles. Discussion among teachers can and does help to clarify these decisions and the teachers gain critical support from their colleagues. The importance of sharing and discussing these strategies and resources as part of a learning team is an important step forward.

Can It Be Done? Reading Comprehension Through Collaborative Learning Teams

The Literacy Assessment Project

In 2004, the Catholic Education Office of Melbourne (CEOM) trialled a range of reading comprehension assessment instruments in 20 Catholic primary schools to examine the benefits and limitations of each. The project evolved in response to schools seeking advice on what was an appropriate approach to the assessment of reading comprehension in years 3 and 4. A whole-of-school commitment to, and by PLTs, was required in order for schools to be accepted into the project.

Assessments Administered

The project involved the use of standardised tests administered to students in years 3 and 4. At the beginning and end of an 8-month period, teachers were asked to administer two reading assessments: a year 3 AIM Reading test (VCAA, 2003–2005) and one of a TORCH (Mossensen, Hill, & Masters, 1993), PROBE (Pool, Parkin, & Parkin, 2002) or DART test (ACER, 1994). It represented considerable work for the teachers who had to mark the tests and record for every student whether the answer to each item was correct. A total of 70 teachers administered the tests to approximately 1640 students each year. The assessment data were analysed to develop a *Progression of Reading Development*, discussed next.

Establishing the Progression of Reading Development

Common item-equating procedures were used to map all the items from the four tests onto the same continuum (Write & Stone, 1979). All but four of the 236 test questions mapped onto a single underlying variable. The skills audit was then used to interpret the variable and a common *Progression of Reading Development* of eight levels was identified. Students were placed at one of the levels according to their test performance.

The test items were content-analysed and calibrated using item-response theory (Rasch, 1960) to determine whether they provided similar information and whether they could be used interchangeably to report progress and identify starting points for learning. As mentioned, a skills audit was performed. The TORCH, DART and

AIM Reading test developers provided some skill descriptors as part of the test documentation, but the PROBE test required a complete item skills audit. The PROBE test questions were classified by the test authors according to six elements of comprehension: literal comprehension, reorganisation, inference, vocabulary, evaluative comprehension and reaction. In some cases, it was difficult to distinguish between the elements of PROBE and confirm the specific skill required to complete a question. When all test items were audited, the skill descriptors were arranged in order of item difficulty and this gave a series of ordered descriptions from which a developmental reading progression emerged. The progression had eight levels. Students were placed at one of the levels according to their two test scores, but a very small number of students had inconsistent scores across their two tests. One test might have had a high score but the second a low score. There were not many of these, but they posed a problem for interpretation of student performance. A decision was taken to use the higher of the two scores.

The teachers were provided with a look-up table that enabled a conversion from a raw score to a level (see Fig. 10.3). Item-response logit values also showed that the width of each of the levels 1–8 were 2, 1.1, 0.4, 0.8, 0.6, 1.7, 1.2 and 2 logits, respectively. The widths of the band levels were important to understand the magnitudes of the growth patterns demonstrated by the students. Repeated studies of development have shown that a growth of 0.5 logits can be expected with a 1-year program for the typical student. This developmental progression therefore represents better than 8 years of development in reading comprehension. The look-up table contains information from the AIM tests, the TORCH and the DART tests. No data have been included in the table for the PROBE because the subtests in the PROBE package were unreliable, and it seriously affected the vertical equating procedures.

The data were collected at the beginning and end of the first year and again in the second year. It became clear that there were irregularities with data from students taking the PROBE test. This was traced to the low reliability of the PROBE test, which was attributed to the design of the tests in the PROBE package. A short, seven-item test, for example, mapped onto an eight-level scale led to unstable results. Compare this to a 45-item test as in the AIM, mapped to eight levels. The problem was accentuated by teacher judgment in scoring the PROBE because of inconsistency in marking stringency. However, teachers indicated that PROBE was a useful tool because it provided exercises in each of the cognitive classifications and the teachers valued the advice on teaching strategies and resources to meet individual students' learning needs. So, while PROBE went some way to providing this advice, the DART, TORCH and AIM Reading tests had greater stability as assessments for progress reporting.

The Professional Learning Teams

Figure 10.4 shows the three collaborating organisations involved in the project. The CEOM oversaw the project. Teachers from years 3 and 4 from each school

Levels and Logits across Literacy Tests Year 3 | Year 4

Level	logit	AIM3 04	AIM3 05	AIM5 04	AIM5 05	D1	D2	t1	t2	t3	Level	AIM3 04	AIM3 05	D1	t1	t2	Level	AIM5 04	AIM5 05	D1	D2	t2	t3
8	4.6						27				I						I						
8	4.5										I						I						
8	4.4			29							I						I						
8	4.3										I						I						
8	4.2										I						I						
8	4.1										I						I						
8	4			28	28						I						I						
8	3.9										I						I						
8	3.8				28						I						I						
8	3.7										I						I						
8	3.6			28					19		I						I	30	28		25	20	
8	3.5				27					21	I		26	27	19	20	I	29	27				
8	3.4		27								H	26		26			I	28		24			
8	3.3						25				H		25				I	27	26				
8	3.2			27		27					H			26			I			23			
8	3.1										H						I						
8	3		26		26						H	24	24	24			I	26	25				
8	2.9						24				H						I						
8	2.8			26					18		H			23			I						
8	2.7	25			25						H						I		24	22			
7	2.6					26				20	H						H	25					
7	2.5			25	24		23				H						H		26				
7	2.4										H		23			19	H			19			
7	2.3		25	24	23		22	17			G	23		22			H	24	23	21		21	
7	2.2					25		18	19		G				18		H						
7	2.1			23	22						G		22				H						
7	2	24			21		21				G						H		22				
7	1.9			24	22	24			16		G			21		18	H			20			
7	1.8				20		20		18		G						H	23			18		
7	1.7			21	19	23		15			G						H	25	21				
7	1.6		23	20	18		19			17	G	22	21	20	17		H	22		19			
6	1.4	23	22	19	17	22	18		14		G						H		20			20	
6	1.3							17		16	G					17	H						
6	1.1	22	21	18	16	21	17				F		20	19			H			18			
6	1			17	15			13	15		F	21				16	H	21	19				
6	0.9		20			20	16	16			F						H					17	
6	0.8	21									F					15	H						
5	0.7		19	16	14	19	15		12	14	F		19	18	16		H	24				19	
5	0.6			15	13					13	F	20		17		14	H	20	18	17		18	
5	0.5	20		14	12	18	14	15	11		F		18			13	H	23			16		
5	0.4		18								F	19		16			H	19	17				
5	0.3	19	17	13	11	17	13			12	E		17	16	12		G	18	16	22	16		
5	0.2								10		E			15			G					15	
4	0.1	18	16	12	10	16	12	14		11	E	18	16		11		G	17		15			17
4	0			11	9				9		E						G		21			14	16
4	-0.1	17	15			15				10	E	17	15	14	14		G		15	20	14	13	
4	-0.2			10	8	14	11	13			E			13	13		G	16	14				
4	-0.3	16	14	9	7	13	10	12	8	9	E	16	14				F	15		19	13		15
4	-0.5	15	13								E					9	F		13		12		
3	-0.6			8	6	12	9		7	8	D	15	13	12	12		F	14			12		14
3	-0.7	14	12			11		11	6	7	D		12	11	11	8	F	13	12	18	11		
3	-0.8			7	5		8				D	14				7	F			17		10	13
3	-0.9	13	11			10		10			D		11	10			F	12	11	16	10	9	12
2	-1.1	12	10	6			7		6	6	C	13		9	10	6	E		10		9	8	
2	-1.2	11				9		9			C	12	10		9		E	11	9	16		7	
2	-1.4	10	9	5	4	8				5	C	11	9	8	8		E					6	10
2	-1.6	9	8	4	3	7	5	8	4		C	10		7	8		E	10	8	14	8		8
2	-1.7							7		4	C			6	7	5	E			13	7	5	7
2	-1.8					6					B	9	8				E	9			12		6
2	-1.9	8	7				4		3		B						D		7	12	6	4	5
2	-2			3	2						B	8	7	4	5	3	D			11			4
1	-2.1	7				5		6		3	B	7			4		D	8	6	10	5		3
1	-2.2		6								B					2	D						
1	-2.3	6					3	5			B	6		3		1	C			9		3	
1	-2.4					4					B		6		3		C		4	8	4	2	
1	-2.5	5	5	2					2		B	5			2		C	7	5	7			2
1	-2.6										B		5				C	6					
1	-2.7		4					4		2	B	4		2	1		C						
1	-2.8					3	2		4		B	3	4				C			6	3		
1	-2.9	4	3								B	2	3	1			B	5		5	2		
1	-3				1			3			B	1	2				B	4	3	4	1	1	
1	-3.1										B						B						
1	-3.2			1							B						B						
1	-3.3	3	2				2			1	B						B						
1	-3.4										B						B						
1	-3.5									1	B						B						
1	-3.6							1	2		B						B						
1	-3.7		1								B						B						
1	-3.8	2									B						B						
1	-3.9										B						B						
1	-4										B						B						
1	-4.1										B						B						
1	-4.2					1					B						B						
1	-4.3							1			B						B						
1	-4.4										B						B						
1	-4.5										B						B						
1	-4.6	1									B						B						
1	-4.7										B						B						
1	-4.8										B						B						
		AIM3 04	AIM3 05	AIM5 04	AIM5 05	D1	D2	t1	t2	t3		AIM3 05	AIM3 04	D1	t1	t2		AIM5 04	AIM5 05	D1	D2	t2	t3

Fig. 10.3 Look-up table for teachers to convert raw scores to levels

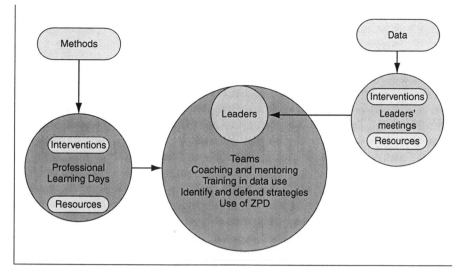

Fig. 10.4 Professional learning teams in a collaborative partnership project

formed the PLTs. The PLT leadership role[1] was undertaken by the school's literacy coordinator. The university provided inputs in two areas. The first was in the field of assessment and the use of data in a developmental assessment framework. The second was in providing an overview of reading comprehension and the associated intervention strategies.

PLTs worked to investigate and extend their knowledge of strategies for comprehension and began to identify a range of intervention strategies that could assist the development of reading skills for students at different comprehension levels. The literacy team leaders also attended professional learning sessions to reflect on the data and build a common understanding of its interpretation and links to teaching strategies. This was consistent with Joyce and Showers (2002), who argued that unless structured opportunities for professional development and training were provided, teachers found it difficult to acquire new teaching skills; and unless adequate follow-up and support was provided in the school, the new skills do not transfer into the classroom. Teachers needed to control their professional learning as a key to the improvement in the quality of student learning and teacher effectiveness.

The PLTs operated in a tiered approach. Each school-based literacy team was led by the coordinator, who in turn belonged to a leaders' team. The leaders' team met with the project specialists and shared results, discussed and critiqued the assessments. They were, at a school level, accountable to other team leaders for their developing expertise and the way in which they understood and used the data. They

---

[1] The leadership role was critical as the PLT leader had to be involved in all project meetings. The PLT leader was also given the opportunity to be both a lead learner who had the 'big picture' of the project and as such could contribute to overall the project design and management.

were also responsible for explaining the evidence to their literacy teachers in the school-based team and for reporting to the leaders' team and the project management the impact and effect on the literacy PLTs. The tiered accountability model ensured that external expertise could be distributed across the schools in an efficient manner. It also meant that accountability was operating at two levels. Team leaders were accountable to other team leaders for the way in which they understood, used and explained the evidence to their colleagues in the PLTs and how this led to improvements in student learning at their schools. Teachers were accountable to other teachers in their school for the way in which the evidence of development was used to identify intervention strategies and relevant resources. They needed to link the developmental level of individual students to an intervention strategy and then discuss it with their colleagues. Team leaders had to summarise the overall strategies of the literacy team and link this to the development and evidence of growth that the data showed for their school. The external specialists were accountable for the quality of the data and their reporting materials that the team leaders and the literacy teachers were using in the schools. It was a multi-tiered accountability approach for the use of data in intervention, and student growth and development in reading comprehension.

School-level aggregated data always showed growth, but this was not surprising given the effects of maturation and normal expected progress for each year level. An example of a typical school's data is shown in Fig. 10.5. The horizontal axis represents the eight levels in the reading comprehension scale. The vertical axis represents the percentage of students at each level. The two superimposed bar charts represent the assessments at October in each of 2005 and 2006. The shift to the right is interpreted as growth. Was it just maturation? It might be, but if it were, it was astonishing and uniform, large, maturation effects across the 20 schools. Based on large-scale studies using item-response analyses, there is evidence of a substantial shift in reading comprehension development. The difference in the item-response measure (logits) between the high and low levels is more than 8 logits. This was

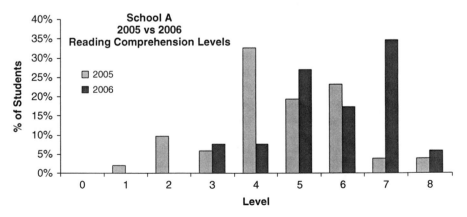

Fig. 10.5 Gains from 2005 to 2006 by years 3 and 4 for school A

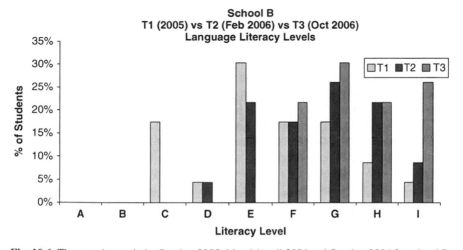

Fig. 10.6 Three testing periods, October 2005, March/April 2006 and October 2006 for school B

approximately 1 logit per reading comprehension level (see Fig. 10.6). As noted, a look-up table was provided to teachers for translating test scores into logits and levels of development. In national, state and international studies the general gain per year level is 0.5 logits per school year. This includes general gains on the AIM test used in this project when it is used in a state-level cohort testing. The average gain per school in this study was approximately 1–1.5 levels or 1.5 logits—three times the normal expected gain. If this is maturation, it is extraordinary. However, the average gain is not the only way to describe the shift. Consider the lowest group. They have moved upwards by two levels and one school had improved by 2.7 logits—four to more than five times the expected growth! Less growth is evident at the upper levels, but this could be because of the limits of the measurement instruments. In any pre-test and post-test design, as used in this program, students who are lower initial performers will appear to grow or improve more than those students at higher initial performance levels. This effect, known as 'regression-to-the-mean', will occur regardless of any intervention (Campbell & Russo, 1999). So while the gains in the lower levels are impressive, some might be attributed to maturation, some to regression and some to practice effect due to the retesting procedures. However, gains are still up to five times the expected gain; gains of such magnitude cannot be dismissed as attributable to design threats to validity.

The collaborative basis of the three-tiered PLTs recognised and developed the knowledge, expertise and skills that the project team brought to it. The results of the *Progression of Reading Development* were provided to the teachers in a discussion forum. Professional learning was shared in these forums and both literacy coordinators and project team members gained insights from each other as the discussions cantered on the application of the *Progression of Reading Development* and its application to targeted and differentiated teaching (Griffin, 2007; Perkins, 2005). Close liaison was maintained between the university, the CEOM and the literacy coordinators in each of the schools. When the literacy leaders examined the data with the CEOM and university staff, no attempts were made to identify the appropriate teaching strategies. The main point was the recognition that intervention was needed, and targeted intervention was essential for students at different levels of development. The emphasis was always on *what* had to be learned and the team leaders then took this information to the professional learning teams in the school to work on strategies and *how* learning was to take place.

The work of *team leaders* was also central to the process of developing the teachers' confidence in using an evidence-based developmental framework. All members of the PLT examined the data in light of their knowledge of individual students, and this also assisted in identifying and remedying any anomalies in the data. The team leaders worked with their *teams* to trial and document appropriate teaching strategies and resources. The substantial growth can be seen in the Figs. 10.5 and 10.6 for two schools over two and three assessment periods, respectively.

A series of reports was provided to teachers. The first represented the individual student performance on the developmental continuum. This has been labelled the 'rocket' report (see Fig. 10.7), and it presents a mix of criterion-referenced and norm-referenced interpretations of the student performance data. The mark on the spine of the report indicates the student's position on the developmental continuum. The box represents the inter-quartile range and enables an interpretation of the student's performance relative to the other students in the school. The descriptions at the side of the 'rocket' describe a summary of each developmental level. The level adjacent to the black marker is a summary description of the ZPD where scaffolding can best be used. It is at this level of development that teachers were encouraged to identify intervention strategies.

The second set of data was the class report (see Fig. 10.8). In this report, it was possible to see, for each student, the results of two or three assessments. In Fig. 10.8, the results for October 2005, March and October 2006 are represented by different shades in the columns in the chart. The descriptions across the top of the report are identical to those in the 'rocket' chart. The top of the bar for each student is at the same position as the marker in the 'rocket'. It indicates the level at which the student is developing. The shaded region is the inter-quartile region for the most recent assessment. The report shows how much progress each individual has made. The report also shows how the rate of change is relative to the group rate of change. The teacher is given an overall perspective of the class and individual achievement levels, rate of change of achievement and the effect of intervention for each individual. It also helps to identify relatively homogeneous intervention groups. It is clear that not all students progress equally, or even at all. Some regress. This was difficult for teachers to accept and, at times, predictably from a teachers' point of view, cast doubt on the measures, but working through the data for each student item by item soon showed that the data were accurate, and the student performance was erratic. Measurement error appeared to have been influenced by student engagement in the assessment as well as by instrument effects.

Team-debriefing sessions at school used these presentations of data analyses by the team leaders, who were trained in the use of the reporting software. The

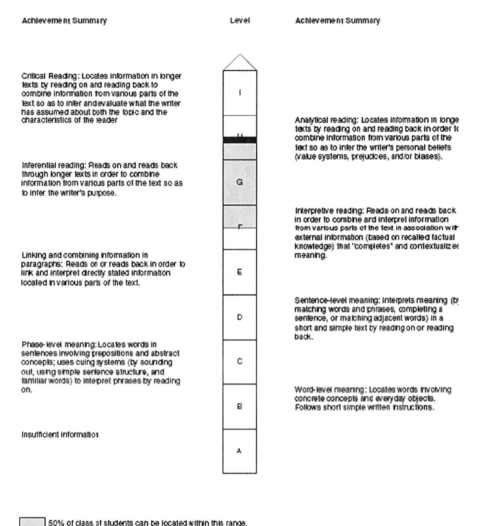

Fig. 10.7 Criterion report for an individual student

teams discussed modifications in teaching, differentiated intervention and targeting in teaching strategies. Project team members held separate meetings with the team leaders. After 1 year, there had been a substantial change in discourse, intervention practice and resource use linked to change in student literacy development. School teams also selected an area of inquiry about the learning and teaching of reading and their investigation was linked to both student and teacher learning. It helped to highlight the importance of the assessment data. At project meetings, team leaders shared with colleagues from other schools their resources for teaching intervention, and these materials were prepared for a website for all schools to use.

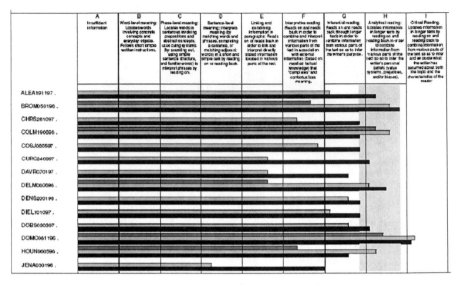

Fig. 10.8 Class-level report showing change against levels for individual students

The importance of PLTs cannot be overstated. Each school allocated time for their teams to meet and examine the data and its connection to their intervention practices. The team leaders shared teaching experiences among colleagues during team meeting days and with leaders from other schools during project meetings. Through these professional learning sessions, all teachers had the opportunity to engage with new and challenging understandings that were directly relevant to improving student outcomes in reading. Professional learning opportunities were drawn from research, ensuring that input was theoretically based and situated within school data. The knowledge and experience bases of teachers were valued and incorporated into the theoretical framework upon which the work was based. Consideration was given to ensuring there was a mix of both input from outside experts and opportunities for teachers to work through issues and engage in learning activities. The ongoing nature of the project, with a consistent cohort of schools and team leaders engaged in the project for over 4 years, has provided time for an action research cycle to occur, with an emphasis on reflective practice (Kemmis & McTaggart, 2000).

Project Outcomes

An analysis of student data over the period of 2005 and 2006 indicated that students had made progress as measured across the developmental progression. Not only had the cohort moved up the scale, but also the spread had not increased. This suggested that all students were developing and the 'tail' of the distribution was not being left behind or remaining static, as was the expected case if the data from Rowe and Hill (1996) study were to be replicated. It was also clear from the measures described above that a year's expected gain (about 0.5 logit) was exceeded many times over by groups, but there were also individual students who appeared to regress. Teachers set about specific intervention with those individuals but always emphasised the readiness issue in determining the 'what' and 'how' of teaching and learning.

The project's success in 'raising the bar' and 'closing the gap' (Fullan, 2005) coincided with a deepening of teacher knowledge and discourse. Confronting the teachers with the evidence of student development and the heterogeneity of the class with respect to reading comprehension development caused an inescapable shift in emphasis.

At no stage were any teaching strategies prescribed, or even recommended. Teachers were shown the data, provided with an interpretation and asked what they would do about it. An external opportunity for discussion and discourse on reading instruction was attended by all members of the school teams after the leader had had a chance to discuss class and individual student results with their team members. They had also had a chance to search for suitable intervention strategies and resources before the professional development day.

A marked shift was identified in the discourse of the literacy team leaders. The same was true of the in-school team members due to their engagement in discussions about the targeted and clinical, interventionist evidence-based approaches to learning and teaching of reading. At the beginning of the project, the initial focus of the discourse centred on the reading acquisition as a discrete set of skills to be taught, learned, practiced and applied. It also focused on resources for their own sake without connection to the level of development of the students. Assessments were used to identify students' mastery (or non-mastery) of discrete skills, and intervention was viewed as a direct approach to teaching specific skills that had not been mastered, using texts and other resources written for specific skill acquisition. It was a clear example of a deficit approach to teaching and intervention. The reading curriculum was being defined in terms of discrete skill acquisition. After the first annual cycle of data interpretation and targeted intervention, aimed at personalised learning plans for students at each level on the developmental progression, the discourse had changed, the view of reading development had changed, the approach to intervention had changed and, more importantly, the results showed obvious gains for students. Every school group had moved upwards on the scale, some more than others. The 'tail' was moving up at the same or a better rate than the 'top'.

A developmental progression on its own, however, will not result in student learning improvement unless there is accompanying change in teacher behaviour and a relevant change in curriculum and resources. When a developmental progression was used in conjunction with targeted instruction, gains were achieved. Changes in teacher behaviour depended on being able to use the evidence appropriately and these, in turn, were dependent on opportunities to learn from externally provided professional development at team leader level, internal development within the teams and whole-of-team professional development provided externally. The combination led to whole-of-school changes in pedagogy. It was never assumed that teachers working in isolation had the expertise or opportunity to design the effective learning opportunities to move the students along the continuum, even when they had identified a starting point for a student's learning. This understanding developed with exposure to evidence, experience in PLTs and opportunities to learn abut data and its links to intervention, and their accountability to each other as members of the learning teams.

Perceptions of Professional Learning

In the PLTs, teachers acknowledged that they generally had a range of data that they consistently used. The practice of placing students on the developmental continuum not only confirmed their teacher perceptions but also gave them a framework and a language that enabled their perceptions to be shared with other members of the team. This meant that data were examined by the entire team, and that all members of the team shared teaching and learning needs and addressed teaching strategies, supporting each other. They gained input from both the assessment project data, from the professional team learning days (offsite, in which specialists presented on teaching strategies for reading development) and from their team meetings (onsite).

Identifying students' levels on the developmental reading progression or their ZPD for scaffolding purposes were not on their own translated directly into effective teaching. This decision needed opportunities for the teachers to develop their knowledge of developmental learning and their understanding of appropriate targeted intervention practices. The teachers drew on the examples learned at the professional learning days (offsite) and emphasised the importance of their own and their colleagues' knowledge and experience in identifying appropriate intervention strategies together with the need to develop personalised learning plans for each student based on readiness to learn. In order to achieve this, they had to learn to use the data, link the data to an interpretation of each student's development and then match a teaching and resource strategy to the student's readiness to learn. This was the fundamental link between practice and theory, coupled with focused professional reading and professional learning opportunities. It underscored the importance of data-driven instruction accompanied by an emphasis on teacher learning and professional development.

Implications for Teacher Education

An important series of questions remain. Can this be applied to pre-service teacher education? Can it be developed into packaged in-service teacher education? Is it possible to establish PLTs consisting of teachers and student teachers, with a team leader? Can the teams be given the opportunity to address specific learning issues in a school, supported by the university-backed 'offsite' and 'in-school' professional development with team leaders steering the professional learning 'onsite'? How can a developmental learning progression underpin each target problem, if, for example, the development is in arts, aesthetics or another discipline which does not normally develop this way? Would this be a successful approach in pre-service teacher education?

It is clear that teachers do not work effectively as solo teachers. Some can, but maximum gains are achieved under the following conditions.

1. Teachers need to learn how to work as members of PLTs.
2. Teachers need skills in interpreting and using data to make decisions about teaching and learning intervention.
3. The teams have to have an approach to peer accountability at a within-school level.
4. Accountability has to be linked to the way teachers use data to make decisions about intervention.
5. Intervention decisions have to be matched with the right resources.
6. Team leaders need to be accountable to other team leaders at a between-school level.
7. The team leaders have to be accountable for the way in which they use the training to inform and lead their colleagues at the within-school level.
8. Project leaders and specialists (if there are any) have to be held accountable for their advice and input to the team leaders.
9. Accountability at every level consists of transparent decision making and collaboration with the members of the learning community.
10. Central to the teacher learning teams is the use of an interpretation framework that links learning and teaching. This is usually in the form of a developmental learning progression. Where this is available, teachers have a common framework to identify intervention points and appropriate teaching strategies for individual students.
11. Discussion of these intervention points and resources appropriate to the intervention is an essential aspect of the professional learning team and peer accountability.

Glossary

Assessment A process of gathering, interpreting and using information about learning. The process of gathering can take many forms, from tests to performances or work samples. The interpretation usually involves some form of measurement or coding and their use leads to decisions about teaching and learning

Calibration A process that assesses the accuracy of the modelling process described in the item-response modelling explanation. Calibration establishes the errors of measurement and the accuracy of the modelling process

Construct and latent construct A construct is a framework we create in our minds to help us understand our observations. An example is 'intelligence', which does not exist, but psychologists use it to explain different levels of cognitive ability demonstrated by people. 'Latent' means unseen or hidden. Usually constructs are hidden and the term latent could be considered redundant. Constructs are hidden because we observe evidence of the construct and then infer the presence or amount of the construct present in a person

Content analysis A systematic, qualitative process used to identify common meanings among different verbal descriptions

Criterion referenced Criterion-referenced interpretation of performance data focuses only on what a person can do. There is no allowance given for group membership or personal characteristics. In teaching and learning, this is 'what a person can do'; it is not about how they learn

Developmental progression and developmental continuum The developmental continuum or progression is a series of descriptions that demonstrate growth in a specific direction; the progressions describe an accumulation of skills and knowledge and can be divided into levels or bands. Glaser called them 'stages', but this might be misinterpreted as a lock-step development

Item-response modelling A mathematical procedure that examines how a mathematical equation can be used to describe how people answer questions on a test, questionnaire or observation report. The extent to which the equation can 'fit' the person's responses to test questions is called 'modelling the response patterns'

Measurement error Every instrument has error associated with it. Measurement error indicates how accurate a test is in providing information about the amount of a person's cognitive skill. Large errors make the test interpretation invalid and the measurement error is usually reported in terms of a reliability index. Values near zero indicate a poor test. Values near 1.0 indicate an accurate test but do not imply correct interpretation

Measurement A process of assigning numbers to things. In education it is a matter of using numerical codes to designate learning. The measures are always codes and measurement needs to provide a way to decode or interpret what the numbers mean

Psychometric basis The term psychometric basis of an interpretation means that the issue is considered only in terms of the quantifiable data. The link to learning or teaching implications is not paramount. Psychometrics is an exact science, mathematically based, and needs to be interpreted carefully to decode the information for teaching and learning implications

Standardised test A test that is administered in a standardised way. No allowance is made for varying the method of administering the test

Test instrument A test. It is common for tests, questionnaires and observation schedules to be called instruments and the questions on them to be called items; hence the test instrument consists of test items to which pupils respond

Variable A way of describing how people differ in some specified measures

References

ACER (Australian Council for Educational Research). (1994). *Developmental assessment resource for teachers*. Melbourne: Author.

Adams, R. J., & Khoo, S. T. (1995). *Quest: Interactive test analysis*. Melbourne: ACER.

Ball, D., & Cohen, D. (1999). Developing practice, developing practitioners: Toward a practice based theory of professional education. In G. Sykes, & L. Darling-Hammond (Eds.), *Teaching as the learning profession: Handbook of policy and practice* (pp. 3–32). San Francisco: Jossey Bass.

Bransford, J., Derry, S., Berliner, D., & Hammermass, K. (2005). Theories of learning and their role in teaching. In L. Darling-Hammond, & J. Bransford (Eds.), *Preparing teachers for a changing world* (pp. 40–87). San Francisco: John Wiley.

Campbell, D. T., & Russo, M. J. (1999). *Social experimentation*. California: Sage Publications.

Embretson, S., & Reise, S. (2000). *Item response theory for psychologists*. Mahwah, NJ: Lawrence Erlbaum and Associates.

Fullan, M. (2005). *Leadership and sustainability: System thinkers in action*. California: Corwin Press.

Glaser, R. (1963). Instructional technology and the measurement of learning outcomes: Some questions. *American Psychologist, 18*(5), 19–521.

Glaser, R. (1981). The future of testing: A research agenda for cognitive psychology and psychometrics. *American Psychologist, 36*, 923–936.

Glaser, R. (1990). Expertise. In M. W. Evnsenk, A. N. Ellis, E. Hunt, & P. Johnson-Laird (Eds.), *The Blackwell dictionary of cognitive psychology*. Oxford, UK: Blackwell Reference.

Greaney, V. S. R., Khandker, S. R., & Alam, M. (1990). *Bangladesh: Assessing basic learning skills*. Bangladesk Development Series. Dhaka: University Press Ltd.

Griffin, P. (1997). *Assessment in schools and workplace*. Inaugural professorial lecture, University of Melbourne, September.

Griffin, P. (1998). *Vietnamese national study of student achievement in mathematics and Vietnamese*. Hanoi: National Institute for Education and Science.

Griffin, P. (2007). The comfort of competence and the uncertainty of assessment. *Studies in Educational Evaluation, 33*(1), 87–99.

Griffin, P., & Forwood, A. (1990). *The adult literacy and numeracy scales*. Canberra: Department of Education, Employment, Training and Youth Affairs.

Griffin, P., & Nix, P. (1990). *Assessment and reporting: A new approach*. Sydney: Harcourt, Brace, Jovanovic.

Halverson, R., Grigg, J., Prichett, R., & Thomas, C. (2005). *The new instructional leadership: Creating data-driven instructional systems in schools* (WCER Working Paper No. 2005–9). Madison: University of Wisconsin-Madison, Wisconsin Center for Education Research. Retrieved November 3, 2005, from <www.wcer.wisc.edu/publications/workingPapers/Working_Paper_No_2005_9.pdf.

Hawley, W. D., & Valli, L. (1999). The essentials of effective professional development: A new consensus. In L. Darling-Hammond, & G. Sykes (Eds.), *Teaching as a learning profession* (pp. 127–150). San Francisco: Jossey-Bass.

Joyce, B., & Showers, B. (2002). Student achievement through staff development. In B. Joyce (Ed.), *Designing training and peer coaching: Our needs for learning*. VA, USA: ASCD.

Kemmis, S., & McTaggart, R. (2000). Participatory action research. In N. K. Denzin, & Y. S. Lincoln (Eds.), *Handbook of qualitative research* (pp. 567–606). Thousand Oaks: Sage Publications.

Ladson-Billings, G., & Gomez, M. L. (2001). Just showing up: Supporting early literacy through teachers' professional communities. *Phi Delta Kappan, 82*(9), 675–680.

Mossensen, J., Hill, P., & Masters, G. (1993). *Test of reading comprehension*. Melbourne: Australian Council for Educational Research.

Murimba, S., Nzomo, J., Keithele, M., Leste, A., Ross, K., & Saito, M., et al. (2002). *Monitoring the quality of education for all: Some examples of different approaches used by The Southern Africa Consortium for monitoring educational quality.* 20. Paris, France: IIEP, UNESCO (International Institute for Educational Planning).

Perkins, D. N. 2005. *Understanding, thinking, and education.* Workshop held at Bialek College, Melbourne, April.

Phillips, G., McNaughton, S., & MacDonald, S. (2004). Managing the mismatch: Enhancing early literacy progress for children with diverse language and cultural identities in mainstream urban schools in New Zealand. *Journal of Educational Psychology, 96*(2), 309–323.

Pool, B., Parkin, C., & Parkin, C. (2002). *PROBE* (2nd ed.). New Zealand: Triune Initiatives.

Rasch, G. (1960). *Probabilistic models for some intelligence and attainment tests.* Copenhagen: Paedaogiske Institut.

Richardson, V. (1990). Significant and worthwhile change in teaching practice. *Educational Researcher, 19*(7), 10–18.

Robinson, V., & Lai, M. K. (2006). *Practitioner research for educators: A guide to improving classrooms and schools.* Thousand Oaks, CA: Corwin Press.

Rowe, K. J., & Hill, P. W. (1996). Assessing, recording and reporting students' educational progress: The case for 'Subject Profiles. *Assessment in Education, 3*(3), 309–352.

Stanovich, K. E. (1986). Matthew effects in reading: Some consequences of individual differences in the acquisition of literacy. *Reading Research Quarterly, 21,* 360–406.

Tayler, C. (2007). *Challenges for early learning and schooling.* Education, Science & the Future of Australia: A public seminar series on policy. University of Melbourne, Woodward Centre, 23 July.

Thurstone, L. L. (1959). *The measurement of values.* Chicago: University of Chicago Press.

Timperley, H. S., & Robinson, V. J. M. (2001). Achieving school improvement through challenging and changing teachers' schema. *Journal of Educational Change, 2,* 281–300.

VCAA (Victoria Curriculum and Assessment Authority). (2003–2005). *The Achievement Improvement Monitor.* Melbourne: Author.

Vygotsky, L. S. (1986). *Thought and language.* Boston: MIT Press.

Wright, B., & Masters, G. (1983). *Rating scale analysis.* Chicago: MESA Press.

Wright, B. D., & Stone, M. (1979). *Best test design.* Chicago: MESA Press.

Chapter 11
A Problematic Leap in the Use of Test Data: From Performance to Inference

Gabrielle Matters

Introduction

Despite all the rhetoric about the new millennium, few assessment issues thus far belong exclusively to the 21st century. An issue spilling over from the 20th century is the demand for schools and teachers to use assessment information to improve student achievement and enhance educational systems more generally. Among the myriad possible mechanisms for improving student achievement through the efficient use of assessment information by schools and teachers is feedback to the student learning process along with enhancement of teachers' pedagogical repertoires. When the assessment instrument is a standardised test, the product (student responses) gives information not only about what was learnt and how well it was learnt but also about what was not learnt and hints as to why this might be so.

The first section in this chapter provides an organisational framework for description of the generation of assessment data, and applies that framework to standardised testing, focusing on the interactions between student (and student dimensions) and tests (and test items). The section includes a typology for classifying sources of item difficulty. The second section discusses the efficient use of assessment information. It promotes the view that the use of test data by time-poor but intellectually and professionally curious teachers, while requiring rigour, can be a creative and imaginative process. The third section challenges the prevailing way of operating in a world that is 'awash with data' (Hattie, 2005, p. 11), but uncritical of test construct.

The concept of test *construct*, not to be confused with the act of test *construction*, is 'a psychological characteristic (e.g., numerical ability, spatial ability, introversion and anxiety) considered to vary across individuals. A construct (sometimes called a latent variable) is not directly observable; rather, it is a theoretical concept derived from research and other experience that has been constructed to explain observable patterns. When test scores are interpreted by using a construct, the scores

G. Matters (✉)
Australian Council for Educational Research, Suite 1, 165 Kelvin Grove Road, Kelvin Grove QLD 4059, Australia
e-mail: matters@acer.edu.au

C. Wyatt-Smith, J.J. Cumming (eds.), *Educational Assessment in the 21st Century*,
DOI 10.1007/978-1-4020-9964-9_11, © Springer Science+Business Media B.V. 2009

are placed in a conceptual framework' (American Education Research Association, American Psychological Association, & National Council on Measurement of Education, 1985, p. 90).

Ultimately, assessment involves making inferences about student achievement on the basis of the evidence available. One of the essential leaps in the assessment process is from performance to inference (that is, scoring the underlying attribute from what students do). Theoretically, this leap is problematic but most approaches to the use of test data fail to problematise it. Accordingly, in this chapter, I point teachers and schools to talking about the significance of student responses at the item level and seeing what it is that each item actually measures before necessarily concluding from the evidence of a low score on, say, a mathematics test (just a score derived from a collection of items), that the student actually knows no mathematics.

Methodologically, to approach test results at this level could be helpful to teachers and schools because it is not at the level of abstraction of ability: it is about what teachers have to do with their students; that is, to identify the things that students can do, the things they cannot do and things they have trouble with, and understand the source of difficulty.

Reference is made to how this approach could be used in specific forms of external standardised tests. Special mention is made of the Programme for International Student Assessment (PISA) because of the significance that PISA has gained in countries in all corners of the globe (see <http://www.pisa.oecd.org>). By design, PISA assesses the 'aptitude to undertake tasks found in everyday life' (OECD, 2001, p. 20).

The Generation of Assessment Information

This section sets the scene for discussion of schools' and teachers' use of assessment information, with a framework for describing the generation of assessment data and for interpreting patterns and relationships in data. The model is then applied to a specific assessment situation, standardised testing. The section focuses on the student–item interaction through a discussion of student characteristics and features of the testing process that might affect test results.

Organisational Framework in an Assessment Situation

The framework is any adaptation of the 3P model of learning and teaching (Biggs, 1999; Biggs & Moore, 1993), which portrays learning as an interactive system, identifying 'three points at which learning-related factors are placed: *presage*, before learning takes place; *process*, during learning; and *product*, the outcome of learning' (Biggs, 1999, p. 18).

The linear progression from presage to process to product tracks the characteristics of the student that exist before the student enters the learning situation (plus environmental factors related to the institution, the teacher and the curriculum) through the student's engagement with the learning environment to the outcome —'how much was learned, how well and in what way' (Biggs, 1993, p. 76).

Although teachers and schools have a causally central role in the learning process, students are equally causally central. Student as serious variable in student's own learning is not just student as self. 'Each student is an amalgam of their genetic code and everything that has influenced them. And they continue to be shaped by current influences, both internal and external to the school' (Ericson & Ellett, 2002). In the spotlight in this section is the individual student in the assessment process.

The presage–process–product model, which could also be viewed as a before–during–after model, is adapted to create a framework for describing the generation of assessment data (see Fig. 11.1). In a given assessment situation, for a given student and a given assessment instrument, say a standardised test, there is a definite product—the student's responses, which can be measured (test score); that is, information on what was learnt and how well or, what was not learnt with hints as to why.

These stages tend to be multifaceted, so I focus on one or two particular facets in each stage. For *presage* to the assessment experience (here, testing), I take student characteristics; for assessment *process*, the interaction between the student and item on the test and, for the assessment *product*, test responses and test scores.

This model differs from that used to describe the classroom learning situation (there are different labels on the components for a start). However, it remains a useful model, one that is capable of generating predictions and of providing feedback, both of which are relevant to the study of assessment information.

Elements in bold typeface in Fig. 11.1 are further elaborated later in this chapter. An understanding of them, or indeed, of the elements not in bold type is not necessary at this stage.

Application of Organisational Framework to Standardised Testing

Standardised testing is taken to be the process of administering a test that is the same for all students in the testing population (for example, from group of countries to group of schools to group of students in a subject) or a wide cross-section thereof, taken under the same conditions and marked according to a commonly applied rubric (such as the key for multiple-choice questions, or marking scheme for constructed-response items).

In this section, I choose the external standardised test as the specific form of assessment instrument to illustrate the application of the general organisational framework. The reason for this choice is the significance of PISA in many countries. A quick glance through the presage elements in Fig. 11.1 reminds us of many of the explanatory factors that have come up in conversations and articles about high- and low-scoring countries.

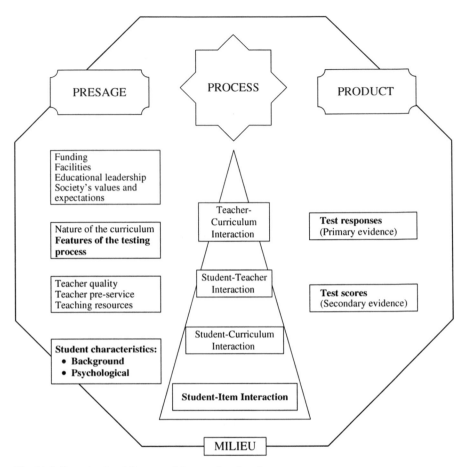

Fig. 11.1 Organisational framework in a testing situation

From Presage to Product

This section focuses on the interaction of student with test item. The student–item interaction is in the 'process' component of the 3P model.

One of the most creative uses of assessment information looks at the products of the assessment process (output data that relate to student achievement) and takes note of how they link with the presage component (input data such as student characteristics and features of the testing process). Examples include the effect of psychological characteristics on test-taking behaviour and therefore on success on tests, the effect of teacher quality on test scores, and gender differences in achievement on different test formats. Student characteristics (background and psychological) are now discussed.

Dimensions of the Student

Students come from different backgrounds, are of different abilities, go to different schools (and keep company with different kinds of children) and have different levels of test preparedness. They also experience different kinds of test items ('hard' compared with 'easy'; 'open' compared with 'closed'), as well as differences in their sources and levels of extrinsic and intrinsic motivation.

Of the myriad characteristics that define an individual at a certain point in that person's life, there are some that the person is born with and others that are the product of a person's environment, in this case, home plus school. Whatever the relative contributions of nature and nurture to the formula for ability, ability is not the same thing as achievement, nor is it the same thing as aptitude, even though doing well at school (academic achievement) is a function of ability, and those who do well at school are taken to have an aptitude for education at this level and the next level. In a nutshell, achievement is what you did, ability is what you could have done and aptitude is what you might be able to do. Ability is the first of the student background characteristics of interest when looking for explanations of patterns, trends and relationships in data.

Other background characteristics that are often included in datasets about students are gender, type of school attended and ethnicity. Although the list is not intended to be exhaustive, the exclusion of socio-economic status (SES) is a deliberate decision. It is my opinion that, on an ethical level, we should refuse to include, at the outset, SES as belonging to the presage component. Otherwise the notion of causality would lead us to the inevitability of low achievement from students from low SES backgrounds.

Achievement is influenced by factors internal to the student as well as to those imposed by features of the assessment environment, which include the assessment instrument itself, preparation for it and conditions under which it is applied. One cluster of internal factors includes the psychological characteristics of the student. Each of the psychological characteristics appearing in the following list is likely to have an impact on the student–item interaction, and therefore the potential to influence the outcome in terms of the quality or accuracy of the response given by this student on a particular item. These factors include achieving motive (motivation), test anxiety, academic self-concept and attributive style.

Throughout the very large and ever-increasing volume of literature on the topic, test anxiety and motivation are deemed to be major factors contributing to test-score variance. Various models have been used to explain the link between test anxiety and academic achievement. Sarason (1984, p. 936), who views anxiety as 'self-preoccupation over the inability to respond adequately to the call', conceptualises test anxiety on four dimensions: worry, tension, test-irrelevant thinking and bodily symptoms.

According to Marsh (1990), highly motivated students are likely to agree strongly with the following statements: 'I see doing well in school as a sort of game, and I play to win.' 'I will work for top marks in a subject whether or not I like the subject.'

'I have a strong desire to do best in all of my studies.' 'I try to obtain high marks in all my subjects because of the advantage this gives me in competing with others when I leave school.'

Marsh's (1990) 20-item questionnaire for measuring 'school-subjects self-concept' includes items such as: 'People come to me for help in most school subjects.' 'If I work really hard I could be one of the best students in my year at school.' 'I learn things quickly in most school subjects.' 'I do well in tests in most school subjects.'

Some students attribute their success and failure to internal stable factors: 'I bombed out on that test because I have no talent.' Other students attribute their success and failure to external, unstable factors: 'I bombed out on that test because the teacher set stupid questions.' These two sets of students have different attributive styles; the former students have an internal locus of control, the latter an external locus of control.

When teachers and schools use assessment information, whether from international and national tests of generic skills, or from systemic tests of discipline-specific knowledge, they should not limit their explanations of low (or high) scores to teacher or school effect.

Features of the Assessment Process

The student–item interaction is also affected by features of the assessment process, which includes all those things that are experienced by the student as a result of decisions made by those who develop and administer the assessment instrument. The testing process (assessment under standardised conditions on an instrument that has been trialled beforehand) is obviously multifaceted, from what is put in front of the student to what the student is required to do, to the conditions under which the student is to function.

Features of the assessment process impose difficulty on the item that is not simply a function of its intrinsic difficulty (that is, nature of the cognitive task)—some concepts are, quite simply, 'hard' for most people. It could be a function of the way the test is designed, for example, format (multiple choice or extended writing) and mode (written or oral). Design-imposed difficulty exists and it affects different students in different ways. For example, Willingham and Cole (1997) note gender differences related to test format (multiple choice and free response); Stage (1994) notes gender differences in spatial ability (and its consequences for test design).

What Makes an Item Difficult?

Intrinsic difficulty and design-imposed difficulty are alluded to above. Together with the notion of self-imposed difficulty, these potential sources of empirical (statistical) difficulty provide a typology for explaining item difficulty (Matters, 1997).

A common question asked by teachers when examining aggregated data from standardised tests is: 'What made this multiple-choice item so difficult that only a small proportion of students chose the correct answer?' Setting aside the possibility that the keyed response for marking was actually wrong, some of the questions in the set below might be useful in formulating an answer. The questions are composed for application to formats beyond multiple choice, to constructed response (active or passive) and extended response (as in a writing task or providing the solution to a substantial physics problem).

- What kind of thinking was involved: concrete, conceptual or personal?
- What abilities were required: verbal, numerical or spatial?
- What emphases were placed on the treatment of the stimulus material: Did the student need to absorb it, operate on it or transform it into something new?
- Is it possible that a student's (or the student group's) perception of success on the item was influenced by features of the stimulus material such as *context*?

The possibility that the context in which a test item is set imposes differential difficulty on students is of serious concern to some researchers investigating effects of the design of OECD's PISA (which by nature is context-bound, the context for the items being 'real life').

Design-Imposed Difficulty and PISA Results

A curious by-product of the release of comparative data from PISA (Thomson, Cresswell, & De Bortoli, 2004; Thomson & De Bortoli, 2008) is the almost-palpable performance anxiety at the level of participating countries and states. Even more curious is the not-infrequent spectacle, at conferences and other national and international gatherings, of countries defining themselves in terms of their PISA results. This phenomenon is observed from low- as well as high-performing countries.

The purpose of this short section is not to till the fertile ground of social, methodological and theoretical issues regarding PISA. The purpose is merely to tell a story that illustrates the explanatory power of the concept of design-imposed difficulty and, to a certain extent, self-imposed difficulty. For this I draw on Rochex's (2006) secondary and complementary analyses of the PISA 2000 literacy tests:

> Many of the PISA literacy tests required students to mobilise various fields of reference and various registers of resources and to combine and organise the elements that they could draw from these fields and registers into a hierarchy. The issue of hierarchy was all the more the case given that the goal of the PISA designers was to assess 'the skills to carry out tasks that belong to real-life situations', rather than specific knowledge, and that their themes were often close to the social and cultural references and experiences of the young people taking the test. (p. 185)

One of the conclusions of the study of students' methods (part of the larger study) was that, 'for a great number [of students], these methods varied more in relation to the texts and *contexts*, topics, and *type of tasks or question formats* than to their sole text treatment and reading and writing competencies—what was supposedly being assessed' (Rochex, 2006, p. 204) (my emphasis).

Rochex's finding has implications for the preparation of students for international surveys and also for national and state tests of generic or cross-curriculum skills, where skills that have been developed through the experienced curriculum (the study of several academic subjects) are then tested in unfamiliar contexts.

Effective Use of Assessment Information

Policy makers and practitioners demand to know what works, to know when it works and for whom, and to know how it works and why. At the simplest level, getting to know *what works* comes from inference (and requires a plausible model for causality and a study of the data and their associations); getting to know *when it works* and *for whom* comes from generalisation; and getting to know *how it works* and *why* requires other methods.

Teachers and schools mostly want to know what students have achieved. Teachers, schools and policy analysts often want to know the conditions under which students or certain groups of students achieve. Responses to these demands can be found in the data through inference and generalisation. Responses to demands for explanations about the 'how' and 'why' can be sought in the fields of neurobiology, sociology and psychology.

Bialecki (2008, p. 91) describes how, based on data obtained through PISA surveys on literacy in 2000, 2003 and 2006, the distribution of low literacy has changed in Poland. Five factors were identified as contributing to differential performance on PISA literacy in Poland; two of those five factors were identified as changing after a targeted intervention (see Table 11.1).

Some of the variables are stable within an individual and some can be changed. The finding of interest is that, in response to intervention, it was possible to change student motivation and the literate environment (part of the milieu created by school life and home life). The significance of the literate environment seems to prove what many of us have always suspected about students whose milieu values the various ways in which the life of the mind manifests itself in everyday surroundings (books, images and so on). This finding has implications for countries or jurisdictions that are considering the possibility of joining the 'PISA club'.

Another example of how testing information can be used effectively is the examination, by teachers, of test data that illuminate students' misconceptions (some of which are classic). Because the possibility of having electrodes attached

Table 11.1 Factors influencing PISA literacy scores in Poland

Factor influencing PISA literacy scores, Poland	Classification according to framework in Fig. 11.1	Direction of change
Student ability	Background	↔
Student motivation	Psychological	↑
Parent social status	Background	↔
School attended	Background	↔
Literate environment	Milieu	↑

Source: Bialecki, 2008.

to the student's brain is not yet an option for obtaining more direct information about the student–item interaction, studying individual test responses seems to be a promising compromise as a tool for understanding errors in student reasoning. Other than students' misconceptions (or mere lack of knowledge), there is another oft-overlooked source of incorrect responses on a test—the instrument itself. Sometimes, no evidence of learning is to be found in student responses—not because there was no learning but because the items for bringing forth evidence of learning were flawed.

In the early 21st century climate of comparative test data, teachers, schools and even countries appear to be spending a disproportionate amount of time devising hypotheses to account for underperformance on assessment instruments such as PISA and national testing programs in literacy and numeracy, rather than having first studied the content and construct of the tests. If teachers and schools were to transfer some of that energy to a critique of the test items per se, they would be in a strong position to comment on the quality of the instrument, their own assessment/test development skills would be enhanced and they would be in a better position to prepare students for the test (a good test is worth teaching to).

None of the above is intended to undermine the importance of professional conversations about differential performance by country. International comparisons are seductive. Finland, a top scorer on PISA, is the target of interminable questioning about its success. Australians would be better off asking why it is that results from the Australian Capital Territory, one of the eight states and territories that make up the nation, are similar to those of Finland, and then leave it to policy makers in all countries to ponder the effects of highly trained subject-matter experts in the primary school and of promotion from one year level to the next that is not automatic.

Turn now to the proclivity to fixate on test data without ever querying the quality of the assessment instruments from which the data were generated. Conference papers and media reports are filled with references to information derived from test scores. Three examples of the thousands that exist are how different countries score on PISA, how different Australian states and territories score on national tests of literacy and numeracy and how bad the level of mathematics or science knowledge is in a certain place at a certain time.

It is quite extraordinary that there are so few, if any, conference papers and media reports that point out flawed items on high-stakes tests or query the key for a multiple-choice item or demand to know anything of post-test analyses. It is acknowledged that test development is a sophisticated industry circa 2008 and that test-development agencies have sophisticated quality assurance procedures. It may be the case that an infinitesimal proportion of flawed items appear on high-stakes tests around the world. It may be the case that the wrong option is never marked as correct on a high-stakes test anywhere in the world. It may be the case that post-test analyses always deliver acceptable values for vital parameters. What is surprising is that people, particularly students and teachers in a testing situation, usually challenge information that is not flattering to them, or attribute their lack of success to external factors such as the test itself. Cronbach (1988, p. 7), citing Campbell, declares that highlighting uncertainties can contribute to validity arguments and that 'a community should be disputatious'. Teachers and schools would do well by becoming part of the dialogue through evaluation and challenging of conclusions.

In order to illuminate a different approach to engaging with data generated by standardised tests, I draw attention to the fact that, while we religiously invoke the two main purposes of using assessment data (for learning and for reporting), we often forget the worthwhile learning experience that students get when they receive feedback from tests (not just learning about themselves, meta-cognition and so on, but learning to understand material that was originally not understood by them). For a teacher, the central purpose of using assessment information is to improve the learning of one or more particular students; that is, the individual teacher and the school take the students who come to them and seek to improve the learning of those students. Another purpose—pure intellectual curiosity about how students think—is not so prominent in today's discourse.

I have sat through a 3-hour discussion about the functioning of a multiple-choice mathematics item on a nation-wide test. This item had been trialled before selection for the test. The lively discussion was not in English, although at regular intervals I was informed of the various hypotheses being devised to explain the high value for empirical difficulty: some plausible explanations included the use of vague language, verbal loading noted in mathematics testing, the non-parallel use of terminology in curriculum documentation and test item, the ambiguity in terms used from geometry (side versus edge; size versus volume), and even the possibility that the distracters were not tapping into classic misconceptions of students of this age in this domain. There had obviously not been a study of the variation in location of the item on the item–person map between trial and live administration. Nor was this information requested at any stage in the post-test discussion session. Mathematics and music are, arguably, two of the subjects in which one is most likely to be able to engage if the language being spoken is foreign, while the test item under discussion is highly visual or numerical. With great trepidation I ventured that I could not see how they had reached the 'correct' answer . . . and it transpired that there had been a clerical error in recording the keyed response. Was this discussion time wasted? No, for two reasons. First, there was the hard lesson learnt about transcription errors, which I will not labour here. Second, there was the sustained conversation, albeit for the wrong reasons, about how students think.

Items are relatively simple things compared with people, even though the mathematics of item analysis (Crocker & Algina, 1986; Hambleton, Swaminathan, & Rogers, 1991; Holland & Wainer, 1993) might create a different impression. But computer packages can give instant access to the world of item statistics and item-response modelling, and rules of thumb are composed within testing agencies on the use of information thus generated about items and students. It does little good to use a rule of thumb if a deeper understanding of its meaning could have led, instead, to the occasional (*and* profitable) breaking of the rule (for example, in selecting items on the basis of their trial statistics for inclusion in a test) . . . or, in the case of teachers and schools being provided with information about students' test performance, to their being given an insightful reading of the data rather than being fobbed off by a confidently stated rule of thumb that had been applied.

What Information Is Worth Looking at?

It would take a text book to cover all the issues surrounding the use of assessment information. This section describes just two issues that teachers and schools need to look out for when presented with assessment information for their use.

This School Is More Successful than That School

Using information about school performance in ways that might damage individuals and organisations is an ethical issue.

Schools do not automatically increase the achievement level of their cohort of students over a given period of time to the same extent. That is, students at one school gain an additional advantage over students at another school. This relative advantage is known as 'value-added'.

The call for fair measures of school performance has generated statistical models with an emphasis on value-added (Goldstein, 2001; Kingsbury & Houser, 1997; Rowe, 2005). It is what the school has been able to add to the achievement of its cohort of students, given the ability of the students. Statisticians call it 'the residual' because it is that which is left over after they have taken student ability into account in their multiple-regression analyses. Thus, the residual is not just a measure of the influence of the school. Although there are measurement errors in its calculation, it is a more respected indicator of the net effect that schools have on student progress than a set of 'league tables'.

Through these value-added models, school or teacher effects are derived from complex analyses of limited datasets. The use of measures of 'value-addedness' is accompanied by serious difficulties in principle and in practice, not to mention the fact that the use of multi-level modelling creates a structural misalignment between the humane missions espoused by schools and the technocratic ways in which society increasingly measures the success of schools. League tables, for example, do not recognise a schools' success in adding value in *all* the main ways identified as critical to students' social and economic futures. They do not even recognise a schools' success in adding value in an academic way because they only indicate academic achievement at a point in time (when students 'graduate' from high school), thus assuming that all students were equivalent when they entered school. On the other hand, value-added measures, although restricted to academic achievement, do take account of ability.

Distasteful as these measures might be to some teachers and schools, 'we no longer have the luxury as a society to view comparisons [between schools] as invidious' (Allen, 2007, p. 12). If we accept the political reality of comparisons of school performance, we then encounter another problem—a dearth of sophisticated methods for making the comparisons. If we use the available technology to manipulate large datasets (for example, for cluster analysis), we then impose clusters on the data. In some Australian states, each cluster comprises the so-called 'like schools'. Allen (2007, p. 11), with a dash of acerbity, writes what many have only thought:

'we can no longer restrict comparisons to "like schools" because it is abundantly clear that it is not the schools that are alike [in fact the schools are simply not alike]'.

Female Performance Is Better than Male Performance

Using only means and standard deviations (or just means) for reporting differences in achievement between subgroups of the population has limitations that need to be recognised.

Reports in the media about gender differences tend to focus on mean performance when comparing the test results of females and males when, in fact, there may be much more to say than that one group or other has a higher average. It is possible, for example, for one group to have a higher mean but for the other group to have more of the higher results. This sort of relationship can be captured in a single picture, the Q–Q plot as in Fig. 11.2. It is a plot of the quantiles of the male achievement distribution against the corresponding quantiles of the female achievement distribution. If the points lie along the straight line, $y = x$, the distribution of male achievement matches the distribution of female achievement. A segment of the points above the straight line means that the boys in that part of their achievement distribution did better than the girls in the corresponding part of their achievement distribution.

Figure 11.2 compares the overall achievement indicators, from which tertiary entrance ranks were determined for males and females in Queensland, Australia, in 1988. The graph shows that the males in the top third do better than the females in the top third, whereas the males right at the bottom do much worse than the females. The segment of points below the straight line ($y = x$) covers most of the range of achievement plotted. This tells us that the girls are ahead of the boys over most of

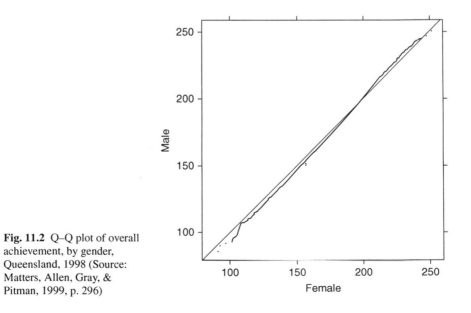

Fig. 11.2 Q–Q plot of overall achievement, by gender, Queensland, 1998 (Source: Matters, Allen, Gray, & Pitman, 1999, p. 296)

the range *but* the boys are ahead at the top. In common parlance, the boys both shine most at the top and 'bomb' out best at the bottom.

Had only the summary statistics been presented, the lingering piece of information would have been that the female group had the higher average score—which could lead to newspaper article headlines of the style 'Girls outperform the boys', when in fact the boys have more of the higher results.

What Has Changed?

Towards the end of the 20th century, Linn (1989, p. 1) listed the advent of hugely sophisticated methods for *measuring* student performance as one of the three most significant changes in educational measurement over the preceding 18 years. Matters (2006, p. 5) argues that over the last decade of the 20th century (the dawning of a new accountability age), the locus of interest moved to the practice of *using* information from the assessment process. I now argue that, at the beginning of the 21st century, when results from international tests and surveys stimulate educational discussion and debate, the significance of student responses at the item level is in the spotlight. If this is the case then teachers and schools should demand streamlined publications containing information about items and students on external standardised tests (and not just PISA).

There is no point in using assessment information for any purpose unless the assessment instrument is good. Mapping backwards and forwards from Bennett's (2006) take on Mislevy, Almond, and Lukas (2003) produces a dependency sequence in two directions: one, useful assessment information comes from good design (design that proceeds after attending to the precursors); and, two, good assessment tasks come from paying attention to what is going to happen with the data on student achievement.

There is no point in using assessment information if the user does not understand the form and purpose of assessment and the act of assessing (whichever paradigm dominates—judging or measuring), including the nature of admissible evidence of student learning. There is no point in using assessment information if the user is not aware of the psychometric underpinnings of assessment or does not possess the skills necessary for interpretation of student achievement data. There is no point in accepting the total score on a collection of test items as a measure of the underlying construct if there is any doubt at all about the properties of individual items in the test.

Conclusion

This chapter is part of a collection of writings around the theme 'assessment issues for the 21st century'. It documents differences in the use of assessment information between the late 20th century and the 21st century thus far, and it underlines schools' and teachers' use of assessment information, especially information from external standardised tests. In the case of well-designed standardised tests, the product (student responses) gives information not only about what was learnt and how well it was learnt but also about what was not learnt and hints as to why this might be so. This chapter also attempts to convince teachers and schools to study tests and student responses at the item level in order to confirm the existence of evidence to support the proposed construct interpretation of test scores.

When Socrates, on trial for heresy, said 'the life which is unexamined is not worth living', he was not referring to the need for public examinations or standardised tests; but if he did say just that in today's educational environment, it is unlikely he would be put to death for it. The role of assessment, and of assessment information, in educational debate and policy in the early 21st century is an extremely powerful one. This chapter contends that this role can be justified only if two conditions (at least) are met: that the assessment itself is of sufficient strength and quality to support the uses to which it will be put, and that the users of the assessment data—the analysts, the teachers, the administrators, the policy makers—have sufficient expertise and imagination to see beyond the rules of thumb and piece together the true underlying story (whether the story in question is about a student underachieving in one subject, or a country outperforming Finland on international standardised tests).

Then it is possible to make the links (forward and backward) between the three points of presage, process and product, in ways that maximise the usefulness of the information obtained not only about the tangible product but also the process (the intangible student–item interaction). Without this level of rigour and expertise being applied to the assessment on which so much today is based, we could adapt what Socrates said, and say that the assessment which is unexamined is not worth using.

Theoretical and Methodological Framings

Paradigms: Measurement Versus Judgment

Educational assessment is the collection of information about student learning in numerous ways for two main purposes: for feeding back into the learning process and/or for reporting to various audiences. Evidence of student learning is obtained in response to assessment instruments. Decisions about the extent of that learning are coded as assessment results. Two paradigms operate: *measuring* how much of a certain quality (single underlying dimension) is evidenced in student responses; and *judging* what the evidence says about what the student has learnt and how well.

The psychometric model that 'observed score = true score + error' suits notions of reliability and validity for multiple-choice testing. Assumptions of the true-score model do not readily suit notions of reliability and validity for testing in open-ended response modes and do not at all suit notions of validity and reliability for school-based assessment. Here, assumptions of the true-score model do not hold, in particular, assumptions about infinite populations, about markers, items and tasks being sampled at random from a universe of markers, items and tasks, and about identical and independent Gaussian distributions. In many school settings, split-half reliability estimates are not possible and the practice of inter-rater agreement studies is beyond the resources of most schools. According to Moss (1992, 1994) the epistemological and ethical purposes served by reliability can be broadened to include the practice of contextualised judgment. One of her three warrants for reliability is the privileging of contextualised (teacher) judgments. This involves the use of a criteria and standards schema against which teachers judge the quality of student work.

Glossary

Constructed response   Refers to assessment items in which students are required to produce a short answer (as opposed to, for example, writing an essay, doing a project or selecting the correct response from a list of options). Responses might involve writing a paragraph of exposition or explanation, performing a calculation, constructing a graph, compiling a table, or producing a sketch or drawing.

> *Active constructed-response items* require the candidate/student to take the stimulus material and do something with it, as in calculating and summarising, or even transforming it into something new, as in composing a poem or devising a plan.
> *Passive constructed-response items* require the candidate/student to treat the stimulus material in a reflexive way, to absorb it as in interpretation or in searching/locating in order to quote extracts

Empirical (statistical) difficulty   In a multiple-choice test, the facility index (f) for an item is defined as the proportion (percentage) of candidates giving the correct response. The lower the value of f, the more difficult the item experientially

Item-response modelling/item-response theory   Item-response theory combines psychology and mathematics in determining the probability p that an examinee with ability θ correctly answers an item. Modern test theory (after Rasch) estimates item parameters and person ability, placing items and students on the same scale

Item statistics   In terms of classical test theory, key statistics for an item (from trial test or 'live' test) are:

> *Difficulty* (see *empirical difficulty* and *facility index*).
> *Discrimination* (usually the point biserial correlation, which is a form of product–moment correlation, between item score and test score)

Quantile   The quantile of a distribution of values is a number that indicates the proportion of the values that are less than or equal to that value. For example, the 0.75 quantile of a variable is a value below which 75 per cent of the values of the variable fall

Socio-economic status   A measure of an individual's or group's position in the social order in terms of income, occupation, educational attainment, wealth, etc.

Standardised testing   Involves all, or a wide cross-section of, students across a jurisdiction, of the same year or age sitting (versions of) the same test under the same conditions and, usually at the same time, with results being reported in a common format (on the same scale and/or according to a commonly applied marking scheme)

Test/test item A published instrument constructed by persons technically trained in mental testing and statistical methods. Its *items* have been thoroughly tried out beforehand, and the test is accompanied by norms or standards of performance that enable the tester to interpret how far a student's score or mark is superior or inferior to those of other similar students

Underlying attribute The theoretical, intangible quality or trait that allows for individual differences in that quality or trait to be measured

References

American Education Research Association, & American Psychological Association & National Council on Measurement of Education. (1985). *Standards for Educational and Psychological Testing*. Washington, DC: American Psychological Association.

Allen, J. R. (2007). *Fair measures of school performance*. Paper presented at the 2007 ACACA Annual Conference, Melbourne.

Bennett, R. E. (2006). Foreword. In G. N. Matters, *Using data to support learning in schools: Students, teachers, systems*. Camberwell: ACER Press.

Bialecki, I. (2008). *Assessment measurement and evaluation of literacy levels and of basic competencies in Poland*. Paper delivered at UNESCO Regional Conference (Europe) in Support of Global Literacy, Baku, Azerbaijan.

Biggs, J. B. (1993). From theory to practice: A cognitive systems approach. *Higher Education Research and Development, 12*, 73–86.

Biggs, J. B. (1999). *Teaching for quality learning at university*. Buckingham: SRHE & Open University Press.

Biggs, J. B., & Moore, P. J. (1993). *The process of learning*. (3rd ed.). New York: Prentice Hall.

Crocker, L., & Algina, J. (1986). *Introduction to classical and modern test theory*. Belmont, CA: Wadsworth.

Cronbach, L. J. (1988). Five perspectives on validity argument. In H. Wainer (Ed.), *Test validity*. Hillsdale, NJ: Erlbaum.

Ericson, D. P., & Ellett, F. S. (2002). The question of the student in educational reform. *Educational Policy Analysis Archives, 10*(31), Retrieved June 19, 2008, from <http://epaa.asu.edu/epaa/v10n31/>.

Goldstein, H. (2001). Using pupil performance data for judging schools and teachers: Scope and limitations. *British Educational Research Journal, 27*(4), 433–442.

Hambleton, R. K., Swaminathan, H., & Rogers, H. J. (1991). *Fundamentals of item response theory*. Newbury Park, CA: Sage.

Hattie, J. A. C. (2005). *What is the nature of evidence that makes a difference to learning?* Paper delivered at the ACER Conference, Melbourne.

Holland, P. W., & Wainer, H. (Eds.). (1993). *Differential item functioning*. Hillsdale, NJ: Lawrence Erlbaum.

Kingsbury, G. G., & Houser, R. (1997). Using data from a level testing system to change a school district. In J. O'Reilly (Ed.), *The Rasch tiger ten years later: Using IRT techniques to measure achievement in schools*. Chicago: National Association of Test Directors.

Linn, R. L. (Ed.). (1989). *Educational measurement* (3rd edn.). Washington, DC: The American Council on Education and the National Council on Measurement in Education.

Marsh, H. W. (1990). A multidimensional, hierarchical model of self-concept: Theoretical and empirical justification. *Educational Psychology Review, 2*(2), 77–172.

Matters, G. N. (1997). *Are Australian boys underachieving?* Paper presented at 23rd annual conference of the International Association for Assessment in Education. Durban, South Africa.

Matters, G. N. (2006). Using data to support learning in schools: Students, teachers, systems. Camberwell: ACER Press.

Matters, G. N., Allen, J. R., Gray, K. R., & Pitman, J. A. (1999). Can we tell the difference and does it matter? Differences in achievement between girls and boys in Australian senior secondary education. *The Curriculum Journal, 10*(2), 283–302.

Mislevy, R. J., Almond, R. G., & Lukas, J. F. (2003). *A Brief Introduction to Evidence-Centered Design.* Retrieved June 19, 2008, from <http://www.ets.org/Media/Research/pdf/RR-03-16.pdf>.

Moss, P. A. (1992). Shifting conceptions of validity in educational measurement: Implications for performance assessment. *Review of Educational Research, 62*(3), 229–258.

Moss, P. A. (1994). Can there be validity without reliability? *Educational Researcher, 23*(2), 5–12.

OECD (Organisation for Economic Co-operation and Development). (2001). *Knowledge and skills for life: First results from PISA 2000.* Paris: Author.

Rochex, J. Y. (2006). Social, methodological, and theoretical issues regarding assessment: lessons from a secondary analysis of PISA 2000 Literacy Tests. *Review of Research in Education, 30*(1), 163–212.

Rowe, K. J. (2006). *Evidence for the kinds of feedback data that support both student and teacher learning.* Paper delivered at the ACER Conference, Melbourne.

Sarason, I. G. (1984). Stress, anxiety, and cognitive interference: Reactions to tests. *Journal of Personality and Social Psychology, 46*(4), 929–938.

Stage, C. (1994). *Gender differences on the SweSAT: A review of studies since 1975.* Department of Educational Measurement, Umeå University, EM No. 7.

Thomson, S., & De Bortoli, L. (2008). *Exploring scientific literacy: How Australia measures up. The PISA 2006 survey of students' scientific, reading and mathematical literacy skills.* Camberwell: ACER Press.

Thomson, S., Cresswell, J., & De Bortoli, L. (2004). *Facing the future: A focus on mathematical literacy among Australian 15-year-old students in PISA 2003.* Camberwell: ACER Press.

Willingham, W. W., & Cole, N. S. (1997). *Gender and fair assessment.* Princeton, NJ: Lawrence Erlbaum.

Chapter 12
Educational Assessment in Norway—A Time of Change

Sverre Tveit

Introduction

This chapter discusses the context, problems, historical background and new approaches to student assessment in Norway. The beginning of the 21st century can be characterised as a time of change in Norwegian education. Based on the disappointing results obtained by Norwegian students on international comparative tests, the educational reforms of the 1990s were determined to have failed. Following implementation of a new reform, 'the Knowledge Promotion' of 2006, the regulations and practices for student assessment are among the areas that are being questioned.

Norway is distinguished from many countries by not grading students through formal assessments until they are 13–14 years old. Few countries have seen the ideological fights over student assessment that have occurred in Norway; conflicts which reached a peak in the 1970s when a national committee suggested the further abolition of formal grading in lower secondary school. Although the fight against formal grading did not result in any significant immediate changes to practices of the time, the controversy has remained a latent conflict that typically ignites when new educational reforms are introduced. In 2004, assessment again became a matter of considerable national policy debate when a controversial new framework for national testing was introduced. As authorities and schools are developing new regulations and practices for student assessment for the new curricula of 2006, controversy continues.

The first section of the chapter briefly presents the context of educational assessment in Norway. The next section discusses problematic issues related to student assessment, such as comparability of teachers' judgments, external examinations and formative feedback. The third section is a short, retrospective analysis of the evolution of assessment regulations in Norway in the 20th century. I argue that the lack of theoretical foundation of the approaches to student assessment is one of the main causes for the problems now faced. The fourth section presents and comments on the recent initiatives by the Norwegian government to address identified

S. Tveit (✉)
Postgraduate student, University of Oslo, Norway and Griffith University, Queensland, Australia
e-mail: sverrtv@student.uv.uio.no

C. Wyatt-Smith, J.J. Cumming (eds.), *Educational Assessment in the 21st Century*,
DOI 10.1007/978-1-4020-9964-9_12, © Springer Science+Business Media B.V. 2009

problems and to develop a thorough approach to student assessment. The chapter concludes by identifying three key strategies considered crucial for Norway to develop a successful approach to student assessment for the 21st century.

Investigation of regulations, government documents and research studies in Norway form the framework for the chapter. The text reflects my background as a student representative, calling for reforms in the systems for educational assessment in Norway and continued work in learning and understanding assessment theories and practices in other nations.

The Context of Educational Assessment in Norway at Glance

Being previously a part of Denmark for more than 400 years (1380–1814), and for almost a century in a union with Sweden (1814–1905), Norway shares important parts of its history with its Scandinavian neighbours. 'The countries are tied together through history, common cultural traditions, the same basic values and the same democratic ideals' (Lysne, 2006, p. 329). Continuous assessment, conducted by the teacher, is the most significant type of summative assessment in Norway. This allows emphasis to be placed on students' development over the course of the school year, and the development of global cognitive areas such as creative and collaborative skills. This clearly reflects social constructivist theories of learning. The constructivist theoretical rationale for teaching and learning in Norway has its basis in the work of Piaget and Vygotsky. The 'Core Curriculum', which was introduced in 1993 and still forms the basis for all subject-specific curricula, has a number of references to these theoretical perspectives (NOU, 2003, p. 15).

Organisation of Education in Norway

For most Norwegians, education is free throughout the compulsory and upper secondary years, and even tertiary years. There are 10 years of compulsory education, starting when children are 6 years old. In 2007, 97 per cent of Norwegian students undertook the compulsory years in schools governed by local municipalities; 93 per cent attended upper secondary schools governed by the regional municipalities[1] (Statistics Norway, Undated-a). In 2007, 96 per cent of students continued to upper secondary education after completing year 10 (Statistics Norway, Undated-b). Fifty-six per cent of these students attended 3-year upper secondary programs for general studies, which qualify for university or university college enrolment, while the rest

---

[1] The term compulsory education refers to the rights and obligations children have for education. Parents may teach their children themselves, but in practice almost all children undergo the compulsory years in schools. Private schools in Norway can get 85 per cent public funding; however this is only granted to schools that represent religious or pedagogical alternatives to the public schools. As the extent of private schooling is limited, the arrangements for assessment in these schools are not discussed.

attended vocational educational programs, which are normally 2 years of schooling followed by 2-year apprenticeship programs (Statistics Norway, Undated-a).

Democratic Education

In order to understand the reactions of students to changes in national assessment policy, and the government response to the student actions, it is necessary to understand the power that students in Norway have in affecting policy. An important aspect of Norwegian education is the emphasis on democratic education. Not only are there powerful teacher unions in Norway, but school students also have their own union protecting their civil rights and allowing the expression of students' opinions in public debates and towards the government and regional authorities.

Norwegian students have the opportunity to have their views taken into consideration through student councils comprised of class representatives. These councils comprise students starting as early as year 5 (when the students are 10–11 years old), with members gaining more responsibility as they get older. Interestingly, Norwegian students have excelled in international comparative studies of students' basic knowledge and skills about the democracy and democratic institutions (Mikkelsen, Buk-Berge, Ellingsen, Fjeldstad, & Sund, 2001, p. 240).

The school-student union of Norway (hereafter called 'the student union'), for which policy is decided by student council representatives from all 350 member schools and groups (mainly public upper secondary schools), is an important participant in the public debates over education and has showed strength in two particular cases related to student assessment: the fights over national testing and the calls for a thorough review of the regulations and practices for student assessment. Both are discussed further in the last sections of the chapter.

General Concept of Student Assessment

New national curricula were introduced with the educational reform known as 'the Knowledge Promotion' in 2006. The new curricula state competence aims (Norwegian terminology) the students are to achieve, but provide few regulations or requirements on how to organise teaching and how to assess student learning. The previous curricula had more comprehensive statements about what the students were meant to do. Standards for assessing the students' learning outcomes, however, have never been stated on a national level. This may change following the Norwegian government's initiative in 2007 to conduct a thorough investigation of the entire assessment system, including trialling national criteria for student assessment, as discussed later.

A strong tradition in Norway is the absence of grading of students until they attend lower secondary school (13–14 years old). Since 1972, the policy in Norway has been not to grade students until it is necessary for selection purposes in lower secondary schools (NOU, 1974, p. 16). There have been strong advocates for the abolition of student grades at this schooling level, as well. The fight against formal grading in the 1970s did not result in any significant immediate changes of existing practices, but the controversy has been a latent conflict that has had a major impact on the evolution of the assessment systems present today (Lysne, 2006, p. 327). The absence of formal grading in primary school is different from many other countries, and calls for an explanation. Rationales for grading students typically follow three lines—selection, motivation and information (Wikström, 2006)—all of which appear to have been generally rejected in Norway.

In Norway, most students go to the local school they 'belong to' throughout the compulsory years of education, hence no selection procedures are necessary until towards the end of lower secondary school. The notion that students should be graded for the sake of their motivation has been repeatedly rejected over concerns about the negative impacts on low achievers (Tønnessen & Telhaug, 1996, p. 25). In discussions about assessment principles, the information purpose is typically being addressed as a key argument for preferring criterion-referenced assessment over norm-referenced assessment. The argument is that grades should express what the students can achieve, and how they progress, rather than comparing their performances relative to that of others (Wikström, 2006, p. 118). As discussed below, Norway has never had a distinct criterion-referenced approach; hence grades are less likely to provide information about progress and achievement levels.

High-Stakes Assessment

Referring to their importance in qualification procedures for education and jobs, grades reported on the students' transcripts are often called 'high-stakes' assessment. The Norwegian approach to high-stakes assessment is to a large extent dependent on teachers' assessment. Students receive one grade for each subject they study, apart from language subjects, which have separate grades for written and oral achievements. There are no national regulations on how these grades should be determined; typically they are based on a number of tests, assignments and other student work that have been graded throughout the year.

In Norway, the national authorities' responsibility for high-stakes assessment has traditionally been limited to the examination system. On the one hand, the national authorities have produced and organised the grading of *external* examinations; on the other hand, they have been responsible for regulation of the *local* examinations. While the external examinations are in written form only, local examinations can take written, oral or practical forms. The local and regional municipalities are responsible for producing, implementing and grading local examinations, responsibilities that typically have been delegated to schools or responsible teachers within schools.

In principle, students can be sampled to undertake examinations in every subject; however, in practice, each student only undertakes a few examinations. Students are normally not notified about what examination they have been sampled to sit until two days before the examinations occur, providing an incentive to prepare well for all subjects throughout the whole school year.

In *lower* secondary school, a student undertakes one external exam and one oral local examination at the end of year 10. In *upper* secondary school, the numbers of examinations vary according to programme of study. In the programme for general studies, 20 per cent of the students are sampled for one examination after the first year and all students for one examination in the second year. In the final year all students undertake three to four examinations. The type of examination varies according to the programmes of specialisation the students are enrolled in. However, all students undertake the external examination in the Norwegian Subject Curriculum (Utdanningsdirektoratet, 2007b). The examinations are reported separately on the students' transcripts and typically make up less than 20 per cent of the grades on their transcripts, while the continuous assessment conducted by teachers in each subject forms the rest of the transcripts (Tveit, 2007b, pp. 194-195, 212).

Global Influence on Education and Student Assessment Policy

International comparative tests of student achievement, which have been conducted over the past 5–10 years (PISA—Programme for International Student Assessment; PIRLS—Progress in International Reading Literacy Study; TIMSS—Trends in International Mathematics and Science Study), have had a major impact on the public debate about schooling in Norway in general. As Norway is among the countries in the world that spend the most money on education (Utdanningsdirektoratet, 2007a, p. 34), one would expect that students in Norway would be among the highest achievers in these tests. However, this is not the case. Despite a few comparative studies conducted in the 1980s and 1990s, which could have triggered an alert, it was not until the results of the PISA2000 tests were published in 2001 (Lie, Kjærnsli, Roe, & Turmo, 2001) that the quality of the education system became a great public concern in Norway.

PISA2000 placed Norway as number 13 of the 31 OECD countries in reading and science, and number 17 in mathematics. These rankings made the front pages of all the major newspapers in Norway, with headlines such as 'Norway is a school loser' and 'Typical Norwegian is average'. The fact that the 'winner' in this 'contest', Finland, is one of Norway's neighbouring countries made the results even harder to accept. The Norwegian Ministry of Education was famously quoted as saying 'This is disappointing, almost like coming home from a winter Olympics without *one* Norwegian medal. And this time we cannot accuse the Finns of being drugged' (my translation) (Bergesen, 2006, p. 41). The PISA2003 and PISA2006 studies confirmed the dismal picture (Kjærnsli, Lie, Olsen, Roe, & Turmo, 2004). In PISA2006 Norway generally scored significantly lower than the mean of the OECD countries in science, reading and mathematics (Kjærnsli, Lie, Olsen, & Roe, 2007, pp. 18, 24).

For Norway, these results are identified as not acceptable by authorities and the general public and have become a driving force towards reforms in the education systems in general. So, for assessment systems, in 2004, the Norwegian Minister of Education introduced new systems for monitoring the quality of the education system, of which national testing was a key component. As the outcomes of the evaluations of the educational reforms of the 1990s were published, possible causes for the disappointing results were addressed, providing the foundation for a comprehensive reform of primary and secondary schooling. The name of the reform, 'the Knowledge Promotion', reflects the main goal of the reform: to improve the learning outcomes for all students (Kunnskapsdepartementet, 2007, p. 2). A thorough investigation of the regulations and practices for student assessment were to accompany the reform after its implementation in 2006.

Problematic Issues in Educational Assessment in Norway

In this section, some problematic issues in educational assessment in Norway are discussed. The discussion is limited to comparability of assessments and teachers judgments, confusion about what to assess and lack of formative feedback.

Comparability of Assessments and Teacher Judgments

In 2003, the Norwegian authority responsible for the development of primary and secondary education (now called the Norwegian Directorate for Education and Training) concluded that 'there appear to have evolved different cultures for grading students across schools, subjects and teachers' (my translation) (Læringssenteret, 2003, p. 35). In a white paper presented to the Norwegian Parliament in 2006, the government stated that the regulations for student assessment are not clearly understood, there is not sufficient competence in student assessment, in teacher education and in schools, and little research on student assessment has been conducted (St.meld. nr. 16, 2006–2007, p. 79).

There seem to be few studies of comparability of teachers' judgments across schools in Norway (Tveit, 2007a). Two statistical studies that compare the grades given in continuous assessment with grades achieved on external examinations indicate significant differences in the interpretations of standards across schools (Hægeland, Kirkebøen, & Raaum, 2005; Kristensen, 1999, Unpublished.). Neither of these studies, however, investigates teachers' judgments of student work; there appear to be no such studies of how continuous assessment is conducted in Norway. A study of teachers' judgments of achievement levels in the test of writing in English, which formed part of the evaluation of the national testing framework in 2005, revealed that the teachers lacked references to an overall standard and used the group as a reference (Lie, 2007, p. 89).

As previously mentioned, examinations play a significant role in high-stakes assessment in Norway, supplementing the continuous assessment conducted by the teachers. A problem, however, is that the purposes and theoretical rationales for these examinations, and how they are linked to the continuous assessment, are not defined (Tveit, 2007a, p. 215). Rather, the combination of the two can be seen as reflecting a compromise between two ideological positions towards student assessment. Those opposing external examinations typically argue that these tests do not measure relevant subject content. From this perspective, capacity to assess student work produced throughout a whole school year is a key argument for emphasising continuous assessment. Those calling for more external examinations typically argue that such tests provide a more reliable measure and prevent biased assessments undertaken by the teacher.

Those in favour of keeping or expanding the external examination system appear to base their point of view on an assumption that the external examinations represent an important incentive for the teachers to make valid and reliable judgments in their continuous assessment of students' achievement levels. This concept, however, has not been supported in research and can be questioned logically. Students' learning outcomes measured on a one-day examination, in a restricted assessment mode, can simply not be compared to their achievements measured throughout a number of assignments, tests and collaborative projects through the course of a year. Teachers are likely to argue that they know their students' achievements and abilities better than an examination can measure. This notion is understandable, considering the lack of theoretical linkage between the grades achieved in continuous assessment and the external examinations. This also appears to be the reason why there are no procedures for sanctioning teachers who may be making wrong judgments of the students' achievement levels (Tveit, 2007a, p. 215). Students have the right to lodge complaints on continuous assessment grades and examinations. For complaints on the continuous assessment, however, the court of appeal only considers whether the formal regulations have been followed—it does not judge the teacher's judgments on achievement levels. One reason for this lack of legal protection of students is the absence of requirements for collecting and storing evidence (Tveit, 2007a, p. 212; 2007b, p. 196).

While there is weak empirical evidence on the comparability of teacher judgments in the continuous assessment, a study of the external comparability of judgments in the external examination at the end of year 10 in the Norwegian subject curriculum indicated relatively high levels of comparability of judgments (Vagle, Berge, Evensen, & Hertzberg, 2007, p. 76). It can be assumed, however, that the level of comparability across schools in continuous assessment is considerably weaker than in the external examinations, as the national authorities' programmes for training teachers in making judgments on achievement levels historically have been reserved for the examination assessors only. As the vast majority of the students' school leaving certificates, which form the basis for tertiary education qualification in Norway, is based on continuous assessment conducted by the teacher, this is a major concern. The available evidence indicates that consistency in assessment has not yet been achieved. The absence of national criteria or standards, and the fact that the regulations do not state any requirements for moderation (neither social nor statistical), imply that significant injustice to individual students may occur.

Confusion About What to Assess

The lack of comparability across schools in Norway is due to a large extent to the lack of formal regulations for student assessment. This has resulted in confusion about what should be assessed: Should the students' efforts be assessed? How should their 'order' and 'behaviour' be assessed? Should verbal activity and participation in class be included in the judgments?

Grades for effort were abandoned in Norway in the 1920s. Since then there have been several attempts to reintroduce the concept, but those attempts have never succeeded, as such assessment clearly is difficult to do without bias (Lysne, 2004, p. 200; Tveit, 2007a, pp. 204–207). However, although such assessment has been politically discussed and rejected several times, it has not been clearly stated in the assessment regulations that students' effort should not be taken into consideration when assessing their work.

A study of upper and lower secondary school teachers' and students' views on assessment conducted by Dale and Wærness (2006) showed that teachers to a large extent take students' effort into consideration when grading (pp. 192–193). Verbal activity in class is often regarded as an indication of good effort. When placing too much emphasis on verbal activity without stating explicit criteria, one risks valuing activity regardless of the content and level of the students' contribution. Some students are better at this game than others, and receive better grades from the teachers by simply being verbally active. This disadvantages students who are well prepared for the class, but are less extroverted (Tveit, 2007a, p. 210).

According to Wynne Harlen (2004), strong evidence shows that 'using grades as rewards and punishment is harmful to students' learning by encouraging extrinsic motivation' (p. 5). Hence, it is important that subject grades are not used as a disciplinary tool. It should be clear to students that subject grades are judgments and feedback on the quality of their work only. In the assessment regulations in Norway, there are two specific grades for assessing students' 'order' and 'behaviour'. One should therefore expect that such factors were not an issue when grading students' work within each subject.

Dale and Wærness (2007), however, showed that many teachers tend to mix these two grading processes. One of the teachers in their qualitative study was quoted '[. . .] Positive attitude in the classroom is important. [This] 'Trynefaktor' [Norwegian term for a sense of 'face factor'] should not be underestimated. It counts in the working life [. . .]' (my translation) (p. 194). Many students report that the so-called trynefaktor—the concept of judgments being biased based on whether one likes the appearance and attitude of the person or not—is a big problem. Although there are no known studies that have investigated this particular problem, it is a topic of general concern among students, parents and teachers.

Lack of Formative Feedback

Rumours about 'face factor' gain ground if students are not provided with good explanations for the grades they receive. In the Dale and Wærness (2006) study, a student said that 'I don't really know what their assessment is based on. I never really get the criteria stated. We've asked for it before and then we've been told that it is an overall assessment' (my translation) (p. 197). A reference to 'an overall assessment' does not help students understand what they should have been doing different to achieve better results. The image drawn by this student was confirmed in a survey undertaken in 2005. A majority of the students said that the teachers to a limited extent told them what they were good at and what they needed to improve (Furre, Danielsen, & Stiberg-Jamt, 2006, p. 62). An evaluation of the previous reform of education for the compulsory years also identified that teachers are not good at expressing their expectations to students. Considerable positive feedback was given; however, this feedback was not sufficiently based on the quality of the students' achievements (Klette, 2003, p. 53).

The lack of explicitness in assessment criteria must be understood in the context of national curricula, which historically do not state how to assess levels of achievement. In guidelines developed for the grading of state-wide external examinations, however, there are nationally stated criteria. Dale and Wærness (2007) have also examined the criteria used in some of these examinations, which are commonly used by teachers in the continuous assessment in the following years. They found that the criteria used for describing achievement levels on all levels but the two highest are written and characterised with reference to the highest level and the lack of obtaining those standards. If these criteria were to be used in the continuous assessment, low achievers would be described in terms such as 'Your text has no clear structure, incoherent logic, the message has little relevance, the content is poor and your language is imprecise and characterised by many mistakes' (my translation) (Dale & Wærness, 2007, p. 106). Such an approach to stating expectations to students has limited formative assessment effect and is not useful for assessment practices in the classroom.

Underlying Factors for the Problems of Educational Assessment in Norway

In this section I argue that one of the underlying causes of the confusion about student assessment in Norway is an indistinct adoption of fundamental principles for student assessment. Historically, two distinct approaches to student assessment have been applied in the Western world: *norm referencing* and *criterion referencing*. Generally, one can say that in terms of theoretical development of the concepts in international literature, the former had its peak in the first half of the 20th century, while the latter concept gained ground in the second half and was dominating towards the beginning of the 21st century, whether approached through assessment or measurement paradigms.

The Evolution of the Assessment Regulations

In Norway, grade inflation became a major concern in upper secondary education in the 1920s, when a statistical review showed that the distributions were very much skewed, a concern shared by most of the countries in the Western world. The first national regulations for grading came with the national model plan of 1939 (*Normalplanen*), in which a principle of norm referencing based on a normal distribution was implemented for a five-step scale: *Outstandingly good*: 4%, *Very good*: 24%, *Good*: 44%, *Fairly good*: 24%, *Good*: 4%. It was made clear that the distribution guide should apply only to large groups, and not small groups such as single classes. 'The so-called "relative grading system" had never been critically discussed, not even the fact that it doomed a certain percentage of the students to fail' (Lysne, 2006, p. 343). An obvious problem was that most teachers did not have any references to the levels of other students than their own and, therefore, to a certain extent, applied normal distributions within their own groups. This concept typically results in its being easier to get a high grade in a low-achieving class and vice versa (Wikström, 2006, p. 118). In the 1960s and 1970s, new concepts of grading, inspired by United States theories, collided with calls from the political left wing in Scandinavia for the total abolition of formal grading (Egelund, 2005, p. 208). According to Lysne (2006), Bloom and Tyler had a great influence on theory and practice of education in Scandinavia in the 1960s. In 1963, Robert Glaser defined the distinction between criterion-referenced and norm-referenced testing and assessment, and within a few years a significant body of literature had been written about the concept of criterion-referenced assessment (Lysne, 2006, p. 348).

At this time, the frustration with regulated distribution of grades reached its peak in Norway and formed the ground for what can be argued was the most passionate debate over school politics in Norway ever, perhaps unparalleled in the world (Lysne, 2004, p. 113). The ultimate consequence of the system—that it made classmates compete against each other—was used as one of the arguments for the total abolition of formal grading. A way out of the problems with norm-referenced grading had to be found. For those opposing formal grading, most commonly among the influential politicians and researchers on the left wing in the 1970s, being compared to an objective standard, as criterion-referenced assessment was represented, was no better than being compared with other students. They feared too much emphasis on knowledge as a means to monitor and control (Lysne, 1999, pp. 37, 39).

The 1980s in Norway was the time for recovering from the debate over formal grading of the 1970s. The upper secondary school students' union had in 1978 collected 60 000 signatures for retention of a grading schema in both lower and upper secondary schools. The Labour party lost the majority in the Parliament after the election in 1981 and attempts to abolish formal grading at these levels were not continued by the incoming government (Lysne, 2004, p. 113).

Instead, the new conservative government used the opportunity to introduce what Lysne (2004, p. 120) calls 'adapted goal-referenced assessment' (my translation of the Norwegian term '*tillempet målrelatering*') (p. 120), which had already been applied in upper secondary school since 1968. The concept of 'adapted goal-referenced assessment' was to abandon the norm-referenced principle but not to entirely apply a criterion-referenced system: absolute learning outcomes or evidence of specific skills should not be required in the curricula. Emphasis was placed on the choice of learning content, teaching aids and learning methods that were focusing on the students' personal development towards a wide range of goals (Lysne, 2004, pp. 120, 197). The teachers, however, had doubts about how to put this into practice. In an attempt to clarify the regulations 'the norm-referenced model was involved again, and thus the new system became sort of a bastard of those two principles' (Lysne, 2006, p. 352).

Assessment Regulations in the Reforms of the 1990s

When new curricula for the entire school system were introduced in Norway in the 1990s, it was attempted to formalise the principle of 'adapted goal-referenced assessment' by the introduction of a core curriculum that stated the general objectives of schooling in 1993. In 1994, a form of holistic assessment was prescribed in an operational directive for the new reform of upper secondary school. A concept of 'overall competence' (my translation of the Norwegian term 'helhetlig kompetanse'), which referred to a broader understanding of competence than subject-specific competence, was to be emphasised when grades were given in each subject. This concept included students' ability to cooperate with each other and develop their personality and character (Lysne, 2006, p. 353). It is easy to agree that these are important aspects of schools' and teachers' mandates. A problem, however, is that if there is no clear-cut distinction between these general goals and the assessment of specific learning objectives, there is again a great risk of the assessment being biased (Tveit, 2007a, p. 206).

Sweden had been experimenting with regulations for holistic assessment in the 1970s; however, the concept was abandoned there a few years later. According to Lysne (2006), a special feature of Norwegian school politics is that '[m]ost of the ideas Sweden had tried and found not to work, Norway was inclined to try over again, and as a rule to come to the same conclusion as in Sweden' (p. 354). In Norway, the principle of 'overall competence' made the confusion about what the learning objectives were and how to make judgements on the students' achievements even worse. As Lysne (2006) noted, (p. 353) teachers and parents protested spontaneously because they could not understand what was meant—the directive was withdrawn and replaced by a new one that was more in accordance with traditional prescriptions for grading. However, the regulations remained obscure. In the preparations for the educational reform of 2006, the Norwegian government acknowledged that the concept of emphasising holistic assessment had contributed to the obscurity of the regulations for student assessment (St.meld. nr. 30, 2003–2004, p. 39).

Despite the alleged rejection of the concept of norm-referencing, the prevailing regulation during the educational reform for upper secondary school of 1994 (Reform 94) had distinct references to norm-referenced assessment: the six grade levels were grouped in three levels 'Above average' (6 and 5), 'Average' (4 and 3) and 'Below average' (2 and 1). This way of expressing the achievement levels can be seen as legitimating the concept of applying a norm-referenced strategy to grade small groups of students (Dale & Wærness, 2007, p. 105). While other parts of the assessment regulations were changed when implementing the new reform in 2006, this remained unchanged. I argue that the government's reluctance to change this essential part of the regulations was owing to apprehension of reigniting the debate over formal assessment—and thereby jeopardising the generally broad consensus about the new reform.

New Approaches to Students' Assessment in the 21st Century

The new educational reform of 2006 implied a wide range of changes in response to the disappointing results on the international comparative tests in the first years of the 21st century. The introduction of *basic skills* and *competence aims* (learning outcomes) are among the most significant changes in the curricula. The basic skills are defined as being able to *express oneself in writing and orally, being able to read, do mathematics and use digital tools* (Utdanningsdirektoratet, 2007a, p. 73). All basic skills were attempted to be included in all subject curricula; the concept being that all teachers share a responsibility for supporting the students' development of the basic skills.

The curricula state the competence aims the students are expected to achieve at the end of years 2, 4 and 7 in primary school, the end of lower secondary school (year 10) and for each year in most subjects in upper secondary school. The introduction of competence aims is a response to the lack of explicitness in the learning objectives addressed earlier; a move accompanied by a range of changes in the regulations of student assessment. It was made clearer that subject-specific achievements, on the one hand, and behaviour, order and effort, on the other hand, should be kept apart, clarifying for students the basis for judgment of students' achievement levels. Only evidence of achievement of the competence aims should form the judgment when grading students. The curricula, however, include no shared criteria or standards for judging whether the competence aims are being achieved. Instead, the local authorities and schools were encouraged to develop criteria themselves.

New Approach to National Testing

As mentioned in the introduction, an initiative for national testing of students' basic skills had been introduced already in 2004, 2 years before the implementation of new curricula. Back in 1988, a report from the OECD (1988) had questioned whether Norway had sufficient tools for monitoring the quality of its education system. Throughout the 1990s, a system for national evaluation of schooling was discussed in several documents by the government and the Parliament, but no centrally coordinated system was implemented until an official committee suggested so in 2002. Then, the first results of the PISA tests had already ignited a heated debate about the quality of schooling in Norway. National tests, a key element of the national quality monitoring system, were implemented hastily, and the government highly misjudged the controversies that evolved from their initiative. Not only were there substantial ideological battles over the principle of publishing the schools results and thereby promoting competition, but the quality of the tests was also found by researchers to be poor (Hølleland, 2007).

The government, however, continued its approach despite critique from researchers, teacher unions and the student union. When the second circle was introduced in 2005, it became clear that the student union had achieved significant support for the boycott actions it had started the year before. Between 36 and 45 per cent of students boycotted the tests in mathematics, reading and English writing in upper secondary school (Hølleland, 2007, p. 30). The boycott established the controversies over national testing as one of the key issues addressed by politicians in debates over education policy before the parliamentary elections later the same year. Following the election, a new government was formed, which soon announced that it would follow the advice of the researchers who had conducted an even more critical evaluation, and institute a one-year moratorium in order to develop a more solid framework for national testing. In this process, more influence has been given to the stakeholders, and the teacher and student unions have been making a significant contribution to the debate about how the testing framework can be improved (Hølleland, 2007, p. 37; Lie, 2007, p. 88).

While merely the question as to whether publishing schools' results on the tests along with their mean grades was the main concern addressed in the media, the Norwegian 'experiment' was interesting from a research perspective. It revealed a number of problems related to student assessment in general, which provided strong arguments for a broader examination of the systems and regulations of student assessment that were to come (Tveit, 2007a, p. 202).

The problems of the first tests, acknowledged later, was indistinctiveness on at least two levels: the purposes of the tests and the design of the different types of tests (Utdanningsdirektoratet, 2007a, p. 82). Furthermore, there were mixed messages on whether the results should be taken into account when giving final grades for the individual student, or whether they were measures of group performance only (Hølleland, 2007, p. 37). The new framework introduced in 2007 was limited to year 5 and year 8 in primary and lower secondary school, in mathematics and in reading in Norwegian and English (Utdanningsdirektoratet, 2007a, p. 82). The implementation of these tests was more in accordance with the regulations than the implementation of 2005 (Kavli, 2008, p. 4).

By having the test at the outset of the mid-years and lower secondary, it is made clear that the tests for the students are low stakes. The purpose of the test framework is now primarily defined as giving 'information about the group and the year set to teachers, school owners, local authorities and the regional and national level as the basis for improvement and development activities' (Utdanningsdirektoratet, 2007a, p. 82). The results, based on a common scale, will be published and made available to the public; however, the ministry will not introduce a ranking of schools.

New Approach to Criterion-Referenced Assessment?

While the approach to student assessment for quality monitoring purposes was hastily implemented *before* the new curricula, the policy on how to assess the individual students' achievements was not discussed until *after* schools had started to use the new curricula.

In the white paper to the Parliament of 2003, which prepared the new educational reform, it was stated that the continuous assessment should be 'standard based' (St.meld. nr. 30, 2003–2004, p. 40). The theoretical rationale for this assessment principle, however, was never explained in any government documents (a task that was still unaccomplished at the time of publication). Perhaps the government had neither the courage nor the time for the ideological battles over student assessment that surely awaited it; a somewhat latent conflict it indeed was a part of itself. As a result, these fights were postponed until after the new curricula had been implemented. Although it was predictable for those involved in preparing the reform, it was not until the examinations were to be prepared and the teachers were to conduct their final assessments based on the new curricula that controversies over student assessment reached the surface.

In a white paper to the Norwegian Parliament in December 2006, the new government mandated a thorough review of the regulations and systems for student assessment in order to achieve 'more equal and fair student assessment' (St.meld. nr. 16, 2006–2007, p. 79). In August 2007, additional changes were made to the regulations, acknowledging the critique that had been raised about legitimatising the concept of norm-referencing by the way achievement levels were described in the regulations. The achievement levels were to be described on a continuum scale from 'very low competence in the subject' (grade 1) to 'outstanding competence in the subject' (grade 6). At the same time, the Directorate for Education and Training introduced a project called 'Improved Assessment Practices' (*Bedre Vurderingspraksis*), which aims to investigate four models for developing a shared understanding of achievement levels across schools within the subjects Norwegian, mathematics, social science and food and health. The three models being trialled in primary schools range from the schools themselves developing and trialling criteria for one (high) or two (high and low) achievement levels, to trialling pre-stated achievement levels for high and low achievement. In the fourth model, lower and upper secondary schools are developing and trialling achievement levels for each of the six levels of competence stated in the general regulations for grading (Utdanningsdirektoratet, 2007c, p. 12).

This strategy is a step in the right direction, in order to facilitate shared understanding across schools and thereby more consistent and fair grading. However, the approach still suffers heavily because of the lack of theoretical rationale for assessment in the fundamental basis for making judgments—the curricula. A study of experiences with the early launch of the new curricula showed that student assessment was the field where most teachers (65 per cent) expressed that they needed more training in relation to the new reform (Bergem, Båtevik, Bachmann, & Kvangarsnes, 2006, p. 28). Student assessment was therefore stated as one of the national priority areas for professional development in 2007 (Utdanningsdirektoratet, 2007a, p. 36). Projects for trialling assessment criteria and professional development programs are crucial; however, for this to be successful the approach has to be grounded in theory. Whether Norwegian politicians and stakeholders are able to overcome the ideological controversies that have characterised the debate on student assessment since the 1970s and develop a distinct approach to criterion-referenced assessment remains an unanswered question.

Conclusion

What can we learn from the history of educational assessment in Norway? The past decades' ideological controversy over assessment policy can be seen as one of the reasons Norwegian politicians have failed to address the practical problems in the present assessment systems. The theory and practice of educational assessment in Norway can be seen as weak, owing to ideological rather than informed debates over fundamental principles regarding student assessment. While different theories may be seen as underpinning the different styles of assessment that have operated since the early 20th century, these links and bases have not been made overt. The lack of theoretical foundation of the assessment systems may reflect a fundamental fear of acknowledging what formal grading essentially expresses—that some students perform better than others.

The absence of formal grading in primary schools implies that student assessment, particularly in terms of grading, is not likely to form an important part of the teachers' competence. Teachers in Norway appear not to have been provided with sufficient training in student assessment. While the wide concerns for comparability of teacher judgments across schools appear to be owing to a fundamental theoretical and conceptual problem of the approach to student assessment, concerns about the teachers' practical competence is of equal importance.

For Norway to develop a successful approach to student assessment for the 21st century, three strategies can be seen as crucial. First, assessment regulations and practices need to be grounded in theory. This includes both the continuous assessment and the examinations, and not least the linkage between the two. By applying a distinct approach to criterion-referenced assessment, Norway can benefit from the experiences and theoretical concepts of the international community.

Second, considerable changes in the method of administration and reform of education should be applied. In Norway, problems in the educational system tend to have accumulated over a number of years, and often after approximately 10 years an extensive reform has been initiated. In a constantly more global and competitive world, politicians are inclined to introduce major reforms to address the problems their country is facing. Educational systems, particularly student assessment, are vulnerable in such reform strategies. It would be preferable to plan the education system on predictable cycles of revision of the curricula and to establish permanent arenas for professional development in relation to this.

Third, but not least, new strategies for giving the teaching profession the instruments and confidence necessary to make judgments on students' achievement need to be introduced. Resources should be provided to ensure that all teachers can develop quality assessment instruments and arenas where teachers can share experiences and moderate each other's judgments on the quality of students' achievements.

The concepts and processes of grading students are among the most powerful institutions in society—future generations' dreams and ambitions rely to a large extent on the grades they receive in school. Acknowledging that student grading can never be perfectly just, policy makers should provide extensive resources to improve concepts and procedures for student assessment.

References

Bergem, R., Båtevik, F. O., Bachmann, K., & Kvangarsnes, M. (2006). Tidleg oppstart med nye læreplanar: Kartlegging av erfaringar med førebuing og iverksetjing. *Arbeidsrappo rt* no. 196. Volda: Høgskulen i Volda.

Bergesen, H. O. (2006). *Kampen om Kunnskapsskolen*. Oslo: Universitetsforlaget.

Dale, E. L., & Wærness, J. I. (2006). Vurdering og læring i en elevaktiv skole. Oslo: Universitetsforlaget.

Dale, E. L., & Wærness, J. I. (2007). Tilpasset opplæring og elevvurdering. In S. Tveit (Ed.), *Elevvurdering i skolen—grunnlag for kulturendring*. Oslo: Universitetsforlaget.

Egelund, N. (2005). Educational assessment in Danish schools. *Assessment in Education: Principles, Policy and Practice, 12*(2), 203–212.

Furre, H., Danielsen, I. J., & Stiberg-Jamt, R. (2006). *Analyse av den nasjonale undersøkelsen 'Elevundersøkelsen' 2006*. Kristiansand: Oxford Research.

Harlen, W. (2004). *A systematic review of the evidence of the impact on students, teachers and the curriculum of the process of using assessment by teachers for summative purposes*. London: EPPI-Centre, Social Science Research Unit, Institute of Education.

Hægeland, T., Kirkebøen, L. J., & Raaum, O. (2005). *Skoleresultater 2004. En kartlegging av karakterer fra grunn- og videregående skoler i Norge*. Oslo: Statistics Norway.

Hølleland, H. (2007). Nasjonale prøver og kvalitetsutvikling i skolen. In S. Tveit (Ed.), *Elevvurdering i skolen—grunnlag for kulturendring*. Oslo: Universitetsforlaget.

Kavli, H. (2008). *Nasjonale prøver 2007—Brukernes evaluering av gjennomføringen*. Oslo: Synovate.

Kjærnsli, M., Lie, S., Olsen, R. V., & Roe, A. (2007). *Tid for tunge løft. Norske elevers kompetanse i naturfag, lesing og matematikk i PISA 2006*. Kortversjon. Oslo: Universitetsforlaget.

Kjærnsli, M., Lie, S., Olsen, R. V., Roe, A., & Turmo, A. (2004). *Rett spo eller ville veier? Norske elevers kompetanse i matematikk, naturfag og lesing i PISA 2003*. Oslo: Universitetsforlaget.

Klette, K. (2003). Lærernes klasseromsarbeid; Interkasjons- og arbeidsformer i norske klasserom etter Reform 97. In K. Klette (Ed.), *Klasserommets praksisformer etter Reform 97*. Oslo: Pedagogisk Forskningsinstitutt, Universitetet i Oslo.

Kunnskapsdepartementet (2007). *Oppdragsbrev nr. 06 om tiltak knyttet til individvurdering i skole og fag- og yrkesopplæring*. Oslo: Kunnskapsdepartementet.

Lie, S. (2007). Evalueringen av de nasjonale prøvene og hva vi kan lære av dem. In S. Tveit (Ed.), *Elevvurdering i skolen—grunnlag for kulturendring*. Oslo: Universitetsforlaget.

Lie, S., Kjærnsli, M., Roe, A., & Turmo, A. (2001). Godt rustet for framtida? Norske 15-åringers kompetanse i lesing og realfag i et internasjonalt perspektiv: Institutt for lærerutdanning og skoleutvikling, Universitetet i Oslo.

Lysne, A. (1999). *Karakterer og kompetanse. Stridstema i norsk skolehistorie*. Bind 1. Haslum: AVA Forlag.

Lysne, A. (2004). *Kampen om skolen. 1970–2000. Karakterer og kompetanse. Stridstema i norsk skolehistorie*. Bind 2. Haslum: AVA Forlag.

Lysne, A. (2006). Assessment theory and practice of students' outcomes in the Nordic Countries. *Scandinavian Journal of Educational Research, 50*(3), 327–359.

Læringssenteret (2003). *Karakter—mer enn karakterer*. Oslo: Læringssenteret.

Mikkelsen, R., Buk-Berge, E., Ellingsen, H., Fjeldstad, D., & Sund, A. 2001. Civic Education Study Norge 2001. Demokratisk beredskap og engasjement hos 9.-klassinger i Norge og 27 andre land. Oslo: Institutt for Lærerutdanning og Skoleutvikling, Universitetet i Oslo.

NOU (1974: 41). *Karakterer, eksamener, kompetanse m.v. i skoleverket. Norges offentlige utredninger*. Oslo: Statens forvaltningstjeneste.

NOU (2003: 16). *I første rekke. Norges offentlige utredninger*. Oslo: Statens forvaltningstjeneste.

OECD (1988). *OECD-vurdering av norsk utdanningspolitikk*. Oslo: Kirke-og undervisningsdepartementet.

Statistics Norway (2008). Færre grunnskolar. Retrieved May 23, 2008, from <http://www.ssb.no/emner/04/02/20/utgrs/>.

Statistics Norway (Undated-a). Emne:04 Utdanning. Tabell: 05326: Elever i videregående opplæring, etter studieretningstype og skolen sitt eierforhold (F). Reviderte tall for 2007. Retrieved May 29, 2008, from <http://statbank.ssb.no/statistikkbanken/Default_FR.asp?PXSid=0&nvl=true&PLanguage=0&tilside=selecttable/hovedtabellHjem.asp &KortnavnWeb=vgu>.

Statistics Norway (Undated-b). Utvalgte nøkkeltall, fylkeskommuner – nivå 1. Gjennomsnitt alle fylkeskommuner 2007. Retrieved May 23, 2008, from <http://www.ssb.no/kostra/stt/index.cgi?spraak=norsk&nivaa=1&regionstype=fylkeskommune&faktaark=101040642883067 &regioner=default@default&kolonne=0&event=ny&mal=region&cookie=0>.

St.meld. nr. 30 (2003–2004). *Kultur for læring*. Oslo: Utdannings- og forskningsdepartementet.

St.meld. nr. 16 (2006–2007). *... og ingen stod igjen*. Oslo: Kunnskapsdepartementet.

Tveit, S. (2007a). Analyse av retningslinjer og praksis for elevvurdering. In S. Tveit (Ed.), *Elevvurdering i skolen—grunnlag for kulturendring*. Oslo: Universitetsforlaget.

Tveit, S. (2007b). Formål og retningslinjer for elevvurdering i Kunnskapsløftet. In S. Tveit (Ed.), *Elevvurdering i skolen—grunnlag for kulturendring*. Oslo: Universitetsforlaget.

Tønnessen, L. K. B., & Telhaug, A. O. (1996). Elevvurderingen i norsk skole i etterkrigstida. *Karakterboka. Om karakterer og vurdering i ny skole*. Oslo: Universitetsforlaget.

Utdanningsdirektoratet (2007a). *The Education Mirror 2006. Analysis of primary and lower and upper secondary education in Norway*. Oslo: Utdanningsdirektoratet.

Utdanningsdirektoratet (2007b). Høringsbrev om forslag til endringer i forskrift til opplæringsloven 23.06.2006 nr. 724 og endring i Læreplanverket for Kunnskapsløftet. Oslo: Utdanningsdirektoratet.

Utdanningsdirektoratet (2007c). *Vurdering. Et felles løft for bedre vurderingspraksis—en veiledning. Revidert utgave*. Oslo: Utdanningsdirektoratet.

Vagle, W., Berge, K. L., Evensen, L. S., & Hertzberg, F. (2007). Det umulige er nesten mulig. Om norskeksamen på ungdomsskolen og utvikling av vurderingsnormer. In S. Tveit (Ed.), *Elevvurdering i skolen—grunnlag for kulturendring* Oslo: Universitetsforlaget.

Wikström, C. (2006). Education and assessment in Sweden. *Assessment in Education: Principles, Policy and Practice, 13*(1), 113–28.

Chapter 13
Articulating Tacit Knowledge Through Analyses of Recordings: Implications for Competency Assessment in the Vocational Education and Training Sector

Ann Kelly

Introduction

In this chapter I argue that there are oral communication competencies that workers have developed and use to effect in their everyday practices but which have not been articulated and thus are not recognised in assessment measures related to training packages. The analysis of recordings of the talk used in authentic tasks, through which such competencies are made visible, can offer one way to ensure that such competencies become not only available for assessment but also available for formal recognition and credit for trainee employees. Conversation analysis, a broad term that includes the analysis of a range of types of talk, has rarely been used for this purpose[1] and I argue that its application within the vocational education and training sector would increase the repertoire of trainers' and teachers' assessment methods in a valuable way. For readers outside this particular educational sector, however, the analyses of talk that enacts specific practices may also be a worthwhile addition to their pedagogical repertoire.

The articulation and codification of tacit knowledge has been a continuing challenge within the vocational education and training sector since the implementation of competency-based training. However, recently, theorists have differentiated tacit knowledge that has not been articulated from knowledge that cannot be articulated. Using the example of an analysis of a transcript of a service request interaction involving a complainant and an administrative trainee employed in a local government council office, I show how such an approach has the potential to render explicit those otherwise tacit competencies employed by the interactants in constituting and documenting a service request. I then discuss a framework that comprises quality

A. Kelly (✉)
School of Educ & Professional Studies, Mt Gravatt Campus, Griffith University, 176 Messines Ridge Road, Mt Gravatt QLD 4122, Australia
e-mail: ann.kelly@griffith.edu.au

[1] An example of its use is in the diagnostic assessment of aphasia patients (Perkins et al., 1999).

C. Wyatt-Smith, J.J. Cumming (eds.), *Educational Assessment in the 21st Century*,
DOI 10.1007/978-1-4020-9964-9_13, © Springer Science+Business Media B.V. 2009

criteria for evaluating the viability of using recordings as assessment items. Finally, I proffer a case for the development of descriptors that are consistent with an understanding of the sequential nature of oral communication interactions. This contrasts with a more psychometric approach, based on item theory, which separates items from their context.

Background

For more than two decades, most of the accredited vocational education and training (VET) in Australia and in a number of other industrialised countries have been colonised by a highly bureaucratised form of competency-based training (CBT) and assessment. A key feature of the Australian CBT system has been the articulation and codification of work tasks into a framework of competencies (National Training Board, 1992).

In the early identification of work tasks and in the development of sets of competencies relating to those tasks, a narrow, 'functional approach' (Le Deist & Winterton, 2005) or skills perspective (Clarke & Winch, 2006) was implemented (National Training Board, 1990). While this approach continues to characterise competencies in the United Kingdom, a broader conception of competencies, including the recognition of underpinning knowledge, has been adopted in Australia. This articulated underpinning knowledge, however, does not always encompass the relevant tacit knowledge required to enact work tasks successfully. Within the research literature (for example, Cowan, David & Foray, 2000; Johnson, Lorenz & Lundvall, 2002; Stevenson, 2000) there is recognition that some forms of knowledge will always remain unarticulated and uncodified. This may be because such knowledge is inaccessible or it may not be in the interests of industries or employers to render such knowledge explicit (Nelson & Winter, 1982). It follows, then, that in the assessment of competencies, the issue of tacit knowledge becomes problematic. In this chapter I focus on the elucidation of this non-articulated and non-codified tacit knowledge in registered sets of competencies (that is, training packages in Australia) and the resultant implications for the assessment of those competencies.

Tacit Knowledge

Tacit knowledge has been aligned with Ryle's (1963) concept of 'knowing how' in a general sense, and in a more specific sense, has also been linked to Tulving's (1972) term, 'episodic memory', a memory for personally relevant experiential episodes by Connell, Klein and Powell (2003). It is differentiated from explicit knowledge on the grounds that this form of knowledge is difficult to specify (a requirement in competency statements) because it is largely unconscious (Grant, 1996), and is embedded in individuals and organisational structures. In a seminal study of tacit knowledge, however, Nelson & Winter (1982) suggest that, while this knowledge may not be articulated, this does not necessarily mean that at least some of it *cannot* be articulated.

In this chapter I examine a case of unarticulated knowledge relating to the work of an administrative trainee employed in a local council office. The reporting service requests that I present raise subsequent questions about how the trainee's performance on this task might be assessed productively against the relevant elements of competency. This case derives from an ethnomethodological Australian study that investigated the ways in which three different work tasks, namely the reporting of service requests, the receipt of rate payments and the provision of information regarding applications for positions, were accomplished in three separate local council settings by trainees. While the end results appeared to have been accomplished to the satisfaction of the parties concerned in virtually every case, a detailed examination of the different ways in which this was done, using a conversation-analysis approach, sheds light on the specific competencies that the trainee and the customers displayed in effecting this outcome. In the following section, key aspects of conversation analysis are highlighted to support the position I take in this chapter that the development of expertise in the use of this analytical method has the potential to enhance teachers' pedagogical repertoires.

Conversation Analysis as an Assessment Tool

Conversation analysis has its roots in ethnomethodology, which is concerned with 'how order is produced as the local achievement of actors' (Boden, 1990, p. 189). Thus, while there may be common features evident in how outcomes are achieved across a corpus of instances, in a conversation-analysis approach there is an emphasis on the rationality that is displayed by participants in accomplishing social practices in response to local exigencies as they occur progressively in each interaction. The use of recordings of such interactions provides assessors with a depth of insight into how 'institutional identities' (Drew & Heritage, 1992, p. 3) are developed and maintained. This is not otherwise available from electronic or paper-based texts that may result from such work or from participant accounts following such interactions (Afflerbach, 2000). Such use is also consistent with approaches to assessment that reflect authentic social practices.

In the next section, I present the practical application of an oral interaction analysis that focuses on the in situ audio recording of a service request. This provides evidence of the value of such a conversation-analysis approach in the assessment of certain types of competencies. In this recording the actual talk sequence was central to the work of explicating the trainee's competence. However, what are also evident are particular identities that are assumed by the participants in ensuring that understandings by both parties were adequate for the practical purpose of accomplishing the service request. For example, in this transcript of the service request, the caller can be seen to have provided very detailed location details to support a position that he was addressing a council rather than a personal problem. For her part, the trainee, in responding to the call, not only dealt with this focus but also managed to elicit and record required details for later insertion into an official service request form in a way that can be observed to be acceptable to the caller.

Identifying and Reporting a Council Service Problem

Responding to requests to address complaints was a key function of administrative staff in one council office in my study. This process involved a number of discrete stages that are shown in Fig. 13.1. In this chapter I am concerned with stages 1 and 2.

Stage 1	Stage 2	Stage 3	Stage 4
Constitution of the service request by caller and trainee and its documentation as notes by the trainee	Documentation of the request on the Customer Service Request form by trainee	Actioning of response to complaint and documentation of this action by designated council officer	Establishment of satisfaction with the resolution to the complaint by trainee and caller

Fig. 13.1 Stages in responding to a service request

In order to show empirically how an actual telephone service request was negotiated by both parties, a transcript of the interaction that occurred, based on a modified conversation-analysis approach (Psathas, 1995), is shown below. The transcript is sectioned on the right to show the phases of the call. Identifying details such as names and locations have been changed and the initial opening sequence, which included permission to record the call, is not available. A set of notational symbols and their meaning can be found in the description of conversation analysis at the end of the chapter.

Transcript 1
     T is the trainee and C is the caller

```
1    C    ( ) sweet and nice                              ⎫
2    T    hhhhhh okay (.) so you have a leaking            ⎪
3         water                                            ⎪
4         (1.0)                                            ⎬ Summarising the nature of the problem
5         [water pipe do you]                              ⎪
6    C    [yeh::: the the:] water main's leakin (.)        ⎪
7         right out in front of our mail box               ⎭
8         (2.0)                                            ⎫
9    T    out the front of your mailbox=                   ⎪
10   C    =yeh at ninety-one macmillan street (.)          ⎪
11        mangrove (.)                                      ⎪
12   T    how do you spell that sir                         ⎪
13   C    em-ay-see-em-eye-el-el-aye-en                     ⎪
14        (2.0)                                             ⎪
15   T    macmillan street mangrove=                        ⎪
16   C    =street or court whatever you like to put         ⎪
17        down is right                                     ⎪
18   T    o:kay                                             ⎬ Locating the  problem
20   T    sorry                                             ⎪
21   C    off bottlebrush street                            ⎪
22   T    off bottlebrush (.) uh huh                        ⎪
23   C    we live at number ninety-one and it's            ⎪
24        right outside the bloody mailbox (.)             ⎪
25        on the road                                       ⎪
26        (2.0)                                             ⎪
27        it's between the (.) the bitumen and the          ⎪
28        gutter right                                       ⎪
29        (2.0)                                              ⎭
30   T    okay
31        (4.0)
32        what I'll do for you (.) sorry I'm just
33        writing all this down=
34   C    =huh=
```

```
35   T    =what I'll do for you sir is I'll um (.)
36        put in a service request and (.)              Initial actioning of the request
37        hopefully get that fixed up for you=
38   C    =ha ha [ha ha]
39   T           [is it] leaking badly
40        (1.0)
41   C    we:ll (.) it's leakin bad enough
42   T    yeh=
43   C    =it's startin to lift the road
44        (2.0)
45   T    o:okay                                         Warranting of the request

46        (2.0)
47   C    because I walked out a minute ago and
48        it was as ah soft as hell
49   T    ye:h [okay]
50   C         [so I] reckon it's about ready to
51        bust any minute
52   T    well I'll um (.) I'll hopefully get            Confirming action to be taken
53        someone out for you to:day what was
54        your name sir
55   C    bla:ck (.) I live at number ninety-one
56   T    okay and your contact phone number
57        mister black                                   Managing caller details
58   C    five four nine three one three six one
59   T    nine three one three six one=
60   C    =I'm the chap here with the big ugly dog
61   T    o::huh huh kay
62   C    okay
63   T    okay I'll um (.) [put in (  )]
64   C                     [get on to it]
65   T    yeh (. ) [I'::ll I'll]                         Further warranting of the call
66   C             [tell them] don't tell them not to
67        wait for six months cause I won't have
68        enough water to water to water the lawn
69   T    right okay
70   C    okay
71   T    thanks mister black                            Closing of the call
72   C    bye bye
73   T    bye
```

Summarising the Cause of the Problem in Service Request Calls

The interactional work undertaken to summarise the problem in this call request occurs very early in the call. Between lines 2 and 7, beginning with the use of the conjunction 'so' as a sign that she was engaging in formulating work (Heritage & Watson, 1979), the trainee offered a possible specific cause of the problem for confirmation through the use of a question ('so you have a leaking water (1.0) [water pipe do you]). This summation overlapped the caller's initial affirmation and the beginning of his correction of a water pipe to a water main.

Examining the summary statement that was written on the informal note (see Fig. 13.2) during the interaction, it is evident that the cause of the problem was confined to 'leaking water'—the initial formulating terms used by the trainee in lines 2 and 3 of the transcript.

On the service request form, 'leaking water' was converted to a heading 'Water' that served to indicate the department in the council to which the form would be forwarded. Included also was a collocation of terms as subheadings (Mains/leaks/burst) that, though they were somewhat of a departure from the details provided by the caller, for the practical purpose of recording the problem that had been described and clarified, were likely to be satisfactory. In writing a summary of the problem the

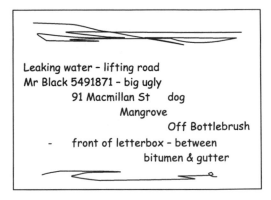

Leaking water – lifting road
Mr Black 5491871 – big ugly
                91 Macmillan St   dog
                        Mangrove
                                Off Bottlebrush
        -       front of letterbox – between
                                bitumen & gutter

Fig. 13.2 Trainee's notes of call

Customer Service Request Provider Services Water Mains/Leaks/burst		12301
		Property No
Summary		
Water leak on the road out the front of the above location between the bitumen and the gutter		

Fig. 13.3 Summary headings and statement on the service request form

trainee rearranged the order of the words of the call and the note marginally to read 'Water leak on the road', followed by two brief locational details (Fig. 13.2).

Managing the Locational Details of the Problem in Service Request Calls

In council service request interactions conducted by telephone, it is imperative that the call taker record information about the location of the problem. In some cases, elicitation questions by the trainee were required to obtain this information. It is necessary, however, that the type of locational information is 'right' (Schegloff, 1972, p. 81) for the particular problem that is being addressed, with the nature of the 'right' details being dependent on a number of local contingencies. In this case, these included an appreciation by both parties to the call that a third party would physically address the problem. Further, both the caller and trainee needed to appreciate that this third party would be using road transport to travel to the problem site. However, there were wider understandings observable as well. For example, in this call, considerations about the source of responsibility for the resolution of the problem were evident in the description of the specific location provided by the caller.

In this instance, the service requester appeared to take considerable trouble to identify exactly the location of the source of the problem. Throughout the three locational sequences in this interaction, the caller repeated his property number twice and the location of the leak—as situated 'in front of', and 'outside', his mailbox—once, that is, *outside* his property. The street number was obviously important to him and, undoubtedly, would be to the council workers who would subsequently address the problem. Equally vital were the other locational details provided. The second item that was repeated, the location of the leak, might be heard as belonging to two categories. It was a relevant geographical item of information, but it was also a jurisdictional one. In reiterating this detail, the caller could be heard to be stating his understanding that the rectification of the problem was a council, rather than a personal, responsibility. Each of these separate details was documented by the trainee on her note. However, once the caller's official address was recorded, only the detail related to the site of the leak was added.

Schegloff (1972) has asserted that the 'right' locational details appear to be recipient designed. Thus, it is evident that the trainee was required to perform quite complicated interactional and cognitive work in locating the source of the problem that was likely to remain tacit if a recording of this work were not available. This would have implications for the assessment of this particular trainee's competence in the recording of complaints, an element of competency upon which she was judged. It would also have ramifications for other trainees engaged in similar practices, albeit in slightly different ways, and to assessment practices generally that involve tacit abilities. We can draw a similar conclusion from the provision and receipt of warrants in service request calls, in other words, justifications for the call.

Determining the Gravity of the Problem Underpinning the Service Request Call

Sharrock and Turner (1978) have noted that not all service calls are supported by warrants. They argue that this is because no accounting is expected when requesting assistance for particular problems. The authors cite the theft of a car as an example in which accounts may not be required. Where an accounting is the norm, however, it is understood that 'there is a need for some documentation of noticings, realisations, suspicions, and so on as an essential component of the complaint—its absence occasioning questions as to its availability' (Sharrock & Turner, 1978, p. 179). Critical to such documentation is the particular 'stance' (Whalen & Zimmerman, 1990, p. 466) that service requesters adopt towards the problem. In elaborating on this notion, Whalen and Zimmerman (1990) argue that when framing their telephone complaints, callers 'orient to displays of a *practical* epistemology—just how, on this occasion, one has come to know about the particular event' [original emphasis] (p. 466). It has been observed, however, that a measure of 'equivocality' (Sharrock & Turner, 1978) pertains with respect to the warranting of complaints in cases in which caller vulnerabilities can be exposed. As a result, complaining and requesting services require finesse if the caller is not to be heard as vindictive or not credible.

Call takers, on the other hand, engage in 'verifying' behaviour in response to the warrants that are proposed by the callers. Zimmerman (1992) defines a 'verification' activity as 'a form of a repetition of the caller's previous turn, or some portion of it ... [which] thus displays the information that the call-taker has received from the caller' (p. 445). Verification is also discussed by Meehan (1986), within a context similar to that of Zimmerman's. Meehan suggests that *formulations* (Heritage & Watson, 1979) are often a useful way to accomplish the work of verification. Formulations are an important medium whereby the gist of a problem is verified. In the following fragment, excerpted from the transcript of the call, formulations are observably performing the critical work of justifying the call and providing information about the immediacy of the response that is required.

In this call, the warranting work, in relation to the water that was leaking from the main, was undertaken towards its conclusion. In addition, in contrast to some of the other service request calls that comprise my corpus, it was initiated by the trainee, who enquired whether it was 'leaking badly' (line 39), that is, whether the problem was serious. Relevant transcript fragments of the warranting phase of the call are shown below.

Excerpt from Transcript 1

```
39   T                    [is it leaking] badly
40           (1.0)
41   C       we:ll (.) it's leakin bad enough
42   T       yeh=
43   C       =it's startin to lift the road
44           (2.0)
45   T       o:kay
46           (2.0)
47   C       because I walked out a minute ago and
48           it was as ah soft as hell
49   T       ye:h [okay]
50   C            [so I] reckon it's about ready to
51           bust any minute
52   T       well I'll um (.) I'll hopefully get
53           someone out for you to:day
...
64   C                       [get on to it]
65   T       yeh (. ) [I'::ll I'll]
66   C                [tell them] don't tell them not to
67           wait for six months cause I won't have
68           enough water to water to water the lawn
69           right okay
70   T       okay
```

In choosing the modifier 'badly' (line 39) over a less serious term (for example, 'much'), the trainee appeared to recognise that a leak in a water main was a legitimate reason for contacting the council. In the first warranting phase, the caller first described the effect of the leaking main in the following way: 'it's startin to lift the road' (line 43). There was a longish pause following this claim, during which time the trainee completed her informal notes relating to the call by inserting the warrant: 'lifting road' (see Fig. 13.4)

In the second warrant offered, the caller began by informing the trainee that the evidence for his concern was gathered very recently—'I walked out a minute ago (to inspect the problem)' (line 47). At that time, 'it' (presumably the road) was as 'soft as hell'. This opinion was accepted by the trainee in her next turn ('ye:h okay') but her second acknowledgment marker was overlapped with a formulation by the caller: 'so I reckon it's about ready to bust any minute' (lines 50–51). A high level of seriousness of the problem was recognised by the trainee as evidenced by her assurance to the caller that she would 'hopefully get someone out for you **to:day** [my emphasis]'. This level of urgency is also evident on the service request form that was developed from the call through her insertion of the abbreviation, 'ASAP', when recommending action to be taken (see arrowed sentence in Fig. 13.5).

The third warrant given, however, appeared to be much weaker than the previous two in this interaction. The excerpt relating to this part of the call is shown below.

> Leaking water – lifting

Fig. 13.4 Warranting details on trainee's notes

Excerpt 2 from Transcript 1

```
66      C              [tell them] don't tell them not to
67                     wait for six months cause I won't have
68                     enough water to water to water the lawn
69      T      right okay
```

In line 66, it can be seen that the caller advised the trainee to '[tell them] don't tell them not to wait for six months cause I won't have enough water to water to water the lawn right ↑'. While the trainee acknowledged hearing this directive, as evidenced by her use of the marker 'okay', the warrant was not recorded either on her notes or on the resultant organisational form. That is, she used her judgment to hear this warrant as a post 'agreement-to-act' and not as a serious matter to be recorded on the form.

As with all the service request calls recorded, the trainee was required to make a decision about the seriousness of the alleged problem. In this call, as in other calls, she allowed the requester to present his perspective. However, in contrast to some other responses in which she queried the caller's warrants, in this instance she accepted the first two warrants that were offered and informed the caller that she would endeavour ('hopefully') to have the problem addressed that same day.

Summary:	
	Water leak on the road out the front of the above location between the bitumen and the gutter

Details:	
	Mr Black, 91 Macmillan Mangrove 5491871

Please investigate and arrange appropriate action ASAP as it is lifting the road. Thankyou.

Fig. 13.5 Warranting details on service request form

The three key components of the task of identifying and reporting council service problems, that is, the summarising of their cause, the managing of their locational details and the determination of their gravity, were evident in all of the calls in the corpus that was recorded, although the way in which they were addressed differed across the calls. These particular components obviously reflected the information that was required on the service request forms that were developed from the calls. What is not known, though, is whether the same types of information are required for responding to complaint calls by other councils or, indeed, how complaints are addressed and managed generally. These questions are important for assessors of Level III administrative trainees such as the one in my study because their role is to determine whether such trainees are competent in 'responding to complaints' (National Training Information Services (NTIS), n.d., n.p.).

In the following section, I examine the endorsed elements of competency relating to addressing a complaint. In comparing these with the work of the trainee that is visible in the transcript above, it is evident that much of the interactional accomplishment inherent in documenting a complaint would remain tacit if audio or video recordings were not available to assessors as a resource for judging competence in this task.

Assessing Competence in Recording Complaints

The accredited element of competency related to the recording of complaints as service requests is shown in Table 13.1.

In addition to elements of competency and performance criteria, the documentation accompanying units of competency also contain *required skills and knowledge*, a *range* statement and an *evidence guide* that provides advice on assessment. Required skills include:

Table 13.1 BSBCMM301A: Process customer complaints

Element	Performance criteria
1. Respond to complaints	1.1 Process customer complaints using effective communication in accordance with organisational procedures established under organisational policies, legislation or codes of practice.
	1.2 Obtain, document and review necessary reports relating to customer complaints.
	1.3 Make decisions about customer complaints, taking into account applicable legislation, organisational policies and codes.
	1.4 Negotiate resolution of the complaint and obtain agreement where possible.
	1.5 Maintain a register of complaints/disputes.
	1.6 Inform customer of the outcome of the investigation.

Source: National Training Information Services, n.d., n.p.

- communication skills to interpret customer complaints, and to monitor and advise on customer service strategies and resolutions
- culturally appropriate communication skills to relate to people from diverse backgrounds and people with diverse abilities
- literacy skills to read and understand a variety of texts; to prepare general information and paper according to target audience; and to edit and proofread texts to ensure clarity of meaning and accuracy of grammar and punctuation and
- problem-solving skills to deal with customer enquiries or complaints, to apply organisational procedures to a range of situations and to exercise judgement in this application' (National Training Information Service (NTIS), n.d., n.p.).

The required knowledge is concerned with applicable legislation, government policies and conventions, and the trainee's role in addressing complaints or service requests. The range of variables listed for consideration comprises different customer characteristics, different types of complaints and communication practices such as speaking and writing clearly and concisely.

Thus, this unit of competence is conceptualised in a very general way. However, it is recognised that this is necessary because of the high number of Level III trainee administration staff[2] who are likely to process complaints, the range of modes in which such complaints are made and the diversity of contexts in which they are employed. However, this generality has implications for assessment, which I address in the final section of the chapter.

The Assessment of Complaint Recording

The evidence guide relating to the unit of competence focusing on the processing of complaints states that examples of customer complaints (and presumably, the documentation that ensues from their processing) must be available to assessors. However, in the list of 'appropriate' methods of assessment, no explicit mention of the review of recordings of actual interactions in which complaints are framed in an acceptable bureaucratic form [3] are made. The question then arises: What would be the implication for quality assessments if such reviews were to be used as one component of an assessment framework?

In reviewing possible 'quality' criteria for inclusion in a competency assessment framework, Baartman, Bastiaens, Kirschner and van der Vleuten (2006) built on earlier work by theorists, such as Birenbaum (1996, 2003), Gulikers, Bastiaens & Kirschner (2004), Linn, Baker and Dunbar (1991) and van der Vleuten & Schuwith (2005), to identify possible criteria. Fifteen international experts on assessment and quality criteria for assessment subsequently validated these criteria. The resultant

---

[2] In September 2007, the number of elementary clerical, sales and service workers in training was 21 000 (National Centre for Vocational Education Research, 2007).
[3] Mention is made, though, in the NTIS literature relating to this competency that audio-visual tapes may be used to document customer complaint reports.

Fig. 13.6 The Wheel of
Competency Assessment
Framework (Source:
Baartman, Bastiaens,
Kirschner & van der
Vleuten, 2006, p. 166)

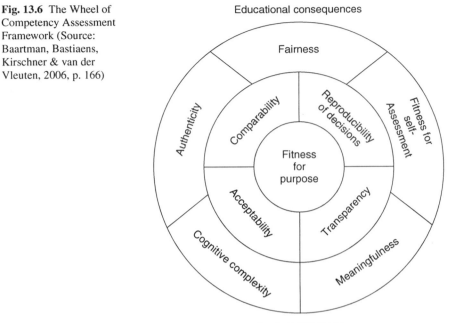

'Wheel of Competency Assessment' framework, reproduced with permission,[4] is shown in Fig. 13.6.

The authors note that the adjacent placement of criteria both within the circle segments and across them is arbitrary. However, the positioning of criterion *Fitness for purpose* is placed deliberately at the centre of the arrangement because it is foundational to the framework. The rationale for the placement of the criteria in the inner circle is their importance and pervasiveness, while the criteria on the outer circle and further out within the square reflect recent ideas about competency assessment. In applying these criteria to the use of a selection of audio or video recordings, resources relating to the assessment of complaint processing within one particular occupational environment, it is possible that they would be considered *meaningful, authentic, fit for the purpose* and *for self-assessment* as well as having educational *consequences*. However, additional work by at least one panel of experts across employment sites, who have responsibility for assessing the competency *Process customer complaints*, would need to be expended in developing rating rubrics in order to determine whether such assessment resources would prove to be *transparent, comparable, fair, reproducible of decisions, cost- and time-effective* and

---

[4] Reproduced from *Studies in Educational Evaluation, 22*, Baartman, L. K., Bastiaens, T. J., Kirschner, P. A. & Van der Vleuten, C. P. M., 'The wheel of competency assessment: Presenting quality criteria for competency assessment programs', pp. 153–170, Copyright (2006), with permission from Elsevier.

reflective of the *cognitive complexity* required of a Level III administrative officer. As Connally, Jorgensen, Gillis and Griffin (2002) have noted:

> The use of criterion referenced definitions for rating scales convey far greater information about the quality of performance, discriminates more accurately between individuals, and allows for candidates to be given more diagnostic feedback, feedback that they likely perceive as more constructive and valid. (n.p.)

While certain types and forms of information may need to be conventionalised for the bureaucratic purposes of employment situations, what must be kept in the forefront of such criteria-development work is the sequential nature of oral communication interactions in which tasks are accomplished and the local rationalities, contingencies and co-operation displayed by the participants in the tasks (Kelly, 2003). While research by Griffin (2007) and his colleagues (Bateman & Griffin, 2003; Connally et al., 2002) have provided a model for such developmental work that has, as a central feature, the use of the Rasch notion of a continuum of competence with a candidate being positioned at a point relative to the amount of latent trait that is demonstrated, it is important that the special features of conversation analysis not be lost in such a psychometric approach (Schegloff, 1993).

With respect to the unit of competency relating to the processing of customer complaints and other competencies that involve interactive work, it is recognised that, in addition to reviews of audio recordings, it would be necessary also to consider face-to-face interactions. It is likely, however, that these could be observed. A similar process of developing descriptive rating scales, some of which are likely to overlap with those developed for audio recordings, would be necessary. Further types of evidence are also likely to be necessary. For example, in the case of the local council recordings of complaints, a relevant measure would be the proportion of documentations that led to successful outcomes of complaints and the number of recalls to complainants that were made by the trainee to meet the content requirements of relevant forms.[5] Another source of evidence that might be appropriate is the judgment of supervisors with respect to the trainee's competence. All of these aspects could be incorporated into a valuable multi-evidential assessment approach that is currently missing from both the formal requirements of the CBT assessment process in Australia and the practices of assessors.

A qualitative study using conversation analysis as presented in this chapter might be dismissed for being inconsequential because only one task was examined, and therefore the study is limited in its objectivity, empiricism and rigour (Freebody, 2003, p. 69). However, as a counter to such criticism, Freebody asserts that qualitative studies might be perceived as being:

- more *objective*, in the sense of understanding what constitutes a cultural 'object' ...
- more *empirical,* in the sense of attending meticulously to the anomalies and contradictions evident in the findings, as well as to the foreseen and unforeseen consistencies ...

---

[5] In my corpus of 30 such calls, one follow-up call was made.

- through the use of transparent and consistently applied techniques for analysis and interpretation, more *rigorous*, in the sense of resisting the 'escape of the phenomenon' into pre-emptive explanatory formulas, into the a priori commitments of the researchers or the participants, or into the themes extracted from other studies or other sites in the study at hand (italics and quotations marks in original) (Freebody, 2003, p. 70).

In determining employees' competencies in performing work tasks, it is critical that there be an understanding of what constitutes these tasks. When this understanding is available and known, multiple observations of behaviour or products over a period of time, or even objective tests of knowledge, are likely to be appropriate. In other cases, though, where the elements of work tasks are tacit, then audio or video recordings of performances of such tasks would allow such elements to become more explicit and thus available for assessment in a more objective, empirical and rigorous way.

Conclusion

In this chapter I argued that the use of recordings (with an exemplar using an audio recording) should be considered as a strategy for making explicit the knowledge, skills and attitudinal requirements inherent in the successful accomplishment of particular units of competency, which would otherwise remain tacit. Specifically, such recordings capture the competencies that are used interactionally and in situ in enacting actual work—a feature that cannot be discerned through an analysis of textual outcomes or the verbal recounts of practices. While the analysis of the recording of service requests is located within the vocational education and training sector, readers are urged to consider its applicability to other learning and assessment contexts.

However, it is recognised that any recordings that are made of authentic practices need to be judged with respect to a set of quality criteria, one framework for which is presented for consideration (Baartman et al., 2006). In addition, rating scales would need to be developed to assess the competence demonstrated in these recordings as well as the results from other assessment measures against which employees' competencies could be assessed. It is further argued that the recent work by Griffin (2007) and his colleagues (Bateman & Griffin, 2003; Connally et al., 2002) may serve as a useful model to guide this work.

One of the rationales for adopting a competency-based approach to training and assessment was that *all* workers should be able to be credited for the competencies they display at work. If these remain tacit, this goal will not be achieved. On the other hand, if these tacit knowledges, skills and attitudes can be made visible, assessment practices for the 21st century will be rendered more meaningful, authentic and fit for the purpose, and for self-assessment, and will have more beneficial educational consequences.

Theoretical and Methodological Framings

Conversation Analysis as a Method for Explicating and Assessing Competencies at Work

Conversation analysis has been used as a research method within a number of disciplinary areas to gain an understanding of how work tasks are constituted. These areas include medicine, law, education, journalism and international trade. However, with the exception of Linda Tapsell (for example, Tapsell, Brenninger, & Barnard, 2001), Lisa Perkins (for example, Perkins, Crisp & Walshaw, 1999) and Kelly (for example, Kelly, 2003), there appears to be little application of conversation analysis within the vocational education and training research literature. A list of the basic principles relating to the analysis of conversation, as initially developed by Sacks (1995) and more recently applied, is shown below.

- Conversation analysts assume that, when people talk, they are engaging in a social activity. In examining talk, they seek to 'uncover, describe and analyse the ways in which social order is ongoingly produced, achieved and made recognizable in and through this action' (Psathas, 1995, p. 65).
- The research data derive from audio or video recordings of the talk that is generated by people as they use language to engage in everyday activities, including those enacted at work. While such recordings cannot be undertaken on a large scale, for example, compared with a survey, the level of authenticity of the data is high. In addition, the detailed transcripts are available to others for independent analysis.
- In analysing transcripts, researchers assume an *indifferent* stance. That is, they do not bring prior expectations to this process. Rather, the transcripts themselves are read for the logic and accounting practices that are used by the participants in the talk. This transparency contrasts with a number of other research methods that use pre-determined coding systems to organise and interpret data.
- Conversation analysts have shown talk to be organised in systematic ways. A particular focus of analytical work has been 'turn-taking'. Researchers have demonstrated that the organisation of turns by speakers in a conversation is an important feature in accomplishing activities.

The first step in undertaking an analysis of interactions in both face-to-face and other modes is to audio or video record the focal activity in which the participants are engaging. These recordings are then transcribed in fine detail using established conventions of notation, with the transcriber checking continually that the transcription is accurate. While the transcription of the talk used is important in both audio and video recordings, obviously, features of the interaction additional to those listed below (for example, body movement, gestures, gaze, etc.) must be included in video transcriptions as they impact on how the activity is undertaken. Selections of particular instances of items of interest evident in the transcriptions that have emerged are then made (for example, the way a teacher deals with the students' prior knowledge in lessons). The next step involves deriving meaning from what is evident to the analyst as well as the participants in the interaction and then explicating this meaning. Finally, these explications are compared with understandings that prevail in the research literature (Freebody, 2003). Instances of these analytical features are then compared and contrasted both within the analysts' data and across the literature, and themes and issues are identified.

For some purposes, for example, in rendering tacit knowledge observable through the use of transcriptions of interactions, as exemplified in this chapter, a conversation-analysis methodology would appear to be particularly applicable.

The notational symbols (Psathas, 1995, pp. 70–85) used for transcribing the telephone complaint and their meaning are shown below:

[ ]	simultaneous utterance
=	latching of utterances
(1.0)	timed intervals in seconds between and within utterances
(.)	untimed intervals within utterances of less than a second
(())	description
XYZ	loud delivery
°	soft delivery
:	sound stretch
underlining	stressed phonemes or words
↓↑	intonational markers

Glossary

Accounting The provision of one or more reasons for an action

Codification The reduction of a phenomenon to a short series of letters and/or numbers

Competency-based training Training that focuses on sets of related knowledge, skills and attitudes that can be demonstrated by individuals and measured against formalised standards

Criteria A set of standards against which judgments are made

Interactional work An activity that is performed in a mutual or reciprocal way by participants

Modified conversation-analysis approach While most of the rigorous notational conventions employed in conversation analysis have been used, some intonational features have not been recorded

Tacit knowledge Knowledge that is implicit and therefore difficult to access

Turn-taking Warrants: grounds used in justifying an action or belief

Warranting phase A complete stretch of talk whereby grounds are offered and accepted to justify an action or belief

Work tasks Actions employed to achieve a particular goal in a work setting

References

Afflerbach, P. (2000). Verbal reports and protocol analysis. In: M. L. Kamil, P. B. Mosenthal, P. D. Pearson, & R. Barr (Eds.), *Handbook of reading research, Vol. III* (pp. 163–179). Mahwah, NJ: Erlbaum.

Baartman, L. K., Bastiaens, T. J., Kirschner, P. A., & van der Vleuten, C. P. M. (2006). The wheel of competency assessment: Presenting quality criteria for competency assessment programs. *Studies in Educational Evaluation, 32*, 153–170.

Bateman, A., & Griffin, P. (2003). The appropriateness of professional judgement to determine performance rubrics in a graded competency based assessment framework. Unpublished manuscript retrieved May 16, 2008, from <www.edfac.unimelb.edu.au/arc/PDFs/2003-667.pdf>

Birenbaum, M. (1996). Assesment 2000: Towards a pluralistic approach to assessment. In: M. Birenbaum. & F. J. R. C. Dochy (Eds.), *Alternatives in assessment of achievement, learning processes and prior knowledge* (pp. 2–29). Boston, MA: Kluwer.

Birenbaum, M. (2003). New insights into learning and teaching and their implications for assessment. In: M. Segers, & F. J. R. C. Dochy & E. Cascallar (Eds.), *Optimising new modes of assessment: In search of qualities and* standards (pp. 13–36). Dordrecht: Kluwer.

Boden, D. (1990). The world as it happens: Ethnomethodology and conversation analysis. In: G. Ritzner (Ed.), *Frontiers of social theory: The new synthesis* (pp. 185–213). New York: Columbia University Press.

Clarke, L., & Winch, C. (2006). A European skills framework?—but what skills? Anglo-Saxon versus German concepts. *Journal of Education and Work, 19*(3), 255–269.

Connally, J., Jorgensen, K., Gillis, S., & Griffin, P. (2002). *An integrated approach to the assessment of higher order competencies.* Paper presented at the Australian Association for Research in Education Annual Conference, Brisbane, Australia, December 2002. Retrieved May 16, 2008, from <www.aare.edu.au/02pap/con02630.htm>.

Connell, N. A. D., Klein, J. H., & Powell, P. L. (2003). It's tacit knowledge but not as we know it: Redirecting the search for knowledge. *Journal of the Operational Research Society, 54*, 140–152.

Cowan, R., David, P. A., & Foray, D. (2000). The explicit economics of knowledge codification and tacitness. *Industrial and Corporate* Change, 9, 211–253.

Drew, P., & Heritage, J. (1992). *Talk at work: Interaction in institutional settings.* Cambridge, UK: Cambridge University Press.

Freebody, P. (2003). *Qualitative research in education: Interaction and* practice. London: Sage.

Grant, R. M. (1996). Towards a knowledge-based theory of the firm. *Strategic Management Journal, 17*, 109–122.

Griffin, P. (2007). The comfort of competence and the uncertainty of assessment. *Studies in Educational Evaluation, 33*, 87–99.

Gulikers, J. T. M., Bastiaens, T. J., & Kirschner, P. A. (2004). A five-dimensional framework for authentic assessment. *Educational Technology Research & Design, 52*, 67–87.

Heritage, J. C., & Watson, D. R. (1979). Formulations as conversational objects. In: G. Psathas (Ed.), *Everyday language: Studies in ethnomethodology* (pp. 123–162). New York: Irvington Publishers.

Johnson, B., Lorenz, E., & Lundvall, B. (2002). Why all this fuss about codified and tacit knowledge? *Industrial and Corporate* Change, *11*(2), 245–256.

Kelly, A. (2003). The work of clerical trainees in local government council offices: An eth-nomethodological study of competence and competency standards. Unpublished doctoral dissertation. University Of Queensland: THE17370.

Le Deist, F. D., & Winterton, J. (2005) What is competence? *Human Resource Development International, 8*(1), 27–46.

Linn, R. L., Baker, E., & Dunbar, S. B. (1991). Complex, performance-based assessment: Expectations and validation criteria. *Educational Researcher, 20,* 15–21.

Meehan, A. J. (1986). Assessing the 'police-worthiness' of citizen complaints to the police: Accountability and the negotiation of 'facts'. *Zeitshrift für Soziologie, 15,* 341–362.

National Centre for Vocational Education Research (2007). *Australian vocational education and training statistics: Apprentices and trainees—September quarter.* Retrieved May 16, 2007, from <www.ncver.edu.au/statistics/aats/quarter/sept2007/sum_sept07.pdf>.

National Training Board (1990). *Setting national skills standards. A discussion paper.* Canberra: The National Training Board Ltd.

National Training Board (1992). *National competency standards: Policy and guidelines.* (2nd ed.). Canberra: The National Training Board Ltd.

National Training Information Services. Process client complaints. Retrieved May 16, 2007, from <www.ntis.gov.au/Default.aspx?/trainingpackage/BSB07/unit/BSBCMM301A>.

Nelson, R. R., & Winter, S. (1982). *An evolutionary theory of economic change.* Cambridge, MA: Harvard University Press.

Perkins, L., Crisp, J., & Walshaw, D. (1999). Exploring conversation analysis as an assessment tool for aphasia: The issue of reliability. *Aphasiology, 13*(4), 259–281.

Psathas, G. (1995). *Conversation analysis: The study of talk in interaction.* Qualitative Research Methods Series No. 35. Thousand Oaks: Sage.

Ryle, G. (1963). *The concept of mind.* London: Penguin.

Sacks, J. (1995). *Lectures on conversation. Vols 1 & 2.* Oxford, UK: Blackwell.

Schegloff, E. A. (1993). Reflections on quantification in the study of conversation. *Research on language and Social Interaction, 26, 99–128.*

Schegloff, E. A. (1972). Notes on conversational practice: Formulating place. In: D. Sudnow (Ed.), *Studies in social interaction* (pp. 75–119). New York: Free Press.

Sharrock, W. W., & Turner, R. (1978). On a conversational environment for equivocality. In: J. N. Schenkein (Ed.), *Studies in the organisation of conversational interaction* (pp. 173–197). New York: Academic.

Stevenson, J. (2000). Codification of tacit knowledge for the new learning economy. In: *Learning together, working together.* Proceedings of the 8th Annual International Conference on Post-compulsory Education and Training, Gold Coast, Australia, 4–6 December, 2000.

Tapsell, L., Brenninger, V. & Barnard, J. (2001). Applying conversation analysis to foster accu-rate reporting in the diet history interview. *Journal of American Dietetic Association,* 100(7), 818–824.

Tulving, E. (1972). Episodic and semantic memory. In: E. Tulving & W. Donaldson (Eds.), *Organization of memory* (pp. 1236–1247). New York: Academic.

Update of the Administration Training Package. *News: Newsletter of the Admin Training* Company, 24, July, 4.

Van der Vleuten, C. P. M., & Schuwith, L. W. T. (2005). Assessing professional competence: From methods to programmes. *Medical Education, 39,* 309–317.

Whalen, M. R., & Zimmerman, D. H. (1990). Describing trouble: practical epistemology in citizen calls to the police. *Language in Society, 19,* 465–492.

Zimmerman, D. H. (1992). The interactional organization of emergency assistance. In: P. Drew, & J. Heritage (Eds.), *Talk at work: Interaction in institutional settings* (pp. 418–469). Cambridge, NY: Cambridge University Press.

Chapter 14
Defining Standards for the 21st Century

Graham Samuel Maxwell

Introduction

Most countries around the world have entered the 21st century with increased focus on and requirements for educational accountability, expressed through a variety of assessment regimes and policies. Common to these directions is talk about 'standards' in education. For example, there is talk about setting standards (preferring high standards and eschewing low standards), monitoring standards (emphasising school and teacher accountability), raising standards (improving educational outcomes) and reporting on standards (saying how well students are progressing in school). Talk about standards pervades current discussions about education, particularly, for the focus of this book, discussions that involve educational assessment.

But what exactly are standards and how are they expressed? Discussions about standards are not all about the same thing. The term 'standards' has a variety of meanings in different contexts and different countries. These different meanings can have quite different implications for educational practice. Clear communication depends on identifying which meaning is intended. However, there is no agreed conceptual structure for identifying different kinds of standards, the ways in which they are expressed and their consequences or effects. In order to support meaningful educational theories and practices both within and across countries in the 21st century and to address educational issues on a global basis, there is an urgent need to dispel some of the confusion surrounding standards and to develop some clearer conceptual structures.

In this chapter, I examine different perspectives on standards and suggest some ways in which to clarify their different meanings and uses. I draw some distinctions between different kinds of standards, especially those relating to expected student learning outcomes. I discuss how standards are represented or expressed, consider some unresolved issues and suggest some desirable directions of development for the 21st century.

G.S. Maxwell (✉)
Educational Consultant, Brisbane, QLD, Australia
e-mail: gsmax@bigpond.net.au

C. Wyatt-Smith, J.J. Cumming (eds.), *Educational Assessment in the 21st Century*,
DOI 10.1007/978-1-4020-9964-9_14, © Springer Science+Business Media B.V. 2009

The chapter is presented in three sections, with the first discussing the dimensional meanings of standards and the second analysing some of the current discourse around standards. The final section considers some current educational realisations and uses of standards, and their import for education and students.

While the focus of this discussion is on different meanings of standards and their implications for educational practice, I also explore the consequences of different realisations of standards, especially from the perspective of implications for the student as learner. My underlying philosophical position or assumption is that the purpose of education is to enable the advancement of the personal knowledge and capabilities of each student to the fullest extent possible and to prepare them for further learning and development throughout their life. For children just beginning school now, this can mean throughout the whole of the 21st century.

Charting the Different Meanings of Standards

In educational discourse, standards differ in their characteristics along at least four dimensions:

- the *type* of standard
- the *focus*; that is, the thing or event to which the standards are being applied
- the underlying characteristic or *construct*
- the *purpose* or use to which standards will be put.

These four dimensions affect the way in which standards are talked about and represented. Standards with different characteristics typically invoke different terminology, concepts and connotations. That is, once the type, focus, construct and purpose are settled, other characteristics follow. Different kinds of standards are (or should be) expressed differently, are related to a constellation of other concepts and carry hidden implications for educational practice and outcomes. These implications can be intended or unintended as well as desirable or undesirable. Consequently, choices need to be made. We should consider carefully whether some ways of talking about standards and some ways of representing them may not be benign, especially for individual students, and therefore whether alternative approaches would be more beneficial.

The following parts of this section discuss each of these four dimensions in turn. Each involves several categories and, in some cases, subcategories. It will be evident that there are some restrictions on relationships between the dimensions. That is, a choice of category on one dimension may exclude some choices on another dimension. It is best to consider this classification scheme as suggesting a series of questions to ask when someone refers to standards; that is, 'which of these types, focuses, constructs and purposes do you mean?'

Different Types

In a previous paper (Maxwell, 2002a), I argued that there are at least five different meanings of the term 'standards'. These will be referred to here as different types of standards (since I am extending the discussion here beyond that single dimension):

- standards as moral or ethical imperatives (what someone should do)
- standards as legal or regulatory requirements (what someone must do)
- standards as target benchmarks (expected practice or performance)
- standards as arbiters of quality (relative success or merit)
- standards as milestones (progressive or developmental targets).

The first three types are, respectively, desirable, necessary or appropriate; the last two are outcome levels. The first is usually expressed through guidelines or professional codes, the second through performance requirements that imply the possibility of failure (such as requirements for approving a program or awarding a certificate) and the third through statements detailing expected (or targeted or typical) outcomes.

The last two categories highlight two different ways of representing categorically different levels of learning, performance or achievement (see the section on constructs below for a discussion of these three terms): levels of merit (or quality) and levels of development (or progress). These are two sides of the same coin—both are concerned with identifying a range of ordered categories against which educational outcomes can be judged. An important difference is the time frame for referencing the performance: for merit standards, a set of comparative levels of merit (for example, on a task, course or program that is considered to be finished and done with); for developmental standards, sequential stages of possible improvement over time (requiring periodic re-assessment to determine current status). Some examples are discussed later in the third section of the chapter.

Different Focuses

Three important questions define focus: What facet of educational expectations are we focusing on? What units of analysis are we interested in? What is the scope of the assessment? A range of indicative possibilities for each of these can be summarised as follows:

- *facet*: educational content; or educational delivery; or educational outcomes
- *unit*: country; or system; or school; or program; or student
- *scope*: test, or task; or portfolio; or semester; or course; or certificate.

All three questions need to be considered in identifying the focus. For example, it is possible for the focus to be on the content of a course within a school (such as for school registration or approval to teach science). Alternatively, say, the focus might be on the individual student's performance on an assessment task. Yet again, the focus might be on country performance on an international test. The permutations and combinations are clearly too many to consider them all in this chapter.

Because of the prevalence of content standards and performance standards in educational discourse, attention is given in the third section of this chapter to the distinction between them. Content standards typically apply to schools and systems (what they ought or must teach); performance standards typically apply to students (what and how well they have learned), although with a shift of focus performance standards could also apply to schools and systems. Of course, all outcomes are gauged by assessing students, but the way this is done can differ according to whether the focus is the individual student or a whole system—for example, a sample of students rather than a full census can be used for system monitoring, which practice has shown allows richer and more authentic assessment to be conducted (see, for example, the United States National Assessment of Educational Progress <http://nces.ed.gov/nationsreportcard/>).

Different Constructs

Another important question is what characteristic or construct is being assessed. The choice of constructs shapes how we represent and express any relevant standards.

Some contrasting constructs in this context include:

- learning versus performance
- development (time-extensive, assessing interim progress) versus achievement (time-limited, assessing degree of success)
- criterion-referencing versus norm-referencing
- quality (how well) versus quantity (how much).

Each of these warrants some discussion.

Learning Versus Performance

The contrast between learning and performance is a persistent one, stemming from the claim that learning itself is unobservable and that we must depend on observable performances (including, especially, those involving speaking and writing) to infer its existence. Strictly, of course, this is true. Nevertheless, dropping reference to learning entirely focuses attention only on the observables. These are merely indicative of the learning. They need to be referenced to the underlying dimensions of the student's learning, such as developing concepts and skills.[1] Keeping learning as the primary goal, with performance being indicative of it, situates the student's present performance in the context of their ongoing development as a learner. To see

---

[1] We can learn much from other areas of human endeavour. For example, in Olympic swimming, swim time against other competitors is the determinant of a standard. While this is a helpful reference for progress and the likelihood of being an Olympic swimmer, it provides no evidence to the trainer or swimmer about how to improve time until consideration of components (dive, turns, stroke style) is undertaken.

the student as a learner is to see the student as more than a performer of separate, isolated tasks. Standards that service learning may need to be represented differently from standards for performing a task. This idea connects with the next distinguishing achievement and development.

Development Versus Achievement

In common language, achievement is defined as: 1. something successfully accomplished, especially by hard work, ability or heroism; 2. successful completion (*Collins English Dictionary and Thesaurus*, 1993). An alternative term is attainment. The reference is to effort and striving as well as accomplishment—a journey completed and done well. The implications are all positive. Unfortunately, that is not how the term is used in education, where typically it refers to comparative performance; that is, 'how well did you do compared to other students?' When we talk of reporting achievement, it is not typically a description of the things that have been successfully accomplished but a rating or grading of performance on a task, semester or course; that is, reporting not what was done but how well it was done.

For example, the five grades reported on the Queensland Certificate of Education at the end of year 12 are called Levels of Achievement <http://www.qsa.qld.edu.au>. These grades are criterion-referenced, in the sense that they have pre-specified descriptions (requirements) for what constitutes achievement at each level and provide the benchmarks against which student achievement is referenced.[2] Although the intention is to judge each student's achievement against the requirements for each grade and not relative to other students' achievement, nevertheless it is expected that the grades will differentiate the range of student achievement across the state (generally it is expected that most students will not reach the top two levels, High Achievement and Very High Achievement). Therefore, for many students the message is negative (the lowest two levels, awarded to large numbers of students, carry the labels Limited Achievement and Very Limited Achievement—not exactly indicating successful accomplishment of anything—and even the middle category of Sound Achievement seems to damn with faint praise). Grades such as A–E are somewhat less assertive in their connotations of relative success and failure but the underlying conceptualisation is the same—students must be measured against a set of differentiated standards that are designed to discriminate the students as well.[3] While this might be appropriate for awarding certificates, diplomas, degrees and professional licences (satisfying a passing standard is often sufficient—for example

---

[2] This form of criterion referencing is referred to, in this instance, as standards referencing. This accords with defining the five grade levels (standards) as defined by (referenced by) particular achievement requirements (standards). This sounds tautological—the 'standard' is defined by a 'standard' but highlights the focus on the standards of achievement. Terminological debates and different practices surrounding the terms 'criterion' and 'standard' are beyond the scope of this chapter.

[3] Discriminate is the term used in educational measurement. It has a neutral meaning (tell apart), not a pejorative one (treat unfairly).

in awarding PhDs), it is unclear that grades are an appropriate way to register student progress at most stages of schooling, where a more descriptive approach to reporting progress (or achievement in the dictionary sense) would seem preferable.

Achievement reported through grades contrasts with charting development over time. Development suggests progress and elaboration over time. This could imply something that is 'natural', but it could also imply effort and striving. In education, it ought to reference both: the natural unfolding of human development needs to be coupled with experience and challenge that encourages and shapes that development. The time frame here is more extended; that is, point-in-time reporting is situated within a longer process of increasing strength and complexity of knowledge and proficiency. In that case, development can be represented by a continuum, with the student advancing progressively through the steps or stages along the continuum. Properly executed, progression of students at different rates along such a continuum can be accepted as normal and unexceptional. Examples of such developmental standards or progression targets are found in Judo rankings (*kyu* and *dan* ranks), English–language-proficiency scales (such as the International Second Language Proficiency Ratings), attainment targets for Key Stage Assessment and Reporting in England, and the six levels (and part levels) for the Victorian Essential Learning Standards (Years P–10).[4]

The contrast between graded achievement and developmental targets is discussed again in the third section of this chapter. It is a key issue in relation to how educational standards might best be represented.

Criterion Referencing Versus Norm Referencing

Another well-known distinction in assessment is between criterion referencing and norm referencing. The key idea in criterion referencing, in the form referred to here, is the specification of a number of ordered categories representing different levels of performance, preferably with each defined by explicit statements of the characteristics of each category and preferably also with exemplars to illustrate each category; assessment involves judgment of which category best fits the performance. The key idea in norm referencing is deliberate rank ordering along a scale, usually through aggregating scores on items; this may be followed by subdivision of the scale into a smaller number of levels defined by cut-scores, often by fitting an a priori distribution.

In practice, these distinctions are blurred. Thus, in criterion referencing, it is anticipated that the categories typically will capture a range of possible performances, since some degree of differentiation among students is expected; that is, there is an element of norm referencing underlying generation of the categories. Conversely, in norm referencing, each level can be described in terms of the characteristics typical of that level. An important difference is that criterion referencing

---

[4] Information on Judo ranks can be found at <http://www.judoinfo.com/obi.htm>, on the International Second Language Proficiency Ratings in Wylie and Ingram (1999), on Key Stage Assessment and Reporting at <http://www.qca.org.uk/>, and on the Victorian Essential Learning Standards at <http://www.vcaa.vic.edu.au/>.

establishes the categories or levels prior to assessment, whereas norm referencing does this afterwards. In addition, criterion-referenced categories serve as targets for student learning, whereas norm-referenced categories can only do so if they are carried over from one testing occasion to the next, in which case, for the second testing occasion they are predetermined and therefore criterion referenced.[5]

Quality Versus Quantity

Sometimes, a distinction is made between standards defined by quality (how well has the student performed?) and quantity (how much has been learned?). This is essentially an inappropriate distinction. The tradition of multiple-choice testing with a focus on right/wrong answers has not helped because better performance is equated to number of correct items. This can easily end up valuing more knowledge rather than more sophisticated and elaborated knowledge. As Shepard (2000) has pointed out, such practices are largely based on outmoded psychology. Current understandings of knowledge go much beyond recall and recognition (Pelligrino, Chudowski, & Glaser, 2001), and learners are better seen as charting a course from novice (the beginning learner) to expert (the proficient performer) (Bereiter & Scardamalier, 1993; Bransford, Brown, & Cocking, 2000a; Chi, Glaser, & Farr, 1988). Education needs to be concerned with understanding and using knowledge, including problem solving, creative endeavour and habits of mind (Costa, 2001; Costa & Kallick, 2000; Wiggins, 1998). As more is learned, it needs to be expressed and used in qualitatively different ways. Standards need to incorporate the qualitative progression from less complex to more complex knowledge and skill.

Different Purposes

Some possible purposes for standards include:

- setting targets for student learning
- showing students how they are progressing
- promoting consistency in judging achievement/progress
- setting requirements for qualification (certification)
- interpreting performances on tests
- setting benchmarks for system monitoring
- accountability for schools and systems

These purposes could be held in conjunction with each other. On the other hand, that could depend on choice of type, focus and construct. For example, as already

---

[5] There are, however, important differences between situations in which student performance is judged directly (classified) against a set of such standards (descriptive categories) and situations in which such standards are the basis for determining cut-scores on a continuous distribution (such as scores produced on a test). The language used to represent the standards could be similar but the processes for applying them are quite different, as too are the performances to which they refer. See, for example, Bennett (1998).

discussed, developmental standards could be more appropriate for showing students how they are progressing, while merit standards might be more appropriate for test results. In addition, accountability of schools and systems could be norm referenced but consistency in judging achievement depends on criterion referencing. Setting targets for student learning could be for individual students or systems and be linked to accountability or merely offered as a guideline (desirable but not mandatory). And so on.

Three of these purposes warrant special comment here.

Setting Requirements for Qualifications For qualifications, the critical standard is the minimum (or passing) standard required for receiving the relevant qualification (though this might be constituted of several standards, or requirements, in combination). This standard determines the qualification's social acceptability and credibility. Its function is sometimes to provide protection against professional incompetence (by only qualifying those with an acceptable level of capability) and sometimes simply to provide a 'tick of approval' (recognition for achievement). However, sometimes the relevant standard is determined by use of the qualification as a selection gateway, in which case the standard is set implicitly by the imposition of a quota rather than explicitly by a predetermined benchmark.

Setting Benchmarks for System Monitoring Another common purpose of standards is to establish benchmarks for system monitoring and/or accountability. For monitoring purposes, there are differences between setting benchmarks within a country or state linked to a specific curriculum (allowing teachers to use them formatively as targets for student learning) and setting a range of performance levels *ex post facto* on national or international testing programs (to allow richer comparison through descriptive performance levels rather than simply through scores).

Accountability for Schools and Systems Setting standards for accountability based on country or state testing programs is controversial and can have unfortunate side-effects. Sometimes, the target is unachievable, for example, the 100 per cent benchmark success target for literacy and numeracy benchmarks in Australia (<http://www.dest.gov.au/sectors/school_education/>) and the average yearly progress targets under No Child Left Behind (NCLB) in the United States (<http://www.ed.gov/nclb/>). The former was considered as a desirable goal (ought) but the latter was a required goal (must) so the consequences have been different. Failure to consider the consequences, such as narrowing of the curriculum, can be damaging.

This concludes the consideration of the different meanings of the term 'standards'. As previously suggested, I have suggested some questions that should be asked in any discussion of standards—questions concerning the intended type, focus, construct and purpose. Unless these questions are asked, it will often be the case that different participants in discussions about standards will have different implicit understandings of what is being discussed and will accordingly talk past each other.

The next section of this chapter considers some other aspects of the way we talk about standards and their implications for educational practice and student learning.

Setting Standards for Student Learning

Setting standards as targets for student learning is one possible purpose for having standards, as discussed in the previous section of this chapter. Two key ideas warrant further discussion: setting minimum standards and setting high standards.

Setting Minimum Standards

Setting minimum standards for student learning sounds like a good idea because it affirms an interest in and commitment to focused and purposeful learning. However, setting minimum standards implies the possibility that some may fail to reach them. How we handle such failure, whether we even refer to it as failure, is very important for the students concerned. While some educational commentators consider that the threat of failure is motivating, and it can be for some students, this is not so for all. In fact, it is bad psychology. The threat of failure can generate feelings of panic and inadequacy (Hodgson & Spours, 2005), often disrupting rather than supporting effective learning. Furthermore, failure itself can be accompanied by feelings of shame and rejection. The effects on students of being repeatedly classified as a fail-ure (for some, over 24 semesters of schooling) can be catastrophic for the individual, and later for society through transformation of feelings of failure and inadequacy into anti-social behaviour. In the 21st century, we need to recast the educational language and practice so that such negative consequences are ameliorated.

For students, satisfying the minimum requirements for satisfactory completion of a stage of education is about 'permission to proceed' (that is, move on to some new endeavour to which the qualification provides access), 'permission to practice' (that is, admission to the profession or trade) or at least 'permission to claim the qualification' (that is, simply holding the certificate, diploma or degree as part of a curriculum vitae). In some situations (for example, in some countries for high school diplomas or university entrance examinations), students who fail in their attempt to gain a passing standard may have to redirect their energies and try something else. In other situations they may be able to try again. Also, in some countries, 'permission to proceed' is still relevant at points earlier than the end of secondary education, whether for access to the next stage of schooling or for streaming into different sec-ondary schools or programs. Sometimes this involves a qualification (for example, in England, General Certificate of Secondary Education) and sometimes not (for example, primary school examinations as early as year 3 in some countries), but the effects of failure are similar—denial of access to further education or to particular programs.

The application of minimum standards where there is no selection or streaming is a futile practice unless failure is followed by some helpful action, such as remedi-ation, or repeating the year or program, or redirection into some other activity. Some school systems, for example, in the United States, require such 'failing students' to repeat the year (but how many times before the student drops out?). Other school systems, for example, in Australia, value keeping the student age cohort together (hence 'years' not 'grades'). Repeating a year rarely leads to better performance the second time around and in some cases to worse performance (as shown by Heubert & Hauser, 1999; Shepard & Smith, 1989). Typically, neither approach (repeating or progression) involves a tailored response to individual student needs. It is peculiar and damaging, therefore, to classify students as above or below an expected standard when there is no systemic way of properly managing students labelled as failed learners. There is an element of blaming the learner for this rather than blaming the inbuilt assumptions of school and curriculum structures. An aim for the 21st century should be to find a way of designing learning systems that are more personalised and adaptive.

A softer version of minimum standards is expected standards. How much softer depends on the force behind the word 'expected'. Leaving aside 'have to' (essentially the same as 'required'), expected can mean either 'ought to' (a moral or ethical imperative, but not one with serious consequences for failure, merely disappointment) or 'desired' (a learning target—what we would like to achieve if at all possible and therefore should work very hard to reach). Such expectations are typically framed for years (grades) or junctures (stages) and considered applicable to all students. This is again insensitive to individual student development and the diversity of student characteristics and capabilities in a classroom. Any such standards are typically directed at a level that some students will not reach within the designated time frame (such as before the end of year 7). Human development is too varied for that. It is futile to express such expectations if we know in advance that all students will not reach them (and, on the other side of the coin, that some students will exceed them by the proverbial mile). In the 21st century we should move to establish individualised learning targets that challenge students while respecting their own developmental possibilities (a *zone of proximal development* approach) (Chaiklin, 2003; Daniels, 1993). Maybe, with proper support, some students, rather than differing in ability, just need more time than others to attain a desired standard—something first suggested by John Carroll in the 1960s (see Carroll, 1963, 1989).

High Standards

Another part of the discourse on standards refers to 'high standards'. These are really 'high expectations'. For example, Wiggins (1991) says: 'A school has high standards when it has high and consistent expectations of all students in all courses' (p. 18). Also, Hill and Crévola (1999) talk about setting 'high and challenging standards that most students are expected to achieve' and suggest that 'low standards' are unacceptable ('zero tolerance of educational failure'). Is this reasonable?

Some research suggests that people respond to challenging or demanding expectations (the Pygmalion effect), though this is not necessarily so—there are interactions with various personal predispositions (Ng & Bahr, 2000). The assessment literature carries many exhortations for teachers to set high standards for their students as a powerful strategy for increasing overall performance levels. The success of this strategy depends on continual encouragement and support, continual feedback that shows progress towards the target and personal belief that the target is achievable. Targets that are too high and believed by the student to be unreachable within the constraints of time and opportunities for learning are counterproductive, merely leading to frustration (Schunk, 1984). What is a high standard for one student may be too high for another student (beyond their zone of proximal development) or too low (undemanding and unchallenging) for another.

Another aspect of this stress on high standards is raising the ante with students pedagogically: 'by requiring students to work until standards are met, we teach students and teachers that work is not done until it is done right' (Wiggins, 1991, p. 22) which suggests a polishing of meta-cognitive skills, not just acquiring a lexicon of knowledge. There is also a value dimension operating here:

> When we speak of persons or institutions with standards—especially when modified by the word high—we mean they live by a set of mature, coherent, and consistently applied values evident in all their actions. (p. 20)

> Higher standards are not stiffer test-result quotas but a more vigorous commitment to intellectual values upheld consistently and daily in the face of entropy, fatalism, and the occasional desire on everyone's part to not give a damn. (p. 20)

> High standards are only to be found in completed tasks, products, and performances that require such intellectual virtues as craftsmanship, self-criticism, and persistence; when complex tasks are done consistently well, we easily and validly infer that the worker has high standards. (p. 21)

In fact, having high standards (expectations) in this sense is not just a matter of 'expecting a lot' and 'pushing the pace'. Expectations have to be realistic, that is, achievable with reasonable effort in the available time and prevailing circumstances. Even then, what may be realistically achievable in general or on average or by some is not necessarily achievable by everyone. The very concept of high standards in education has a norm-referenced underpinning. Standards reached easily by most people are ordinary, not high. There must be at least a sense that most people will struggle to achieve high standards. In other words, high implies contrast and comparison. However, the comparison need not be with other students in the same group; 'other people' can refer to other groups (other schools, other states or other countries) or other times (groups in previous years). Maybe, asking how high is high, in some objective sense, is a bit like asking how long is a piece of string.

Educational policy currently is awash with the need for 'high standards'. However, unreasonable expectations at the personal level, pursued inexorably, have dire consequences for student engagement and self-image. The resolution of this tension between group and individual expectations and progress remains an unresolved issue in educational theory and practice. Perhaps we will learn how to address this issue by the end of the 21st century—but only if we work on it.

Some Implementations of Standards

This section deals with three specific ways in which standards are characterised: content standards; performance standards (focusing on merit or proficiency standards); and developmental standards. These were chosen for their prominence and importance in educational discourse and practice. Examples are drawn from several countries around the world.

Content Standards

Sometimes, especially in the United States, 'standards' mean 'content standards'. These standards attempt to list the concepts and skills that should be the focus of teaching in schools and are usually organised by school subjects and by year/grade. In other places, they might be called a syllabus or a curriculum framework. Such standards could be considered as a moral or ethical imperative (type), specifying educational content for schools to use in framing their whole curriculum (focus), deal with what schools should teach (construct) and for target setting and accountability (purpose).

Content standards provide a 'road map' for schools and teachers, providing an overall structure of knowledge for each domain of knowledge and a framework for planning and delivering the curriculum. Their purpose is to ensure orderly progression and comprehensive coverage of important concepts and skills. Schools may, of course, repackage them to fit the way they wish to deliver the curriculum, including, for example, problem-based or interdisciplinary studies, though some content standards may constrain the extent to which they are able to do this.

Various United States agencies have developed standards for particular subject areas, for example, science standards by the National Research Council (1996), English, mathematics and science standards by New Standards (1997) and mathematics standards by the National Council of Teachers of Mathematics (2000). Every state has now developed its own standards for the core subjects. A recent review of these state standards by the Thomas B. Fordham Foundation (Finn, Julian, & Petrilli, 2006) claimed that only California, Indiana and Massachusetts had acceptable standards (their criteria being 'clear, rigorous, and right-headed [sic] about content'). For example, they considered that excellent English standards expect students to read and understand important literary genres, worthy science standards place the teaching of evolution at the centre of biology instruction and strong United States and world history standards are organised around a chronology of key events with an ample supply of fascinating and important individuals. Another highly critical review of state standards, specifically for science, is found in Wilson and Bertenthal (2001).

Content standards have the strength of giving teachers clear guidelines concerning the structural features of each subject and what may be appropriate for their students to learn at particular year levels. They provide scope and sequence for subjects.

However, content standards have the weakness of confusing what is being taught with what is being learned. They represent a 'backwards mapping' of each subject from the perspective of the 'expert' to fit the stages of schooling. Students do not necessarily learn according to the straightforward framework and sequence suggested by the content standards. The learning steps and sequences of the individual learner tend to be rather messier and unpredictable.[6]

Where content standards are packaged into tidy parcels of content to be taught to each year cohort, this inevitably means that some students will be left behind through not consolidating earlier material. Some other students may be bored by the lack of challenge unless given supplementary or accelerated learning opportunities. This phenomenon was well researched in the 'steering group' research of the 1960s and 1970s (Dahllöf, 1971; Kallos & Lundgren, 1979; Lundgren, 1972). That research showed that in teacher-centred classrooms where content is delivered in common to all students in a year cohort, the teacher typically and intuitively determines the pace of presentation (when to move on) by the rate of progress of the 'steering group'—students lying roughly between the 10th and the 25th percentiles of ranked achievement. In a curriculum organised and delivered by years (grades), the bottom 10 per cent of students are left progressively further behind because they cannot cope with the pace of new content. We have still not solved the problem within schools of how best to manage, both structurally and pedagogically, the substantial diversity within any group of students who typically are at different stages of development and learn in different ways and at different rates.

It is claimed sometimes that such (content) standards set uniform and high academic expectations for all students (Cohen, 1996; Darling-Hammond, 1997; Rowan, 1996; Sandholz, Ogawa, & Scribner, 2004). That is, the standards are what all students should know and be able to do (see earlier discussion). However, this makes them aspirational and idealistic. That is, it is unlikely that all students (strictly, perhaps, *any* student) will acquire all the knowledge and skills mentioned. Realistically, most students (perhaps all students) will acquire only some of the knowledge and skills (and retain some misconceptions and faulty skills as well).[7]

---

[6] Wilson and Bertenthal (2001) do call for content standards to reflect how students learn and develop understanding. While this can be broadly achieved by ensuring that more difficult concepts build on simpler ones, this still assumes that what works in general (for a typical student) will work for all.

[7] This is a necessary consequence of an expectation that all students will learn everything. Since clearly all students do not learn everything, the expectation that they will do so represents an unrealistic, aspirational target. The response to this is usually to recognise the spread of learning in some way, typically a range of performance standards. The top standard is the aspirational standard. Every other standard falls short and indicates some deficiencies of knowledge and skills. Students who just satisfy minimum requirements for a 'pass' standard (as opposed to the 'top' standard) are especially deficient and typically hold many misunderstandings, wrong ideas and inappropriate strategies. In systems that set 50 per cent success as a pass, students who just satisfy the pass requirement presumably do not know half of what was expected (or at any rate half of what was tested). Sequential content maps tend to assume that most students learn most of what was taught, which is clearly fallacious.

Performance Standards

A distinction is made typically between content standards and performance standards. For example, Stites (1999, no page numbering) says:

> Performance standards are specifications of 'how much' students should know and be able to do. Thus, while content standards shape what goes into a curriculum, performance standards set benchmarks—specified levels of achievement—that shape expectations for educational outcomes, provide a basis for measuring learning outcomes, and provide the criteria for imposing rewards and sanctions. Performance standards for mathematics, for example, specify the mathematical operations and concepts that should be mastered at each grade level as well as the types of assessments that should be used to measure that mastery.

The language in this quote may not be universal but it is instructive. It refers to benchmarks (type) for educational outcomes achieved by students (also implicitly teachers, schools and systems) at each grade level (focus), for measuring learning outcomes, quantity of knowledge and skills, level of achievement or mastery (constructs) and for accountability through rewards and sanctions (purpose).

Sometimes the line between content and performance standards is blurred, and performance standards become merely a more elaborated version of content standards. For example, The Georgia Department of Education provides the following explanation of its performance standards:

> Performance standards go into much greater depth than the content standards used in the previous curriculum. The performance standard incorporates the content standard, which simply tells the teacher what a student is expected to know (i.e., what concepts he or she is expected to master), and expands upon it by providing three additional items: suggested tasks, sample student work, and teacher commentary on that work. <http://www.georgiastandards.org/faqs.aspx>

Are these performance standards? Not really. Performance standards need to reference actual performance in some way. Where assessment is based on standardised tests, this might be represented by a cut-score (or several cut-scores if there are several standards). These can be arbitrarily defined (perhaps by an imposed distribution of levels or by natural breaks in the distribution of scores) and then given descriptive labels. Preferably, adopting a criterion-referenced approach, levels are defined by benchmark descriptions and cut-scores determined through a process of expert judgment (Cizek, 2001).

Another, now widespread, approach treats the benchmark descriptions as the performance standards against which assessors (typically teachers) make judgments of the level of achievement demonstrated by students. For example, in Canada, the British Columbia Ministry of Education defines performance standards in literacy and numeracy for each year/grade using generic labels that are elaborated by snapshot descriptors for each grade as well as by further elaborations for each 'aspect' (dimension) (see <http://www.bced.gov.bc.ca/perf_stands/>).

Interesting features of the British Columbia example are:

- The standards labels reference 'expectations' (not yet within expectations, meets minimal expectations, fully meets expectations, exceeds expectations): these labels signal a meaning for the standards beyond their indicating simply an ordered set of categories (range of proficiencies).

- The snapshot descriptors refer to the degree of completeness, familiarity and independence evidenced by the student.
- The descriptive elaborations of each standard reference specific and observable actions.
- The snapshot descriptors and descriptive elaborations bring in additional factors at higher levels.[8]

These performance standards are applicable to semester reporting by teachers of their students' achievement (and therefore could also be called achievement standards). They provide sufficient detail to identify performance characteristics that differentiate one level of achievement from another.

Sadler (1987) provided an influential analysis of these types of standards, in which he drew an important distinction between criteria (dimensions) and standards (levels). He also pointed out that standards defined by verbal descriptions are necessarily fuzzy (not sharply differentiated), indicative (not prescriptive or definitive), imprecise (because language is) and contextual (assuming familiarity with intended meanings and applications). Common interpretation and consistent use of such standards can be assisted by exemplars but may also need deliberate action such as assessor training and moderation (Maxwell, 2001, 2002b).

A typical way of representing such performance (achievement, merit or proficiency) standards is through a rubric (criteria-and-standards matrix). Rubrics are arbiters of quality (type), applicable to a variety of assessment artefacts (focus could be task, portfolio, semester, course, certificate). When developed by teachers for local application, their purpose is to make marking more objective, consistent and defensible, as well as to guide student learning (the latter by creating a language for discussing what distinguishes better performance from weaker performance). Rubrics have become a common feature of educational practice and satisfy a need to make explicit the basis on which judgments of performance quality (merit) are made.[9]

How explicit a rubric should be depends on the circumstances of its use. The general intention is to signal the performance characteristics in sufficient detail to support consistent judgment of the fit between performance and level. It is possible to frame the levels without connotations of failure if positive statements are made about the characteristics of each level. However, lower levels are often framed as deficient in some of the characteristics of higher levels, implying failure; also, a particular (expected) level is often designated as a satisfactory or passing level. Sometimes, an overall grade (level) is reported for each student, requiring a 'best fit' judgment that considers trade-offs between several dimensions (criteria); the specifics for each student are 'lost' and the grade description depicts only a 'typical' student. This may be adequate for certification. However, the specifics are important

---

[8] In other words, these are not in the form of a rubric (a fully crossed matrix of criteria by standards). New criteria emerge at higher levels of performance as the essence of differentiating higher levels from lower levels.

[9] One website <http://www.rcampus.com/indexrubric.cfm> provides a tool for developing rubrics and claims to have some 30 000 'ready to use' rubrics.

for feedback (formative purposes), where the detailed profile of performance on separate dimensions would be more useful.[10]

Developmental Standards

In England, although there is no explicit use of the term 'standards' in relation to the national curriculum and its assessment,[11] each national curriculum subject charts progress through nine levels (1–8 plus exceptional) along several attainment targets (strands) in each subject. The levels are represented through paragraph-length level descriptions (LDs) that summarise the characteristics of performance typical of each level. Progress against the levels is assessed at the end of each key stage (Stage 1: Year 2, Age 7; Stage 2: Year 6, Age 11; Stage 3: Year 9, Age 14). A holistic, on-balance judgment is made of which level best fits each student's performance. These levels represent standards in the sense that they involve milestones (type), individual student educational outcomes for junctures or stages (focus), development judged against specific criteria (constructs) and showing students how they are progressing in terms of a common national framework (purpose).

The complete attainment targets and levels are found on the Qualifications and Curriculum Authority website <http://curriculum.qca.org.uk>. The following extracts for English: Writing are illustrative:

Level 2
Pupils' writing communicates meaning in both narrative and non-narrative forms, using appropriate and interesting vocabulary, and showing some awareness of the reader. Ideas are developed in a sequence of sentences, sometimes demarcated by capital letters and full stops. Simple, monosyllabic words are usually spelt correctly, and where there are inaccuracies the alternative is phonetically plausible. In handwriting, letters are accurately formed and consistent in size.

Level 3
Pupils' writing is often organised, imaginative and clear. The main features of different forms of writing are used appropriately, beginning to be adapted to different readers. Sequences of sentences extend ideas logically and words are chosen for variety and interest. The basic grammatical structure of sentences is usually correct. Spelling is usually accurate, including that of common, polysyllabic words. Punctuation to mark sentences—full stops, capital letters and question marks—is used accurately. Handwriting is joined and legible.

Level 4
Pupils' writing in a range of forms is lively and thoughtful. Ideas are often sustained and developed in interesting ways and organised appropriately for the purpose of the reader.

---

[10] Comprehensive advice on designing rubrics is given by Wiggins (1998).

[11] There has been much debate in the United Kingdom about standards, whether they are being maintained from year to year for the General Certificate of School Education at Year 10 and the General Certificate of Education: Advanced Level at Year 12, but this is a different issue. See Aldrich (2000), Baird, Cresswell, and Newton (2000), Goldstein and Heath (2000) and Wolf (2000) for some background.

> Vocabulary choices are often adventurous and words are used for effect. Pupils are beginning to use grammatically complex sentences, extending meaning. Spelling, including that of polysyllabic words that conform to regular patterns, is generally accurate. Full stops, capital letters and question marks are used correctly, and pupils are beginning to use punctuation within the sentence. Handwriting style is fluent, joined and legible.

Sainsbury and Sizmur (1998), in their analysis of the complexities of the LDs, highlight the challenges caused by clustering several (somewhat disconnected) dimensions into each statement and also by needing to look outside the wording of the statements to professional understandings of the underlying constructs. Further, Hall and Harding (2002) found little evidence of the development of the communities of assessment practice needed to generate consistent interpretation and use of the LDs. Beyond these challenges there are clear advantages in reporting progress in age-independent (and year-independent) steps along a continuum. Green (2002) suggests several: the efficiency of a common set of benchmarks across all years; depiction of progress as movement along a continuum; focus on achievable progress rather than fixed ability; and 'natural' differentiation at each age or year level. To these could be added feed-forward opportunities, that is, higher levels as targets for learning (Sadler, 1989) and the motivating effects on students of experiencing growth and success rather than receiving the same grade year on year (Dweck, 1986).

Another realisation of the notion of developmental standards is the Primary Language Record (PLR) (Barrs, Ellis, Hester & Thomas, 1988) which has been highly influential (over 100 000 copies sold) in the United Kingdom, United States, Canada and Australia. Originally developed for multilingual inner London schools, but then expanded to fit the national curriculum, it is adaptive to cultural and linguistic diversity within common reporting frameworks. Five levels are defined for each of two age ranges (Scale 1: 6–8 years and Scale 2: 8–12 years) in both reading and writing.[12] Levels have labels (for example, beginning to fluent) and paragraph descriptions. Scale 1 charts progression from dependence to independence and Scale 2 from being inexperienced to experienced.[13] The PLR has been popular because of its emphasis on careful observation and documentation of student performance in authentic situations, charting their progress in a positive and supportive way and using this to plan next steps in learning.

The Australian state of Victoria offers another example of developmental standards. The roots of this approach go back to the attempt to create a national curriculum in the early 1990s. A key feature of this curriculum was levels of progression across the years of schooling (Willis & Kissane, 1997). Each Australian

---

[12] Details are available on the Research and Projects page of the Centre for Literacy in Primary Education website <http://www.clpe.co.uk/>. See also Falk (1998).

[13] There is implicit overlap between the scales but no natural transition—a single scale might work better. An exemplary single scale was developed by the Queensland Studies Authority (QSA) for the writing component of the Queensland Years 3, 5 and 7: Literacy and Numeracy Tests (QSA, 2007). This had four dimensions and 12 levels, for ease of use divided into sections typical of each year level.

state and territory soon decided to go its own way, with some erosion of the original ideas. Victoria remained committed to levels of progression for curriculum planning, assessment and reporting. In 2006 the state implemented the Victorian Essential Learnings Standards (VELS), which builds on and incorporates the previous Curriculum Standards Framework (CSF) <http://vels.cvaa.vic.edu.au/>.

VELS has three strands (Physical, Personal and Social Learning; Discipline-based Learning; and Interdisciplinary Learning), interrelated through what is characterised as a triple helix. Each strand has several domains, which are split further into several dimensions. For each domain there is a table of 'standards and progression points' that describes six developmental levels over the 11 years of compulsory schooling, together with three progression points between each level. The levels represent typical progress at 2-year intervals from end of Prep to end of year 10.

The term 'standards' is here used in three different ways: first, the knowledge and skills expected to be taught in each of the strands (content standards); second, the levels and progression points for assessing progress (development standards); and, third, the typical or targeted level for each year level (expected standards). To complicate this further, the Australian government imposed a national requirement in 2006 that all schools report student performance to parents each semester on an A–E scale (Commonwealth of Australia, 2005). Under VELS, Victoria maintains an expectation that schools will continue to assess the standard (level) and progression point reached by each student, with computerised conversion to an A–E grade appropriate for each year level (and representation of the levels in terms of their year of typical attainment). These characteristics of VELS are both visionary and realistic, adhering to the benefits of charting student progress developmentally but acceding to governmental and parental expectations. Whether this will be successful or confusing remains to be seen.[14]

Benefits of developmental standards include that they: provide a clear set of steps from novice to expert; emphasise language and expectation of progress; allow for student spurts and plateaus; and make evident to students the progress they have made. Difficulties include that: the progression of steps may not apply universally and levels typically cover several dimensions (with problems of best fit, as for performance standards). Challenges include: how to combine developmental levels with expected levels without reverting to a language of failure and how to develop school structures to support developmental progression of students better.

---

[14] Referents for A–E in Victoria are defined relative to the expected level for each year: well above, above, at, below, well below. Other Australian states and territories have adopted similar generic descriptors (for example, excellent, good, satisfactory, limited and poor) that offer crude comparative indicators (almost certainly inconsistently applied by different teachers and schools) but convey no information about what the student knows or can do.

Conclusion

This chapter provides an analysis of some different understandings and applications of standards in educational assessment. The intention has been first to provide a framework of different meanings and referents for standards, second to analyse the implications for educational practice of some prevalent ways of talking about and using standards and third to consider some contrasting implementations of standards and their strengths and limitations.

The framework of meanings and referents provided in the first section of the chapter suggests some ways of asking questions (about type, focus, construct and purpose) to clarify which of many possible meanings is intended in any discussion of standards. This can help to ensure that when people are talking about standards they are all talking about the same thing and not talking past each other because their focus is different.

The analysis in the second section of the chapter focuses on two prominent calls in current discourse on standards: setting minimum standards and high standards. This analysis suggests that there are some situations where setting minimum standards may be necessary and even beneficial, but others where they can be inappropriate and even damaging; similarly, there are some situations where expecting high standards may be desirable and motivating, but others where they can be unhelpful and even destructive. Further, minimum standards are written for the typical or average student, and high standards are by their nature not achievable by everyone, so both represent 'a bridge too far' for some students. Assessment practice and educational structures need to become more adaptive to personal circumstances and needs.

The third section of the chapter looks at some salient kinds of standards (content standards, performance standards, and developmental standards), examples of their implementation around the world, roles and uses, assumptions and connotations and strengths and weaknesses. Each was seen to have some virtues but to face challenges. Each should not be confused with the others. Some overall conclusions can be drawn.

Content standards. These can provide useful structuring of domains of knowledge, signalling important concepts and skills that schools should teach and students should learn. However, two types of adaptation are needed. First, content standards are not themselves the curriculum but inform its construction; schools need to devise their curriculum to fit local circumstances using the content standards as an input. Second, individual students do not necessarily learn at the standard pace and in the logical sequence laid out by the content standards; student learning is dependent on a variety of factors that disrupt any such 'assembly line' expectation. Rather, the general flow of student development contains lots of eddies where learning needs to revisit and consolidate before moving on. The notion of a spiral curriculum, with its constant revisiting and extension of central ideas and themes (Bruner, 1966), another idea from the 1960s, is worth revisiting as a way of resolving this lack of fit between a linearly sequential curriculum and the idiosyncrasies of human development.

Performance standards. In the form of merit, proficiency or achievement standards, these are the most widespread kind of standard. They are presented as levels, represented by labels, descriptors and (sometimes) exemplars to indicate and instantiate their conceptual meanings. Performance standards are used summatively to report differences in quality of performance and formatively to acquaint students with differences between better and weaker performance. Handled well, performance standards can challenge students towards excellence. Handled badly, their latent competitive nature and potential for failure can destroy incentive. Working out a helpful and balanced role for performance standards is a challenge for the 21st century.

Developmental standards. One of the problems with performance standards is that they fail to make explicit how students change over time, especially where the same labels (for example, A–E) and sometimes also the same descriptors (when generic descriptors are used) are continually applied. Students can appropriate the label to describe themselves (a C-student; a failure). Developmental standards provide progressive labels and descriptions that indicate the unfolding journey of learning and the milestones passed. Examples are not widespread and those that exist are struggling to justify themselves. Yet, they have enormous potential as a replacement for or supplement to performance standards. More development is needed, and it may be best to start with those areas of learning that are naturally developmental, such as language learning. This is an important agenda for the 21st century.

One issue that keeps recurring is that of target setting. The setting of a blanket target for all students, whether it be for the content to be learned, the proficiency standard for satisfactory performance or the developmental level to be reached, *by a particular point in time*, fails to recognise and respect the diversity of background and circumstances, stage of development, existing knowledge and skill, personal characteristics and learning needs of individual students. This poses a dilemma: How to indicate desirable targets for learning and performance while respecting the individuality of the learner and providing positive feedback for progress made? This dilemma is especially pertinent in the compulsory years of schooling, when support and encouragement are so important and the conditions for life-long learning are being established.

Setting expected standards as general targets can be useful for defining what it would be good or desirable to achieve in various stages of learning, as a guide to curriculum implementation. However, this is likely to characterise a typical or 'average' student and therefore miss the mark for individual students. How these targets are represented, talked about and assessed is therefore important. Targets will function better if they are negotiated to fit the circumstances and if students have continuing opportunities to meet them over time. That is, flexibility is needed for schools to determine what the targets should be for each student. The notion of individual learning plans is one that should be applied to all students. In the secondary school, this should be broadened to encompass the notion of differentiated pathways (Grubb & Oakes, 2007).[15]

---

[15] Grubb and Oakes (2007) argue for schools as collaborative learning communities, for differentiated pathways based on multiple conceptions of standards and for stakeholder involvement in setting target standards.

Throughout this chapter, the focus has been on the welfare of the learner. Equity considerations require that every student be treated as an individual. A challenge for the 21st century is to work out how to reconcile representations of standards at a general systemic level with the idiosyncratic circumstances and needs of the individual student. In order to maintain a focus on the learner, we need ways of talking about and applying standards that reflect the 21st-century state of knowledge about learning. This knowledge is certain to keep growing and we need to be ready to absorb that knowledge into educational, and especially educational assessment, practice and recast that practice accordingly. There are three ideas that may prove productive lines of enquiry: personalised learning; brain research; and being more descriptive.

Personalising. A conclusion of this chapter is that an aim for the 21st century should be to find a way of designing learning programs and assessment systems that are more personalised and adaptive. Personalised learning has already captured considerable attention as a key concept in future delivery of educational services (see Keamy, Nicholas, Mahar & Herrick, 2007; OECD, 2006). This is a promising direction of development. Further consideration is needed of how notions of standards can fit with processes of personalised learning.

Brain research. At the beginning of the 21st century we are just in the infancy of neuroscience research on the brain. Such research will eventually revolutionise our understandings about how people learn. The implications for educational practice in the future are likely to be profound (OECD, 2007). Some scepticism is warranted for some current claims on the implications of brain research (McCandliss, 2002), but some cautious suggestions are already possible (Bransford, Brown & Cocking, 2000b; Jensen, 2005: Wolf, 2001). What is clear is that each brain, and therefore each student, is different and distinctive. This has implications for the tailoring of learning expectations, and consequently learning opportunities, to the individual student.

Being more descriptive. Both performance and developmental standards require a judgment of best fit to a standard that is represented by a description that typifies the standard but will not, in general, exactly describe the individual performance. This gives a broad overview of the performance in terms of the level reached in relation to other possible levels (and also, consequently, in relation to the performance of other students). In other words, it is a summary. If the level labels only are reported, then it is a very broad summary indeed, carrying no information about the characteristics of the performance. While this is useful for some purposes, such as certification and accountability, it is useless for others, such as providing feedback to assist further learning. Furthermore, greater emphasis on the personal advancement of students against tailored targets means attending more carefully and deliberately to the detail of each student's learning. Consequently, an important challenge for the future is developing ways of characterising and recording student achievement to keep better track of student learning and to make transparent to both teacher and student what next steps are needed for the student to make further progress. Technological advances may assist in doing this more easily, but successful implementation depends on clear thinking about how to set personalised targets for student learning. This is where the emphasis needs to be in assessment strategies of the future.

References

Aldrich, R. (2000). Educational standards in historical perspective, *Proceedings of the British Academy, 102*, 9–37. London: The British Academy. (Also in Goldstein & Heath, 2000). Retrieved June 19, 2008 from <http://www.proc.britac.ac.uk/cgi-bin/somsid.cgi?page=volumes/pba102&session=770884A>.

Baird, J., Cresswell, M. & Newton, P. (2000). Would the real gold standard please step forward? *Research Papers in Education, 15* (2), 213–229.

Barrs, M., Ellis, S., Hester, H. & Thomas, A. (1988), *The primary language record handbook for teachers*. London: Centre for Literacy in Primary Education. Retrieved June 19, 2008 from <http://www.clpe.co.uk/researchandprojects/research_06.html>.

Bennett, J. (1998). *Setting standards and applying them across different administrations of large-scale, high-stakes, curriculum-based public examinations.* Sydney: New South Wales Board of Studies. Retrieved June 18, 2008, from <www.boardofstudies.nsw.edu.au/archives/occasional_papers/occasionalp1_assess.htm>.

Bereiter, C. & Scardamalier, M. (1993). *Surpassing ourselves: An enquiry into the nature and implications of expertise.* Chicago: Open Court.

Bransford, J. D., Brown, A. L., & Cocking, R. R. (Eds.). (2000a). How experts differ from novices. In *How people learn: Brain, mind, experience and school* (pp. 31–50). Washington, DC: National Academy Press.

Bransford, J. D., Brown, A. L., & Cocking, R. R. (Eds.). (2000b). Mind and brain. In *How people learn: Brain, mind, experience and school* (pp. 114–127). Washington, DC: National Academy Press.

Bruner, J. S. (1966). *The process of education.* Cambridge, MA: Harvard University Press.

Carroll, J. B. (1963). A model of school learning, *Teachers College Record, 64* (8), 723–723.

Carroll, J. B. (1989). The Carroll model: A twenty-five year retrospective and prospective view, *Educational Researcher, 18* (1), 26–31.

Chaiklin, S. (2003). The zone of proximal development in Vygotsky's analysis of learning and instruction. In A. Kozulin, B. Gindis, V. Ageyev, & S. Miller, S. (Eds.), *Vygotsky's educational theory and practice in cultural context.* Cambridge: Cambridge University Press.

Chi, M. T. H., Glaser, R., & Farr, M. J. (1988). *The nature of expertise.* Hillsdale, New Jersey: Laurence Erlbaum Associates.

Cizek, G. J. (Ed.) (2001). *Setting performance standards: Concepts, methods, and perspectives.* Mahwah, NJ: Lawrence Erlbaum.

Cohen, D. K. (1996). Standards-based school reform: Policy, practice, and performance. In H. F. Ladd (Ed.), *Holding schools accountable: Performance-based reform in education* (pp. 99–127). Washington, DC: Brookings Institution,

Commonwealth of Australia (2005). *Schools Assistance (Learning Together—Achievement Through Choice and Opportunity) Regulations 2005.* Canberra: Federal Register of Legislative Instruments. Retrieved June 19, 2008, from <http://www.dest.gov.au/sectors/school_education/publications_resources/profiles/Schools_Assistance_Regulations_2005.htm>.

Costa, A. L. (Ed.) (2001). *Developing minds: A resource book for teaching thinking* (3rd ed.). Alexandria, Virginia: Association for Supervision and Curriculum Development.

Costa, A. L., & Kallick, B. (2000). *Habits of mind: A developmental series.* Alexandria, Virginia: Association for Supervision and Curriculum Development.

Dahllöf, U. (1971). *Ability grouping, content and process analysis.* New York: Teachers College Press.

Daniels, H. (Ed.) (1993). *Charting the agenda: Educational activity after Vygotsky.* London & New York: Routledge.

Darling-Hammond, L. (1997). *The right to learn: A blueprint for creating schools that work.* San Francisco: Jossey-Bass.

Dweck, C. S. (1986). Motivational processes affecting learning. *American Psychologist* (special issue: psychological science and education), *41*(10), 1040–1048.

Falk, B. (1998). Supporting diverse learners with the Primary Language Record. In D. Allen (Ed.), *Assessing student learning: From grading to understanding*. New York and London: Teachers College Press.

Finn, C. E., Julian, L., & Petrilli, M. J. (2006). *The state of state standards*. Washington, DC: Thomas B. Fordham Foundation. Retrieved June 9, 2008, from <http://www.edexcellence.net/doc/StateofStateStandards2006.pdf>.

Goldstein, H. & Heath, A. (Eds.). (2000). *Educational standards: Proceedings of the British Academy 102*. Oxford: Oxford University Press. Also available at <http://www.proc.britac.ac.uk/cgi-bin/somsid.cgi?page=volumes/pba102&session=770884A> retrieved June 19, 2008.

Green, S. (2002). *Criterion referenced assessment as a guide to learning: The importance of progression and reliability*. A paper presented at the Association for the Study of Evaluation in Education in South Africa International Conference, Johannesburg. Retrieved June 18, 2008, from <http://www.cambridgeassessment.org.uk/ca/digitalAssets/113775_Criterion_Referenced_Assessment_as_a_Guide_to_Learning._The_.pdf>.

Grubb, W. N., & Oakes, J. (2007). *Restoring Value to the high school: the rhetoric and practice of higher standards*. Tempe, Arizona: Education Policy Research Unit & Education Policy Research Unit. Retrieved 9 June, 2008, from <http://epsl.asu.edu/epru/documents/EPSL-0710-242-EPRU.pdf>.

Hall, K., & Harding, A. (2002). Level descriptions and teacher assessments in England: Towards a community of practice, *Education Research, 44*(1), 1–16.

Heubert, J. P., & Hauser, R. M. (Eds.). (1999). *High stakes: Testing for tracking, promotion, and graduation*. Washington, DC: National Academies Press.

Hill, P. W., & Crévola, C. A. (1999). The role of standards in educational reform for the 21st century. In D. D. Marsh (Ed.), *ASCD Yearbook 1999: Preparing our schools for the 21st century* (pp. 117–142) Alexandria, Virginia: Association for Supervision and Curriculum Development.

Hodgson, A., & Spours, K. (2005). The learner experience of Curriculum 2000: Implications for the reform of 14–19 education in England, *Journal of Education Policy, 20*(1), 101–108.

Jensen, E. (2005). *Teaching with the brain in mind* (2nd ed.). Alexandria, Virginia: Association for Supervision and Curriculum Development.

Kallos, D., & Lundgren, U. P. (1979). *Curriculum as a pedagogical problem*. Lund: LiberLäromedel/Gleerup.

Keamy, R. K., Nicholas, H., Mahar, S., & Herrick, C. (2007). *Personalising education: From research to policy and practice*. Melbourne, Victoria: Department of Education and Early Childhood Development. Retrieved June 24, 2008, from <http://www.eduweb.vic.gov.au/edulibrary/public/publ/research/publ/personalising-education-report.pdf>.

Lundgren, U. P. (1972). *Frame factors and the teaching process*. Stockholm: Almquist & Wiksell.

Maxwell, G. S. (2001). *Moderation of assessments in vocational education and training*. Brisbane: Queensland Department of Employment and Training. Retrieved June 24, 2008, from <http://www.trainandemploy.qld.gov.au/resources/about_us/pdf/moderation_report.pdf>.

Maxwell, G. S. (2002a). *Are core learning outcomes standards?* Brisbane: Queensland Studies Authority (now Queensland Studies Authority). Retrieved June 10, 2008, from <http://www.qsa.qld.edu.au/downloads/publications/research_qscc_assess_report_1.pdf>.

Maxwell, G. S. (2002b). *Moderation of teacher judgments in student assessment*. Brisbane: Queensland School Curriculum Council (now Queensland Studies Authority). Retrieved June 24, 2008, from <http://www.qsa.qld.edu.au/downloads/publications/research_qscc_assess_report_2.pdf>.

McCandliss, B. (2002). Brain-based education in *Encyclopedia of Education*. Farmington Hills, Michigan: The Gale Group. Retrieved June 24, 2008, from <http://www.answers.com/topic/brain-based-education>.

National Council for Teachers of Mathematics (NCTM) (2000). *Principles and standards for school mathematics*. Reston, Virginia: NCTM.

National Research Council (NRC) (1996). *National Science Education Standards*. Washington, DC: National Academy Press. Retrieved June 19, 2008, from <http://www.nap.edu/html/nses/>.

New Standards (1997). *New standards performance standards: Elementary, middle school and high school*. Rochester. Washington, DC: National Center on Education and the Economy.

Ng, C. & Bahr, N. (2000). Knowledge structures and motivation to learn: Reciprocal effects. *Queensland Journal of Educational Research, 16* (1), 76–106. Interaction of knowledge and motivation. Retrieved June 19, 2008, from <www.iier.org.au/qjer/qjer16/ng.html>.

OECD (Organisation for Economic Co-operation and Development) (2006). *Personalising education*. Paris: OECD.

OECD (Organisation for Economic Co-operation and Development) (2007). *Understanding the brain: The birth of a learning science*. Paris: OECD.
dsfsdfsd

Pelligrino, J. W., Chudowski, N., & Glaser, R. (Eds.). (2001). *Knowing what students know: The science and design of educational assessment*. Washington, DC: National Academy Press.

Rowan, B. (1996). Standards as incentives for instructional reform. In S. H. Furhman & J. O'Day (Eds.), *Rewards and reform: Creating educational incentives that work*. San Francisco: Jossey Bass.

Queensland Studies Authority (QSA) (2007). Years 3, 5, and 7 Literacy: Writing. In *2007 Test Reporting Handbook for the Queensland Years 3, 5 and 7 Literacy and Numeracy Tests* (pp. 15–24). Brisbane: QSA. Retrieved June 19, 2008, from <http://www.qsa.qld.edu.au/downloads/assessment/3579_handbook_reporting_07.pdf>.

Sadler, D. R. (1987). Specifying and promulgating achievement standards, *Oxford Review of Education, 13*(2), 191–209.

Sadler, D. R. (1989). Formative assessment and the design of instructional systems, *Instructional Science, 18*, 119–144.

Sainsbury, M., & Sizmur, S. (1998). Level descriptions in the National Curriculum: What kind of criterion referencing is this? *Oxford Review of Education, 24*(2), 181–93.

Sandholz, J. H., Ogawa, R. T., & Scribner, S. P. (2004). The standards gap. *Teachers College Record, 106*(6), 1177–1202.

Schunk, D. (1984). Enhancing self-efficacy and achievement through rewards and goals: Motivational and informational effects. *Journal of Educational Research, 78*, 29–34.

Shepard, L. A. (2000). The role of assessment in a learning culture, *Educational Researcher, 29*(7), 4–14.

Shepard, L. A., & Smith, M. L. (Eds.). (1989). *Flunking grades: Research and policies on retention*. London: The Falmer Press.

Stites, R. (1999). A user's guide to standards-based educational reform: From theory to practice, *Focus on basics: Connecting research and practice*, vol. 3, issue C. Retrieved from <http://www.ncsall.net/?id=352>.

Wiggins, G. (1991). Standards not standardisation: Evoking quality student work, *Educational Leadership, 48*(5), 18–25.

Wiggins, G. (1998). *Educative assessment: Designing assessments to inform and improve performance*. San Francisco: Jossey-Bass.

Willis, S., & Kissane, B. (1997). *Achieving outcome-based education: Premises, principles and implications for curriculum and assessment*. Deakin, ACT: Australian Curriculum Studies Association.

Wilson, M. R., & Bertenthal, M. W. (Eds.). (2001). *Systems for state science assessment*. Washington, DC: The National Academies Press.

Wolf, A. (2000). A comparative perspective on educational standards. *Proceedings of the British Academy, 102*, 9–37. London: The British Academy. (Also in Goldstein & Heath, 2000). Retrieved June 19, 2008, from <http://www.proc.britac.ac.uk/cgi-bin/somsid.cgi?page=volumes/pba102&session=770884A>.

Wolf, P. (2001). *Brain matters: Translating research into classroom practice*. Alexandria, Virginia: Association for Supervision and Curriculum Development.

Wylie, E., & Ingram, D. E. (1999). *International Second Language Proficiency Ratings (ISLPR): General proficiency version for English*. Brisbane: Centre for Applied Linguistics and Languages, Griffith University.

Author Index

Subject Index

Printed in the United States
148587LV00001B/91/P